THE LIMITS OF REASON

The German Democratic Press
and the Collapse of
Weimar Democracy

BY

MODRIS EKSTEINS

OXFORD UNIVERSITY PRESS
1975

Oxford University Press, Ely House, London W. 1

GLASGOW NEW YORK TORONTO MELBOURNE WELLINGTON
CAPE TOWN IBADAN NAIROBI DAR ES SALAAM LUSAKA ADDIS ABABA
DELHI BOMBAY CALCUTTA MADRAS KARACHI LAHORE DACCA
KUALA LUMPUR SINGAPORE HONG KONG TOKYO

ISBN 0 19 821862 1

© *Oxford University Press 1975*

*Printed in Great Britain by
Fletcher and Sons Ltd. Norwich*

FOR MY FATHER

PREFACE

The initial impulse behind this book was a limited one. It was a desire to investigate how a cross-section of the German liberal press responded to the rise and success of National Socialism between 1928 and 1933. A number of newspapers, representative of the variety of liberal political journalism, were to be selected, and their editorial policies on the subject of National Socialism were then to be analysed. The rationale behind such a project was to see what conceptions of National Socialism self-proclaimed liberals held and disseminated in the years immediately prior to the Third Reich.

It soon became clear, however, that the purpose of such a study was questionable. A study merely of editorial opinions will always remain, to a large extent, an exercise in précis and paraphrase. Explanations for shifts in editorial policy will, of necessity, be superficial and usually hypothetical, for after all the lead article in a newspaper is like the visible tip of an iceberg, and unless we explore under the surface, any assertions about the nature of the generic whole will never transcend the realm of conjecture. A newspaper is a product of the intellect but it is also a complex social organism; its character is determined by the dialectical interplay of individual creativity and institutional structures. Unless a newspaper is considered both as a multi-dimensional institution in its own right and as part of a wider social and political context, its utterances cannot be appreciated fully by the historian and they are often even liable to misinterpretation. Therefore an account of the attitudes of the liberal press towards National Socialism, if based exclusively or even largely on editorial articles, would have remained a sterile record and could never have claimed to be a historical analysis of *how* those attitudes towards the Hitler movement evolved and *why* they underwent changes in the course of time. Furthermore, it also became clear that one could not justifiably isolate the attitudes of liberal editors and publishers towards National Socialism from their reactions to the political culture as a whole of Weimar Germany. In its most significant aspects the liberal response to the challenge of National Socialism was determined by the relationship of liberals to the Weimar state, to their own parties, and to the electorate. All liberals, in fact all republican elements, recognized that the success of National Socialism was a result of the lack of success of liberalism, that the weaknesses of the Weimar Republic were a precondition for the strengths of National Socialism. The response of liberals to National Socialism, then, was conditioned by the crisis in liberalism. Hence the focal point of my investigation shifted from expressions of editorial policy to the actual formulation of that policy, in other words to the workings of the press as an institution, and from National Socialism to liberalism as the primary concern of that policy.

In order to keep the project within manageable proportions three newspaper firms were chosen for concentrated study, the Berlin firms of Mosse and Ullstein and the Frankfurt firm of Sonnemann (Frankfurter Societäts-Druckerei). This choice was made not because these concerns were felt to be representative of liberal publishing houses in terms of size, the nature of their publications, their party affiliations, and their political influence. In these respects the Mosse, Ullstein, and Sonnemann houses were by and large atypical, and the provincial liberal press and liberal politicians asserted this day in day out. These particular firms were selected because they identified themselves most closely with the ideals of the Weimar Republic; and if any convinced and resolute opposition to National Socialism could have been expected in the liberal press, it ought to have emanated from this quarter. All three firms were Jewish owned; all were liberal-democratic in political orientation. In November 1918 Mosse and Sonnemann journalists played a leading part in the founding of the left-liberal German Democratic Party, a party which was designed originally to serve as both the main pillar and the fulcrum of Weimar politics. Mosse and Ullstein were the two largest newspaper-publishing houses in Germany; Ullstein's *Berliner Morgenpost* had the highest circulation of any German daily, the same firm's *Berliner Illustrirte Zeitung* the highest circulation of any German periodical publication. Mosse's *Berliner Tageblatt*, Ullstein's *Vossische Zeitung*, and Sonnemann's *Frankfurter Zeitung* were newspapers of high quality, with venerable traditions, and with not only a national but also an international readership. And finally, contrary to the majority of the German press, of all political persuasions, this metropolitan 'democratic' press cherished the ideal and exalted the importance of independence from outside interests in newspaper publishing. Newspapers, said the long-standing credo of this press, had a social and political role to play as intermediaries between state and society, and this function could not be executed properly if a newspaper were not free from the constraints of government, parties, and pressure groups. Consequently, if any liberal papers had reason to resist with vigour a political movement which flaunted its devotion to irrationalism, violence, racism, and a Führer cult, and which regarded its ideological essence as the utter antithesis of liberal democracy, it was the Mosse, Ullstein, and Sonnemann papers. Nevertheless, in 1933 this press adapted its editorial policies and internal organization to suit the new National Socialist regime as rapidly as most other newspapers. The liberal collapse was wholesale.

The growing numerical weakness of organized political liberalism in the Weimar Republic did not in itself dictate a policy of passive 'surrender' by German liberals to the enemies of the Republic in 1933. The fate of political parties, their electoral success or decline, is not always necessarily an accurate indication of a prevailing political mood. Organizational shortcomings, inadequate propaganda and publicity, weak leadership, and tactical mistakes are often more consequential factors in the fate of modern parties than strictly ideological considerations. For the rapid and quiet 'surrender' of 1933 to occur the entire institutional foundation of German liberalism had to be in a state of decay and disarray, and this book seeks to describe and to explain the nature of the confusion prevalent in an important sector of this liberal substructure in the last years of the Weimar Republic and in the early stages of National Socialist rule.

The core of the book focuses on the crisis in the press and in politics in the period between 1928 and 1933, a crisis which terminated with what so many historians have described as 'the Nazi seizure of power'. Germans who con-

sidered themselves opponents of the Hitler regime of course
felt that a 'seizure of power' occurred in 1933. The term
implies, however, that there was an active opposition from
whom power was seized; moreover, that there were peaceful
alternatives to a Hitler-led government at the end of January
1933; and finally, that terror and force were the indispensable keys to success for the National Socialists in the
erection of their dictatorship. The second half of this study
suggests that the notion of a 'seizure of power' should be
reconsidered. The Weimar Republic did not perish simply on
account of the skill and determination, the ruthless 'will to
power', of Hitler and his cohorts. A close study of the press
in the last years of the Republic indicates that the entire sub-
soil necessary for democratic parliamentary government had
been eroded. Despite their interminable rationalizations for
what they regarded as a conscious decision on their part,
liberals had no political choice in 1933 other than to
acquiesce or emigrate. But liberal behaviour in 1933 was
determined not so much by what National Socialism represented as by what liberalism no longer represented. In view
of this, even the use of terms like 'surrender' or 'capitulation'
to describe liberal action in 1933 can be misleading.

The authorities of the German Democratic Republic would
not grant me permission to visit archives there; hence the
private papers of Georg Bernhard and an extensive collection
of government documents on the press had to remain un-
explored. Certain institutions and individuals who could have
provided valuable information and sources were also not
prepared to assist the project. Nevertheless, this book is being
published with the confidence that any further source
material would not have changed the general thesis that is
presented here.

 Some of the sections in this book on the Frankfurter
Societäts-Druckerei appeared in my article 'The Frankfurter
Zeitung: Mirror of Weimar Democracy' in the *Journal of
Contemporary History*, VI/4 (1971).

 The personal debts which I have accumulated while preparing the various versions of this study are indeed many.
The Canada Council was more than generous with its

financial support over the years; the Rhodes Trust and the
University of Toronto also covered certain costs at different
stages. All the archivists and librarians of the institutions
listed in the bibliography deserve individual thanks. Many
other kind people gave unstintingly of their time and energy
to help and guide me. Numerous friends hurled invaluable
criticism and salutary abuse at me. To list every one of these
people would require pages; I hope that all of them see their
names between these lines and accept my very warm thanks.
James Joll, Anthony Nicholls, Michael Balfour, Robert
Spencer, Martin Broszat, and Eberhard Pikart belong in a
very special category. They gave me ideas, advice, criticism,
and friendship; but probably most important, their interest
and encouragement gave me energy and confidence. Of
Oxford, where an earlier version of this work was accepted as
a doctoral thesis, I can only say, along with Henry James,
that it lent 'sweetness to labour and dignity to leisure'.
Finally, to the editors of Oxford Historical Monographs I
express my gratitude for adding this volume to their series.

Scarborough College
University of Toronto
June 1973

CONTENTS

Abbreviations   xv

PART ONE

I.   Liberalism and the Press in Germany in 1918   3

II.   The German Democratic Party   31

III. The Press in the Weimar Republic   70

IV.   The Firms of Mosse, Ullstein, and Sonnemann   104

PART TWO

V.   The Eclipse of Liberalism   141

VI.   Odd Bedfellows: The *Frankfurter Zeitung* and
      I.G.Farben   160

VII. Ullstein *v.* Ullstein   180

VIII. The Advent of Stoicism   194

IX.   The New Relativism   213

X.   'Prelude to Silence': The Liquidation of
      Democracy   247

XI.   Gleichschaltung, Phase One: The Elimination
      of Opposition   264

XII. Gleichschaltung, Phase Two: The End of
      Ullstein, Mosse, and Sonnemann   281

      Conclusion   305

Appendix I: The Political Orientation of the
                 German Press   312

Appendix II: Circulation of Ullstein Publications   314

Bibliography   315

Index   327

ABBREVIATIONS

BM	*Berliner Morgenpost*
BT	*Berliner Tageblatt*
BVP	Bavarian People's Party
BVZ	*Berliner Volks-Zeitung*
DAZ	*Deutsche Allgemeine Zeitung*
DDP	German Democratic Party
DVP	German People's Party
DNVP	German Nationalist People's Party
FSD	Frankfurter Societäts-Druckerei
FZ	*Frankfurter Zeitung*
KPD	Communist Party of Germany
MNN	*Münchner Neueste Nachrichten*
NL	*Nachlass* (Private Papers)
NSDAP	National Socialist German Workers' Party
SPD	Social Democratic Party of Germany
UFA	Universum Film A.G.
VZ	*Vossische Zeitung*

PART ONE

I

LIBERALISM AND THE PRESS
IN GERMANY IN 1918

Ever since Thorstein Veblen's analysis of German industrialization, the view of Germany as a 'belated nation' has proved extremely popular and useful. Certainly when compared to England and France Germany emerged late and then in many respects haltingly from the feudal era. At the end of the eighteenth century German society was still locked in a rigid caste system. The middle estate was small and geographically fragmented. Industry was limited; agriculture was backward; and the quilt-like configuration of sovereign states in the Holy Roman Empire stifled political change. In this environment liberalism, either as a social philosophy or as a political ideology, could sprout no strong roots. Ideas about the vitality and dignity of the human personality and the importance of individual rights, particularly the active pursuit of these rights, in furthering collective progress, had little resonance in society as a whole.[1]

It was, in fact, not until well into the nineteenth century that any substantial social base for liberal ideas emerged. The reforms implemented during and in the immediate aftermath of the revolutionary and Napoleonic epoch, either by direct French intervention or as a prophylactic measure by native administrators, undermined the corporative feudal order, rationalized the state structure, encouraged a hitherto unknown degree of social flux and, in the process, the gradual

---

[1] Thorstein Veblen, *Imperial Germany and the Industrial Revolution* (New York, 1915). Among the many recent studies pursuing this theme from different perspectives are Helmuth Plessner, *Die verspätete Nation* (Stuttgart, 1959); Ralf Dahrendorf, *Society and Democracy in Germany* (London, 1968); and Barrington Moore, Jr., *Social Origins of Democracy and Dictatorship* (London, 1967). The most valuable general treatments of nineteenth-century German liberalism are Heinrich Heffter, *Die deutsche Selbstverwaltung im 19. Jahrhundert* (Stuttgart, 1950); Leonard Krieger, *The German Idea of Freedom* (Boston, Mass., 1957); and Mack Walker, *German Home Towns* (Ithaca, N.Y., and London, 1971).

growth of a self-interested, ambitious commercial and educated middle class. However, the self-confidence, sense of
security, and desire for political responsibility of this social
grouping remained limited, for as industrialization and urbanization accelerated and before the middle classes had attained
either any political cohesion or any significant measure of
political influence, a new urban labouring class appeared
which the propertied and professional stratum, and even the
less well-to-do middle classes, regarded as a greater threat to
their interests and ambitions than the ruling élite. The social
anxieties of the middle strata dominated their attitude
towards politics and consistently vitiated their positive political impulses. The memory of the excesses of the French
Revolution proved to be indelible; and the events of 1848
appeared to underline the lessons of the French experience,
namely that freedom could not exist without a clearly
defined and staunchly defended social order. Furthermore,
Germany's governing authorities, inspired by highly developed efficiency-minded bureaucracies, always found sufficient common ground with middle-class aspirations to
provide a vent for any acute social and political tensions.
Consequently, in the course of the century not only did the
German *Mittelstand* become amenable to, but much of it
eventually favoured, 'reform from above'. Moderation, restraint, and, above all, the wish for a positive relationship
with the existing state, became the hallmark of German
liberalism. The 'attainable' became a more popular political
slogan than the 'desirable' with the German middle classes.

This attitude towards the state and politics enjoyed its
heyday in the 1870s, amidst the exuberance that accompanied the unification of Germany. It was represented and
articulated by the National Liberal Party, which for most
of the decade was by far the largest political grouping and
constituted the nucleus of Bismarck's parliamentary majority. A rump of liberalism refused to endorse the accolades
for Bismarck; however, even in left liberalism—organized in
the Progressive Party, from which the National Liberals had
split off in 1866-7, and in the smaller south-German People's
Party—opposition was evoked, in the final analysis, not so
much by the substance as by the methods of Bismarckian

politics. The liberalism of the left tended to be more ethical than social. A democratic orientation which looked for much of its inspiration to the French radical tradition did exist, but even within left liberalism it remained a distinct, predominantly intellectual, minority throughout the nineteenth century. In fact, as the century advanced, the term 'democrat' assumed an increasingly pejorative flavour. It implied an unpatriotic unwillingness to see the over-all needs of the national community, an inability to place internal political questions in a wider, national and international, context, and an underestimation and even a rejection of Germany's foreign-political interests and aims. To be called a 'democrat' meant that one was associated with the extreme left wing of liberalism, closer on many issues to 'social democracy' than to the rest of the liberal movement. Most left liberals tried to avoid this classification.

In 1879 Bismarck threw down the gauntlet to liberalism when he reintroduced protection and proceeded to consolidate his pseudo-parliamentary state on the twin pillars of heavy industry and large-scale, Junker-dominated agriculture. The response of German liberals to this challenge strikingly revealed their lack of political imagination and independent initiative. The National Liberals were thrown into confusion, but the industrialist wing did then carry the day. The free traders on the left of the party departed, claiming that national liberalism had ceased being a partner and had become a captive of Bismarck. However, the secessionists failed to develop any new ideas or policies, and in 1884 most of them joined the Progressives to form the German *Freisinnige* Party.[2] In the 1880s the depleted National Liberal Party became the casemated representative of the prosperous educated and propertied bourgeoisie, of industrialists, shipping magnates, bankers, and wealthy professional people. Although it still paraded its class interests in the guise of *raison d'état*, its popularity waned abruptly. From a high point of 155 Reichstag seats in 1874 the National Liberals plummeted to 47 in 1881. With the

[2] To translate *Freisinninge* as 'Radical' would be misleading. The 'free thought' of this wing of liberalism did not involve the extensive social and political reform implicit in 'radicalism'.

exception of a brief recovery in 1887, owing to an electoral agreement with the conservative parties, right-wing liberalism stayed roughly at this medium level of parliamentary strength until the First World War. Left liberalism, in turn, under the strong-willed but uninspired leadership of Eugen Richter, sank ever deeper into its sterile policy of 'principled opposition'. By the late 1880s many voters had realized that left liberalism provided no real alternative or effective counterbalance to the ruling forces. The left liberals were unwilling as a whole to commit themselves openly to democratization, and hampered by an almost mystical reliance on their notion of individualism—a notion which internalized the quest for freedom—their social programme was virtually non-existent. Unable to cater realistically to the specific interests of any social group, and devoid of influence on the government except as an irritant, left liberalism was gradually deserted by many of those white-collar employees, small businessmen, intellectuals, artisans, and workers to whom it looked for support. After a peak in 1881 when the Progressives, the German People's Party, and the secessionists from the National Liberals together controlled 115 Reichstag seats, left liberalism suffered several catastrophic setbacks. In 1887 it was reduced to a sum of 32 deputies. In subsequent prewar elections left-liberal parliamentary strength normally ranged between 49 and 36 seats.

Whereas the Catholic Centre Party revealed great constancy in its electoral strength between 1871 and 1914, and the Social Democratic Party (SPD) an awe-inspiring growth, liberalism as a whole underwent an almost uninterrupted political decline. In 1871 the various liberal parties won 172 seats, in 1881 162, in 1890 118, and in 1912 only 87. The obvious inability of German liberalism to reconcile its intellectual principles with the social and political implications of those principles eroded its appeal as the structure and needs of German society changed at an ever quickening pace in the last quarter of the nineteenth century. This conflict between theory and practice was fundamental to western liberalism as a whole, but it revealed itself as particularly acute in Germany, a country which, owing to its late 'modernization', was confronted with a more sudden, pressing, and compact version of the problems which western society in general faced in its transition from an agrarian feudal order to an urban mechanized civilization.

Yet, the mere enumeration of parliamentary representation gives an incomplete picture of the development of pre-war liberalism.[3] In the two decades before 1914 the number of liberals who became convinced that their political movement was going up a blind alley grew. In the 1890s, as Germany embarked on a period of feverish industrial activity, a small group on the left began announcing energetically that without democratization liberalism would suffocate, and that without extensive social reform there could be no genuine and effective democratization. Furthermore, in order to break the political hegemony of agrarians and industrialists, liberalism had to unite its forces, display unequivocally its national loyalty, and expunge its more abrasive class bias; not only that, it also had to seek the political assistance of the labour movement. These views were first enunciated, soberly and almost academically, in the *Freisinnige* Union, a group which broke away from Richter's party in 1893 (the latter renamed itself the *Freisinnige* People's Party) and then with romantic trappings and enormous verve in another quarter, in Friedrich Naumann's National Social Union. In 1903, after the electoral setback which all liberal parties suffered, these two mutually complementary groups merged. Further efforts to advance liberal unity followed. In November 1906, a few months after the death of Richter, who had insisted on remaining aloof from the deliberations on union, the three left-liberal parties agreed to co-operate in the forthcoming Reichstag elections, and this new *rapport* culminated in 1910 in their merger to form the Progressive People's Party.[4]

---

[3] The argument which follows relies on the recent works by Peter Gilg, *Die Erneuerung des demokratischen Denkens im Wilhelminischen Deutschland* (Wiesbaden, 1965); Stuart T. Robson, 'Left-Wing Liberalism in Germany 1900-19', unpublished diss. (Oxford, 1966); Konstanze Wegner, *Theodor Barth und die Freisinnige Vereinigung* (Tübingen, 1968); and Ludwig Elm, *Zwischen Fortschritt und Reaktion: Geschichte der Parteien der liberalen Bourgeoisie in Deutschland 1893-1918* (Berlin [East], 1968).

[4] A very small group of left liberals, who had formed the so-called Democratic Union in 1908, refused to join the new party.

The new positive ideas on liberalism of course contributed to the achievement of unity, but viewed in broad perspective left-liberal consolidation must be seen as essentially an emergency measure, a defensive step designed to shore up a crumbling edifice. Former Richterites were the largest constituent faction in the new party and dominated its organization. The strong petty-bourgeois and provincial base of the Richter wing of left liberalism meant that a good measure of lower middle-class neuroses towards the labour movement was injected into the new party. Thus, in effect, the cutting edge of the new tendencies in left liberalism was dulled. Nevertheless, the creation of the Progressive People's Party did at least enlarge the arena of reformist activity; moreover, developments in other parties enhanced the reformers' hopes and inspired further efforts.

In the socialist party the revisionist wing was beginning to prevail. At their conference in September 1909 the Social Democrats intimated that their previously resolute opposition to political co-operation with bourgeois parties was crumbling. Furthermore, some of the younger generation of National Liberals wished to break with the narrow-interest politics which their party practised and which, they argued, were carrying national liberalism into a stagnant backwater. In response to the rise of the SPD they too became deeply concerned with the need for liberal unity and began to urge a more open-minded stance on social and electoral reform. By 1910 numerical decline and the adroit agitation of the so-called Young Liberals had plunged national liberalism into a severe internal crisis which was to last, apart from a brief respite in the early years of the war, until the reorganization of liberalism in 1918. And finally, after the turn of the century the leaders of political Catholicism were becoming increasingly distressed that their party, despite its stable parliamentary representation, was capturing less and less of the total Catholic vote. The rural and small-town vote remained secure; it was the Catholic urban worker who was deserting the party. A section of the Swabian and Rhenish leadership, the latter connected with the Christian trade-union movement, began to argue that the party had to adopt the cause of political reform if the Centre was to resuscitate its waning appeal for the Catholic working class.[5]

The 1912 elections indicated that the reformers were making some headway in the Progressive Party and also that there was reasonable cause for optimism about the possibility of creating a reformist camp in national politics. In the principal elections the Progressives and the National Liberals co-operated; however, for the ensuing run-off elections which were required in constituencies where no candidate obtained a majority, the Progressives drew up an electoral agreement with the SPD. Albeit many local Progressive committees refused to follow the dictates of the party executive, the arrangement helped the socialists to their landslide gains. In 1912 one out of every three Germans voted for a socialist candidate. The substantial decline of all parties except the SPD and several small splinter groups threw German political life into an excited commotion. The two conservative parties lost 27 seats between them; the two liberal parties 16; and the Centre with a loss of 14 seats suffered the heaviest setback in its history. The Social Democrats added 67 seats to their previous representation. Moderate and left-wing liberals hailed the conservative defeat, but their own losses and the great gains of the Social Democrats elicited intense anxiety and considerable doubt about the wisdom of neo-liberal proposals and strategy. The reformers rationalized the result and contended that it was a victory for reform. Naumann commented that 'something new has begun in Germany in these past days; an era is approaching its end; a new age has dawned.'[6] In February 1913 the ultra-conservative Agrarian League passed the following resolution to summarize its view of the political situation: 'The developments in our internal politics fill us . . . with great concern. We see how democratization is making progress in virtually all areas of legis-

5 For the SPD see Carl E. Schorske, *German Social Democracy 1905-1917* (Cambridge, Mass., 1955). For a clear indication of the internal crisis in national liberalism see Klaus-Peter Reiss (ed.), *Von Bassermann zu Stresemann: Die Sitzungen des nationalliberalen Zentralvorstandes 1912-1917* (Düsseldorf, 1967). For the Centre see Rudolf Morsey, *Die Deutsche Zentrumspartei 1917-1923* (Düsseldorf, 1966), pp. 33ff., and Klaus Epstein, *Matthias Erzberger and the Dilemma of German Democracy* (Princeton, N.J., 1959), pp. 38ff.

6 Cited in Fritz Fischer, *Krieg der Illusionen* (Düsseldorf, 1969), pp. 154f.

lation and public life, and how the larger part of liberalism is increasingly adopting democratic demands, fighting against the right, and begging the favour of the masses, often in contradiction to its own best heritage. In all this liberalism is simply breaking ground for socialism.'[7]

Germans of all political persuasions began to think it possible that in the not too distant future the reform-minded elements would win an absolute majority in the Reichstag, and then a situation in which the government was in open conflict with parliament might result. In the eyes of many a fundamental political and major social crisis was approaching irresistibly. Although the outbreak of the First World War should not be analysed exclusively from the standpoint of the German domestic situation, it is clear that important sections of the ruling classes looked upon war, or at least the threat of war, as a possible answer, in the Bismarckian tradition, to the country's internal difficulties.[8]

At first the war seemed to demonstrate that this thinking was not entirely unsound. All of German society rallied behind the war effort, and a 'domestic truce' was proclaimed. As long as there was still a prospect of quick military victory, political quiescence ruled. However, by early 1915 the question of war aims had reared itself, and the debate on war aims in turn resurrected the subject of political reform. As the war dragged on, frustration mounted on both the right and the left. The military and its political backing wished to remove strategy in all its dimensions entirely from civilian interference; but at the same time the supporters of a compromise peace grew in number, and most of them recognized that the securing of a workable peace could not be left to the military, or even to a civilian government which was not responsible to parliament.

On 6 July 1917 an 'inter-party committee' was established with members from the SPD, the Progressive Party, and the Centre. The National Liberals participated for several days,

7 Cited in ibid., p. 385.

8 Ibid., especially pp. 359f. For a useful discussion see Arno J. Mayer, 'Domestic Causes of the First World War', in *The Responsibility of Power: Historical Essays in Honor of Hajo Holborn*, ed. Leonard Krieger and Fritz Stern (New York, 1967), pp. 286-300.

withdrew, but subsequently sent observers. Within a fortnight, on 19 July, the famous 'peace resolution', calling for a
compromise peace without annexations, was presented to the
Reichstag and passed by a large majority, 212 to 126. Yet,
a fairly loose joint declaration in favour of peace was one
thing; agreement on the exact nature of constitutional reform
was another matter. The committee was constantly rocked
by dissension, resolutions adopted were imprecise, and the
hesitancy of the committee's members unequivocally to
demand responsibility for government was obvious.[9] Finally,
however, the failure of the western offensive in 1918 led the
committee to conclude that if the war was not removed from
the exclusive control of the military a breakdown of social
order would result. In the autumn of 1918, unaware of
exactly how critical the military situation was, the inter-party
committee at last launched a concerted effort to bring about
the introduction of parliamentary government. The initiative
was made independently of the high command's simul-
taneous deliberations about giving the political parties
governmental authority. The constitutional reforms of
October 1918, which introduced parliamentary democracy
to Germany, crowned the work of the committee.

The October reforms certain Progressives considered a
great and, in no small measure, personal achievement.
Although accompanied by impending military defeat, the
reforms, they felt, were not simply the result of the triumph
of external forces over the *ancien régime* in Germany but
also the deserved reward for an energetic effort on the part
of a segment of left liberalism, the climax of a policy of
reconciliation, integration, and positive evolution which had
germinated in the 1890s. The moderate socialists had been
drawn into government and persuaded to accept a parliamentary monarchy; the Catholic Centre had made a preliminary commitment to democracy; and national liberalism,
because of the permanent crisis in its ranks and the sympathy
of its left wing for the accomplishments of the Progressives,
would now probably not survive.

[9] Erich Matthias and Rudolf Morsey, *Der Interfraktionelle Ausschuss 1917-
18*, 2 vols. (Düsseldorf, 1959).

A socially conscious, national-minded democratic liberalism indeed seemed to have triumphed over not only national liberalism but traditional left liberalism as well, and, moreover, to have revived the liberal movement as a whole. The overwhelming popular mandate, 76·2 per cent of the total vote, given in January 1919 in the elections to the national assembly to the three political tendencies which had become allies in a reform coalition during the war suggested that modernism had perhaps finally vanquished traditionalism in Germany. However, the length of time that it had taken for a reform movement to consolidate itself and to register any concrete gains in German politics also suggested that the coalition was perhaps of a Laodicean stripe. In addition, there was reason to believe that the serious divisions within liberalism had only been papered over rather than resolved.

As industrialism progressed in the nineteenth century and as society became more diversified, government and administration became more complex and organizations for group interests sprouted in every sphere of human activity. In the course of this development the horizons of the common man were vastly expanded; he experienced the influences of the world beyond his immediate visible and tangible environment and felt the need to comprehend its workings in order to foresee its threats. In this context the modern press was born, as an intermediary between rational, organized, purposeful public opinion on the one hand and spontaneous, inquisitive, labile public sentiments on the other. In the nineteenth century the press became both the most important avenue for the articulation of organized interests and the staple reading diet of the average man. A dualism, of varying intensity, thus came to characterize the existence of all newspapers: they were tied to the institutional structures of society as well as being dependent, to some degree ultimately, on the less definable general social temper. Because of these ties the German press was naturally closely involved in the confrontation between modernism and traditionalism which developed in German society, and that

confrontation was reflected in turn in the nature and role of
the German press.

A number of newspapers had existed in Germany already
in the early seventeenth century; in the eighteenth century
the first larger *Nachrichtenblätter* had been founded, papers
which concentrated entirely on disseminating news and
information deemed by their publishers to be of interest to
the limited reading public. At the end of the eighteenth
and in the first half of the nineteenth century, revolutions,
wars, and frequent disorders throughout Europe made news a
more immediate public concern in Germany and encouraged
the gradual growth in number of newspapers, their frequency
of publication, and the scope of their coverage. Although
taxes, tight censorship, and the right of confiscation by the
state placed limits on the expansion of the German press
and particularly on its political involvement, an awareness of
the political potential of newspapers mounted among existing
and would-be publishers. This awareness was stimulated
especially by the events of the March revolution of 1848
when for the first time press censorship was briefly abolished. Thereafter the pre-1848 conditions of absolutism
could never be restored in their entirety despite the return
of reactionary rule, and newspapers usurped the role of the
political pamphlet. The consolidation of party politics after
the unification of Germany, the flourishing of economic life,
the process of urbanization, the introduction of universal
suffrage in the Reich and then universal education, the
expansion of communications, the technical advances in
newspaper production; all these developments accounted for
the burgeoning of the German press in the last decades of the
century. In 1866 the number of newspapers stood at about
1,500, of which only 300 appeared daily. By 1900 there were
almost 3,500 papers. By 1914 the figure had reached over
4,200, and nearly half of these papers appeared at least six
times a week. By comparison the British press had only
about 2,400 newspaper titles; and while Germany possessed
close to 2,000 dailies, France had fewer than 500.[10]

[10] For Germany see Kurt Koszyk, *Deutsche Presse im 19. Jahrhundert*
(Berlin, 1966), pp. 307f.; for Great Britain, Max Grünbeck, *Die Presse
Grossbritanniens* (2 vols., Leipzig, 1936), I, p. 117; for France, René de Livois,
Histoire de la presse française (2 vols., Lausanne, 1965), I, pp. 272ff., II, pp.
325ff.

Dispersion was one of the most striking characteristics of the German press. Deep-seated regional and local loyalties, cultural and religious diversity, the lateness of urbanization and unification, the fragmentation of politics, in short the superimposition of modern technical facilities and political and social forms on a society that was still tradition-bound, were mirrored in the decentralization of the German press. In 1906 the 41 cities with populations over 100,000 produced 632 newspapers, an average of slightly over 15 papers per city.[11]

Another prominent feature in the development of the German press in the second half of the nineteenth century was its commercialization. Publishers discovered that a newspaper could be a marketable item like any other piece of merchandise. Impelled entirely by the profit motive and eager to imitate successful precedents in England, France, and America, publishers like August Huck and Wilhelm Girardet designed newspapers to appeal to the largest possible number of consumers. A variant of the mass circulation 'penny press' of western countries, the German *Generalanzeiger*, as this new type of paper was called, catered to the tastes of the mass reading public, emphasizing the human-interest story, giving considerable space to local news, and above all depending on extensive advertising to keep subscription rates low. In order not to alienate possible buyers and advertisers, the Generalanzeiger usually tried to avoid an obvious political bias. However, although political neutrality was the ideal, in practice many of these new papers eventually drifted into specific political attachments. Nearly half of the newspapers founded between 1871 and 1914 belonged to the Generalanzeiger category.[12]

After the turn of the century the *Boulevardblatt* appeared, intended primarily for street sales and patterned on the Pulitzer and Hearst press in the United States and Northcliffe's *Daily Mail* in England. In coverage heightening

[11] Otto Groth, *Die Zeitung* (4 vols., Mannheim, Berlin, Leipzig, 1928-30), I, pp. 217ff.

[12] Koszyk, *Deutsche Presse*, pp. 267ff., 272; see also Emil Dovifat, 'Generalanzeiger', in *Handbuch der Zeitungswissenschaft*, ed. Walther Heide (Leipzig, 1940-1), columns 1217ff.

the sensationalism introduced by the Generalanzeiger, the 'boulevard press' was meant for the hurried reader interested in catching the latest headlines or in preparing for an evening's entertainment. The prose style was declamatory, didactic, omniscient, simple. Pictures were abundant. And as in the case of the Generalanzeiger, advertising was the major source of revenue for these papers.

Traditionalists in Germany never ceased decrying the commercialization process. To introduce the banality of advertisements into what had always been regarded as a product of the intellect they considered as a sacrilege and a prostitution of the press. The influence of big-capital interests was corrupting the press, many claimed; standards were declining, and the intellectual vitality and sense of responsibility of newspapers were being destroyed. Such complaints were, of course, not limited to Germany: Northcliffe, Hearst, and Millaud all stirred immense controversy with their innovations in their respective countries. The very deep-seated reservations against commercialization in Germany, however, meant that the changes in the nature of German newspaper content and in the approach to journalism were not on the whole as far-reaching as in the west. The German press generally retained a more ponderous tone; the newspaper was supposed not only to inform but to instruct as well. The prominence given to this educative ideal most German newspapermen regarded as a worthy and distinctive feature of their press. In practice, however, given the political fragmentation in the country, education by means of the press often amounted to political indoctrination.

Until the turn of the century politics in Germany was the pursuit of active amateurs and of notables. Before 1906 Reichstag deputies did not receive a salary and they rarely campaigned in their constituencies. Party organizations were still extremely loose. Consequently newspapers were felt to be indispensable as a link between parties and their prospective voters. Both politicians and those newspapermen who were conscious of their own political function agreed on this point. The result was that alongside the commercialization of the German press in the last decades of the nineteenth century there occurred a determined politicization as well.

At the beginning of this century approximately one half of all German papers admitted some political commitment.[13] Thus the intense factionalism in German politics was carried over into the press, and a large proportion of newspapers addressed themselves exclusively to specific, narrow groups in society.

In sum, the most striking features of the German press on the eve of the First World War were its abundance, its decentralization, and its growing commercialization and politicization. The press by nature was an eminently modern institution. It was a direct offspring of the liberalization and fragmentation of society; at the same time it was a generator of change, even if to a lesser degree than the nineteenth-century observer assumed. Since in pre-1914 Germany modernism and traditionalism were not yet reconciled in the structure and functioning of society, the press found itself in conflict between its inherent nature and the ambiguous demands of the environment which was its life-blood. The innate impulse of a newspaper was to communicate with increasingly larger numbers of people. However, social and political conditions in Germany stunted the natural development of the press. Instead of being catholic in its appeal, the press in Germany was sectarian; instead of prospering, much of the press struggled to survive.

In politics elements on the liberal left eventually played a leading role in the effort to break the shackles of traditionalism. That progressively inclined liberal publishers should have played a similar role in the press was not a coincidence.

Rudolf Mosse came to newspaper publishing through advertising. With a precociously developed business instinct, unbounded ambition, and remarkable psychological intuition, he founded in 1867, at the age of twenty-two, a newspaper advertising agency in Berlin. At the time advertising was still in its infancy, and the world of publishing, in Germany at any rate, still looked upon this business as an unsavoury activity. Mosse revolutionized the business: he undermined

---

[13] *Handbuch der deutschen Zeitungen*, ed. Oskar Michel (Berlin, 1917), p. xiii.

much of the public prejudice against the advertisement, introduced it not only into newspapers but also periodicals and magazines, and by emphasizing the striking catch-word and visual appeal brought imagination and artistic creativity to advertising. Very rapidly he became a rich man, and his subsequent career epitomized in many respects the ebullient, expansive upsurge of imperial Germany.[14]

In 1871, partly from business ambitions and partly as an irate reaction to the demeaning treatment which his advertising agency received at the hands of the highbrow *Vossische Zeitung*, Mosse founded the *Berliner Tageblatt*. The newspaper at the start was entirely a commercial and by no means a political venture. Mosse's own political ideas were not clearly defined; he had no great passion for politics. However, as a Jew, and as a self-made man who in his business life had to do battle against the conservative mentality, he naturally inclined towards a progressive liberalism. His greatest concern and most intense pride, as Theodor Wolff was to point out on Mosse's death in 1920, was the complete independence of his paper from outside influence.[15] With only these two basic interests—a liberal tendency and editorial independence—as conditions, Mosse gave his chief editors a free rein. While generally sympathetic to Bismarck's foreign policy after 1871, the paper became an increasingly virulent critic of his absolutist manipulation of domestic politics. The irritation of the chancellor at this outspoken criticism was immense and at least on one occasion he attempted to bribe Rudolf Mosse.[16]

The *Tageblatt* rapidly became a success among the Berlin public. By 1886 it had a circulation of 70,000, almost three times that of its rival, the *Vossische Zeitung*; in 1906 the paper had a printing of 112,000 copies, and in 1913 228,000, outstripped only by Ullstein's *Berliner Morgenpost* (360,000)

[14] See Werner E. Mosse, 'Rudolf Mosse and the House of Mosse 1867-1920', in *Year Book IV* of the Leo Baeck Institute (London, 1959), pp. 239ff.; Peter de Mendelssohn, *Zeitungsstadt Berlin* (Berlin, 1959), pp. 63ff.; Margaret Boveri, *Wir lügen alle* (Olten and Freiburg i.B., 1965), pp. 18f.; and Joachim Klippel, *Geschichte des Berliner Tageblattes von 1872 bis 1880* (Dresden, 1935), p. 17.

[15] Koszyk, *Deutsche Presse*, p. 278.

[16] Mosse, 'Rudolf Mosse', p. 244.

and Scherl's *Berliner Lokal-Anzeiger* (*c.* 250,000).[17] Over one quarter of the subscribers lived outside Berlin.

The year 1906 marked a decisive turning point in the history of the paper. The chief editor, Arthur Levysohn, fell seriously ill and Rudolf Mosse summoned one of his own nephews, Theodor Wolff, to take his place. Wolff had come to journalism from the world of theatre; in his youth he had been active in the naturalist *Freie Bühne* movement in Berlin, and two of his plays were eventually produced with success by Max Reinhardt. He had earned his journalistic spurs in twelve years as the Paris correspondent of the *Tageblatt*, particularly through his stirring coverage of the Dreyfus trial. He was thirty-eight years old when he was called to take over the editorship of the paper. Wolff introduced a fresh atmosphere: he gathered a new staff about him, built up the Mosse news service, removed the paper from many of the rather hazy, imprecise formulations of the old-style liberal left, and bestowed on the *Tageblatt* a more coherent and more pronounced radical tone.[18]

A few years later Wolff was to outline his concept of a political paper in a letter to Conrad Haussmann: '. . . in my opinion a political newspaper is effective and valuable only if it follows a straight path, on all questions if possible, and if not, then at least definitely on every major issue. It should not waver to and fro but work entirely consistently and resolutely.'[19] This equation of ideological firmness with political effect was at the core of Wolff's journalistic activity. His insistence on his paper's complete political independence, in other words on the voluntarism which governed its support for any party, and his strict editorial methods reaped respect and admiration but also resentment and

---

[17] See Horst Heenemann, *Die Auflagenhöhen der deutschen Zeitungen* (Berlin, 1930), pp. 75f. Heenemann's figures are, however, occasionally suspect.

[18] For a fuller treatment of Wolff's career see Gotthart Schwarz, *Theodor Wolff und das 'Berliner Tageblatt'* (Tübingen, 1968). Wolff's articles on the Dreyfus affair were published as *Pariser Tagebuch* (rev. edn., Berlin, 1927). For Wolff's impact on the *Tageblatt* see Rudolf Schay, *Die Juden in der deutschen Politik* (Berlin, 1929), pp. 264f. Schay was a member of the editorial board of the paper.

[19] Letter of 10 April 1917, *Nachlass* (hereafter abbreviated as NL) Haussmann, folder 117, Hauptstaatsarchiv Württemberg, Stuttgart.

hatred. Prior to the war Wolff was an untiring advocate of the introduction of parliamentary responsibility in government and of a clinical approach to foreign policy. Under Levysohn the *Tageblatt* had backed the navy and had even spurned publicly the diplomatic overtures of the British government towards Germany between 1898 and 1901.[20] Under Wolff the paper opposed Tirpitz's naval schemes, promoted the idea of alliance with England and friendship with France, and warned against unreasonable support for Austria-Hungary.

Encouraged by his success with this paper, Mosse began to expand his publishing interests, first to a variety of supplements for the *Tageblatt*, then to journals, and finally to more newspapers. In 1889 he started the *Berliner Morgen-Zeitung* and in 1904 he took over from his brother-in-law, Emil Cohn, the failing *Berliner Volks-Zeitung*. This paper, which dated from 1848, was one of the most radical voices of German liberalism and for a time was even edited by the Social Democrat Franz Mehring. With the Mosse advertising and news services available to the paper, it was soon revitalized and within ten years its circulation had climbed from 34,000 to 140,000; in 1916 its sales passed 200,000.[21] In 1910 Mosse also contracted an agreement with the owners of the *National-Zeitung*, a former leading organ of the National Liberal Party in Berlin which had run into financial difficulties after 1900. He was instrumental in having its name changed to the *8-Uhr-Abendblatt* and helped turn it into a popular evening *Boulevardblatt*. In 1914 Mosse's newspapers had a combined circulation of close to half a million.

Leopold Ullstein came to Berlin in 1848 at the age of twenty-two to found a paper wholesale firm. Since Berlin devoured a great deal of paper, Ullstein's firm prospered, and by the time the city became the capital of Germany his fortune was established. In 1871 he turned to politics personally and achieved election to the Berlin city assembly, where he acquired a reputation as an embattled proponent of social and communal reform. However, his political ambitions were

[20] See Wolff, *Das Vorspiel* (Berlin, 1924), p. 70.
[21] Heenemann, *Auflagenhöhen*, p. 76.

frustrated when he was defeated in the next city elections in 1877. He then decided to launch himself into a publishing career.

In the autumn of 1877 Ullstein bought the *Neue Berliner Tageblatt*, a rebellious offshoot of Mosse's *Tageblatt*, turned it into an evening paper, and called it *Deutsche Union*. His main interest at first was, like Mosse's, purely commercial, for, although dissatisfied with the editorial policy of the paper, he allowed the editorial staff to carry on unimpeded until he had established a foothold in the Berlin publishing world. At the beginning of 1878 he purchased the progressive *Berliner Zeitung* and announced that the paper would represent 'a thoroughly left-liberal attitude, independent of all cliques and parties'.[22] Soon afterwards the *Deutsche Union* was dropped. On 29 September 1878 the *Berliner Zeitung* issued a statement of its politics: 'The *Berliner Zeitung* desires constitutional government, not chancellor-absolutism. We demand that the German people be free and not be treated like a conquered nation.'[23] Thereafter its editors repeatedly spent months in prison, charged with *lèse-majesté* because of their remarks about Bismarck and the imperial regime. On account of its severe criticism of Bismarck's anti-socialist legislation and because no readable Social Democratic newspaper appeared in Berlin until 1884, the *Berliner Zeitung* harvested a large working-class readership.[24] Henceforth every new Ullstein venture seemed to spell success. In 1887 an expanded, less political version of the *Berliner Zeitung*, the *Berliner Abendpost*, was begun. By 1889 both papers had a circulation of approximately 100,000.[25]

In 1898 Ullstein introduced a new type of newspaper to the Berlin public, the *Berliner Morgenpost*, styled on the lines of the Generalanzeiger but with clear political opinions. It carried extensive advertising but also pronounced in its first issue that Germans should be 'active political partisans,

[22] Cited in Mendelssohn, *Zeitungsstadt Berlin*, p. 73.
[23] Cited in Georg Bernhard, 'Die Geschichte des Hauses', in *50 Jahre Ullstein 1877-1927* (Berlin, 1927), p. 22.
[24] Ibid., pp. 23f.
[25] Ibid., pp. 30ff.

not merely passive party followers'.[26] The success of the venture surprised even its inspirers: in two months the paper had a circulation of 40,000, in seven months 100,000, and by February 1914 it had reached the 400,000 mark.[27] The avid acceptance of the *Morgenpost* seemed to confirm that the Berliner had an appetite for a newspaper with a firm political inclination, which at the same time offered him the variety and general human-interest coverage of the Generalanzeiger, at a popular price.

Leopold Ullstein died in 1899. Encouraged by the success of the *Morgenpost*, his five sons—Hans, Louis, Franz, Rudolf, Hermann—decided in 1904 to attempt another innovation in German newspaper publishing: to produce a newspaper geared to the street sale, which could quickly inform the interested public of latest developments in a politically impartial manner. On 22 October 1904 the first German *Boulevardblatt* appeared, the *BZ am Mittag*. The paper adopted the American mottoes 'Get it first but get it right' and 'Divorce the news from the views.'[28] Within a year it had swallowed its predecessor, the *Berliner Zeitung*. In 1909 yet another paper was launched, the *Berliner Allgemeine Zeitung*, which eventually absorbed the *Abendpost*.

The Ullsteins, like Mosse, also published popular supplements to their newspapers, and founded magazines for an assortment of interests and readers. The weekly *Berliner Illustrirte Zeitung*, a lively illustrated magazine, became the most successful of all Ullstein publications. In 1910, following the example of Thomas Nelson & Sons in England, the Ullsteins began publishing inexpensive editions of novels. Each *Ullstein-Buch*, with a printing ranging between 50,000 and 100,000, sold for a mark. An immense advertising

---

[26] Lead article, *Berliner Morgenpost* (hereafter *BM*), Nr. 1, 20 September 1898.

[27] Arthur Bernstein, 'Wie die "Berliner Morgenpost" wurde', in *50 Jahre Ullstein*, pp. 153ff.

[28] See Gustav Kauder, 'Bezett! - Bezett am Mittag!', in *50 Jahre Ullstein*, pp. 191ff.; and Egon Jameson, *Wenn ich mich recht erinnere* (Berne and Stuttgart, 1963), pp. 229ff. In an interview in New York in 1912 Franz Ullstein admitted that the *BZ* had been modelled on American popular papers; *New York Times*, 18 September 1912.

campaign for the books was launched and the venture
became an enormous success.[29]

When Leopold Ullstein died in 1899 he left his sons a
publishing firm which had already developed a distinct tradition in its approach to newspapers and their readers.
Leopold Ullstein had concentrated on reaching the mass of
Germans with products tailored to their tastes but at the
same time incorporating certain broad political ideals. The
entire range of newspapers and magazines postulated a kind
of 'Ullstein man': an individual characterized by catholic
interests and open-mindedness, well informed and yet always
seeking new experience and knowledge, humane, progressive,
and conciliatory. In the 1920s the term *Ullsteindeutscher*
was to become a part of the colloquial vocabulary.

For the conservatives of the German publishing world the
Ullsteins represented the worst side of the effervescence of
imperial Germany; their innovations were looked upon with
supercilious disdain, their firm slightingly labelled a 'department store of public opinion'.[30] Even Mosse did not
encounter the same degree of snobbish derision for he at
least published a paper of some intellectual standing, the
Berliner Tageblatt. In 1912-13 the Ullstein brothers were
offered the opportunity of countering these opinions. The
oldest newspaper in Berlin, dating back to the year 1705, the
*Vossische Zeitung, Königlich privilegirte Berlinische Zeitung
von Staats- und gelehrten Sachen*, was put up for sale by the
Lessing family and the Ullsteins could not resist 'the idea of
becoming the publishers of this ancient, respected journal'.[31]
Ownership changed hands on 1 January 1914. The oldest,
stylistically most conservative Berlin paper became the
eminent show-piece of the most progressive and inventive
German publishing firm. The transfer was full of symbolic
meaning and underlined the vigorous ferment in the German
newspaper industry. Prejudices and bigotry were stirred up

---

[29] See the account in Peter de Mendelssohn, *S. Fischer und sein Verlag*
(Frankfurt a.M., 1970), pp. 530ff.

[30] Cited in A.H. Kober, *Einst in Berlin* (Hamburg, 1956), p. 16.

[31] Hermann Ullstein, *The Rise and Fall of the House of Ullstein* (New York,
1943), pp. 118f.; see also Max Osborn, 'Die Vossische Zeitung seit 1904', in
50 Jahre Ullstein, pp. 223ff.

by the sale, and enraged Guards' officers, East-Elbian Junkers, and *Korps* students renounced their subscriptions, claiming that they could not read a 'Jewish rag'.[32] A number of editors of the old *Voss* also refused to join the Ullsteins.

Previously the *Vossische Zeitung* had always displayed a very cautious liberalism, avoiding polemics, emphasizing tradition, but also recognizing the need for gradual political reform. The Ullsteins did not insist that this editorial policy be changed at once; in fact the majority of the old editors remained with the paper. The editor-in-chief Hermann Bachmann stayed on at his post until 1920, although he was joined by a co-editor, Georg Bernhard, in 1914. A few technical changes were instituted and the paper became more colourful, but that was the extent of the immediate alterations. Circulation, which had formerly never exceeded 25,000, rose very slightly, but the paper failed ever to become a successful financial proposition for the Ullsteins. It was acquired for prestige and was maintained for prestige; 'our highest trump', according to Hermann Ullstein, 'but a devilishly expensive one'. In the course of twenty years it was to devour no less than thirty million gold marks.[33]

The installation of Georg Bernhard as co-editor of the *Vossische Zeitung* was as significant a move for that paper as Theodor Wolff's appointment was for the *Berliner Tageblatt*. Bernhard was one of the most colourful, ambitious, and yet erratic figures of the German newspaper world. He had begun his chequered career as a lowly bank employee, had then studied economics and finance, and subsequently had moved into journalism as a business-page editor, for a short time with *Die Welt am Montag* and then with Ullstein's *Berliner Morgenpost*. His first political affiliations had been with the SPD, where he stood on the revisionist flank. At the turn of the century the debate between revisionism and orthodoxy rocked the socialist party, and the party congresses of 1901 and 1903 ended with the tactical defeat of the ideological reformers. The debate was accompanied in the ranks of the

---

[32] See Kober, *Einst in Berlin*, p. 16; and Paul Fechter, *An der Wende der Zeit* (Gütersloh, 1949), pp. 44, 52f. The disdain for the Ullsteins still emerges in Fechter's remarkably contemptuous account.

[33] H. Ullstein, *Rise and Fall*, p. 125.

party by a veritable persecution of intellectuals, particularly of those with bourgeois associations.[34] At the Dresden party conference of 1903 Bernhard, together with Georg von Vollmar, Paul Göhre, Heinrich Braun, and Wolfgang Heine, had come under such sharp attack, from August Bebel among others, for working for bourgeois publications[35] that some months later, after additional differences with the Ullsteins, he had quit the firm and founded his own journal for business news and comment, *Plutus*. In 1908, however, he had resigned from the SPD as a result of disagreements over economic questions and shortly thereafter he had been lured back to the Ullstein firm with the offer of the managing directorship of the Ullstein dailies. Bernhard's personal features and dress—his short-cropped hair and enormous mouth, his rimmed spectacles and bull-like countenance, the three-piece suits, the inseparable black cigar, and the high collars—fitted well with a pugnacious and at times insensitive character and also made him the natural butt of caricature, particularly from anti-Semites. His spontaneity and aggressiveness quickly made him the best-known public personality in the Ullstein firm.

The liberal economist Moritz Julius Bonn, reminiscing about experiences in the German capital in the last years of the nineteenth century, noted that in Berlin 'everything was new and extremely clean; streets and buildings were spacious, but there was a lot of tinsel meant to look like gold. . . . The place was not unlike an oil city of the American west, which had grown up overnight and, feeling its strength, insisted on displaying its wealth.'[36] For Bonn Berlin was a parvenu city which lacked historic roots and traditions. In relation to Berlin which he described as Roman, his birthplace Frankfurt was in his mind Greek. This comparison was not merely the emotional response of a Hessian liberal to the Prussian

[34] See Julie Braun-Vogelstein, *Was niemals stirbt* (Stuttgart, 1966), p. 282; and the same author's *Heinrich Braun* (Stuttgart, 1967), pp. 162ff.

[35] *Protokoll über die Verhandlungen des Parteitages der Sozialdemokratischen Partei Deutschlands, abgehalten zu Dresden vom 13. bis 20. September 1903* (Berlin, 1903), pp. 196ff.

[36] *Wandering Scholar* (London, 1949), pp. 44f.

dominance of the empire; the comparison was apt on many
levels. It certainly held true for the leading left-liberal
publishing houses in the two cities.

By the turn of the century the most prominent provincial
newspaper in Germany was the *Frankfurter Zeitung*. Its
owner was Leopold Sonnemann, a Jew born in 1831 in
Höchberg near Würzburg, who at the age of twenty-two had
inherited the wholesale trade of his father, had shortly
thereafter turned to banking and investment, and in 1856
had founded a financial paper in Frankfurt together with
another banker.[37] Made intensely aware of politics through
his father's and his own business experiences and possessing a
keen and sensitive social conscience, Sonnemann within three
years turned the financial news-sheet into the political organ
of south-German social-liberal tendencies. In 1866
Sonnemann became the sole owner of the paper. Originally
in close touch with the developing workers' movement, he
was greatly distressed when in 1869 the newly founded
Social Democratic Workers' Party emphatically pronounced
its class character. Nevertheless, he remained sympathetic to
the movement in the hope of bridging the gap between the
working class and the socially conscious liberal bourgeoisie.
In 1876 it was revealed that Sonnemann had lent funds to
local socialist party organizations and even to August Bebel
personally.[38]

Adamantly opposed to Bismarck's political methods,
Sonnemann's newspaper withdrew to Stuttgart for three
months when Prussian troops occupied Frankfurt in 1866.
Subsequently, between 1866 and 1868 Sonnemann played a
prominent role in the founding of the left-liberal southern
German People's Party. From 1871 to 1877 and again from
1878 to 1884 he himself was a deputy to the Reichstag and
leader of the parliamentary delegation of the party. He also

---

[37] On Sonnemann see Heinrich Simon, *Leopold Sonnemann* (Frankfurt a.M.,
1931); and Klaus Gerteis, *Leopold Sonnemann* (Frankfurt a.M., 1970). An
elaborate history of the *Frankfurter Zeitung* up to 1911 is available: *Geschichte
der Frankfurter Zeitung*, ed. Verlag der Frankfurter Zeitung (Frankfurt a.M.,
1911).

[38] Koszyk, *Deutsche Presse*, pp. 196ff.

served as a city councillor in Frankfurt for thirty-one years of his life.

Although not strictly a party newspaper, the *Frankfurter Zeitung*, owing to Sonnemann's intimate ties with the People's Party, was a reliable representative of the political attitudes of south-German left liberalism. The untempered attacks of Sonnemann and his paper on Bismarck and the parties in the chancellor's coalitions brought bitter reactions from these forces, ranging from Bismarck's accusations in the Reichstag in 1878 that Sonnemann was in league with the French to direct opposition by the National Liberals and Bismarck to the re-election of Sonnemann to the Reichstag in 1884. Bismarck's fall in 1890 was greeted with enthusiasm in the offices of the *Frankfurter Zeitung*.[39] In the Wilhelmine Reich, the paper continued its appeal for reforms in domestic politics, opposed the government's exorbitant financial outlay for military purposes, advocated closer ties with England, and criticized the excesses of the Kaiser's *Weltpolitik*.

Sonnemann, unlike Mosse and Ullstein, was never interested in building up a newspaper empire. The *Frankfurter Zeitung* was never intended to be a mass-circulation paper but rather an influential, carefully edited and therefore respected, journal of political and economic views. Sonnemann was satisfied if the paper supported itself financially, and for personal gain he invested his money in other economic propositions.[40]

In 1875 the *Frankfurter Zeitung* had reached a circulation of only 20,000; by 1914 this figure had barely doubled. A former editor of the paper estimated that only about one fifth of the subscribers actually lived in Frankfurt.[41] Over one half of the paper's readers belonged to the world of business, industry, and banking, and only an insignificant portion consisted of non-professional people. The *Frankfurter Zeitung* developed over the years the most factual and reliable financial section of all German news-

---

[39] *Geschichte der Frankfurter Zeitung*, pp. 409ff., 438, 450f.

[40] See Gerteis, *Sonnemann*, p. 19.

[41] Wilhelm Cohnstaedt, 'German Newspapers Before Hitler', in *Journalism Quarterly*, XII (1935), p. 158.

papers and became virtually indispensable reading for the business community.[42] Actually, a striking discrepancy existed between the political orientation of the paper and the political inclinations of much of its readership. The political grouping which the paper represented provided only a small percentage of its subscribers. Leopold Sonnemann never revealed any intention of trying to expand the readership of the newspaper. He seemed satisfied that he at least had the ear of the moneyed class, the wielders of considerable power in the German Reich.

The *Frankfurter Zeitung* did not have an editor-in-chief. Instead, the policy of the newspaper was decided in a daily meeting of the entire editorial board which Sonnemann chaired. Not only was editorial policy discussed by this board but also the hiring and dismissal of editors. The only condition to free discussion in the meetings was that all editors had to accept the basic political guidelines of the paper.[43] This corporate decision-making, according to a former member of the board, 'gave a great sense of independence and much satisfaction to the individual editor'.[44]

Leopold Sonnemann died in 1909. In 1893 he had turned his publishing house into a company of limited liability in order to circumvent future problems of inheritance and help ensure the continuity of the political views of the paper.[45] In 1909 Therese Simon-Sonnemann, the only child of Sonnemann, inherited the majority of the company's shares as well as her father's fortune, which in 1908 was valued at between seventeen and eighteen million marks. Her two sons Kurt and Heinrich Simon were eventually to become the major shareholders and leading figures in the firm. Sonnemann in his will also expressed the wish that the paper continue its established political course: 'politically liberal, in social-political matters always just and friendly to reform,

[42] See Ernst Kahn, 'The Frankfurter Zeitung', in *Year Book II* of the Leo Baeck Institute (London, 1957), pp. 233f.

[43] This *Kollegialsystem* was introduced in 1866 after a number of the paper's editors had been arrested. See ibid., p. 235; and Artur Lauinger, *Das öffentliche Gewissen* (Frankfurt a.M., 1958), p. 6.

[44] Kahn, 'The Frankfurter Zeitung', p. 235.

[45] *Geschichte der Frankfurter Zeitung*, p. 641.

always inclined to support the economically weak. As a foundation I would suggest the Munich programme of the German People's Party; of course, this foundation would always have to be adapted to new conditions.' A large part of the success of his enterprise, he recognized, had rested in the ability of the financial section of the *Frankfurter Zeitung* to maintain its independence. 'This must remain so in the future as well.'[46]

Industrialism and the whole modernization process in German society prior to 1914 had brought about striking changes in the form and content of newspapers. Yet the social and political context in which the press functioned authorized the continuing dominance of residual paternalistic attitudes about the role of the press in society. The press was generally not regarded as an independent element in the political process; it did not act as a check on government and administration and on the conscience of political parties. Instead newspapers were utilized as instruments of specific interests, as means of sectionalist propaganda, and as tools for biased pedagogy. Those profit-oriented Generalanzeiger papers which proclaimed political neutrality and struggled to preserve the semblance of impartiality went to the opposite extreme, and by avoiding any contentious issues they served as agents of the *status quo*. The number of newspapers which asserted that the press had a responsibility to the public independent of parties, economic interests, and government and managed to perform according to this belief, was very small indeed. The newspapers of the Mosse, Ullstein, and Sonnemann firms all subscribed to this liberal-democratic conception of the role of the press. Although many of these firms' publications admitted and encouraged party sympathies, they denied that they were in any respect under the control of a party, and they often in fact did not hesitate to criticise their own political allies.

The *Burgfriede* which was called for and established in German politics and society at the outbreak of the war in 1914 extended, of course, to the press as well. The demand

<hr>

46 Cited ibid., p. 1056.

for news in time of war caused the circulation figures of newspapers to soar; many papers doubled the size of their daily printings.[47] However, to use the phrase of one Ullstein journalist, 'a state of siege on truth' set in,[48] and the filtered news which one newspaper had to offer was virtually the same as that of the next. Censorship eliminated any information of a demoralizing nature, from reversals on the war fronts, to train collisions, industrial accidents, strikes, and the food shortage. But instead of producing the uniformity of will and determination among the nation desired by officialdom and the nationalists, newspapers invoked distrust of all their contents. Censorship eroded their credibility.

The war gradually exacerbated the tensions that had existed in German society and politics prior to 1914 and provoked many Germans to reconsider their loyalties to traditional institutions and ideas. Censorship and government directives to the press, accompanied by knowledge of the very different and apparently successful press policies of some of the enemy states, Great Britain in particular, elicited a similar re-examination by newspapermen in Germany of the news and editorial content of their papers. The concept of news, that is factual reporting, acquired a new meaning for much of the German press and public during the war; but, at the same time, the right and responsibility to interpret news was irrevocably imprinted upon the minds of many publishers and journalists. The upshot was that news coverage was expanded and improved in most larger papers, but the war also rang the death-knell of the 'unpolitical' newspaper, even though much of the German press after the war still considered itself *parteilos*, politically unattached. Moreover, government policy towards newspapers during the war made the press more convinced that it possessed political power. In the leading newspapers on the liberal left a heightened sense of political responsibility, independent of the established parties of the empire, and a revitalized confidence in the influence and authority of the press as an institution induced

---

[47] Groth, *Die Zeitung*, I, p. 252.

[48] From an article by Arthur Bernstein of the *Berliner Morgenpost*, which, significantly, was never printed; see Mendelssohn, *Zeitungsstadt Berlin*, pp. 195ff.

a number of prominent journalists and publishers to undertake an active, direct, political initiative in the midst of the confusion and bewilderment which, together with military defeat, overwhelmed Germany in November 1918.

II

THE GERMAN DEMOCRATIC PARTY

On the morning of Sunday, 10 November 1918, only hours after the Kaiser had abdicated and fled to Holland and a day before the armistice was signed, seventeen Berlin industrialists, intellectuals, and civil servants assembled at the home of the Jewish industrialist Theodor Vogelstein in the Kurfürstenstrasse in the heart of Berlin.[1] For some time now Vogelstein had been concerned with the dire economic prospects that faced Germany if the war dragged on much longer. At the end of October he had helped organize, from industrial and commercial circles, a representation to the chancellor for an immediate cessation of hostilities before the enemy armies crossed the boundaries of Germany.[2] With the worsening of the military situation, with the spread of mutiny in the navy and army in early November, and with the burgeoning of revolutionary agitation throughout Germany, Vogelstein, together with three other industrialists who were supporters of the petition, Hjalmar Schacht, Sali Segall, and Count Bethusy-Huc, had decided that a political initiative should be inaugurated immediately since the old political order was on the point of dissolution. They were also of the opinion that fresh blood had to be injected into German politics. An effort had to be made to avoid a total social and economic collapse, and urgent action was imperative.

On 10 November the men assembled discussed the founding of a new liberal party, the basis of which should be a 'truly democratic and social policy'.[3] Since the country,

[1] For a list of those present see the galley proofs of Richard Frankfurter's essay 'Zur Geschichte der Deutschen Demokratischen Partei und ihres Programmes', in NL Haussmann, 100; also in NL Richthofen, 18, Bundesarchiv Koblenz.

[2] See the four letters of Vogelstein to Carl Friedrich von Siemens, 25 to 29 October 1918, and the text of the petition, in NL Siemens, 4/Lf513, Werner-von-Siemens-Institut für die Geschichte des Hauses Siemens, Munich.

[3] Frankfurter, 'Zur Geschichte'.

however, was in a state of turmoil, with public transportation widely disrupted and telephone and postal services utterly unreliable, a major problem existed in communicating with similarly minded groups of individuals, in assembling their representatives, and in disseminating information.[4] Although, of course, the press too suffered from the confusion, a national newspaper was nevertheless still the quickest available means of communicating with a large number of people.

Among the men present at the meeting was Martin Carbe, the general director of the Mosse publishing firm, and, presumably at his instigation, Theodor Wolff was telephoned and asked whether he would consider making the *Berliner Tageblatt* available for the proposed project. Wolff welcomed the idea, and at noon a delegation of five men led by Vogelstein visited him at his home where the decision was taken to proceed with the founding of the new party.[5] Whether these men actually intended that Wolff should now assume the initiative in the new effort is not entirely clear. Wolff himself had the impression that the delegation which visited him had requested that he take the lead in the formation of the new party because he was a figure who had an unscarred political reputation.[6]

During the war, after a brief initial period of reflection, he had rejected any annexationist war aims and had consistently opposed the introduction and use of unrestricted submarine warfare. After the fall of Bethmann Hollweg and the initiation of tighter controls over the press, the *Tageblatt* had been banned on a number of occasions.[7] Also, in the course of the war Wolff's paper had become not only an accepted avenue for sponsoring and publicizing the cause of peace and reform among the liberal left but, more generally, the principal forum for the intellectual opposition to the manner in which the war was being prosecuted. In 1915 Conrad Haussmann had appealed to Wolff to make his paper

[4] Similar discussions were apparently taking place in Jena, Weimar, and south Germany; see ibid.

[5] See ibid., and Wolff's diary for 10 November in his *Through Two Decades* (London, 1936), p. 138.

[6] Wolff, loc. cit.

[7] See Schwarz, *Theodor Wolff*, pp. 46ff.; Schay, *Juden*, p. 264; and Wolff's article in the *Berliner Tageblatt* (hereafter *BT*), 551, 28 October 1918.

available to the anti-annexationist forces in the Progressive Party and Wolff had eagerly complied. In June of the same year, at the request of Professor Hans Delbrück, Wolff had drawn up a public statement signed by a large number of professors, industrialists, and liberal aristocrats, denouncing the annexation of territories which were accustomed to or ready for political independence. Among the extreme nationalists Wolff's criticisms of government policy were regarded as a treasonous campaign of slander, the product of 'a basic perversion of political instincts', and he came to be cast as a 'November criminal', who had played no mean role in sabotaging national solidarity and in undermining Germany's war effort.[8]

A man of sensitivity, an *homme de lettres* whose concern with politics ensued from an acute insight into human foibles and weaknesses, Wolff embraced a liberalism which diagnosed political, social, and economic conditions in terms of individual action and the free will of human beings. For Wolff, society consisted of individuals whose moral, spiritual, and intellectual capacities determined events. He was not unaware of the less tangible significance of social and economic forces, but these forces were of secondary importance in his interpretations of events. Having begun his journalistic career at the turn of the century, a time of considerable national impetuosity and pompousness, irritated by what he regarded as the philistinism and irrationality of *fin-de-siècle* man, and made profoundly aware of social injustice by the Dreyfus affair in France, which he had covered as a journalist, Wolff believed that the duty of the publicist was to reveal the inconsistencies, the deviousness, in a word the illiberality of human behaviour. Wolff was by no means naive enough to believe that the constant revelation of mistakes would necessarily lead to the victory of reason and to the establishment of the democratic, tolerant, cosmopolitan political and social order that he craved for Germany. Rather his belief in reason was based on a '*heroic pessimism*' which commanded as duty the struggle for the postulates of reason, regardless of

8 Gustav Blume, *Herr Theodor Wolff und das Ressentiment* (Berlin, 1920), pp. 5, 39; and Alfred Rosenberg, *Dreissig Novemberköpfe* (4th edn., Munich, 1939), pp. 177ff.

whether they prevailed tomorrow or in five hundred years or in fact never'.[9] Wolff, the inveterate Francophile who chain-smoked Gauloises, stood in the highest tradition of French rationalism.

In November 1918 Wolff was not looked upon simply as another journalist in a country which was littered with newspapers. He was the editor-in-chief of a paper which was considered to represent an entire section of political sentiment. A critic of his was to write to him in 1920: 'I read your newspaper because undoubtedly it has had, and continues to have, such a great significance and impact in public life that one can say without exaggerating that it is impossible to understand the German public of recent years, particularly since 1914, if one is not familiar with the *Berliner Tageblatt*.'[10] On the occasion of Rudolf Mosse's death in September 1920 a Viennese commentator remarked: 'A few more Mosses and Theodor Wolffs could perhaps have averted some of the disaster.'[11] Prior to the autumn of 1918 Wolff and his paper disclaimed subservience to any particular party; rather the *Tageblatt* proffered a *Weltanschauung*, a liberalism which believed in the possibility, if not necessarily in the likelihood, of freeing man from the shackles of unreason and of evoking systematized deliberation. *Erziehungsarbeit*, education, was the concept which lay at the heart of this liberalism.

After Wolff had agreed on 10 November to join the Vogelstein project; he immediately took charge and enlisted his friend Alfred Weber, the Heidelberg professor of sociology and brother of Max Weber, now residing in Berlin. In recent years Alfred Weber, whose political views coincided with those of Wolff, had been a regular contributor to the *Berliner Tageblatt*. The same afternoon Max Wiessner and August Stein, the Berlin correspondents of the *Frankfurter Zeitung*, were reached by telephone and persuaded to co-operate. In the following days Munich and Hamburg were also contacted and the support of the *Münchner Neueste*

9 Kurt Hiller, *Köpfe und Tröpfe* (Hamburg und Stuttgart, 1950), pp. 366f.
10 Blume, *Herr Theodor Wolff*, p. 5.
11 *Wiener Illustrierte Zeitung*, 8 September 1920.

Nachrichten and *Hamburger Fremdenblatt* obtained. Emil Faktor, editor-in-chief of the *Berliner Börsen-Courier*, Hellmut von Gerlach of *Die Welt am Montag*, Robert Hieronymus of the *Holsteinischer Kurier*, Otto Nuschke of the *Berliner Volks-Zeitung*, and Rudolf Mosse all shortly declared their support. This formidable and quickly assembled press backing brought, within a few days, well over one million subscribers, and probably between two and three million readers, into touch with the emerging party.[12]

The Wolff-Weber-Vogelstein group met again on 11 November to draw up more concrete plans for procedure. Despite some differences among the participants, agreement was reached that the new party should have a relatively broad base and that the only requirements for membership should be a professed adherence to democratic principles, the acceptance of the *faits accomplis* of recent days, and a political past that was not marred by pro-annexationist activities during the war. An attempt would be made to absorb the Progressives and those elements in other parties who met and accepted the general conditions. Wolff was to draft a public manifesto to this effect.

Wolff's paramount passion hitherto was to witness the introduction of responsible cabinet democracy in Germany, according to the English example. Prior to the war, and most acidly in 1917 during the deliberations surrounding the peace resolution, Wolff had criticized the representatives of left liberalism for not showing sufficient devotion to the idea of parliamentary sovereignty. Tactical considerations always appeared to relegate this Progressive demand to a secondary position. For Wolff, a political party, like a newspaper, had to radiate clarity, precision, consistency, and confidence in its platform and principles. Compromises and contradictions were like poison in the system of a political organization; they would eventually destroy it.

In the official account of the founding of the Democratic Party Otto Nuschke stated that 'a number of intellectuals, who undoubtedly formed the majority within the leadership

---

[12] See Hjalmar Schacht, *My First Seventy-Six Years* (London, 1959), pp. 150f; Frankfurter, 'Zur Geschichte'; and the list of signatories of the manifesto in the *BT*, 587, 16 November 1918.

of the new party, believed that a small but pure party, a party true to its principles, could, together with the Social Democrats, win a majority in the elections to the national assembly and take in hand the constitutional reconstruction of the state'.[13] Foremost among the intellectuals to whom Nuschke was alluding were Theodor Wolff and Alfred Weber. As a colleague of Wolff in the Mosse firm, Nuschke was in constant contact with the editor of the *Tageblatt* and followed his thinking closely, but in his brief account of the origins of the DDP he oversimplified Wolff's intentions and those of Weber.

Wolff and Weber believed, as did many other politically concerned Germans at the time, that the old liberal parties should be interred together with the empire. The birth of a German republic and of a new political system required new institutional forms and political groupings.[14] Most German liberals doubted whether the nation could afford the 'luxury of two liberal parties' any longer,[15] and in the distressing days of November 1918 the most common political slogans on the lips of the German middle class—a class, in Wolff's words, 'frightened and at its wits' end . . ., fluttering like birds who have fallen out of their nest and do not know where to go'[16]—were liberal unity and a bourgeois front against socialist terror and anarchy. For Wolff, however, liberal unity was not a question of political relevance. A truly democratic party had to be a 'people's party', not a middle-class party. 'The ideas of those politicians urging concentration and consolidation [*Sammlungspolitiker*], who formerly saw a panacea in hotchpotch plans', in lame compromises and tactical somersaults, would find no place in the new party, Wolff wrote. 'We do not want a democracy which

[13] Otto Nuschke, 'Wie die Deutsche Demokratische Partei wurde, was sie leistete und was sie ist', in *Zehn Jahre Deutsche Republik*, ed. Anton Erkelenz (Berlin, 1928), p. 27.

[14] Even Stresemann wrote in *Deutsche Stimmen* of 26 November 1918 that the war and revolution had produced a situation where the prewar parties 'belong only to the past and to history'; reprinted in Gustav Stresemann, *Von der Revolution bis zum Frieden von Versailles* (Berlin, 1919), p. 47.

[15] The quotation is from a speech by Jacob Riesser on 13 October 1918, cited in Wolfgang Hartenstein, *Die Anfänge der Deutschen Volkspartei 1918-1920* (Düsseldorf, 1962), p. 10.

[16] Wolff, *Through Two Decades*, p. 138.

is adulterated either from the right or the left, but a true democracy. . . . Men with fresh, sharp. perceptive minds— together with a number of parliamentarians who accept our views and whom we should not like to do without—must take political leadership and be sent to the national assembly. This is how we conceive our great democratic party.'[17]

Wolff and Weber did not think in terms of a small intellectually élitist party, but rather of a party whose clear forthright approach to political problems and whose decisive leadership would act as a powerful magnet within a nation which had completely lost confidence in its old political leaders. Indeed, their primary concern was not about the size of the party—they assumed it would attract widespread public support—but rather about the character and attitudes of its leadership. It was in the choice of its prominent political lights that the most careful deliberations had to take place. The ideals of the party and consequently its political vigour should not be jeopardized by an over-zealous preoccupation with size. The party would gather adherents through the attractiveness and suitability of its ideas, not as a home for political orphans.

The intention of Wolff was to create in Germany a counterpart to the French radical socialist party. The new democratic party would 'organize those strata of the non-Catholic middle class who are at all inclined toward democratic ideas';[18] it would not attempt to compete with the Centre Party or the SPD, but it was to be hoped that together with these two parties it would provide the pillars of the liberal republican state. The new party would attach great emphasis to social reform, not simply to try and drain away support from the socialist parties but because of genuine conviction.

Despite his belief in the primacy of ideas as a constructive force, Wolff was not unaware of the tangible organizational needs of the new party. He realized that it was imperative that the Progressives be immediately persuaded to join the emerging party so that their organization could be put to use.

17 *BT*, 588, 16 November 1918.
18 Wolff diary for 10 November 1918, *Through Two Decades*, p. 139.

For this reason Georg Gothein, who had been with Haussmann the staunchest opponent of annexationist tendencies within the Progressive Party, was contacted and urged to give his support to the new political initiative.[19]

With these considerations in mind, Theodor Wolff had drafted his manifesto to announce the new party. Addressing the 'men and women of the new Germany', he began by proclaiming that the imperial order was 'irredeemably dead', the 'old party structures shattered', the 'piously guarded party programmes rendered meaningless', and many of the former political leaders of the country 'left behind by the double-quick step of history'. The manifesto appealed to all those Germans who were interested in taking an active part in the construction of a new republican Germany, in which 'freedom', 'legality', and 'the political equality of all citizens' were part of one indivisible concept of liberty and justice, in which every form of terror, whether that of Bolshevism or reaction, would be combatted. 'A *great democratic party for a unitary Reich*' would be formed by those who responded to the call. No clear programme could be announced as yet, but Wolff did devote one quarter of the manifesto to suggestions for social and economic reform. Some proposals were precise: the confiscation of private profits from the war, the institution of a progressive capital levy, legislation to guarantee the claims of war veterans, their widows and orphans, the partition of state lands, restrictions on large land-holding. Others were more vague: 'the international implementation of a socialist minimum programme' and the socialization of certain monopoly-controlled areas of the economy.[20] Wolff intentionally did not once use words such as 'liberal', 'bourgeoisie', 'middle-class centre'. He was not interested in a class party, or in middle-class unity.

Ideas akin to Wolff's were being voiced at the same time by a number of other prominent German newspapers of

---

[19] See Gothein to Haussmann, 13 November 1918, NL Haussmann, 114.

[20] The manifesto appeared in the *BT*, 587, 16 November 1918, and in a large number of other papers throughout the country. A copy of Wolff's original draft is available in NL Harden, 113, p. 43, Bundesarchiv Koblenz. The emphasis is in the original.

liberal persuasion. Several had effected astonishing about-turns once the military leaders had admitted defeat and particularly when the revolutionary events of November had erupted. One such paper was the former National Liberal *Münchner Neueste Nachrichten*. On 15 November the paper received a new editor-in-chief, and editorial policy turned suddenly against the National Liberals. The pacifists Ludwig Quidde and Friedrich Wilhelm Foerster now frequently appeared as contributors; an article by Foerster was even published which placed the burden of war-guilt squarely on Germany's shoulders.[21] Urging liberal consolidation, the paper nevertheless warned against making bourgeois unity a negative goal, that is a purely defensive action directed against the Social Democrats.[22] Another paper enacting an about-face was the *Hamburger Fremdenblatt*, which had been considered left-liberal prior to 1914 but during the war, overcome by an aggressive patriotism, had supported Tirpitz, unrestricted submarine warfare, the goals of the military leadership, and had opposed the peace resolution of 1917.[23]

The volte-face of these two journals was representative of the reactions of many liberals to the sudden demise of the old political system and to the alarming popular agitation which surrounded and accompanied this demise. In many cases the *renversement des alliances* which a significant number of liberals enacted was prompted by simple opportunism. Many liberals diagnosed a distinct 'pitch to the left',[24] a genuine radicalization of political opinion, and acted quickly so as not to be stranded politically. Most, however, without necessarily being convinced democrats, felt that the confrontation which had been brewing in Germany for several decades between the conservative establishment and the reformist opposition had been resolved suddenly. Now it was a question of giving democracy a chance and preventing reform from becoming a purely socialist pursuit.

[21] *Münchner Neueste Nachrichten* (hereafter *MNN*), 643, 20 December 1918.

[22] *MNN*, 605, 30 November 1918.

[23] Alfred Herrmann, *Hamburg und das Hamburger Fremdenblatt* (Hamburg, 1928), pp. 503ff.

[24] August Weber to Stresemann, 15 November 1918, Deutsche Volkspartei files, R45II/1, pp. 13f., Bundesarchiv Koblenz.

The closest spiritual ally of Wolff and the *Berliner Tageblatt* among German newspapers was the *Frankfurter Zeitung*. The Frankfurt paper, on 25 October, had been one of the first public voices to demand the abdication of Wilhelm II. With the outbreak of the revolution, a significant section of the editorial staff, particularly some of the younger members such as Wilhelm Cohnstaedt and Arthur Feiler, was seized by a rebellious, reforming enthusiasm, and the pages of the newspaper became the platform for some of the most radical non-socialist utterances in the country. On 11 November the editorial article expressly welcomed the revolution in Germany and urged the progressive bourgeoisie to associate with it, for not just the aims of the workers were being realized. This point was emphasized repeatedly in the following days. New political leaders for the bourgeoisie were called for to rouse the middle class from its 'death-like sleep'. Even the temporary dictatorship of the socialists was accepted as unavoidable and necessary in the circumstances. The mere acceptance of the republic was not enough: 'the new Germany must be radical and socialist to the core! . . . Only with a radical programme can the middle class dare to engage in politics with a prospect of success and enter the elections to the national assembly. The bourgeoisie must be radical—or it will cease to be!'[25] For the *Frankfurter Zeitung*, the manifesto of Wolff, though welcomed when it was published, was hardly radical enough. The mention of socialization did not suffice; the *Frankfurter Zeitung* demanded 'extensive socialization'.[26]

After coming to Berlin for a meeting to discuss the manifesto, Georg Gothein returned to Breslau and on 13 November sent out a letter to twenty-one Progressives urging them to declare their adherence to the new party and to canvass further support in their respective constituencies.[27] That the names of only six Progressives (four Reichstag deputies) appeared under the manifesto published in the press on 16 November was probably due mainly to the slowness of the mails but presumably also in part to the hesitation

[25] *Frankfurter Zeitung* (hereafter *FZ*), 316, 14 November 1918.
[26] *FZ*, 318, 16 November 1918.
[27] A copy of the letter sent around is in NL Haussmann, 114.

and unwillingness of some of the Progressives approached to commit themselves before the party as a whole had taken a position. A reflection of the state of disarray and confusion of the National Liberal Party was the fact that fourteen National Liberals (nine deputies) were among the sixty signatories.

Almost one half of those who endorsed the manifesto held the title of doctor; one third were active as publicists or academics; and the majority of the signatories came from Berlin.[28] There was thus a strong intellectual and idealistic strain among the founders of the party. Most of them had been outsiders to active politics in imperial Germany; many were frustrated by the dilemma of their position as critics of society and politics and yet concurrently as intellectual servants of the same society and political system. In the turmoil of November 1918, during the apparent collapse of the old social and political order, and amidst the general indecision and confusion evident in the German middle classes, this frustration erupted in some intellectuals, and they were seized by a missionary zeal that was composed of a sense of opportunity, a feeling of responsibility, and in no small measure an attitude of moral righteousness. These intellectuals sensed that it was their duty to become actively engaged in the political reconstruction of Germany.[29] Of all the ideas which received expression, the most popular was that of 'newness': the lost war and the revolution heralded a new beginning, a rebirth, springtime, fresh ideas, and, above all, new uncompromised political leadership. An individual like Alfred Weber even left the impression of being infused with messianic aspirations. The experienced liberal politicians, whether Progressive or National Liberal, whether annexationist or unerringly opposed to aggressive German nationalism during the war, tended to be regarded with distrust simply because they were considered to have been tainted by active participation in a political establishment which had gone bankrupt.

[28] Hartenstein, *Anfänge*, pp. 56f., presents a valuable analysis of the signatories.

[29] See Gordon A. Craig's remarks on artists, 'Engagement and Neutrality in Weimar Germany', *Journal of Contemporary History*, II (April 1967), pp. 51f.

Theodor Wolff and Alfred Weber, in particular, came to regard the new democratic party as their brain-child and tended to picture themselves in the role of a selection committee by which all prospective members had to be screened.[30] They were faced, however, with a delicate problem: their political venture, in order to gain any momentum, required the organizational apparatus of at least the Progressive Party. Their resolution of this difficulty—that all could join who wished to do so, but that only those with an 'uncompromised' political past could assume prominent positions in the party—was bound to break down in practice, for it was difficult to counter rationally the argument of Meinecke that 'we all share a part of the responsibility through our actions and our words, for the fate which has befallen us, and only Pharisees could dare attempt to deliver themselves of this shared responsibility.'[31]

After the democratic manifesto had appeared in the press on 16 November—in all the major liberal newspapers and in a considerable portion of the provincial press—declarations of support began to flood into the offices of the new party. Wolff felt 'rather like old Noah facing a vast crowd pushing to get into the Ark'.[32] The sociological spectrum of support for the party was very broad. Heavy industrialists like Hugo Stinnes wished to join; every section of the middle classes was represented; and the endorsement of the party by the liberal trade-union representatives stemmed, at least in part, the flow of formerly liberal workers to the SPD.[33] The social heterogeneity of the new support made it inevitable that sooner or later an intense conflict of opinion would develop over two questions which had plagued the past history of German liberalism and were to remain unresolved in the Weimar Republic: the questions

[30] See Otto Fischbeck to Gothein, 18 November 1918, NL Gothein, 20, pp. 39f., Bundesarchiv Koblenz.

[31] Article in *Norddeutsche Allgemeine Zeitung*, 563, 3 November 1918, reprinted in Meinecke, *Politische Schriften und Reden*, ed. Georg Kotowski (Darmstadt, 1958), p. 259.

[32] Wolff, *Through Two Decades*, p. 152.

[33] See the correspondence for November 1918 in NL Erkelenz, 12, Bundesarchiv Koblenz; especially the letter from Karl Hartmann, a trade-union leader in Duisburg, 15 November 1918.

of liberal unity and of attitudes to the Social Democratic Party.

The re-establishment of liberal party unity had been a constant issue for liberals, even if at times subdued, ever since the split in the Progressive Party in 1866. At the turn of the century, with two decades of steady decline behind them, many liberals on both the right and left were sympathetic to the gradual consolidation of liberalism. During the war the matter was not forgotten and prominent voices were often raised in favour of the union of the Progressive and National Liberal parties. Negotiations about the fusion of the two parties had already been going on in secret prior to 8 November 1918.[34] After the abdication of the Kaiser and the assumption of governmental control by a 'council of people's commissars', calls for liberal unity to oppose 'socialist dictatorship' multiplied and open negotiations between the two liberal parties began.[35]

Gustav Stresemann, the leader of the National Liberals, was weighing seriously the possibilities of a complete merger with the Progressives but did not wish to commit his party irrevocably before the elections to the national assembly—the first elections in over six years—had revealed what the public's response to his party would be.[36] This flexible position became untenable, however, as soon as it was clear that the Wolff-Weber democrats were intent upon drawing the Progressives into their new party and as soon as a number of eminent Progressives and their followers showed a distinct interest in joining the new creation. The reasoning of most Progressive leaders was that it would be disastrous for left liberalism as a whole if an independent party inserted itself in the political spectrum between them and the Social Democrats. Conrad Haussmann noted that public sentiments were swinging sharply to the left; the old Progressive programme was no longer adequate; and if, therefore, the

[34] Oskar Maretzky to Stresemann, 8 November 1918, NL Stresemann, 180, 133670ff., Politisches Archiv des Auswärtigen Amtes, Bonn.

[35] For the best accounts of the negotiations see Hartenstein, *Anfänge*, pp. 14ff.; and Robson, 'Left-Wing Liberalism', pp. 375ff.

[36] See Stresemann to Theodor Boehm, 15 November 1918, NL Stresemann, 180, 133662.

Progressives wished to retain the upper hand in the left-liberal movement they had to adapt their ideas to the more radical public mood.[37]

Stresemann was well informed of the intentions of the Wolff-Weber group of democrats by 14 November at the latest.[38] Of all the critics of Stresemann and the National Liberals during the war Theodor Wolff had been the most severe and unrelenting, and the leader of German right-wing liberalism had developed an intense dislike for the sermonizing, deprecating self-assurance of Wolff. He decided that he personally could never join a political party in which Wolff played a prominent role and was prepared if necessary to retire from politics if there were no alternative to such a party. Many of his National Liberal friends felt the same way. Otto Hugo, the general secretary of the National Liberals in Lower Saxony, wrote to Stresemann on 15 November: 'In the provinces Theodor Wolff has such a horribly deterring effect that our party friends will take a thoroughly negative attitude [to the new party], with exceptions perhaps in areas of south Germany and Silesia.'[39]

At a meeting of the Dresden National Liberal Association, Rudolf Heinze, a leading Saxon politician, remarked: 'A party which includes Theodor Wolff and myself is intrinsically a fiction.' Stresemann agreed and noted that this argument was 'in essence the justification' for the foundation of a separate German People's Party (DVP) which would carry on the true traditions of national liberalism.[40]

Stresemann was to claim that the negotiations for liberal unity had collapsed because of the intransigence and dogmatism of the democrats, but it is clear that he never regarded complete unity as possible. In this respect he and Theodor

[37] 'Notizen 1918', NL Haussmann, 101.

[38] Stresemann's diary for 14 November contains the entry: 'Learn of manifesto for the formation of democratic party (Witting, Theodor Wolff, Kleefeld).' NL Stresemann, 201, 166100f.

[39] NL Stresemann, 187, 134545ff.

[40] Stresemann, *Von der Revolution*, p. 66. In a letter to Brües on 25 November 1918 Stresemann wrote: 'I could not join the other side without being unfaithful to myself, whereas union with the Progressive Party would have been altogether possible and would have corresponded to my wishes.' NL Stresemann, 187, 134608.

Wolff were of the same opinion. Wolff, the intellectual, at least made no secret of his views; Stresemann, the politician, procrastinated briefly for tactical reasons. Both men vied for support—from the Progressives and left-wing National Liberals—for their respective political ideas; both tried to render the other politically impotent. Wolff hinted that Stresemann would be wise to disappear from political life for the time being because of his annexationist past; Stresemann did not hesitate to impute sabotage of the home front to Wolff's war articles—an early variant of the stab-in-the-back theory—and suggested that Wolff and his friends were therefore just as 'compromised' as the annexationists. In Stresemann's mind, those who insisted that he retire from politics without demanding the same of 'the other side' were hypocrites.[41]

It was, however, not only personal antipathies and antagonistic attitudes during the war which separated Stresemann and his associates from the Wolff-Weber camp. Their respective interpretations of the revolution, of the substance and purpose of liberalism, and consequently their attitude towards socialism and its political adherents, were irreconcilably opposed. Wolff saw the revolution as a great opportunity for German democracy and hoped to found a party which would co-operate closely with the Social Democrats; for Stresemann the revolution signified the end 'to everything that had seemed permanent',[42] and in his own mind he readily associated the revolution with Social Democracy and what he regarded as its nihilistic tendencies. As far as he was concerned the gap between the democrats and the National Liberals was far greater than that between the democrats and the Social Democrats.[43]

[41] In the letter to Brües, 25 November 1918, Stresemann added: 'Whether we in our conception of war policy were wrong or not, on this the last word has not yet been spoken. The history of this war will be written, and retrospective criticism will one day establish that the collapse of the home front also led to the collapse of the military front which was holding so courageously. In this disruption of the home front no one took such an enthusiastic part as the *Berliner Tageblatt.*' Ibidem.

[42] Stresemann, *Von der Revolution*, p. 47.

[43] Ibid., pp. 58f.

The German Democratic Party (DDP), comprising democratic, Progressive, and left-wing National Liberal elements, was officially constituted on 20 November. However, the broader issues which separated Stresemann and his followers from the Wolff-Weber group remained matters of bitter contention within the ranks of the new party. Particularly the questions of socialization and of the desired relationship between a predominantly middle-class party and the SPD bedevilled the new creation; they constituted the most difficult issues in the composition of the party's official programme and delayed the drafting of this programme until well into the new year. The prominence accorded these issues indicated that many of the ideas propounded by neoliberal thinkers since the turn of the century had in fact remained hypotheses, and that the reform impulse in German liberalism had gained ground not for positive but largely negative reasons.

The left and the moderate sectors of the new party now began a tug of war for control. The imperious attitudes of Alfred Weber in particular increasingly upset the middle-of-the-road liberals. Otto Fishbeck had the impression that Weber considered everyone but the new democratic elements as 'stupid children or political criminals'.[44] On 30 November the election of the provisional executive revealed the configuration of power in the party. Of the thirty-four members of the executive only nine were left democrats. They included Wolff, Weber, Otto Nuschke, and Arthur Feiler, the latter a political editor of the *Frankfurter Zeitung*.

Towards the beginning of December, the Progressives, who now constituted the majority in the DDP, initiated an offensive against the more radical political novices on the left flank.[45] Men like Fishbeck, Naumann, and even Haussmann found it intolerable that politically inexperienced, self-appointed, and self-righteous 'upstarts' should try to dictate policy to the party. Naumann likened the founding of the party to a *'coup*, which emanated from the *Berliner*

---

[44] Fischbeck to Gothein, 18 November 1918, NL Gothein, 20, pp. 39f.

[45] Vogelstein remarked on this offensive in his letter to Gothein, 9 December 1918, NL Gothein, 32, pp. 89f.

Tageblatt'. 'We have been Bolshevized', he remarked.[46] His disciple Theodor Heuss castigated Alfred Weber for his 'hysterics' and 'demagoguery' and Wolff for his inappropriate 'pacifistic sallies'.[47] Fishbeck worried that the predominance of Berlin Jews among the signatories of the original manifesto would leave the impression that the new party was a 'capitalist-Jewish' undertaking and would provide ammunition for anti-Semitic propaganda against the DDP.[48] The Naumannite journal *Deutsche Politik* pointed out that the magnitude of the tasks facing German left liberals did not permit that 'two or three newspapers, two or three new party leaders should possess unlimited powers to pronounce the opinion of the party'.[49] These voices were also echoing opinions which were widespread in the provinces. A Düsseldorf liberal reported that campaign efforts for the party in December constantly encountered the response: 'I can't join a party which is led by *those* papers which did so much to subvert national unity during the war and which are under Jewish influence.'[50]

On 1 December Alfred Weber committed an enormous political blunder which not only revealed his political *naiveté* but also rendered him defenceless before his critics in the party, who only too gladly took the opportunity to expel him from his executive position. In a speech in Berlin Weber spread a rumour that the Rhenish industrialists August and Fritz Thyssen and Hugo Stinnes were negotiating with the Entente powers to establish a separate Rhenish federation. On 6 December the industrialists were arrested and transported to Berlin, with absolutely no concrete evidence against them. On 11 December they were released at the

---

[46] Naumann to Georg Hohmann, 25 November 1918, cited by Theodor Heuss, *Friedrich Naumann* (rev. edn., Tübingen, 1949), p. 453.

[47] Heuss to Haussmann, 13 December 1918, NL Haussmann, 115.

[48] Fischbeck to Haussmann, 1 December 1918, NL Haussmann, 114. Ministerialdirektor Kirchner, for example, in a letter to Siegfried von Kardorff, 25 December 1918, called the 'German Democratic Party (Theodor Wolff)' a tool of 'Jewish capitalism' and 'a pace-maker for Social Democracy'; NL Kardorff, 11, p. 35, Bundesarchiv Koblenz. See also Erich Koch-Weser's diary entry for 23 December 1918, NL Koch-Weser, 14, p. 203, Bundesarchiv Koblenz.

[49] From editorial remarks, III (13 December 1918), pp. 1569f.

[50] Otto Erbslöh to Erkelenz, 14 December 1918, NL Erkelenz, 12.

intervention of the council of people's commissars and the Prussian ministry of interior. Weber drew the consequences of his mistake and offered his resignation to the managing committee of the DDP; it was accepted on 13 December with enthusiasm.[51]

On 19 December the general congress of workers and soldiers' councils, meeting in Berlin, voted that a national assembly be convened to draft a new constitution for the Republic. National elections would be held in a month's time. The election campaign began immediately and forced the bourgeois parties, all of which had been undergoing some degree of reorganization, to consolidate themselves quickly on the basis of the old organizations and established politicians. In the candidate lists drawn up by the DDP there was scarcely a new radical face in the lead positions on the lists. The left democrats complained bitterly about their exclusion, but to no avail.

The case of Max Weber was instructive. At the end of November he had written a series of articles for the *Frankfurter Zeitung*[52] discussing mainly the possible nature of Germany's constitution but at the same time ranging over many of the wider political problems that would prove inseparable from the constitutional deliberations. Among other things Weber came out for a large measure of socialization. The articles received considerable attention in political circles, but also infuriated a great many people. The *Frankfurter Zeitung* accepted Weber as an unofficial political adviser, and he exerted a noticeable influence on the editorial views of the paper.[53] Supported strongly by the paper, Weber agreed to seek election to the national assembly as a candidate in Hessen-Nassau, but the Democrats in Cassel and Marburg expressed such strong opposition to the candidacy

[51] Deutsche Demokratische Partei files, R45III/9, p. 17, Bundesarchiv Koblenz. In the speech, on 1 December, in which Weber made his false accusations against the Thyssens and Stinnes, he challenged his audience to elevate 'spiritual ideas' above material concerns. See the report in the *FZ*, 334, 2 December 1918.

[52] The articles were entitled 'Die Staatsform Deutschlands', *FZ*, 324, 22 November; 326, 24 November; 330, 28 November; 332, 30 November; 337, 5 December 1918.

[53] See the letter of Marianne Weber to the *FZ*, 805/6, 29 October 1931.

that Weber in the end let it fall. Hermann Luppe, the mayor of Frankfurt, eventually led the list, followed by the mayor of Cassel, Erich Koch-Weser. Koch-Weser's diary for 23 December expressed well the mood which determined the exclusion of Weber:

The intolerance of our left democrats is daily becoming more insufferable. They have commandeered the right to speak for the entire middle class. Whoever refuses to swear by them is rejected. In this manner they are strengthening the [political] right. Is it not outrageous that the *Frankfurter Zeitung* wishes to bless the province with 5 deputies whose main merit is that they write for this paper?[54]

Already the notion was emerging that the prominent left-liberal press, or democratic press, as it now described itself, was perhaps more harmful than beneficial to the interests of the DDP. The independent initiative of the Berlin-Frankfurt democratic newspapers in the founding of the new party and in proposals for policy and leaders was resented by the professional politicians, most intensely by those like Koch-Weser and Luppe who hoped that the new democratic republic would provide them with an opportunity for rapid advancement from the relative obscurity of civic politics to national prominence. The *Frankfurter Zeitung* castigated the party leadership for not making room for 'striking personalities' and denounced the rule of the party bosses.[55] Luppe, who later was to become the mayor of Nuremberg, complained that subsequently the paper attacked him more often than it supported him.[56]

Max Weber was not the only political hopeful who was run over by the party machine. Walther Rathenau, Hugo Preuss, Martin Carbe, Kurt Kleefeld, Heinrich Gerland, were others who suffered similar exasperating fates. In some cases the party leadership was only indirectly responsible for the exclusion of men with slightly radical views. At the end of December a '*Kuratorium* for the reconstruction of German economic life', based on the Berlin electro-technical industry, but including bankers and merchants, had been formed with the expressed purpose of guaranteeing 'trade and industry a

54 NL Koch-Weser, 14, p. 203.

55 *FZ*, 2, 1 January 1919.

56 See the unpublished memoirs of Hermann Luppe, NL Luppe, 9, p. 87, Bundesarchiv Koblenz.

greater role in political life' and of providing Germans 'with a wider knowledge of the importance of economic affairs for the Fatherland'. The AEG and Siemens firms each contributed one million marks to a fund which was to be used in the elections explicitly 'for the battle against Social Democracy'.[57] On 31 December this Kuratorium met with representatives of the executive committee of the DDP and agreed to donate one million marks to the party, with the provision, however, that the Kuratorium could stipulate the electoral areas (and therefore candidates) to which financial support was to be supplied.[58] This financial assistance, about whose exact nature only a small number of the party's leaders was informed, ensured that not many avid proponents of socialization would appear in the DDP's parliamentary party. The party, by accepting this aid with its provisos, surrendered its right to independent action and established a connection with business and industry which was to reduce a significant number of its leading members, in view of their many genuinely democratic goals, to a state of acute political schizophrenia.[59] The need for substantial financial support from business concerns and the desire for complete independence from outside interests in formulating policy were to prove irreconcilable. Many younger idealistic democrats referred cynically to the Reich list as the 'price list'.[60] All non-socialist parties received assistance from the Kuratorium

[57] Carl Friedrich von Siemens to A. von Rieppel, 14 February 1919, NL Siemens, 4/Lf514, pp. 55f. See also Lothar Albertin, 'German Liberalism and the Foundation of the Weimar Republic: A Missed Opportunity?', in *German Democracy and the Triumph of Hitler*, ed. Anthony Nicholls and Erich Matthias (London, 1971), pp. 37f. The same author's *Liberalismus und Demokratie am Anfang der Weimarer Republik* (Düsseldorf, 1972) appeared too late to be integrated into this work.

[58] Siemens to Deutsch, 2 January 1919, NL Siemens, 4/Lf514, p. 13.

[59] Without being aware of the financial details, Georg Bernhard nevertheless described perceptively the effect on the DDP of the influx of men from banking, business, and industry, in *Die deutsche Tragödie* (Prague, 1933), pp. 65f.

[60] Lilo Linke, *Restless Flags* (London, 1935), p. 287. The system of proportional representation adopted after the war stated that for every 60,000 votes won in a constituency a party could send one deputy to the Reichstag from that constituency. The residue of votes from all constituencies was then tallied and applied to a 'Reich list', a slate of names drawn up by the national office of each party; again for every 60,000 votes one name from this list was elected. The top names on the Reich lists of the larger parties were sure of a seat in the Reichstag.

but in 1919 the DDP received the largest sum, an indication of how industry assessed the political mood in Germany after the war.

By January 1919 many of the more radical liberals who had placed such high hopes in the revolution and in the new party had become sorely disillusioned. Left-liberal intellectual critics began to regain their sense of detachment. For almost six weeks the *Frankfurter Zeitung* and *Berliner Tageblatt* had come close to adopting the role of a 'party press'. During the election campaign the papers backed the DDP strongly but at the same time retreated some distance from the party. Hellmut von Gerlach captured many of the sentiments of the more radical democratic press in an article which he wrote on 20 January 1919, the day after the elections to the national assembly. The DDP had just become the third largest party with seventy-five seats.

At the end of 1918 the German Democratic Party, in its budding youth, appeared on the political horizon like a brand new, splendidly radical and brilliant constellation [said Gerlach]. Its founding manifesto resounded like a fanfare. After mature reflection, only those persons were permitted to sign who during the war had not revealed themselves as either reactionaries or imperialists. . . . The new era was to produce something quite new. It seemed that Germany was finally to acquire what almost every European state possessed: a radical middle-class democratic movement, not socialist, but still much less anti-socialist. . . . Alas, how quickly beauty and form fade! The German Democratic Party of today has a devilish similarity to the Progressive People's Party of yesterday. To be sure, the transition from monarchy to republic has been effectively executed. . . but otherwise little has changed either in personnel or in essentials. . . . The election speeches, proclamations, and other manifestations taste of *ancien régime*, of course not in the sense of feudalism, but rather in the direction of the *juste milieu* of the upright citizen-king Louis Philippe. The left is being damned with a rigour, as if the dangers from that quarter were at least as great as those from the right. One hears less talk of pacifism than of a powerful army. Nationalism is so strongly emphasized that it sounds almost nationalistic. The 'middle class' is talked about so much that one could sometimes feel transferred back to the blissful times of the conservative guild agitation. . . . The young bourgeois democratic movement seems to be, all in all, far more *opportunistic* than *principled*.[61]

---

[61] *Die Welt am Montag*, 20 January 1919, cited in Ruth Greuner, *Wandlungen eines Aufrechten: Lebensbild Hellmut von Gerlachs* (Berlin [East], 1965), pp. 106f.

Hopelessly outnumbered in the party committees, the left democrats had less and less influence on party decisions. The sole left democrat to be elected to the national assembly was Otto Nuschke. For Theodor Wolff the atmosphere in the party's executive committee became ever more stifling, and the *Berliner Tageblatt* began to adopt an increasingly critical tone towards the DDP. The managing committee even asked Nuschke to point out to Wolff the harm that his paper was doing to the party.[62] Wolff decided that independent criticism of the party and active participation in its ranks were incompatible. At the end of April 1919 he resigned from the executive.

The reason Wolff gave for his resignation was that the executive committee no longer asserted the 'political leadership' which the statutes of the party had accorded it and that this leadership had been assumed instead by the parliamentary party. 'The members of the party executive share responsibility for political decisions of which they know nothing and which they can in no way influence.'[63] Wolff's complaint was relevant, but it was none the less merely a pretext. He was not as deeply disturbed by the shift in the source of political initiative within the party as by the individuals who had moved into the foreground of the party's policy-making forums and who were instrumental in drowning out the radicals. Conrad Haussmann read Wolff's letter and felt compelled to reply to his charge that the parliamentary party had seized the reins of leadership. 'You said it, Rabbi. And I level the serious charge that the Berlin executive, in which Theodor Wolff was a leading figure, did *not* lead.' Liberals in the provinces, continued Haussmann, had joined the Democratic Party at Wolff's request in mid-November and had waited for leadership, for weeks and months had waited for a party programme, which never came and still had not been drafted. 'Is that what you call leadership?' he asked Wolff. Haussmann told Wolff that he and the left democrats in Berlin had failed miserably in their duties.

<hr>

62 Minutes of the meeting of the managing committee, 18 March 1919, NL Richthofen, 16.

63 A hand-written copy of the letter of resignation to Otto Fischbeck, dated 'end of April 1919', is in NL Haussmann, 102.

The parliamentary party had been forced to fill the leader-ship vacuum. Its task was a difficult one, but now the democratic press was deserting it and seeking to undermine its authority with the 'mistaken teaching of [Georg] Bernhard and Heinrich Simon' that 'the democratic press must be independent from the parliamentary party.' 'In truth *unanimity* [between party and press], in *principle* and in *fact, must* exist. Its lack means the neutralization of both.' Haussmann concluded by saying that the conception of Germans (i.e. Wolff) about what the relationship between press and parliament should be was wrong, and that the cleavage between party and press was 'in the final analysis an expression of the unpolitical mind of Germans'.[64] The last remark was an oblique stab at what Haussmann considered to be the unreal, impractical, idealistic political notions of men like Theodor Wolff, Georg Bernhard, Hellmut von Gerlach, Heinrich Simon, Wilhelm Cohnstaedt, in other words of the left-democratic press.

Haussmann's irritated outburst against Wolff, and the Berlin-Frankfurt democratic press in general, implied a belief that the party and the independent, generally more radical, press could and should work closely together. Haussmann and Friedrich von Payer tried hard to re-establish the intimate ties between the Württemberg left liberals and the *Frankfurter Zeitung* that had existed while Leopold Sonnemann had been alive.[65] During the war these ties had loosened considerably, and in November 1918 a gush of 'enthusiasm for the revolution' (*Revolutionsschwärmerei*) engulfed the editorial staff.[66] Payer was aghast at some of the paper's attitudes and, as an old friend of the Sonnemann family and minor shareholder, decided to join the super-visory board of directors to try and exert an influence on the paper.[67] However, to think that papers like the *Frankfurter*

[64] Haussmann to Wolff, 2 May 1919, NL Haussmann, 102.

[65] Haussmann to the *Frankfurter Zeitung* (Heinrich Simon), 29 November 1918, NL Haussmann, 87.

[66] See Haussmann to Wilhelm Cohnstaedt, 12 February 1917, NL Haussmann, 114; and August Stein to Payer, 5 January 1919, NL Payer, 12, Bundesarchiv Koblenz.

[67] See Therese Simon-Sonnemann to Payer, 23 December 1918, NL Payer, 16, pp. 60ff.; and Payer to H. Rössler, 31 January 1919, NL Payer, 12, pp. 221ff.

Zeitung and *Berliner Tageblatt* might allow themselves to be considered by the party as completely subservient required blind disregard of the past history of these papers and especially of the effect of the war experience on them. During the war these two papers had stood steadfastly by their principles and beliefs while the vast majority of liberal politicians had wavered or capitulated at some point to nationalist instincts. Payer who had been vice-chancellor in the Hertlins government from late 1917 until October 1918 was often accused by the left democrats of having betrayed left liberalism with his equivocation on the war-aims issue. The failure of the party's appeals to these papers to be more responsible and loyal in their editorial line exacerbated the differences and led to mutual recriminations. At the first general party conference of the DDP in July 1919 Wilhelm Cohnstaedt of the *Frankfurter Zeitung* complained that the left wing of the party had been entirely ignored by the central organizers, and he protested that the Democratic Party appeared capable of neglecting its political principles in internal party affairs. And Arthur Feiler, of the same paper, denounced vigorously those in the party who were saying that 'politics is today more than ever the art of the possible and attainable.' 'No,' he countered, 'politics today must be, and more so than ever, the art of bold and inspiring action'; and he called for a thorough reorganization of the national economy and of social policy. Democracy finally had its great opportunity in Germany, he said; it would win the masses only if it showed fervour and determination.[68]

No representative of the Ullstein firm played a prominent role in the events leading to the founding of the DDP. The abstention of the Ullstein Verlag from direct involvement in the reorganization of liberalism in the autumn of 1918 was prompted by the political stance of the firm during the war.

In the war years Georg Bernhard became Ullstein's chief emissary and a figure of considerable importance in domestic

---

[68] *Bericht über die Verhandlungen des 1. Parteitags der Deutschen Demokratischen Partei abgehalten in Berlin, vom 19. bis 22. Juli 1919* (Berlin, 1919), pp. 53f., and 223ff.

politics. From 1915 to 1918 he was the elected spokesman of the press in the official press conferences. Of the two chief editors of the *Vossische Zeitung*, he soon achieved by far the greater prominence and influence. Bernhard belonged to that small group of socialists, among them Paul Lensch and August Winnig, who, faithful to a fundamentally economic interpretation of events, believed that the world war, once it had begun, was a necessary evil and that Germany's principal enemy in the struggle was not Russia but England, an imperialistic, in essence anti-socialist, and repressive state. For Bernhard, the war had to be won by Germany if the country was not to be thrown back decades in its economic development and if industrial society in Germany was quickly to reach that stage where socialism would become viable. Bernhard's grand design for the future was a *Kontinentalpolitik*—'the gradual unification of all of Europe and the opening up of trade routes to the east, via Tokyo, deep into China'[69]—the initiation of which required above all peace with Russia, and hence a renunciation of any annexationist aims in the east. With England as the main enemy in his view, Bernhard supported Tirpitz's proposals for unlimited submarine warfare, and broke with him only in 1917 when, a year after his resignation as head of the admiralty, Tirpitz openly adopted annexationist goals in the east together with the new ultra-nationalist Fatherland Party. As director of the Ullstein daily papers and as the link between the management and all the editorial personnel, Bernhard exerted great influence on the political position of the Ullstein papers. If he was absent from Berlin, he remarked to Franz Ullstein in August 1918, he noticed in reading the Ullstein papers that his personal touch was missing: 'Usually it's only a question of details, the last pinch of salt administered by a good cook.'[70] In a book published in 1920 Walter Nicolai, the head of the information bureau of the chiefs-of-staff, indicated that Bernhard's influence had amounted to more than 'a pinch of salt'. 'Gratefully acknowledged was the intercession of the Ullstein papers, which were

---

[69] *Vossische Zeitung* (hereafter *VZ*), 2, 2 January 1918.
[70] Letter of 10 August 1918, Ullstein file, Leo Baeck Institute, New York.

under his direction, in favour of the vigorous conduct of the war', wrote Nicolai. 'Especially appreciated was the support of the *Berliner Morgenpost*, which . . . had a wide circulation among the middle class and workers in Berlin. This was in stark contrast to the papers of the Mosse firm.'[71]

The associations with the ultra-nationalist right naturally made Bernhard and the whole Ullstein press suspect to the left-liberal leadership, even after the Ullstein papers, without exception, had promptly declared their support for the Republic on 9-10 November. Bernhard quickly joined the Democratic Party but, while not hesitating to contribute ideas,[72] nevertheless maintained a critical distance. In contrast to the *Berliner Tageblatt* and *Frankfurter Zeitung*, which fervently urged their readers to vote for the DDP in January 1919, Bernhard and the *Vossische Zeitung* displayed a laconic reserve towards the actual party-political campaign. In the week prior to election day, advertisements in the paper for Stresemann's German People's Party, the Catholic Centre, and even the right-wing German Nationalist People's Party far outnumbered those for the DDP. On the day of voting, 19 January, Bernhard restricted himself in his lead article to developing his view that 'the commanding idea of the future lies in the organizational principle of socialism.' He believed that the socialization of monopoly industry and capital was essential, but that within the context of state ownership and of a planned economy the maintenance and encouragement of private initiative were possible and indispensable. The economy should be regulated in such a way that both corporate public interests and private enterprise were served; to achieve this synthesis the state had to control productivity, wages, and prices.

Bernhard's aloofness from the DDP was partly imposed, partly self-willed. First, within the party he was classed with those members who, because of their attitudes during the war, were not to be admitted into the forefront of party

[71] *Nachrichtendienst, Presse und Volksstimmung im Weltkrieg* (Berlin, 1920), p. 176.

[72] See, for example, the pamphlet by Bernhard, *Demokratische Politik: Grundlinien zu einem Partei-Programm* (Berlin, 1919), which was based on a series of articles published by Bernhard in the *VZ* at the end of December 1918.

activity. In December 1918 the Democrats in Upper Silesia wanted to nominate him as the German all-party candidate for the area, but the DDP managing committee turned down the request.[73] Bernhard's usual choleric reaction to reproaches probably led him to swear that he would make the party regret its decision to insist on a period of atonement. Secondly, he was an avid proponent of liberal unity and, as a close friend of Stresemann, tended to sympathize with the latter's exasperation at the treatment which he had received from the left democrats. During November liberal unity appeared inevitable. When Stresemann finally put an end to these hopes by founding the DVP on 15 December, he induced certain members of the DDP to question their previous decision to join the new party, Bernhard perhaps among them. Thirdly, Bernhard could not accept the DDP's interpretation of the revolution, namely that it was in essence only a national 'nervous breakdown'[74] suffered by an army and a civilian population which were totally exhausted by the war effort. Bernhard, who, like the vast majority of Germans, had placed all his faith in the military for over four years, could not believe that the revolution had not been made but had more or less simply happened. And finally, as a renegade Marxist, who nevertheless still adamantly propagated the blessings of socialization,[75] Bernhard was all the more a *persona non grata* to the high priests of left liberalism who by the beginning of 1919 had established their control over the Democratic Party. He therefore insisted on keeping the *Vossische Zeitung* entirely independent of the DDP, a policy which soon led to very strained relations. In the summer of 1919 the parliamentary party of the DDP decided that it would no longer permit representatives of the paper to attend the 'consultative sessions' for the party's press because the paper had taken a position opposed to that of the DDP on the most important internal and external questions of the day.[76]

[73] Minutes of the session on 30 December 1918, DDP files, R45III/9, p. 36.

[74] Nuschke, 'Wie die Deutsche Demokratische Partie wurde', pp. 24f.

[75] See Bernhard's remarks on socialization to a session of the DDP Hauptvorstand, 13 April 1919, DDP files, R45III/15, p. 90.

[76] Groth, *Die Zeitung*, I, p. 821.

Thus, within months of the founding of the DDP the relationship between the party and the distinguished Berlin-Frankfurt press of democratic persuasion had evolved into a love-hate partnership. Theoretical differences about the role and purpose of the political press were only a secondary cause of the difficulties. The estrangement was rooted primarily in basic discrepancies in the interpretation of liberalism and of its responsibilities. Even in the case of Bernhard, who until 1920 co-ordinated the editorial policies of all Ullstein papers, differences with the DDP eventually revolved essentially around his economic and foreign policy ideas rather than his political record during the war.

The clash of ideas and personalities which had surrounded the launching of the German Democratic Party had inflicted deep wounds on many of the participants, particularly on those who were inexperienced in the techniques of party-political infighting and whose sudden active engagement in party politics was motivated by idealism and a sense of duty. The emotions aroused by the military collapse and by the revolutionary disturbances, the effervescent hopes placed in liberalism, the ensuing disappointment in developments within the party, pervaded the subsequent political thinking and attitudes of many of the editors of the leading democratic newspapers, affecting vitally their relationship with the party and also their degree of attachment and commitment to the Republic.

The hopes placed initially in the German Democratic Party by its founders were majestic. The party would attract to its banner the moderate non-Catholic middle classes and even a significant section of the working class. It was envisaged as the party-political and ideological corner-stone of the new Republic.

The history of left liberalism in the Weimar Republic was, however, a history of disappointment, disenchantment, and after 1928 increasingly of despair. Corroded by internal dissension between conflicting and competing wings, inability to reconcile ideals and practical political demands, and bedevilled by the psychological insecurity resulting from constant decline, the DDP underwent a visible process of dissolution even before the acute economic and political crisis set in at the end of the 1920s. In January 1919 in the elections to the national assembly the party collected 5,641,800 votes and 75 seats, to become the third strongest political grouping in the country; seventeen months later the DDP vote plummeted to 2,333,700, its parliamentary representation to 39. In May 1924 the party lost another eleven seats, gained four in December of the same year, but in the state and local elections between 1925 and 1928 continued to lose heavily. The downward trend appeared inexorable. In 1922 Moritz Julius Bonn stated privately that the party would not last another three years.[77] In July 1919 there were 900,000 card-carrying Democrats; in 1925 only 117,000. By 1928 many of the party's leading personalities had departed: Hellmut von Gerlach in 1922, Eugen Schiffer, Heinrich Gerland, Otto Keinath, and Carl Friedrich von Siemens in 1924, Hjalmar Schacht and Theodor Wolff in 1926, Otto Gessler in 1927. Friedrich Naumann, Max Weber, Conrad Haussmann, Walter Rathenau, and Ernst Troeltsch were dead. In April 1928 Richard Frankfurter remarked that the party had become merely a *Stammtisch*.[78]

The Weimar Republic was begotten in crisis; it lived in crisis. After the war the German public, forced suddenly to cope with new democratic institutions, was confronted at the same time with problems of a hitherto unknown magnitude and frightening immediacy: peace terms which indicted the entire nation as responsible for the war, instead of just its political leaders; a disastrous inflation which affected adversely all but a small segment of the very wealthy entrepreneurial and propertied class; reparations payments to the victor states and the occupation of parts of the country by foreign troops, a situation which was a permanent reminder of humiliation and defeat; and a constitutional system which was geared for confident and circumspect leadership, and not for a confused and insecure body of politicians who were inexperienced in the responsibilities of parliamentarianism. In the distressing social and economic conditions of postwar

---

[77] In a letter to Hermann Fischer, 25 July 1922, NL Erkelenz, 127.
[78] In a letter to Erkelenz, 27 April 1928, NL Erkelenz, 125.

Germany, political opinion began to polarize as soon as the fright, induced by the revolutionary agitation immediately after the war, had subsided and as soon as a semblance of order had returned to the political and administrative substructure. Much of the population, especially among the middle classes, came to feel that Germany's dire misfortunes demanded solutions not debates, answers not suggestions. Reason, discussion, and compromise, the conceptual basis of liberal democracy, were eventually regarded by the public at large as an inexpedient means for assaulting the country's acute difficulties.

The Democratic Party was offered to the electorate in January 1919 as a rock of stability in a frightening crisis. When the party did not live up to its voters' expectations, they deserted it. The DDP was intensely conscious of its political responsibility in the new state and assiduously participated in governments on the national and state level. Of the sixteen Reich cabinets between February 1919 and May 1928, the DDP was represented in thirteen. The imprint of the party's ideologues, men like Hugo Preuss, Max Weber, Friedrich Naumann, and Conrad Haussmann, on the constitution was also profound. In 1926 Anton Erkelenz surmised that although the DDP was supported by only 6 per cent of the nation's voters, its influence in national politics stood at about 40 per cent.[79] A few months later he wrote: 'The construction of the Republic is neither socialist nor clerical, but liberal and democratic. These ideas originated in our movement and we also provided a large part of the leaders who developed these ideas.'[80] Even though many Democrats did not approve of the manner in which the Republic was born in November 1918 and, to cite Gothein, thought the revolution 'unnecessary' in view of the constitutional reforms promulgated in October,[81] the DDP on the whole felt obliged to identify with the Weimar state; the voter in turn tended to identify the DDP with political instability, economic insecurity, and national humiliation.

[79] Manuscript entitled 'Von der Aufgabe der Demokratischen Partei', dated 30 June 1926, NL Erkelenz, 91.

[80] In *Führer-Stimmen*, VI (25 February 1927), in NL Erkelenz, 93.

[81] In a letter to Breitenfeld, 15 November 1918, NL Gothein, 16, p. 133.

The DDP was not capable of counterbalancing its image as a party of ideas (*Weltanschauungspartei*) with a persuasive appeal to the interests of specific social groups, although it did spend a great deal of energy in trying to formulate such an appeal. Members were not lacking who asserted that the party would become merely a decorative element in German politics if it did not consolidate its social backing. 'Only the energetic, positive promotion of systematic middle-class policies and, at the same time, a policy of reconciliation and compromise can firmly anchor democracy in what is actually its oldest and most natural social grouping', wrote one commentator, who reflected widely held sentiments, in July 1920. The enormous electoral setback suffered by the DDP a month previously, he continued, could be attributed to the failure of the party to appeal to 'certain definite social strata'.[82] The party as a whole, however, prided itself on standing ultimately above classes and particular group interests. By publicly distancing itself from the *Interessentenstaat*, the state of interest politics, the hard core of Democrats, for all their laudable intentions, were ignoring the foundation of practical politics in a democracy, that foundation being the mandate of the voter who instinctively interprets the commonweal in terms of his own welfare and security. The party leadership could hardly ignore subsequently that the DDP's strength in 1919 had been due in large part precisely to the opportunism of middle-class voters, who flocked to its banner not because they had become zealous democrats overnight but essentially because the DDP appeared for the moment to represent both the rising star of democracy and the best defence against socialist domination of parliament. As the Republic had its *Vernunftrepublikaner*, so too the DDP had its *Vernunftdemokraten* in its early years. In most cases neither these 'republicans from reason' nor these 'Democrats from reason' developed a commitment to the republican or, respectively, democratic cause. The majority of the DDP's fair-weather friends abandoned the party once their 'reason', or more accurately their anxieties, told them that it was no longer

82 In *Das demokratische Deutschland*, II (18 July 1920), pp. 451ff.

particularly advantageous, for them personally, to remain.
But while being aware that the voter's material concerns
played an enormous role in his voting habits, the Democratic
policy-makers nevertheless believed that in the final analysis
the political struggle in Germany was one of ideas, and they
insisted to the end on remaining faithful to this tenet.

Those Germans who renounced their membership in the
DDP or simply ceased supporting it in elections did so
primarily because they felt that the party was incapable of
relating its rhetoric to reality. A full year elapsed, for
example, before the party finally succeeded in drafting a
genuine official programme at its second national conference
in December 1919. Already in November 1920 Eugen
Schiffer, a member of three Reich cabinets, expressed
succinctly his dissatisfaction with the DDP; 'We have neither
a cultural, nor a political, nor an economic idea which could
be used in any way to make propaganda or elicit enthusiasm
for our cause; . . . I continually ask myself, without finding
an answer, how it is that anyone out in the country still
votes Democratic.'[83] Democrats who impatiently criticised
'the idleness and lack of imagination'[84] of their party were
often in evidence, but they usually succeeded only in
aggravating the indecision and imprecision of their colleagues. As a result the DDP was deserted not only by
members of the middle classes frightened by the predatory
leviathans of monopoly capitalism and proletarian socialism
but also by former party stalwarts who simply became
disillusioned by the ideological corpulence, the obdurate
theorizing, and hence the immobility of the party.

The exodus of supporters from the party flowed largely,
but not exclusively, to the right. A significant segment of
its former ardent backers, who had conceived of the party
as a vibrant and dynamic spearhead in the drive to establish
a well-functioning, fully democratic and humane system of
government became disillusioned when they realized that the

---

[83] From a letter to Walther Schreiber, 17 November 1920, NL Schiffer, 12,
p. 380, Geheimes Staatsarchiv, Berlin.

[84] These words were used by Gustav Stolper in his speech to the DDP
Mannheim party conference, 5 October 1929; printed as *Die wirtschaftlich-
soziale Weltanschauung der Demokratie* (Berlin, 1929), p. 41.

party was dominated by a defensive mentality and was clinging to a policy of entrenchment. Carl von Ossietzky quickly lost his enthusiasm for the party because it concentrated, in his opinion, on 'balancing' rather than 'fighting'.[85] Walther Rathenau was not speaking only for himself when he claimed that the DDP had in effect remained the old Progressive People's Party and when he charged that the party had failed its responsibilities by not developing any new social, economic, or political ideas after the collapse of the empire. Instead the DDP had recorded only 'irksome concessions', and, in essence had become a 'conservative party'.

It wishes to maintain the existing order, namely the bourgeois-individualistic Republic, and regards every step towards social improvement as a concession, not a basic necessity. A party which defends the existing order is uncreative and barren, doubly so at a time of new birth. . . . I can hardly approve of the reactionary policies of the parties of the right but I can understand them. They are fighting for an ideal which I reject, but they are fighting. The DDP is not fighting. It takes pleasure in its comfortable existence and believes that it can hold back its collapse by subscribing to the law of inertia.

Rathenau indicated in the autumn of 1919 that for these reasons he could no longer belong to the DDP.[86] The indictment here was that the leaders of the party had betrayed and sabotaged the mission of the DDP. Instead of vigorously promoting a radical policy of social, economic, and administrative reform, imperative if the country was to recover properly from the disaster which had befallen it and if it was to embark on a new political course, the party had procrastinated and become paralysed by an excessive concern with maintaining its numerical strength, and with not alienating the variegated electoral support and sources of financial backing which it had attracted in the wake of the revolution.

The desertion of the party by voters was naturally accompanied by the erosion of its financial strength. The

---

[85] Cited in Raimund Koplin, *Carl von Ossietzky als politischer Publizist* (Berlin and Frankfurt a.M., 1964), p. 74.

[86] From a letter of Rathenau, reprinted in *Walther Rathenau, Ein preussischer Europäer: Briefe,* ed. Margarete von Eynern (Berlin, 1955), pp. 341f. Criticisms similar to those of Rathenau were numerous at all the early party conferences; for the reports of these conferences see the bibliography.

inflation also cut drastically the income from members' fees. In 1924-5 members' dues brought only RM 2,859 into party coffers. Other sources in that financial year, largely business and industry, provided about one million marks.[87] However, as the party's popular appeal waned and as its weight in government was eclipsed, former financial mentors abandoned it as well. By 1924 the Kuratorium which had underwritten the DDP in the election campaign of 1919 had given up hope in the future of the party.[88] The only major collective source of funds that remained was the Hansabund, but this association of light industry, like the Kuratorium earlier, now insisted on distributing its donations directly to particular Democrats friendly to industry rather than to the party as a whole.[89] As a result the DDP's Reichstag delegation had a strong commercial representation, and in fact leading Democrats held a larger total number of directorships in business and industry by the end of the decade than the prominent members of any other party.[90] The powerful grip of moneyed interests on the party successfully cordoned off radicalism within the DDP on social and economic questions.

The DDP like all the parties of the Weimar Republic was split basically into two wings. Although the divisions— between pacifists and nationalists, unitarians and federalists, supporters of a planned economy and doctrinaire *laissez-faire* liberals, agnostic intellectuals and Protestant believers, employee and employer representatives—were not always entirely consistent in terms of personalities, the Democratic Party nevertheless was plagued, in the words of Gertrud Bäumer, by 'two souls in its breast'.[91]

---

[87] Hermann Fischer, the party's treasurer, to Erkelenz, 20 March 1926, NL Erkelenz, 132.

[88] See the correspondence in file 31 of the NL Erkelenz, especially the letters to Gerland, 8 April, Hummel, 17 April, and Mendelssohn, 20 May 1924.

[89] Fischer to Erkelenz, 20 March 1926, NL Erkelenz, 132.

[90] In 1931 Hermann Fischer, the chairman of the Hansabund, sat on over fifty different boards of directors; Peter Reinhold, who was Reich finance minister in 1926-7, sat on about seventeen; and August Weber on thirty-four. See Ernst Saemisch, 'Volksvertreter und Wirtschaftsmächte', *Die Tat*, XXII (February 1931), pp. 880ff.

[91] *Die Hilfe*, Nr. 12 (15 June 1928), p. 270.

The more conservative wing found its greatest source of popular strength in the Protestant middle strata—small farmers, artisans, small businessmen—of Baden, Württemberg, and Bavaria, where alone in November 1918 liberal union between the Progressives and the National Liberals had been achieved formally. At the popular level, not only in the south but throughout Germany, the party's right emphasized the notion of individualism, middle-class values, the import- ance of the home, family, and religion as the cement in the social fabric, and the need for a community and national spirit based on mutual tolerance and transcending social barriers. Liberalism in the provinces—in the rural areas and smaller cities and towns—was perceived primarily as a personal code of behaviour, directed by religious and moral considerations and rooted in tradition and *Volkstümlichkeit*. Here 'liberal' and *bürgerlich* were virtually synonymous terms in the popular political vocabulary and were readily associ- ated with value judgements such as 'decency', 'patriotism', 'reliability', and 'respectability'. At the national level the DDP's right was dominated by commercial people and by lawyers who retained an undaunted trust in the practica- bility of a society governed essentially by *laissez-faire* prin- ciples. Through their connections with industry and banking, these men, either directly or as agents, supplied the vital financial backing for the party, and their control of the party's purse guaranteed them a firm hold on policies. The conservative wing of the democratic movement saw in socialism a depersonalized, ungodly doctrine of materialism and urged the party as a whole to dissociate itself, openly and clearly, from the economic, and many of the cultural, ideas of Social Democracy. Co-operation in government with the SPD was viewed, however, as a burden of responsibility which the DDP had to bear; the party had to act as the anchor which tied the moderate socialist left to the liberal- democratic state. When Koch-Weser wrote, 'We are trying— not always without success—to educate the Social Demo- crats', he expressed well this attitude.[92]

[92] In a letter to E. Rocholt, 15 March 1919, NL Koch-Weser, 77, p. 4. Koch-Weser, a bureaucrat and excellent administrator rather than an ideologue, actually stood more or less in the centre of the party. He was the party chairman from 1924 to 1930.

The party's left wing was radical, progressive, tolerant, and cosmopolitan in spirit and character. It was based in the major cities, particularly Berlin and Hamburg, had a talented and vocal Jewish element, and drew much of its impetus and support from the Hirsch-Duncker trade unions and from the intellectual community, from journalists, artists, and some academics. This group of Democrats, too, saw the role of the DDP as that of a mediator between liberalism and socialism, between the bourgeoisie and the working class, between the mentality of enterprising capitalism and that of exploited labour. But it believed, contrary to the more conservative elements in the party, that the concepts of liberalism and socialism, if shorn of their dogmatism, could be complementary and need not be antithetical. These Democrats still subscribed to the sanctity of individual initiative, which they considered as the propellant force in progress, but, at the same time, they believed first and foremost in the sanctity of human dignity. A journalist of the *Frankfurter Zeitung* summarized this tenor of thinking during the war: 'Even if liberalism and socialism are still contradictory as concepts, in practice they belong together, because without socialism liberalism turns into pure aristocratism.'[93] Close co-operation between the DDP and SPD was regarded as indispensable if Germany could ever hope to establish a liberal and social democracy.

Outside the large city this approach to liberalism was unattractive; it was associated with 'asphalt culture', with a lack of *Innerlichkeit*, with a disrespect for tradition and heritage. On the other hand the provincial 'liberalism of the hearth' Theodor Wolff dismissed sarcastically as *Bliemschen-kaffeegeist*,[94] a women's-knitting-circle mentality. Within a few years of the founding of the DDP the two wings were defaming each other for controlling the party and destroying it. Theodor Heuss accused the leftists in the party, their 'souls mangled by urban culture' (*vom GrossStädtertum innerlich aufgefressen*), of trying arrogantly to dictate political standards to the party; and Anton Erkelenz complained

[93] W.K. [Walter Kamper], *Vorfragen innerer Politik* (Frankfurt a.M., 1917) p. 34.
[94] *BT*, 248, 27 May 1928.

bitterly about the 'old cab-horses' and 'syndic types' who ran the party and blocked 'capable leaders' from coming to the fore.[95] 'Whoever has to do political work in the "provinces" ', Gertrud Bäumer sighed, 'constantly faces the ideological incompatability of these two elements. This incompatability prevents the realization of a common political "faith" and therefore of the momentum which is needed to overcome the conflict of interest in a democratic party.' The differences and clashes within the DDP led to the split of the parliamentary delegation on virtually all important votes; and this lack of unity in turn reduced the attraction of the party for the voter and for wealthy interest groups.

The Weimar Coalition, consisting of the SPD, DDP, and Centre, which was established as the government of Germany in February 1919 lasted only four months despite its large majority in the national assembly. It fell in June when the socialist chancellor and the Democrats refused to participate in a cabinet that would have to preside over an 'unacceptable' peace settlement. The quick demise of the first government was a harbinger of the subsequent unsettled political life of the Republic. In October 1919 the Democrats returned to the government; in March 1920 the abortive Kapp Putsch brought another reshuffling of the cabinet; and some weeks later the decision was taken to call new elections. In June 1920 the Weimar Coalition was decimated by the negative response of voters to the events of the previous eighteen months, and the long line of heterogeneous, in most cases minority, governments began. The co-operation of the moderate socialists, Centrists, and Democrats had helped restore a semblance of order in the country, but beyond a new system of government and administrative accomplishments little of substance in the social and economic structure of Germany had been changed. Whereas the imperial authorities had been unwilling to give Germany a form of government consonant with the social and economic forces at work in the country, the framers of the Weimar constitution assumed that those

---

[95] Heuss to Koch-Weser, 29 October 1924, reprinted in my *Theodor Heuss und die Weimarer Republik* (Stuttgart, 1969), pp. 145f. Erkelenz to Messrs. Sallmann and Arns, 24 January 1924, NL Erkelenz, 126; and Erkelenz in *Die Hilfe*, Nr. 2 (15 January 1921), p. 20.

forces were willing, of their own accord, to make democracy, in a highly idealized form, work properly.

Between 1920 and 1924 the Republic, buffeted by foreign political, military, and economic pressures, by political assassinations, by a spiralling inflation, and by repeated attempts to overthrow the government by force, merely struggled to survive. In the mid-twenties, however, once the inflation had become only a nightmarish memory and a certain confidence had returned to the economy with the modification of the reparations arrangements and the influx of foreign capital, once tangible progress was registered in the effort to have the Versailles treaty revised and to stabilize Germany's relations with at least France and England, in this period a mood of cautious optimism returned to the liberal ranks despite continuing disheartening results in regional elections. The Hamburg Democrat Peter Stubmann wrote in November 1926: 'The Republic is entrenched. That has become a general conviction.'[96] A year later in a diagnosis of German affairs the Baden Democrat Willy Hellpach asserted that 'the German Reich has become, for an unlimited length of time, a democracy with a republican face.'[97] There was even some feeling in the Reichsbanner that this paramilitary organization which had been formed for the defence of the Republic had fulfilled its purpose and should dissolve itself.[98] Foreign observers, too, remarked on the 'consolidation of the Republic'. Two British authors compared the history of postwar Germany to a drama: 'The fifth and probably last act is now being played, and promises something more heartening than a catastrophic ending.'[99] Many Democrats simply assumed that their party would reassert itself in the general elections of 1928. One young Democrat subsequently remembered the optimism that pervaded party youth meetings before those elections: 'We were all wrapped in dense clouds of cigarette smoke, but in spite of it and other inconveniences we were as happy as children

[96] *Deutsche Einheit*, VIII (20 November 1926), pp. 1097f.

[97] *Politische Prognose für Deutschland* (Berlin, 1928), p. 116.

[98] See Karl Rohe, *Das Reichsbanner Schwarz Rot Gold* (Düsseldorf, 1966), p. 357.

[99] Hugh Quigley and R.T. Clark, *Republic Germany* (London, 1928), pp. 3f.

playing in a spring meadow. In a few weeks our efforts would be rewarded by a great victory.' The DDP, with its thirty-two seats at present, would certainly win at least ten more. 'We were absolutely sure of it since every sign pointed in that direction.'[100]

[100] Linke, *Restless Flags*, p. 286.

III

THE PRESS IN THE WEIMAR REPUBLIC

Article 118 of the Weimar constitution announced that 'every German has the right, within the bounds of the general laws, to express his opinion freely in word, writing, print, picture, or in any other manner. . . . There is no censorship. . . .' The Reich press law of 1874 had guaranteed the right to print established facts; this article, in the section on fundamental liberties, went a step further by proclaiming the freedom to print opinions. However, the qualification contained in the article—'within the bounds of the general laws'—in fact put distinct limits on this freedom. The freedom of expression was subjected to the penal laws, police ordinances, and to the regulations on trade and business practices; and the Reich president, with the emergency powers granted him by article 48, could extinguish the operability of article 118. If opinions expressed in public threatened, directly or indirectly, the security of the state and its citizens, their dissemination could be suppressed.[1] Thus, for example, the 'decrees for the protection of the Republic' of 26 and 29 June 1922, after the murder of the foreign minister, Walther Rathenau, placed tight controls on the press, as did later emergency legislation during the French occupation of the Ruhr and from 1930 on during the deepening political crisis.

The constitutional limitation of the freedom of expression stemmed from a conviction, carried over from the empire and intensified in the democratic Republic, that the printed word, and particularly the press, represented a power of immense proportions in the political process. The prevalent

---

[1] See Gerhard Anschütz, *Die Verfassung des deutschen Reichs* (Berlin, 1933), pp. 550ff.; Willibalt Apelt, *Geschichte der Weimarer Verfassung* (Munich, 1946), pp. 313ff.; and the discussion in Peter J. Fliess, *Freedom of the Press in the German Republic 1918-1933* (Baton Rouge La., 1955), pp. 11ff. Kurt Koszyk's mine of information on the press in Weimar, *Deutsche Presse 1914-1945* (Berlin, 1971), appeared too late to be included in this study.

theories on the press in the political and sociological thinking of the Weimar Republic maintained that the newspaper press carried a burden of 'public responsibility' equivalent to that of the government and parliament. By some observers the press was considered to be a force of greater political significance than the political party, since the party depended on the press as a link with its voters and particularly since, under the ticket-election system (*Listenwahlsystem*), individual politicians had relatively little contact with their constituents. 'What effect can even the greatest open-air meeting have', Rudolf Kircher of the *Frankfurter Zeitung* asked rhetorically, 'as compared with the permanent influence a daily newspaper may exert on hundreds of thousands or even millions?'[2] The institutions of government were regarded by virtually all as dependent, for their proper functioning, on a press which understood and was sympathetic to the principles of democracy.

At the root of these theories lay the firm conviction that Germans accepted the ideas expressed by their newspapers as the gospel truth in spite of the war experience and the strain which the war had placed on the credibility of the press. Georg Bernhard asserted in 1929 that a German viewed his favourite newspaper as 'not merely a source of information, but also an organ of instruction. . . . The German believes what his paper tells him. Men to whom much space is devoted are to him great men.'[3] A year later, the year Hitler and the National Socialists increased their strength in the Reichstag ninefold despite the fact that the total circulation of all their newspapers barely reached 100,000, Richard Lewinsohn, the financial editor of the *Vossische Zeitung*, could still write of the German man in the street: 'The spoken word does not have as great an effect on him as the written and printed word. He does not allow himself to be carried away very easily. What he is to believe, he wishes to see in black and white. His penchant for authority and also his concern for thoroughness and accuracy demand this.'[4]

2 Rudolf Kircher, *Powers and Pillars*, trans. C. Vesey (London, 1928), p. 295.

3 Georg Bernhard, 'The German Press', in *Der Verlag Ullstein zum Welt-Reklame-Kongress 1929* (Berlin, 1929), p. 59.

4 *Das Geld in der Politik* (Berlin, 1930), p. 156.

This confidence in the persuasive powers of the press naturally induced all politically active organizations to devote great attention to their relations with the press. Political parties believed more than ever that extensive and well-organized press backing was a prerequisite to electoral success. Pressure groups were also convinced that control over at least a section of the press was indispensable for the furthering of their interests, both economic and political. Government ministries were of course extremely sensitive to press treatment of their portfolios, and press clippings occupied a substantial portion of their files. The foreign office, and especially Stresemann as foreign minister, repeatedly voiced the view that, considering Germany's unfavourable position in international politics, a successful foreign policy was dependent on virtually unquestioning backing from the press. Opinions abroad about Germany were gleaned primarily from the German press, and therefore, the foreign office felt, unanimity within the press on the goals of Germany's foreign policy and on the means of achieving these goals was essential, so as to illustrate to the outside world how committed the country was to revision of the degrading peace arrangements to which it had been subjected.[5] In 1926 Stresemann arranged for the purchase of the *Deutsche Allgemeine Zeitung* by the Reich, so as to have an influential mouthpiece for his foreign policy.

In the rivalry and interplay of political and economic forces, the press was therefore regarded as a tool, essential for the advancement of particular group interests. This widespread utilitarian attitude to the institution of the press, continued from the imperial era, resulted in the constant subjection of newspapers to pressures which aimed at restricting or eliminating editorial independence and at reducing the press that still retained some autonomy to the role of a loudspeaker for partisan views.

In Germany basic attitudes towards journalism continued to be markedly different from those in Anglo-Saxon countries. Whereas in America and England the first lesson

[5] See in particular Stresemann's speech on 'Presse und Aussenpolitik' to the general meeting of the Union of German Newspaper Publishers in 1925, published in the special Festschrift issue of *Zeitungs-Verlag* (July 1925), p. 3.

taught to an aspiring young journalist was the importance of an impersonal, objective reporting of the facts, in Germany correspondents were encouraged to express opinions and judgements in their coverage, to become participants in controversies rather than to remain spectators.[6] Impartiality was not celebrated as an idea. 'It would be false to assume', said Georg Bernhard, 'that the primary purpose of the press is to provide information. . . . What the newspaper wishes to provide is views. It wishes to bring order into things which the reader sees before and around himself every day; it wishes to bring the events in the world to the attention of the reader from a definite point of view.'[7] 'Facts', another German editor is reputed to have said, 'are not fit for the reader when served raw; they have to be cooked, chewed and presented in the correspondent's saliva.'[8] The emphasis on interpretative reporting had been heightened by the war experience, and the advent of a democratic political system encouraged this tendency in the German press even more. In 1918-19 'the masses' had come to political power, but they exercised this power without the necessary political knowledge or experience. 'Here is where the responsibility of the press begins', a German doctoral student wrote in 1931; 'the press must win the masses and lead the masses.'[9] A journalist consequently thought of himself more in terms of a sage than a purveyor of news, an intellectual, a 'bearer of culture' (*Kulturträger*), rather than a skilled technician. His importance in the political, opinion-making process seemed to be acknowledged and substantiated by the fact that 13 per cent of the Reichstag's deputies in 1924 were publicists by profession.[10]

[6] See the essay by Fred S. Siebert in Siebert *et al.*, *Four Theories of the Press* (Urbana, Ill., 1956), pp. 60ff.

[7] Georg Bernhard, 'Stellungen im Zeitungswesen' (1924), pp. 2f., typewritten manuscript of a speech, Institut für Publizistik, Berlin.

[8] Cited in Arthur Koestler, *Arrow in the Blue* (London, 1952), p. 171. See also the discussion in Walter Hagemann, *Grundzüge der Publizistik* (rev. edn., Münster, 1966), pp. 268f.

[9] Wilhelm Kaupert, *Die deutsche Tagespresse als Politicum* (Freudenstadt, 1932), p. 15.

[10] Fritz K. Ringer, *The Decline of the German Mandarins* (Cambridge, Mass., 1969), p. 66.

In the front ranks of the defenders of the ideological press were the editors of the left-liberal papers. They argued that since democracy was not yet rooted in German political thinking the press carried a great educational responsibility. In urging that the German press preserve its unique character of *Lehrhaftigkeit*, they were in interesting company: another man who saluted the primacy of opinion and called the editorial article the core of a newspaper—'a written poster, or better still, a street-corner address on paper'—was Joseph Goebbels.[11]

The German press remained highly decentralized in the Weimar years, despite a perceptible tendency towards concentration ensuing from the difficulties and dislocation accompanying the world war and the inflationary period which followed. In 1919-20 Germany had 3,689 newspapers; of these only 26 (0·7 per cent) managed to attain a circulation of over 100,000, while 2,470 (67·1 per cent) had printings of 5,000 or less.[12] Whereas in England, America, and France circulations over the one million mark were no longer unusual, in Germany no daily newspaper even approached these heights. The Ullstein *Berliner Morgenpost*, at its peak in April 1930, barely climbed over 600,000.[13] Berlin, albeit the indisputable heart of publishing in Germany, could not rival London, New York, or Paris in newspaper output. By 1932 the total number of papers in Germany had increased to 4,703—including dailies, weeklies, and local editions of parent papers; their total daily printing was in the vicinity of 14 million copies.[14]

Because of their dependence on advertising for their existence, newspapers as a whole, and small papers in particular, were highly susceptible to any virus present in the economy. 'In the way the flag followed trade formerly, the

---

[11] See Ernst Feder's remarks in *Deutsche Presse*, XVIII (2 June 1928), pp. 277f.; also Karl Brammer, 'Presse, Demokratie und öffentliche Meinung', in *Zehn Jahre Deutsche Republik*, pp. 551ff; and Goebbels, *Kampf um Berlin* (Munich, 1939), p. 200.

[12] Groth, *Die Zeitung*, II, p. 257.

[13] See Appendix II, p. 314.

[14] *Handbuch der deutschen Tagespresse*, ed. Institut für Zeitungswissenschaft Berlin (4th edn., Berlin, 1932), p. 27.

newspaper today follows the economy', a commentator on
the press remarked in 1932.[15] During the war the small
provincial press suffered most in Germany, owing to a paper
and manpower shortage. The inflation which followed the
war gave this press no respite from its difficulties. The price
of newsprint and postal charges soared; wages had to be
increased and the tax on advertising became repressive. The
situation was considered so distressing by April 1920 that
Robert Faber, the chairman of the Union of German Newspaper Publishers, cabled the Reich chancellor, Fehrenbach,
saying: 'The German press is on the brink of complete
collapse. . . .'[16] The inflation caused the outright demise of
over 300 papers,[17] but there were other much more important consequences. First, the number of papers which
surrendered their editorial independence and took to relying
entirely on syndicated columns from press agencies increased
sharply. Secondly, a significant segment of the provincial
press, fearing a loss of advertising or subscribers, claimed that
it was renouncing its political bias. In fact this purported
'depoliticization' usually meant a swing to the right politically. And finally, a great many provincial papers slipped,
in the course of the inflation, into financial dependence on
big business and heavy industry and in so doing gave up their
editorial autonomy.

Small newspapers in the provinces could naturally not
afford to employ large staffs. Frequently the owner and chief
editor of a paper with a circulation of only one or two
thousand were one and the same person, and normally any
other editorial personnel that was hired looked after local
rather than national news. All national and foreign news
came to the small provincial paper in the form of reports or
syndicated columns from the news and press agencies to
which it subscribed. Once the original choice of agency was
made, the paper thereafter of course reflected, in its national
and international coverage, the political tone of this service.
After the turn of the century dependence on news columns

15 Friedrich Bertau, ibid., p. 10.
16 Cited in Heinrich Walter, *Zeitung als Aufgabe* (Wiesbaden, 1954), p. 78.
17 Groth, *Die Zeitung*, I, p. 207.

arriving on moulds or stereotyped plates became widespread among small papers because of the enormous amount of time and labour that they saved. The number of local newspapers which adopted this method of gathering their news and commentary material increased vastly during the inflation. By 1926 approximately 1,200 papers were totally dependent on this kind of service.[18] Their editorial independence in matters of national interest was practically non-existent.

There were 593 news and press agencies in Germany in 1932. Some functioned on a national, others only on a regional level, and they varied greatly in size and in the kind of material which they produced. Most restricted themselves to a specific area of interest such as sports, fashion, church affairs, economics.[19] The largest wire service, with over three thousand customers in 1928, was the semi-official Wolff's Telegraph Bureau (WTB). Since 1871 the WTB had a loose unofficial arrangement with the Reich that all government news dispatches would be relayed to the press through its offices. Until 1931 the majority of WTB shares were in the hands of two Berlin banks, the houses of Bleichröder, and Delbrück, Schickler & Co. In that year the Reich government, which on several occasions since 1919 had lent large sums of money to the WTB in exchange for certain supervisory rights, bought the shares owned by Paul Schwabach of the Bleichröder bank.[20] Complaints against the WTB on account of its supposedly one-sided political coverage were voiced occasionally by the parties which stood in opposition to the current government coalition, but on the whole the bureau gave heed to preserving impartiality in reporting meant for domestic consumption. On the other hand, the Telegraph Union, the second largest wire service, was unashamedly nationalist and conservative in political tendency. Next to the party papers of the right, the hard core of its subscribers consisted of the provincial 'non-partisan' press.

[18] Ibid.,I, p. 475.

[19] See the *Handbuch der deutschen Tagespresse* (1932).

[20] The purchase was actually made by an official trustee organization of the Reich, the Cautio G.m.b.H., run by Max Winkler. See the Reichskanzlei file R431/2527, Bundesarchiv Koblenz, on the WTB; especially the memorandum of 16 January 1929 by Walter Zechlin on the relations between the WTB and the Reich, pp. 90ff.

These two news agencies outdistanced by far all their smaller rivals, which ranged from very primitive private undertakings that tried to solicit articles from leading figures in German public life to the press services of the parties. The small news and feature-article agencies which concentrated on political and economic affairs experienced the same financial insecurity as the provincial press, and many of them were eventually swallowed by moneyed interests. If they managed to retain their autonomy they adapted their tone to what they considered to be the political mood of the day. Richard Bahr, to cite one example, offered in December 1918 to change the name of his *Nationalliberale Beiträge* to *Demokratische Beiträge* if the managing committee of the DDP promised to recommend his press agency to all newspapers sympathetic to the party.[21] The Democrats agreed. In March 1920 fifty papers subscribed to Bahr's service. By April 1922, however, the DDP's fortunes had declined to the point where Bahr decided to change the name once again, this time to *Aus Wissenschaft und Politik*. In future, he wrote to Friedrich Meinecke, his agency would no longer have a party bias; instead it would seek 'the co-operation of academics and politicians from all camps, except for the Social Democrats'.[22] A few years later Erich Koch-Weser, then the chairman of the DDP, was accusing Bahr of spreading poisonous remarks about the Democrats in the provincial press.[23]

Those newspapers which were able to remain financially independent during the inflation but nevertheless suddenly announced that they were shedding their previously open political affiliations did so primarily from fear that their continued support for one particular party might alienate some of their advertising clients or their readers. Papers in areas where the strength of the party which they backed was declining were most inclined to take this step. The two parties hardest hit by this political 'neutralization' were the

---

21 Minutes of the DDP managing committee, 30 December 1918, DDP files, R45III/9.

22 27 April 1922, NL Meinecke, 2, p. 49, Geheimes Staatsarchiv, Berlin.

23 Koch-Weser to Peter Bruckmann, 18 February 1927, NL Koch-Weser, 36, pp. 79ff.

DDP and the DVP, both of which had no stringently organized press and depended—unless the owner of a newspaper had a personal stake in the fate of the party—on voluntary support. Papers which proclaimed that they were becoming non-partisan in fact usually simply switched to supporting a political tendency rather than a specific party.

Some of the heavy industrial concerns of the Ruhr and central Germany had acquired newspaper organs to promote their economic and political interests already prior to 1914, but these ventures had all been undeniable financial and journalistic failures because of their all too obvious connections with industry and their blatantly propagandistic nature. During the war, under the guidance of the chairman of the board of directors of the Krupp concern, Alfred Hugenberg, a new approach, carefully planned and organized, was undertaken to try and penetrate the press, 'the channel to the brains of the people', as Hugenberg referred to it.[24]

Hugenberg himself was not an industrialist but a skilled manager who had received his training in the Prussian civil service. In 1909 he had joined Krupp, and within three years his abilities as an organizer and director had brought him the chairmanship of the Bergbauliche Verein, a kind of fraternity of Ruhr industry. When in 1915 the Deutsche Verlagsverein, which had assumed control of the Scherl publishing house just before the war, ran into severe financial trouble, Hugenberg was called upon to restore solvency. Within a year he had drummed up sufficient funds from his industrial contacts to put the firm on its feet again, and, though not a penny of his own money was invested, had taken over the direction of the supervisory board of Scherl. In 1917, backed by the same sources of capital, he founded the Vera Verlagsanstalt, an organization whose purpose was to advise professionally, on contract, provincial newspapers which found themselves in financial distress. The same year the Allgemeine Anzeigen G.m.b.H. (Ala) was formed and became the major rival to Mosse's advertising empire. The war years provided Hugenberg with favourable conditions for an

[24] The following account relies heavily on Ludwig Bernhard, Der 'Hugenberg-Konzern' (Berlin, 1928); and Valeska Dietrich, Alfred Hugenberg (Berlin, 1960).

auspicious beginning; the immediate postwar inflationary period, however, gave him the opportunity for enormous expansion of his activities.

Through two investment-loan companies created in 1922, Mutuum Darlehens A.G. and Alterum Kredit A.G., Hugenberg procured capital for provincial newspapers and also offered them newsprint at reduced cost or on credit. When a publisher received assistance from the Hugenberg 'newspaper banks', he had to agree to accept control of his firm's book-keeping by Vera and was also simultaneously obliged to subscribe to the Telegraph Union (TU),[25] a wire news service, controlled by Hugenberg, which had emerged between 1913 and 1921 from the amalgamation of a number of smaller agencies.

The explicit purpose of this vertical combination of organizations and their functions, like rungs in a ladder, was to strangle the editorial independence of provincial publications. Unless a publisher had idealistic conceptions about his independence, and in fact few provincial publishers could even contemplate strict independence, the facilities provided by Hugenberg's operations had distinct advantages; apart from reducing financial worry, they also reduced work. The further alleviation of a small publisher's work burden was the expressed aim of the Wirtschaftsstelle für die Provinzpresse (Wipro). In 1922 it began offering, at very attractive rates, a news service which reached the customer on moulds ready for casting. These contained every kind of article in which a local newspaper might be interested. Eventually about 350 papers relied entirely on Wipro.

Finally, to round off his empire, Hugenberg in 1927 bought the majority of shares in the Universum Film A.G. (UFA), the largest film-producing company in Germany.

Hugenberg's method of operation was extremely refined. For the outside world the internal workings of this 'opinion factory' were shrouded in a haze of conjecture. Normally the recipient of a loan procured by Hugenberg was kept in the dark as to the actual source of the money. Hugenberg

---

[25] See the anonymous article 'Wie die monarchistische Bewegung "gemacht" wird', *Die Hilfe*, Nr. 3 (1 February 1925), p. 53.

realized that the nature of the press was such that a newspaper could never combine success with its readers and
conspicuously biased promotion of industrial and commercial
interests. 'A great paper can find its point of crystallization
permanently only in an idea', he told the Ruhr magnates who
had provided the original capital to launch his enterprises.

Two ideas are to constitute the foundations of the construction to
which our work is devoted: the principle of nationalism and the re-
instatement of the individual personality in cultural life and in the
economy. . . . While we place general ideas in the forefront, we are at
the same time taking into account the vital interests of the press. For
a newspaper is something other than a rolling-mill or a chemical plant.
No commercial interests should be tacked to a newspaper.[26]

The Hugenberg complex itself was entirely political in
purpose and was not a business venture; all profits were
reinvested and used for further expansion. However, the
press that stumbled into Hugenberg's net was never forced
directly by him to adopt a particular political line; influence
was achieved indirectly and discreetly through the news
agencies and press services under Hugenberg's direction.

Hugenberg was the chairman of all the units within this
massive organization, even though he personally had only an
insignificant amount of his own capital involved. The twelve
'nationally minded' men, as they described themselves—
among them Emil Kirdorf and Albert Vögler—who sat on the
controlling body of the entire complex, the so-called
Economic Association for the Furtherance of the Spiritual
Forces of Reconstruction, agreed that maximum efficiency
could be realized only if one person exercised complete
managerial powers.

A rough estimate would be that Hugenberg enjoyed some
form of control or influence over close to one half of the
German press by 1930. Almost without exception newspapers which professed a right-wing nationalist political
orientation—in 1932 about 1,200 papers—and much of the
so-called non-partisan press—2,029 *parteilose* papers existed
in 1932—had contacts with one or more of Hugenberg's

---

26 Cited in Bernhard, *Der 'Hugenberg-Knozern'*, p. 59.

operations. There were 1,600 papers that subscribed to the TU alone.[27]

Hugenberg's immense power in the newspaper field was generally recognized, but, because of its nature, the exact extent of this power was deceptive, and impossible to counter, except on the same terms. However, no political grouping of the centre or the left could hope to draw on sources of capital similar to those at Hugenberg's disposal. Apart from the publications of the Scherl house—the *Berliner Lokal-Anzeiger, Der Tag,* the *Berliner Illustrierte Nachtausgabe, Die Woche*—and a small number of provincial papers, the Hugenberg concern did not own newspapers directly. Its power lay in its indirect control and manipulation of much of the small decentralized provincial press, whose economic instability and sense of insecurity Hugenberg cleverly exploited.

In October 1928, the German Nationalist People's Party (DNVP), which in the May elections of that year had suffered a sharp setback and therefore was intensely aware of the importance of the press and propaganda, elected Hugenberg as chairman. In 1929 he organized the referendum against the Young Plan on reparations in league with Hitler and threw open his *Meinungskonzern* to National Socialist propaganda. In 1931 he re-established the tie with Hitler in the Harzburg Front. In January 1933 he joined Hitler's government, which in the elections of March that year won a majority victory only with the help of the DNVP's fifty-two Reichstag mandates. Without asserting that Hugenberg's press dominion destroyed the Weimar Republic, one can say that it presented a major obstacle to the implantation of democratic, republican ideas amongst the German public. The pillar on which Hugenberg built his empire was the small provincial newspaper.

A number of Ruhr industrialists wished to exert more overt influence on the press. For a time in the early 1920s Hugo Stinnes, by building up a vertical trust which stretched from pulp-producing forests in East Prussia, a number of

[27] The statistics are from the *Handbuch der deutschen Tagespresse* (1932), p. 27.

provincial presses and newspapers, to the large printing houses of Büxenstein and Hobbing in Berlin, achieved greater notoriety amongst the republican left than Hugenberg. In May 1920 Georg Bernhard could write in the *Vossische Zeitung* that Stinnes 'has, at the moment, turned almost all of Germany into his private business'.[28] Although the Stinnes trust was dissolved after his death in 1924, many of his holdings in the press—the *Deutsche Allgemeine Zeitung* was the most noteworthy example[29]—passed eventually into the hands of other Ruhr magnates or Berlin financial circles. Almost all the more prominent industrialists—Paul Reusch, Fritz Thyssen, Otto Wolff, Ottmar Strauss, for example—tried to further their economic and political interests through the press, either by buying newspapers outright or by bringing pressure to bear on the press in the various, direct and indirect, ways available to them.

Clearly, the arguments used in the Weimar Republic to support the existence of a decentralized press ignored the economic and political realities in the country and also the internal structure and functioning of a newspaper. Since most German newspapers were private enterprises—in 1926 over 80 per cent were still owned theoretically by individual families[30]—and thus by and large guided by commercial interests, many were easy prey, in periods of economic hardship, to the lures and pressures of moneyed interest groups. Consequently, the decentralized German press, dependent as so much of it was after the war on centralized sources of capital and news reports, was on the whole hardly in a position to wield independent political power. Political initiative in much of the press had been surrendered to the barons of the German economy, and the press which functioned within their sphere of influence was a tool, in some cases more sophisticated than in others, of their political aims.

28 *VZ*, 237, 9 May 1920.

29 The *DAZ* was bought in 1925 by the Prussian government, in 1926 was passed on to the Reich, and in February 1927 finally ended up in the hands of a consortium of industrialists, shipping magnates, and financiers.

30 Manfred Rietschel, *Der Familienbesitz in der deutschen politischen Tagespresse* (Leipzig, 1928), pp. 2ff.

By the end of 1925 most sectors of the German economy had recovered from the effects of the war and inflation. In 1926-7 the recovery even appeared to pass into prosperity as foreign investments poured into the country and as commerce and industry modernized and rationalized their structures. The press too revived from the trauma of the inflation, but, on the whole, never really participated in the following upswing. By 1926-7 the increased financial intake through advertising was largely reabsorbed by rising costs of production. In 1928, just as prospects were beginning to brighten for newspapers, a general downward trend in the economy set in. Until near the end of 1929 the effects of the credit shortage and growing unemployment were felt primarily by small papers in rural areas, where the agricultural economy was already in a crisis situation. But by the start of 1930 declining advertising inflicted cramp-like convulsions in the larger newspaper firms as well.

The combination of renewed economic difficulties and a concomitant radicalization of political opinion within the country threw innumerable owners and editors of politically moderate papers into a crisis of conscience. Were they to follow the trend of public opinion in their editorial policies or continue resolutely to propound their political views, at the risk of sacrificing readers and advertising and thus undermining their own livelihood? The experience of the inflation was still fresh in their minds; the aids to alleviating financial worries and work burdens which had been available during the inflationary period were still at hand. The arguments for continuing to support a moderate party of the middle-class centre had, on the other hand, lost meaning. For that section of the press which had already surrendered its editorial independence in the early years of the Republic to right-wing interests or to news services and press syndicates there was no need to take an eleventh-hour decision in these terms. For many of the provincial papers which had managed to preserve their independence and pride earlier, the odds against being able to continue to do so without collapsing entirely now seemed far too great, and they slipped out of the republican, democratic camp into either an illusionary

neutrality or uninhibited partisanship for the forces represen-
ting an 'awakening Germany'.

About one half of the German press in the Weimar Republic
overtly acknowledged some political tendency.[31] Often the
orientation was indicated simply as national, liberal, republican, or even just middle-class; and these newspapers,
which refused to categorize themselves in strict party terms,
frequently reflected the ideas of more than one party on
different political issues. A tightly organized, centrally
directed party press was possessed only by the Social
Democrats, the Communists, and later by the National
Socialists. The newspapers which supported the other major
parties, the DDP, DVP, Centre, and DNVP, usually insisted
that they were free to take an independent stance on party
decisions and policy, to criticize and even to deviate from the
party line. In cases where a paper was financially dependent
on the party or owned by a prominent party member, this
freedom, though repeatedly declared, was almost never
invoked.

The Social Democratic and Communist newspapers were
the party press *par excellence*. Their pages consisted almost
solely of tedious party news and polemical attacks on opponents, and their regular readership came exclusively from
the party faithful who believed religiously in the precepts of
Social Democracy or Communism. In 1925 the 170 existing
SPD papers were organized under the party's aegis in the
Konzentrations A.G., a step which aimed at the consolidation, rationalization, and modernization of the party's
press. Between 1925 and 1930 4·2 million marks were
poured into this organization by the party, but the attempt
to render the SPD press more attractive and perhaps even a
paying business proposition brought accusations of *em-
bourgeoisement* from the old guard in the party and, at any
rate, was destined to be futile as long as the party exercised a
tight bureaucratic control over the choice of editors and
contributors and over the material published.[32] The Com-

[31] See Appendix I, p. 312.
[32] A thorough treatment of the SPD press is to be found in Kurt Koszyk,
Zwischen Kaiserreich und Diktatur (Heidelberg, 1958).

munist press faced similar problems. By 1932 about fifty KPD papers, controlled, like the SPD press, through a central holding company, were published in Germany; of these half were local editions of parent papers.[33]

In contrast to the KPD press, which was carefully planted in the major urban centres by the central party organizers, the National Socialist press sprang up indigenously out of the fervour of local groups or individuals. Whereas the press of the older middle-class parties frequently felt the party to be an uncomfortable yoke and displayed rebellious, individualistic tendencies, National Socialist papers vied for recognition as party organs. Out of the thirty-one Nazi publications in 1928, of which the *Völkischer Beobachter* was the only daily paper, nineteen were classified as official party organs, authorized to carry the swastika on the front page. The rest were merely 'officially recognized' by the party as publications supporting the NSDAP. By late 1930 the party had nineteen dailies, and in 1932 fifty-nine.[34] The National Socialist press was founded in depression-ridden Germany and its sole motivation was a political one. Few of the papers were viable as economic propositions. In the last quarter of 1931 the circulation even of the main Nazi organ, the *Völkischer Beobachter*, was only 41,000.[35] As Goebbels explained of his paper *Der Angriff*, the National Socialist press was not intended to be a purveyor of news and was not interested in replacing the daily paper of information at the breakfast table. The purpose of the Nazi press was 'to incite, to inflame, to urge on'; the effect desired was that of a 'whip, which wakens the dilatory sleepers from their slumber and drives them on to indefatigable activity!'[36]

Of the other major political groupings the Catholic Centre Party and the German Nationalist People's Party were on the whole far more successful in anchoring their press to

---

[33] See Herbert Girardet, *Der wirtschaftliche Aufbau der kommunistischen Tagespresse in Deutschland von 1918 bis 1933* (Essen, 1938), p. 19.

[34] See Oron J. Hale, *The Captive Press in the Third Reich* (Princeton, N.J., 1964), pp. 46f., 59.

[35] This figure is based on mail delivery; see the letter of the minister for postal services Schätzel to Brüning, 3 February 1932, Reichskanzlei files, R431/2683, p. 367.

[36] *Kampf um Berlin*, p. 188.

the party apparatus than the liberal parties. For the Centre, the bond of religion and the active interest in the press of the industrial group within the party tied many of the Catholic papers closely to the party structure. In the immediate postwar years the Nationalists, often independently of Hugenberg's ventures, made a concerted effort to extend their control in the press. In areas east of the Elbe papers were bought up with a zeal verging on fanaticism, often at astronomical prices, to try and eliminate oppositional opinion.[37] Owing to Hugenberg's influence and because the Nationalist political programme during most of the Weimar Republic was essentially one of negativism and opposition to the ruling coalition parties to the left, the DNVP had comparatively little difficulty in the 1920s in maintaining a unified front with its press. Only in the last years of the Republic, when National Socialism was rapidly gaining strength, did dissension arise. Despite their pretentious displays of unity on occasion, Hugenberg and Hitler were more often than not at odds with each other. The Nationalist press, however, frequently refused to publicize differences of opinion in the right-wing camp, feeling that the cause was essentially the same and that only the approach of the two leaders and their parties differed. The Nationalist press thus provided a great service to Hitler; Hugenberg was astute enough to realize this and repeatedly expressed his annoyance at the lack of loyalty to his person.

Both the DDP and DVP always stressed the importance of press support, but neither party, despite the exhortations of certain members, could free itself sufficiently from its liberal ideology and belief in individual initiative in matters of party organization to take coherent steps to guarantee itself any extensive and firm footing in the press. With relatively limited tangible economic ties to the parties and linked, in the main, solely by ideological sympathies, the liberal press proved to be an unstable factor in republican politics, especially in times of economic crisis when its

37 In this connection see the interesting report 'Die Presseverhältnisse in Pommern' (1920), Reichskanzlei files, R43I/2504, pp. 78ff.

existence was threatened and it faced enormous pressures from affluent interest groups.

In some general reflections on the state of the DVP's organization in January 1925, Stresemann noted that much of the provincial press which formerly had backed the People's Party had fallen victim to the inflation and to the Nationalists' drive to expand their control in the press. A number of Prussian provinces, for example, were without a single newspaper on which the DVP could rely. Stresemann insisted that, contrary to a widely held view, his party did not have vast funds available from business and industry and that it was not financed by Hugo Stinnes.[38] In 1924 a plan had been in the air to establish a large fund for the support of the DVP press. Nothing had come of the project, however, because the business concerns that were supposed to provide capital had decided that the poor economic outlook for industry prohibited such speculative investments.[39] As the DVP's strength declined after 1920 newspapers became increasingly reluctant to support the party outright and shifted to a less specific position on the right.[40]

The DDP's experience with the press was even more adverse than that of the DVP. By 1926 left liberalism had lost approximately two-thirds of the sizeable press support which it had enjoyed at the end of the war, and the party secretary, Werner Stephan, estimated that only 180 newspapers remained in the Reich on which the DDP could rely for publicity.[41] Large areas of the country—all of Pomerania, Mecklenburg, and Schleswig-Holstein, most of Bavaria, Saxony, Thuringia, Westphalia, and East Prussia—were without a single paper sympathetic to the party.

[38] Undated, untitled manuscript in NL Stresemann, 92, 172455ff.

[39] Stresemann to the editors of the *Niederschlesische Zeitung*, 12 December 1925, NL Stresemann, 94, 172889f.

[40] For the press of the DVP in general see Heinz Starkulla, 'Organisation und Technik der Pressepolitik des Staatsmannes Gustav Stresemann 1923 bis 1929', unpublished diss. (Munich, 1951).

[41] See Appendix I, p. 312; and the report of the party secretary, Werner Stephan, to the national conference of the DDP in Hamburg, 24 April 1927, NSDAP Hauptarchiv, microfilm folder 39, reel 762. The original riles of the Hauptarchiv are now in the Bundesarchiv Koblenz.

Immediately after the war many publications which had previously backed the National Liberal Party transferred their loyalties to the DDP. Among these papers were such reputable dailies as the *Münchner Neueste Nachrichten*, the *Magdeburgische Zeitung*, and the *Ulmer Tageblatt*. However, when in the course of 1919 Stresemann's DVP began to assert itself and particularly after the resounding defeat of the DDP and the substantial gains of the DVP in the June elections of 1920, many of these papers moved back to the camp of right-wing liberalism.[42] Subsequently many of them moved further to the right, out of the camp of liberalism entirely.[43] The inflation also played havoc with the press inclined to support the Democratic Party. As early as March 1920 the party's press association (*Presse-Verein*) sent out a circular entitled 'The Democratic press is in danger!'[44] and urged that a party fund be set up to assist provincial papers financially. The DDP Presse-Verein admitted in December 1923 that it did not have enough assets to buy even a single postage stamp.[45] One provincial left-liberal paper after another was swallowed by parties to the right, by individuals associated with these parties, or by large capital interests. East of the Elbe press backing for the DDP was almost totally decimated. Everywhere the basic pattern of developments was the same. A provincial paper began to have financial difficulties, not necessarily because circulation was declining but because advertising was falling off and costs were increasing. Appeals for financial assistance to the local Democratic party organization were redirected to the national offices or to individuals like Hermann Fischer, Hermann Dietrich, Otto Gessler, and Hartmann von Richthofen, who were known for their connections with

[42] See the explanation which the editor of the *Magdeburgische Zeitung*, A. Kirchrat, gave to Eugen Schiffer for the withdrawal of the paper's support from the DDP; letter of 4 October 1920, NL Schiffer, 6, pp. 587f.

[43] For the case of the *Münchner Neueste Nachrichten* see Anton Betz, 'Die Tragödie der "Münchner Neuesten Nachrichten" 1932/33', *Journalismus*, II (1961), pp. 22ff.; and Kurt Koszyk, 'Paul Reusch und die "Münchner Neuesten Nachrichten"—Zum Problem Industrie und Presse in der Endphase der Weimarer Republik', *Vierteljahrshefte für Zeitgeschichte*, XX (1972), pp. 75f.

[44] 13 March 1920, NL Haussmann, 105.

[45] Minutes of the meeting of the executive of the Presse-Verein, 28 December 1923, NSDAP Hauptarchiv, 38/757.

moneyed interests. If a loan or some other form of aid was found, it usually was not substantial enough to provide more than a very brief respite, and shortly the alarm was sounded again. If the pleas were eventually not met, liquidation or sale often followed, but more common was the attempt by local publishers to find other sources of capital in order to survive. The tentacles of Hugenberg and heavy industry, or of the more prosperous DNVP, or of a local businessman who was hostile to the DDP, were always waiting. A change in editorial policy invariably attended major alterations in the financial organization of these struggling firms. Of course, in some instances a publisher, while remaining independent, voluntarily changed the political tendency of his paper in the hope of increasing circulation and advertising revenue. Democracy, he decided, was obviously not a marketable proposition. In either case, whether voluntary or not, the political reorientation was often accompanied by staff changes, and journalists who were members of the Democratic Party frequently lost their jobs. The developments in the *Striegauer Anzieger*, a small democratic paper, took on exceptionally grotesque proportions. They became public knowledge when Otto Nuschke disclosed the outlines of the case in the Prussian Landtag.[46] In 1922 the paper was sold, contrary to the promises expressly given to the chief editor, a man called Müller, to right-wing political interests. Müller, who for a time had been chairman of the local DDP organization in Striegau, was dismissed and replaced as editor by a member of the DNVP. Depressed by the breach of promise by the former owners whom he had served for many years and by his own loss of employment, Müller shot himself. If the climax to these events was not the norm, the general pattern certainly was common. Among journalists membership in the DDP came to be considered an unnecessary professional liability. The defeat which the DDP suffered in the May elections of 1924 was attributed in some quarters to the disappearance of much of the party's former press

[46] In a session on 21 October 1922, *Sitzungsberichte des Preussischen Landtags, 1. Wahlperiode*, pp. 12833f.; see also the report in *Der Demokrat*, III (11 October 1922), p. 547.

support; the fact that the DDP's best electoral results were achieved in cities where the party had reliable organs for publicity was used as evidence for this conclusion.[47]

'Today the press means everything; whoever controls the press, controls the mind of the nation', wrote an anonymous contributor to the Naumannite journal *Die Hilfe* in early 1925. Hugenberg's activities in the press and the steady electoral gains of the DNVP, from 44 seats in 1919, to 71 in 1920, to 95 in May 1924, to 103 in December 1924, provided the seemingly unassailable evidence for the assertion.[48] However, in spite of the general conviction among Democrats that press backing was the key to political success, the press situation for the DDP did not improve once the inflation was over. In fact, the continuing decline of the party and its constant financial difficulties undermined further the support that it received from the press.

In January 1924 a number of Democrats, who were particularly concerned about organizational problems and who felt that herein lay perhaps the greatest weakness of the party, began serious discussions which aimed at the establishment of a loan and investment body for the left-liberal press similar to some of Hugenberg's enterprises. Anton Erkelenz, who was chairman of the DDP executive committee from 1921 to 1929 and who unceasingly insisted that the Democrats had a great deal to learn about party organization and political propaganda, was the moving spirit behind the project. In the course of the year he obtained the co-operation of the Mosse, Ullstein, and Sonnemann (FSD) firms which agreed to participate with a modest amount of capital in the operation of a venture called the Verlag Neuer Staat. The stated purpose of the enterprise was to provide financial assistance and advice to provincial papers in distress and, whenever possible, to purchase viable papers for the party.

The plans for the Verlag Neuer Staat were grandiose, the scale of activity in fact very small. After a year the advisory board came to the conclusion that the capital available to the Verlag Neuer Staat did not allow it to fulfil its original

[47] *Der Demokrat*, V (8 May 1924), pp. 153ff.; and VI (16 July 1925), pp. 339ff.

[48] *Die Hilfe*, Nr. 3 (1 February 1925), p. 55.

purpose and that the possibilities of obtaining further funds had all been exhausted. Owing to the general situation in the economy, commerce and industry were simply not prepared to provide money for an unlucrative enterprise. In the course of the year loans had been made to about a half dozen small provincial papers, and minority shares had been purchased in another six publishing firms. Much of the money, however, had been lost when a number of the papers collapsed. Neuer Staat, its advisers reflected, had had the opportunity to invest only in unstable businesses; profitable undertakings had not offered shares and would not offer them.[49] Other matters, which the advisers did not discuss openly, had also harassed the venture. From the beginning the whole operation had been plagued by disagreements, scepticism, and apathy. The party representatives on the advisory board, Erkelenz and Fischer, were constantly feuding because of wider political differences. Erkelenz represented the left wing of the party, the trade-union element, while Fischer, the president of the Hansabund, represented the commercial right wing. Erkelenz, who was absent in America for several months in 1925, was unhappy subsequently about the investments which the Verlag Neuer Staat had made while he was away—he described them as 'gratuities' to hopelessly floundering papers— and felt that Fischer and his business cronies had at least accelerated the failure of the operation. Ullstein had been reluctant to partake in the project from the start and had consented to join only when confronted with the participation of its rival Mosse. Later Franz Ullstein was particularly irritated when he learned that the business manager of the Verlag Neuer Staat, Mathis, was moonlighting and had been involved, in the autumn of 1925, in the purchase, by other interests, of the *Deutsche Allgemeine Zeitung* from the Stinnes holdings. The Ullsteins, who regarded the *DAZ* as a competitor with their financially weak *Vossische Zeitung* and apparently knew nothing of the sale beforehand, claimed that they should have been informed of the negotiations by

---

[49] 'Protokoll der 9. Beiratssitzung', held on 4 May 1926, NL Erkelenz, 115. Minutes of other sessions of the advisory board and business reports are located in folders 37, 130, 136.

Mathis.[50] Furthermore, the intense Mosse-Ullstein rivalry prevented the uninhibited co-operation of either firm in the Verlag Neuer Staat. The FSD, on the other hand, although it contributed capital initially, never played an active role subsequently. Kurt Simon even withdrew from the advisory board in the course of 1925. And finally, the left-liberal provincial press, openly informed by party circulars of the prominent position of the three large Berlin-Frankfurt democratic publishing houses in the enterprise, did not hide their suspicion and anxiety that the Verlag Neuer Staat was merely a disguised scheme by the metropolitan Jewish publishers to infiltrate and buy up the provincial press.[51] In view of all these obstacles the advisory board decided on 4 May 1926 to curtail the recent activities of the Verlag; no new investments would be made and existing ones would be managed by a part-time officer. The Verlag Neuer Staat continued to exist, virtually in name only, until 1934 when it was dissolved.

Once the depression set in at the end of the twenties newspapers deserted the DDP *en masse*. The *Demokratische Zeitungsdienst*, the official news service of the party, barely subsisted after 1927 for lack of subscribers; by December 1932 it could no longer even pay salaries.[52] In April 1932 Karl Brammer, editor of the news service, informed the managing executive of his party that a mere 35 papers remained closely connected with the party while only approximately another one hundred of the thousands of German newspapers were still favourably disposed to its aims and were willing occasionally to print party material.[53]

Neither the magnitude nor the details of the erosion of press support for the Democratic Party struck the layman's eye. Changes in ownership or financial structure in publishing

[50] On the differences between Fischer and Erkelenz see in particular Fischer's letters of 20 March and 7 October 1926, NL Erkelenz, 132 and 129. On Ullstein see Stephan to Erkelenz, 22 September 1925, NL Erkelenz, 130; the minutes of the advisory board session, 18 September 1925, NL Erkelenz, 115; and Franz Ullstein to Erkelenz, 29 December 1926, NL Erkelenz, 41.

[51] See the letter of Theodor Buresch of the *Jauer'sches Stadtblatt* to the executive committee of the DDP, 7 May 1925, NL Erkelenz, 36.

[52] Letters of Brammer to Hermann Dietrich, 26 November 1927 and 3 December 1932, NL Dietrich, 87, p. 313; and 264, p. 16 respectively; Bundesarchiv Koblenz.

[53] Minutes of the meeting, 28 April 1932, NSDAP Hauptarchiv, 39/774.

firms were usually well concealed, and shifts in editorial policy were in many cases gradual and purposely disguised. Much of the public assumed that the DDP possessed powerful press backing simply because a number of the largest publishing houses in Germany described their political orientation as 'democratic', and the average German was unaware of or ignored the difficulties that emerged in the relationship between the DDP and the metropolitan press of similar persuasion.

The Mosse, Ullstein, and Sonnemann papers rarely tried to mask their sympathy for the DDP, but they repeatedly proclaimed their complete editorial independence from the policies of the party and their right to exercise independent judgement on the nation's affairs. Never in the course of the Weimar Republic could the papers of these firms bring themselves to repudiate the Democratic Party, or its successor the State Party, entirely, but a gradual process of disengagement from the party's politics, if not from its fundamental ideas, occurred.

Disenchantment with developments in the party had set in within weeks of its foundation. This chagrin was most pronounced in the *Berliner Tageblatt, Vossische Zeitung, Frankfurter Zeitung*, Hellmut von Gerlach's weekly *Die Welt am Montag*, and the radical pacifist *General-Anzeiger* of Dortmund—the latter had the highest circulation, 250,000, of all dailies outside Berlin.

As with the left wing of the party, the point of departure for all criticism levelled by the leading democratic press against the DDP, and the republican leadership as a whole, was the conviction that the republican, democratic forces in the Weimar state never grasped the initiative proffered to them when the old order collapsed. Democratic journalists like Theodor Wolff, Georg Bernhard, Wilhelm Cohnstaedt, and Hellmut von Gerlach felt that in January 1919 the republican parties of the left, the SPD and DDP, had been given a mandate for thoroughgoing reform, but that the opportunity had not been utilized. Even when the DDP had lost its powerful position in the politics of the Republic, the Mosse, Ullstein, and Sonnemann papers urged the party to be more forceful and insistent in its opposition to the forces of reaction. When the party displayed indecision or weak will on such issues as the socialization of the service industries, the expropriation of crown lands, reform of the taxation system, the lowering of high grain tariffs, and assistance for small farmers in the east, it exposed itself to stinging attacks from the left-democratic press. In its choice of too many uninspiring candidates for its election lists, and in the care it took, by rejecting all traces of radicalism in its personnel and programme, not to estrange any of its supporters and especially its financial patrons, the DDP, so the left-democratic press argued, sacrificed principles, magnetism, verve, and strength for ambiguity, mediocrity, dilatoriness, and decline.

Because the public at large readily associated the *Berliner Tageblatt, Frankfurter Zeitung*, and, to a lesser extent, the *Vossische Zeitung*, with the DDP, the party was acutely irritated and embarrassed by any adverse criticism directed against it by these papers. An intense animosity developed between many Democratic politicians and the metropolitan democratic papers. While the papers often talked of the 'failure' of the party to live up to its responsibilities, DDP leaders threw back the same charge at this press with even greater vehemence. The most scathing recriminations came from those Democratic leaders who had held ministerial posts in Reich governments and therefore felt that they had shouldered the ultimate burdens of decision-making. Men like Otto Gessler, Erich Koch-Weser, Hermann Dietrich, and even Georg Gothein and Friedrich von Payer, did not hesitate to denounce the radical journalists of the democratic press as maverick literati, unconversant in the realities of politics, and their editorials as utopian castle-building and irresponsible self-indulgence. A party committee meeting rarely passed without some negative reference to the major democratic newspapers. Georg Bernhard was virtually ostracized from party affairs in 1919-20. Eduard Hamm, the Democratic economic minister in 1921 called Theodor Wolff and the *Berliner Tageblatt* 'a heavy burden' for the DDP and recommended that 'a line be sharply drawn' between the party and the paper.[54] A few days later Friedrich von Payer wrote

54 In a letter to Schiffer, 2 August 1921, NL Schiffer, 6, p. 696.

a letter of complaint to Wilhelm Cohnstaedt of the *Frankfurter Zeitung* and concluded: 'It is painful to me that your paper, whose views formerly carried such weight in the parliamentary party, for years now no longer has any authority there. One can say that now no paper at all has any influence in the parliamentary party.'[55] If, as Payer indicated, the recommendations and political analyses of the leading democratic papers were no longer given serious consideration by the politicians, the more conservative elements in the DDP none the less continued to be incensed by the stubborn independence of this press. The editors who remained active in the party insisted that closer co-operation between the Democratic Party and the democratic press could only result if the party showed a greater readiness to listen to, and to weigh carefully, the views of the papers before decisions were made.[56] Wilhelm Cohnstaedt, for one, was apparently willing to believe that the *Frankfurter Zeitung* by itself was politically more powerful than the DDP's parliamentary party.[57] He maintained therefore that it was essential that the press be accorded more attention and respect by the party's policy-makers. The DDP executive committee did make room for six representatives of the party's press organization, but usually not more than one of these six came from the metropolitan press. Party leaders and officials, especially in the provinces, gradually built up an unshakeable dislike for the 'ivory-tower' critics in the press who, as Theodor Heuss concluded, had 'given themselves the assignment of deciding just who is still a good Democrat and what democracy actually means'.[58]

There were many Democrats, mainly in the provinces, who alleged that the harsh polemics of the left-democratic press against heavy industry, the army, the judiciary, and against

[55] 26 August 1921, NL Payer, 14, p. 77.

[56] See the remarks of Georg Bernhard to a session of the DDP Hauptvorstand, 13 April 1919, DDP files, R45III/15, p. 90; and of Wilhelm Cohnstaedt to a meeting of the executive, 11 July 1922, NSDAP Hauptarchiv, 38/756.

[57] Payer mentioned this in a letter to Heuss, 1 April 1925, NL Heuss, Theodor Heuss Archiv, Stuttgart. Payer added that Cohnstaedt was a man who confused 'stubbornness with character'.

[58] In a letter to Koch-Weser, 29 October 1924, reprinted in my *Heuss*, pp. 144ff.

the former leaders of imperial Germany, together with the radical proposals for social and economic change propagated in the columns of these papers, were driving voters, and even members, away from the DDP into the arms of the right-wing parties. Because the *Berliner Tageblatt*, *Vossische Zeitung*, and *Frankfurter Zeitung* were newspapers with a nationwide distribution and therefore, it was assumed, had a greater resonance than any other liberal-democratic organs—in government circles, in the parties of the opposition, and amongst the general public—certain Democrats claimed that these papers were distorting the image which the DDP, as an entity, was trying to present to the public. Some went so far as to say that the party was being destroyed by its big-city press.

Resentment between the party and its left-wing press simmered throughout the Republic's existence. On several occasions it exploded openly. On two such occasions leading democratic journalists left the party, Hellmut von Gerlach in 1922, and Theodor Wolff in 1926.

Hellmut von Gerlach was born in Silesia in 1866 and was the descendant of an old family of landed aristocrats. Educated in Geneva and Strasbourg, his political views evolved from an extreme anti-Semitic conservatism, bequeathed to him by his social standing and parental upbringing, through first the Christian socialism of the court preacher Adolf Stöcker and then the democratic national socialism of Friedrich Naumann, ending finally in a radical-democratic pacifism on the extreme bourgeois left.[59] A co-chairman of the Democratic Union, which in 1910 refused to unite with the rest of left liberalism in the Progressive People's Party, and chief editor since 1901 of the outspoken, reform-minded independent weekly *Die Welt am Montag*, Gerlach became one of the most vehement opponents of the war, the manner in which it was conducted, both strategically and on the home front, and, above all, the way in which, in his eyes, the nation was hoodwinked into believing that it was fighting a just war of defence forced upon the country by the Entente powers. At the end of the war, on 15

---

[59] See Gerlach's autobiography, *Von rechts nach links* (Zürich, 1937).

November 1918, Gerlach was appointed under-secretary in the Prussian ministry of the interior and assigned to work on the Polish and Silesian questions. However, in March 1919 he resigned his post, ostensibly on account of differences with the Social Democratic minister of justice in Prussia, Heine, whose policies he considered unduly harsh against the radical left, but primarily because his own opinions on settling the Polish-German frontier dispute were being labelled, even among the left, as treasonable. In mid-November Gerlach had signed Theodor Wolff's democratic manifesto with enthusiasm and great hope. Within weeks, however, not only was his own optimism deflated but sections of the DDP were deeming him a liability.

Gerlach for instance openly announced that, as far as he was concerned, Germany had indeed been responsible for the war and now had to atone for her guilt; the Treaty of Versailles, though harsh and perhaps unjust in some respects, had to be signed. In June 1919 the managing committee of the DDP discussed the possibility of expelling Gerlach from the party but realized that it did not have the competence to do so.[60] A member could be expelled only by the local party organization of the district where he was registered. A local committee had to be set up which would then weigh the evidence against a member and reach a decision. Such an action was never initiated against Gerlach. Instead, in January 1922 Georg Gothein, the chairman of the DDP organization for Berlin West, approached him requesting that he resign from the party voluntarily. He, Gothein, had received numerous petitions from throughout the country urging that Gerlach be expelled. 'Your remaining in the German Democratic Party', Gothein asserted, 'is of advantage only to the parties that stand further to the right, and you should consider that reason enough to reflect whether it would not be in the general political interest if you cut your tie with our party.'[61] Gerlach had grounds to believe that an official attempt to exclude him from the party would not succeed. Anton Erkelenz for one, the chairman of the party's

---

[60] See the minutes of its meeting, 28 June 1919, DDP files, R45III/9, p. 121.
[61] Letter of 10 January 1922, NL Gothein, 21, pp. 91f.

executive committee, felt that there was not sufficient
material for a case against Gerlach.[62] Nevertheless, the latter
complied with Gothein's request. 'Never in my life have I
shyed away from political battle,' he replied to Gothein, 'but
I only fight when the object is worthy of a fight. It seems to
me that is not the case here.' He then outlined his disappointment over the development of the party since its
founding; it had no flair, no vitality, and was full of compromises.

Neither in the question of pacifism, nor in social or fiscal policy,
nor simply in the presentation of the democratic-republican point of
view . . . has the party, in my opinion, fulfilled the responsibilities
which were incumbent upon a radical bourgeois party. . . . You
complain that, on account of my belonging to the party, numerous
members have turned their backs on it and have gone over to the
People's Party. It would appear to me that a truly Democratic Party
should not regret the departure of members who are prepared to use an
excuse like this to justify their action. In their way of thinking these
deserters have obviously always stood with one and a half feet in the
camp of the People's Party. To me their remaining would have been a
burden to the Democratic Party, whereas their departure can be taken
as a great release.

He saw little chance, Gerlach said, of the DDP ever
fulfilling the duties and goals outlined in the founding manifesto, and he concluded his letter with the 'assurance that I
will none the less remain what I was, a convinced democrat,
who sees in true democracy the political cure for his home-
land and for all mankind'.[63]

Gerlach was pressured into withdrawing from the DDP.
Theodor Wolff, on the other hand, gave up his membership
as a gesture of protest against what he viewed as the party's
spinelessness. The occasion was the passing by the Reichstag
in December 1926 of the controversial *Schmutz- und
Schundgesetz*, a bill providing for control of the sale of
pornographic literature to minors. Although much of the
party opposed the bill, three Democrats, Wilhelm Külz, who
was the Reich minister of the interior at the time, Gertrud
Bäumer, and Theodor Heuss, were among its architects and

[62] Mentioned in a letter of Gerland to Carl Petersen, the party chairman, 15
December 1921, NL Gothein, 21, p. 89. See also Gerland's letter to Erkelenz of
the same date, NL Erkelenz, 17.

[63] Letter of 3 February 1922, NL Gothein, 21, pp. 93f.

most vociferous apologists. Of course, the artistic and literary community displayed an almost solid front against any .proposals for censorship. The Ullstein papers were as emphatic in their denunciation of the proposed bill as Wolff.[64] 'Because, in the genesis and treatment of the "law for the protection of youth against pornographic publications", the party has not defended serious literary work and intellectual freedom with the necessary resolve,' Wolff explained to the party chairman, Koch-Weser, 'I find it impossible to belong to it any longer as a registered member.'[65]

Wolff was indeed passionately opposed to the legislation, but nevertheless he also found the bill and the role of the Democrats in its formulation a convenient pretext for renouncing his membership in a party where, for many years now, he had no longer felt comfortable. Wolff was too sensitive a political animal and possessed too much understanding of human nature not to recognize that his own action involved an element of escapism. Ernst Feder, his close associate on the *Berliner Tageblatt*, noted in his diary that Wolff 'senses the error he has committed'.[66] Both Feder and Martin Carbe, the general manager of the Mosse papers, had tried to dissuade Wolff from what they considered to be a rash step. In a further letter to Koch-Weser, a fortnight after the announcement of his withdrawal from the DDP, Wolff's arguments had taken a not very subtle turn. 'Precisely for the sake of the democratic cause and in order to maintain that influence which I do have, did I leave', he wrote, trying to mollify his own feelings of guilt, and

[64] See Hermann Ullstein to Heuss, 6 December 1926, NL Heuss; and Franz Ullstein to Erkelenz, 29 December 1926, NL Erkelenz, 41.

[65] Letter of 4 December 1926, NL Koch-Weser, 34, p. 361.

[66] Diary entry for 10 December 1926. The diaries were consulted in the Geheime Staatsarchiv, Berlin, with the permission of Feder's widow, Erna Feder. Selections from the diaries for the years 1926 to 1932 have since been published: Ernst Feder, *Heute sprach ich mit . . .*, ed. C. Lowenthal-Hensel and A. Paucker (Stuttgart, 1971). The foregoing entry appears on p. 90. Below, references to the diaries are, in the first instance, to the original manuscript; if the relevant passage has been included in the published edition, this is indicated in parentheses.

affirmed that in the long run he could probably be more useful to the party as a non-member.[67] However, a year and a
half later he referred, revealingly, to his departure from the
DDP as his 'step to freedom'.[68]

Gerlach retired from the DDP without a struggle, pleased,
in fact, that he did not have to take the initiative himself.
Wolff eventually found an excuse to justify his break with
the party which he had helped sire. The principal impulse in
both instances was disillusionment with the party and an
unwillingness to be associated with its policies any longer
rather than a positive desire to achieve greater independence
on political matters for the newspapers which the two men
edited. The withdrawal of these leading journalists from the
DDP symbolized the retreat of many idealistic republicans
and democrats from the politics of the Weimar Republic. The
DDP, in many respects, embodied the goals and ideals of the
Republic; not without justification did it proclaim itself 'the
true party of the constitution'.[69] Disengagement from it also
signified disengagement from the realities of the Republic.

The developments in the attitudes of the *Vossische
Zeitung* seemed on the surface to follow a contrary course.
Outwardly, after 1921 a form of reconciliation appeared to
take shape between the paper and the DDP. Because of his
virtual ostracism from the party and because of the frequent
and sharp attacks against him from within its ranks, Bernhard
had maintained a haughty distance from the DDP in the first
two years of the Republic's existence. However, his personal
character did not permit him to remain simply a passive
observer and restrained commentator. He had become, in the
two years, increasingly more outspoken in his views on
foreign policy, advocating friendship with France and a
continental bloc against England, and he had made his
disenchantment with developments in domestic politics clear
by openly promoting corporatist ideas. While not rejecting
parliamentarianism, he argued that the incorporation of class
and professional interests into the structure of government

[67] Letter of 16 December 1926, NL Koch-Weser, 34, pp. 377f.

[68] *BT*, 248, 27 May 1928.

[69] See Ernst Lemmer in *Die Hilfe*, Nr. 19 (1 October 1926), p. 417; and Otto
Nuschke, 'Wie die Deutsche Demokratische Partei wurde', p. 38.

might provide a working formula for greater national harmony. He campaigned, for example, in favour of bestowing some significant legislative authority on the Reich economic council, a body on which he sat as a representative of the journalistic profession. The official inauguration by the Wirth government in 1921 of a foreign policy which corresponded, in its broad outlines, with Bernhard's own concepts marked the turn in his posture towards the Republic and its politics. The DDP staunchly backed the policy of fulfilment. The formation of the great coalition, from the SPD on the left to the DVP on the right, in August 1923 under the chancellorship of Stresemann, the consequent co-operation of the DDP and DVP in government, and the renunciation of passive resistance against the French occupation in the Ruhr, conclusively terminated Bernhard's period of critical abstention. He now ceased propagating corporatist ideas. The more vituperative mutual recriminations between himself and the DDP abated, and the more positive approach which Bernhard manifested towards the Republic and the DDP was rewarded by a Democratic candidacy in Halle in the second national elections of 1924. In 1919-20 he had refused to give his own party any special support in his paper. But in October 1924 he wrote to several party colleagues: 'It is important this time that the Democratic Party should receive its due, in the way of a favourable election result, for its resolute conduct. In order to achieve this success, however, it is necessary that all forces in the party work together to enlighten the public.'[70] Although defeated in these elections, he gradually assumed a more active and prominent role in the party, gaining election to the executive in January 1926, and in May 1928 he was finally sent to the Reichstag by the Potsdam I constituency. However, the reciprocal accommodation worked out by Bernhard and the DDP was one of convenience rather than conviction. In return for an opportunity to satisfy his own political ambitions Bernhard was prepared to swing his paper behind the DDP during election campaigns. Yet, despite his

[70] Letters to Erkelenz and Richthofen, 22 October 1924, NL Erkelenz, 128, and NL Richthofen, 20.

more direct involvement in party affairs he continued to be an unhesitating, even if slightly less emotional, censor of personalities and policies in the DDP. The professional politicians and the party's more conservative wing, in turn, kept a wary and usually disapproving eye on him and his activity. As in the case of Gerlach, many Democrats treated Bernhard as an untouchable and, as the party declined, as a liability; consequently his position in the party always remained tenuous—until he finally left it in 1930.

While many leading DDP politicians looked to the national elections of 1928 with confidence, the principal democratic newspapers warned against a relaxed, cocksure attitude: that the Republic and parliamentary government were not visibly threatened by forces aiming to overthrow them was no criterion for stability. Because Germany had a democratic, republican constitution it did not mean that republican democracy governed the country. In May 1928 the *Berliner Tageblatt* published in its editorial column an article by the police president of Cassel, Ferdinand Friedensburg. The author analysed the political situation and concluded that the Republic was being governed according to the 'guiding principles' (*Richtlinien*) of the German Nationalist People's Party.[71]

By 1928 the cleft had widened between the DDP and the distinguished democratic newspapers of Berlin and Frankfurt which had participated in the party's founding. To be sure, in the campaign for the 1928 Reichstag elections the party still received substantial support from the *Berliner Tageblatt* and *Frankfurter Zeitung* but already in the spirit which was to characterize later support; readers were urged to vote DDP *faute de mieux*. Between the *Vossische Zeitung* and the DDP an uneasy truce reigned. Neither the party nor the press was alone responsible for the conflict between them. The party was singularly incapable of absorbing and pacifying criticism of its policies and tactics. The leading left-democratic news-papers, on the other hand, frequently displayed an exaggerated and unwarranted self-assurance in their judgements; and

[71] *BT*, 213, 6 May 1928.

often revealed great insensitivity for, and even incomprehension of the operative side of politics.

The political journalists of the democratic press did not, of course, function as independent, self-supporting intellectuals. They were the employees of commerical enterprises whose *raison d'être* was to produce marketable newspapers. To a general discussion of the workings and character of the Mosse, Ullstein, and Sonnemann firms, and of their publications, this account must now turn.

IV

THE FIRMS OF MOSSE,
ULLSTEIN, AND SONNEMANN

The new generation of owners that took over the Mosse, Ullstein, and Sonnemann publishing houses after the deaths of their founders inherited not merely businesses but also established political guidelines. For the Jewish proprietors of these firms, prior to the First World War liberalism and personal business success were virtually identical goals. With the advent of parliamentary democracy in Germany in 1918-19, the main objective behind the political commitment of the founders seemed to have been achieved. Concurrent with the apparent consummation of this political ideal, however, was the onset of a period of economic adversity. The Weimar Republic presented the owners of the three firms with the painful evidence that liberal democracy and commercial prosperity were not necessarily related. The natural consequence of this concomitance of success in one respect and incipient difficulty in another was that the paramount and most immediate concern of the owners became a commercial and administrative one. The general political direction of the Ullstein, Mosse, and Sonnemann newspapers was now taken for granted. Yet the predominance of business considerations, which circumstances seemed to dictate, fostered the emergence of an opportunistic frame of mind among the new generation of owners. Most of them became increasingly inclined to look for and to emphasize those nuances in progressive liberalism which might best promote commercial interests.

The founders of the three firms had, in their lifetimes, established a libertarian tradition of owner-editor relations, which accorded editors virtually unimpeded freedom of initiative in formulating day-to-day editorial policy. During the Weimar Republic, economic exigencies, combined with a growing political and ideological scepticism amongst the public, created an electrified atmosphere in these publishing houses, and the inviolability of editorial independence as a governing principle was undermined. With Mosse the difficulties manifested themselves earlier and more clearly than in the other two firms.

After the death of Rudolf Mosse in 1920, the Mosse business remained a family enterprise. The founder's only child, an adopted daughter Felicia, had married Hans Lachmann—who then attached Mosse to his name—and the latter had become a partner in the firm in 1910. Rudolf Mosse, however, came to feel that his son-in-law did not possess all the qualities which he desired in an heir, and in 1920 Lachmann-Mosse inherited only 50 per cent of the *Berliner Tageblatt* directly. The rest of the family fortune went to Felicia, although she did authorize her husband to act as her agent. Mosse's testament, furthermore, guaranteed that his two nephews Martin Carbe and Theodor Wolff were to be irremovable from their posts as managing director of the publishing house and editor-in-chief of the *Tageblatt* respectively. Both these men were thus legally independent of Lachmann-Mosse. Rudolf Mosse hoped, in this way, to assure a certain consistency in the firm's future development.

Lachmann-Mosse, born in 1885, was the son of a Berlin industrialist and a wealthy man in his own right.[1] Highly ambitious and enterprising, he, none the less, had little instinct for business. The Mosse fortune added to his own, he felt compelled to embark on a massive investment spree. To the Mosse advertising organization were added eleven new branch offices in capitals throughout Europe and in New York, when only four branches had existed before. Vast sums of money were sunk into real estate, housing developments, a cinema, a cabaret, and a private art collection which was open to the public at the stately Mosse *palais* on the Pariser Platz. In early 1927 majority shares were purchased in the now foundering *8-Uhr-Abendblatt* for about four million

[1] Some biographical material is available in the Hans Lachmann-Mosse file in the Leo Baeck Institute, New York.

marks. Lachmann-Mosse's enthusiasm for speculative investment led, in the 1920s, to such a sizeable outlay of capital
without promise of early returns that even without the
general economic crisis which struck Germany near the end
of the decade, the Mosse firm would have encountered
serious financial difficulties.[2]

Soon after Rudolf Mosse's death, his son-in-law's rash
financial and managerial proclivities gave birth to a hitherto
unknown tension in the administration of the house and in
the relations of Lachmann-Mosse with the journalistic staff,
thus invariably producing a situation which hampered decisive, energetic, and circumspect directorship. Salaries were
notoriously low. Joseph Schwab, a veteran journalist with
the *Tageblatt*, complained to Ernst Feder, the deputy editor,
that his salary in 1912 had been 750 marks a month; now in
1927 it was only 800 marks a month.[3] The owners paid
little heed to engendering a spirit of devotion to the house as
a whole. In 1926 Erich Dombrowski, Feder's predecessor as
deputy editor of the *Tageblatt*, left the paper partly because
he found the atmosphere surrounding publisher-editor relations in the firm intolerable.[4] Lachmann-Mosse resented
particularly the juridical invulnerability of Wolff and Carbe
as permanent appointments, and he succeeded in making
their professional tasks increasingly trying. Through his
testamentary stipulations, Rudolf Mosse had intended that
Wolff and Carbe be in a position to check any precipitate
deviation from the firm's traditions; however, although the
two nephews were able to block a number of Lachmann-
Mosse's schemes, the arrangement was so inflexible and
Lachmann-Mosse so persistent that gradually Wolff and
Carbe's patience and will to resist the whims of the owners
were worn away.

At first, Theodor Wolff, on the strength of the respect
and long-standing authority which he commanded within the

[2] See Richard Hamburger, *Zeitungsverlag und Annoncen-Expedition Rudolf
Mosse Berlin* (Berlin, n.d.), pp. 18ff.; and Boveri, *Wir lügen alle*, pp. 31ff.

[3] Feder diary, 5 December 1927. The diary is a rich source for the problems
that beset the firm.

[4] Koch-Weser recorded in his diary on 5 February 1926 that 'Dombrowski has
left the Berliner Tageblatt because his master Lachmann-Mosse is obviously a
totally short-sighted and difficult employer'; NL Koch-Weser, 34, p. 23.

firm, was able to act as a shield for the editorial staff against the caprices of Lachmann-Mosse. His colleagues had only words of praise for his aptitude in handling people and editing the *Berliner Tageblatt*. Victor Klages, who worked on the paper from 1923 to 1932, wrote later that Wolff did his job 'without shouting orders, without nagging, and merely through the effect of a personality whose charm overpowered all his closer associates'. Approaching editors personally with suggestions and requests, he ran the paper like a patriarch. The staff called him 'the last gentleman'.[5] Another former editor has remarked that Wolff controlled the large editorial staff 'almost unnoticeably'.[6] Until the early thirties there were no editorial conferences, and policy, if not self-understood, was discussed informally. 'Wolff was not merely in charge of the *Berliner Tageblatt*; he *was* the *Berliner Tageblatt*', yet another of his colleagues wrote.[7]

As long as there were no grave financial problems on the horizon, Lachmann-Mosse made no concerted effort to influence the political orientation of his newspapers. For commercial reasons he favoured a less dogmatic, less critical political attitude than that presented by the *Tageblatt* and *Berliner Volks-Zeitung* and one which underscored 'middle-class interests' more. He strongly supported, for example, the endeavours to unify the DDP and DVP. The Mosse firm normally contributed about RM 20,000 to the campaign funds of the DDP, but by 1928 Lachmann-Mosse was beginning to feel that money was completely wasted on such a cause and asserted that this was the last time such a substantial donation would be made.[8] However, with one exception—dealt with below—concerning the *Volks-Zeitung*, he took no steps before the end of the decade to try and implement any striking over-all changes in editorial direction and restricted his interference to technical and administrative matters.

Wolff and Carbe complained incessantly about Lachmann-Mosse's incapability as a publisher. By 1927 violent verbal

5 *Der Tagesspiegel* (Berlin), 2 August 1946.
6 Hans B. Meyer in *Hannoversche Allgemeine Zeitung*, 2 August 1968.
7 Hermann Sinsheimer, *Gelebt in Paradies* (Munich, 1953), p. 258.
8 Feder diary, 3 December 1927 (*Heute*, p. 147).

exchanges had become almost daily affairs. They concerned
wages, the general treatment of personnel, and the public
image of the firm. The question of the purpose of a newspaper, and consequently of financial priorities, usually lay at
the root of these disputes. Ernst Feder noted in his diary on
one occasion at the end of 1927 that Wolff had returned
from a session with Lachmann-Mosse 'quite pale with rage'.
The latter had insisted that, since the last Sunday edition of
the *Tageblatt* had been two pages longer than usual, the issue
of the following Sunday had to be shortened correspondingly. This had provoked Wolff to shout: 'Every day I have
to protect the paper from you; I reared it, you are destroying
it.' Lachmann-Mosse did far too little to enhance the prestige
of the house, Wolff felt; in public relations he was a complete
failure. Rudolf Mosse had attracted attention by establishing
endowments. The Ullsteins organized large high-society
parties, financed all sorts of competitions, and hence were
constantly in the public eye. Lachmann-Mosse, at most,
arranged only small family gatherings 'with here a Lachmann,
there a Lachmann', as Wolff scurrilously remarked; and his
tight-fisted business methods drove customers into the arms
of competitors. Feder remarked more than once that both
Wolff and Carbe were suffering from insomnia because of
their quarrels with Lachmann-Mosse.[9]

Indeed, in comparison to the energetic and venturous
Ullstein house, the newspaper side of the Mosse concern
appeared to stagnate after the death of Rudolf Mosse. With
the exception of the acquisition of majority control of the
8-Uhr-Abendblatt in 1927, for a sum which was excessively
high, no new newspaper projects were undertaken.
Lachmann-Mosse seemed to take more of an interest in a
number of the firm's other activities, which included the
advertising agency, the production of address directories for
the Reich and eight other European countries, a modest
book-publishing section which even tried earnestly to promote Esperanto as an international language and also
produced Russian-German dictionaries, and finally a small

---

9 Feder diary, 18 December 1926; 2 November 1927 (*Heute*, p. 144); 11
November 1927 (*Heute*, p. 146); 14 November 1927.

music-publishing venture. In March 1928 Lachmann-Mosse told Feder that he had little confidence in the German economy and for the last few years had been conducting his business with this in mind. The investment in foreign address directories, for example, he looked upon as security in the event of an economic collapse in Germany.[10]

Aside from the institution, in May 1928, of roman in place of Gothic type in the *Tageblatt*—a move which was regarded as unpatriotic in some nationalistic circles—neither the formal nor the political inclination of the Mosse newspapers changed substantially in the 1920s.[11] The *Tageblatt*, which appeared twelve times weekly, announced in March 1919 that its Sunday circulation had passed the 300,000 mark;[12] the weekday figure was not given but can be estimated to have stood between 160,000 and 170,000. After the war and revolutionary disturbances the circulation of the paper, following the general pattern for all newspapers, dropped off slightly, and this trend was intensified by the inflation. The losses were not recouped until near the end of the decade. In April 1928 the *Tageblatt* had a daily circulation of 150,000 and a Sunday circulation of 240,000.[13] The readership of the *Tageblatt* came from all sections of the propertied and educated bourgeoisie, ranging from struggling students to wealthy bank directors. The nine different supplements that arrived with the paper in the course of the week indicated that it aimed to reach as wide an audience as possible. The political credo of the paper was unmistakable in all its regular coverage, but, at the same time, Wolff did not hesitate to print articles of a contrary political persuasion, stating, of course, at the outset that the paper disagreed with the views but none the less considered them of value for objective discussion. This open-minded editorial policy, the variety of subject-matter, the stylistic quality of

[10] Feder diary, 6 February and 31 March 1928.

[11] Feder noted that about 1,500 subscribers dropped the paper because of the change in print, diary, 12 April 1928 (*Heute*, p. 173).

[12] *BT*, 139, 30 March 1919.

[13] Feder diary, 12 April 1928 (*Heute*, p. 173).

writing, and the above-average reliability of reporting attracted a readership which extended far beyond the bounds of DDP supporters.

The *Berliner Volks-Zeitung* had a long tradition of political radicalism. Its seventy-fifth anniversary issue of 1 January 1927 reminded readers that the journal had been founded as 'a paper devoted to battling against the forces of darkness'; that it did not serve any particular party but rather 'the Republic and justice, freedom of thought and social equality'. Popular and somewhat sensational in its make-up, the paper enjoyed extensive support among the Berlin working class. Throughout the 1920s, however, it suffered a steady decline in circulation; by April 1928 this had dropped to 70,000,[14] well under half the wartime printing. The reasons for this unabating decline are to be sought more in the low quality of the material production, in the poor layout and unappealing design, and in the competition offered by the Ullsteins and by Scherl, rather than in the paper's contents or political tendencies.

The editor-in-chief after 1915 was Otto Nuschke. As one of the left democrats around Wolff in November 1918, he assisted in the founding of the Democratic Party and was the sole member of the group to gain election to the national assembly. Wolff referred to him in the campaign as 'energetic, popular, brightly enthusiastic'.[15] He had a remarkably flexible personality, for although the newspaper which he edited was strikingly left-wing in its political sympathies, Nuschke was able to work with very little friction within the ranks of the DDP.[16] Losing his seat in the Reichstag in 1920, he was elected to the Prussian Landtag in the following year and kept his seat there until 1933. In 1927 he became business manager of the Verlag Neuer Staat and in December 1930 he even took up the post of general secretary of the State Party, the successor party to the DDP.

In 1923 journalists from the Mosse firm were instrumental for a second time since the end of the war in founding a

14 Feder diary, 12 April 1928 (*Heute*, p. 173).

15 *BT*, 19, 18 January 1919.

16 After the Second World War Nuschke became deputy minister president of the DDR.

political party. In December of that year, Carl von Ossietzky, Berthold Jacob, Karl Vetter, Cheskel Zwi Kloetzel, Henning Duderstadt, Michael Caro, Alfred Krüger, and Heinrich Heppenheimer, all of whom were editors of the *Volks-Zeitung* or contributors to it and outspoken pacifists, established the Republican Party of Germany, whose ultimate aim was to unite in a grassroots radical movement all convinced republican-democrats who recognized the impotence of the traditional parties. The party met with bitter opposition from the left and with embarassing failure in the elections of May 1924, receiving only 50,000 votes in the whole country. It rapidly disintegrated thereafter.[17] The escapade outraged Lachmann-Mosse and he expelled many of the group from the *Volks-Zeitung*.[18] Ossietzky became an uncompromising critic of the Republic; Vetter rejoined the Mosse house in 1930 and, having turned his back on his earlier political activity, proceeded to play a Mephistophelian role in developments there; Duderstadt did a complete aboutface and became an ardent National Socialist.[19]

The two other Mosse dailies, the *Berliner Morgen-Zeitung* and the *8-Uhr-Abendblatt*, were morning and evening papers respectively which only barely managed to keep their heads above water in competition with Ullstein's *Morgenpost* and Scherl's *Nachtausgabe*. The *Morgen-Zeitung* classified itself as 'democratic', the *Abendblatt* as 'democratic without party affiliation'. Both were popular in design but lacked the imagination and verve of their rivals.

Measured by newspaper circulation, political influence, renown, and respect, the Mosse firm reached its peak immediately before and during the First World War, while still under the direction of Rudolf Mosse. For the Ullstein house, on the other hand, the middle years of the Weimar Republic marked

[17] See Koplin, *Carl von Ossietzky*, pp. 67ff.

[18] See Ossietzky, 'Die grosse republikanische Partei', *Die Weltbühne*, 19 June 1928, reprinted in Ossietzky, *Schriften* (2 vols., Berlin [East] and Weimar, 1966), II, pp. 170ff. Wolff tried to intercede to prevent the expulsion of Ossietzky and Vetter.

[19] See Henning Duderstadt, *Vom Reichsbanner zum Hakenkreuz* (Stuttgart, 1933).

the climax of its spectacular development. In the 1920s the Ullstein Verlag became the largest publishing house in Europe and probably the most diversified in the world. Its presses printed everything from books, magazines, and newspapers to currency notes for the Reichsbank during the inflation. Technical inventiveness and publicistic enterprise were unbounded; new projects were always under consideration. Popular Ullstein authors included Carl Zuckmayer, Vicki Baum, Lion Feuchtwanger, Leonhard Frank, and Erich Maria Remarque. The most successful novel of the inter-war period, Remarque's *All Quiet on the Western Front*, was serialized in the *Vossische Zeitung*, appeared then as an Ullstein book in January 1929, and within a few years had been translated into twenty-eight languages and had passed the six-million mark in world sales. Gerhart Hauptmann and Hans Fallada also appeared in serialized form in Ullstein journals. The Ullsteins' Propyläen-Verlag became the respected publisher of serious, exquisitely produced works of non-fiction. Bülow's memoirs and Stresemann's papers (*Vermächtnis*) were Ullstein publications. The weekly *Berliner Illustrirte*, which approached a circulation of two million at the end of the decade, led all similar publications in Europe. Among the other magazines were the light-hearted, satirical *Uhu*; *Koralle*, which was devoted to popular science; the literary and artistic review *Querschnitt*; *Die Grüne Post*, a magazine for country life, which three years after its first issue in April 1927 had acquired over one million subscribers; three women's journals, *Die Dame, Das Blatt der Hausfrau*, and *Praktische Berlinerin*, to which were attached a whole fashion department and dressmaker's shop right in the editorial offices; and in addition, a variety of technical and professional publications. The Ullsteins also continued to publish their four dailies, the *Vossische Zeitung, Berliner Morgenpost, BZ am Mittag*, and *Berliner Allgemeine Zeitung*. In 1920 a new weekly was begun, the *Berliner Montagspost*, and in 1928 another daily called *Tempo* was launched. On a weekday in 1928 the Ullstein daily papers alone were bought by approximately one million Germans.[20]

[20] For the circulation figures of the principal Ullstein publications see Appendix II, p. 314.

In October 1930 forty-eight million pages were printed on Ullstein presses every day.[21] The firm ran its own independent Ullstein News Service, on which ten non-Ullstein papers in Germany and fifteen abroad relied heavily. The Ullstein photo agency was world renowned. Even an efficient travel service was provided by the Ullsteins for Berliners. The firm owned five cinemas and its own film studios; for publicity it organized motor and airplane races, often in co-operation with New York and London papers. 'At the Ullstein house in Berlin', a former editor in the magazine section of the firm has written, 'I felt that I was sitting right in the navel of the world. Life streamed by in thousands of photos, hundreds of people, in the voices from the entire globe.'[22]

The Ullstein house was constantly concerned with growth and modernization. In 1927 the largest printing house in Europe was completed in Tempelhof, and immediately a mortgage was placed on it to take advantage of the favourable money market and thus provide capital for new projects.[23] 'Our technical department was the finest in the Reich', Hermann Ullstein could write later.[24] The firm was not only of great significance in the cultural and intellectual life of Berlin but also in the economic well-being of the capital. In 1918 it employed 5,708 people, of which 129 were journalists; by 1927 these figures had grown to 9,198 and 203 respectively.[25] The total assets of the firm in 1926 amounted to 26·4 million marks; three years later they had climbed to 45·6 million marks.[26] Harold Nicolson was another of those who was greatly impressed by the hive of activity that the Ullsteins ran.

In that vast conglomeration of buildings was assembled every device which science could contrive for the rapid reception and distribution of news and information. Upon the roof the slim antennae of a wireless installation throbbed with messages from Vancouver or Bangkok.

21 *Ullstein-Berichte*, October 1930.
22 Vicki Baum, *I Know What I'm Worth* (London, 1964), pp. 251f.
23 *Ullstein A.G., Geschäftsbericht für das Geschäftsjahr 1927.*
24 *Rise and Fall*, p. 66.
25 *Ullstein-Berichte*, April 1928.
26 *Ullstein Geschäftsbericht* for 1926 and 1929.

Inside the building pneumatic tubes hurled little bombs of paper from one department to another; as one was speaking to an editor or manager there would come a sudden gasp from an orifice beside him and with a faint plop a leading article would drop into the steel basket by his side; and at dawn each day six aeroplanes would rise from Tempelhof to carry the words of Ullstein to the remotest provinces of the Reich.[27]

In the twenties Berliners apparently thought of the Ullstein and Rothschild brothers in the same terms.[28] The mention of either family evoked a kind of reverence. However, despite the personal connotations that the name Ullstein carried for every Berliner because of the Ullstein products which surrounded him from day to day, the formidable size of this publishing enterprise denoted, like the Rothschild banking empire, an immense inscrutable power. This did not mean that the public could not develop a devotion to Ullstein publications, but it did mean that the political discourses of Ullstein journals were not always read without wariness.

Hermann Ullstein later reflected that the size of the firm was also a distinct hindrance to a well-coordinated promulgation of its political interests. '. . .the weakness of our publishing firm', he wrote, 'was that it was too big; there were too many cooks spoiling the broth; too many men without political interest or experience were having too much to say.' Richard A. Müller, for example, who was the manager of the daily papers, having replaced Georg Bernhard in this post in 1920, Ullstein called a 'political greenhorn'.[29] As the firm grew in size and prosperity, the political aggressiveness of much of its publishing flagged, for Ullstein editors had to write increasingly for an audience which, to a large degree, was unsympathetic to the basic political tenets of the house.

The five Ullstein brothers—Hans, Louis, Franz, Rudolf, and Hermann—all complemented one another in their professional abilities. The effective combination of their considerable individual talents constituted the basis of the firm's

---

[27] *Spectator*, CLXXII (10 March 1944), p. 218.

[28] See Emil Herz, *Denk' ich an Deutschland in der Nacht* (Berlin, 1951), p. 308; and R.G. [Rosie Goldschmidt], *Prelude to the Past* (New York, 1934), p. 272.   [29] *Rise and Fall*, p. 168.

rapid expansion. Nevertheless, all five had distinctly individual characters as well, which Leopold Ullstein, their father, had not been able to synchronize. It was in the clash of their personalities and ambitions that fuel for many of the firm's future problems was to lie.

Until the end of 1920 the publishing house was a private undertaking (*Offene Handelsgesellschaft*). As of 1 January 1921 it was listed as a joint-stock company, the Ullstein A.G., a change which meant that the official management was transferred to a board of managing directors, whose administration of business was controlled in turn by a supervisory board of directors. The principal consideration behind the alteration of the administrative structure of the firm was a concern for the future: that, in case of inheritance or serious disagreements among the brothers and the heirs, the business could not be broken up easily. The brothers, owing to their different temperaments and interests, often did not see eye to eye, and the step was looked upon as a safeguard against possible desertion by any one of them or his respective family. Hans, Louis, and Rudolf sat on the supervisory board, with Hans, the eldest, as chairman, and Louis as vice-chairman. Franz led the board of managing directors with Hermann as his deputy. To avoid possible charges of discrimination, the duties of the supervisory board were extended beyond the usual minimum rights of such a board: its members took an active part in the regular business decisions and presided over the meetings of the management.[30]

It was Franz who inspired the change-over to a joint-stock company, against the dogmatic opposition of Louis. The eldest brother, Hans, had been ill since 1914 and had steadily been able to fulfil less of his responsibilities in the firm. Louis, therefore, had assumed many of his functions, among them the chairmanship of the council of brothers, and had come to consider himself as the leading figure in the house. Franz, in turn, had regarded both his elder brothers as an

---

[30] See Gustav Willner, 'The Business Management', in *Der Verlag Ullstein zum Welt-Reklame-Kongress 1929*, pp. 219ff.; Georg Bernhard, 'Die Geschichte des Hauses', pp. 135f.; and Wolfgang Hellwig, *Unternehmungsformen der deutschen Tagespresse* (Leipzig, 1929), p. 37.

uncomfortable check on his ideas and ambitions and consequently had been particularly eager to alter the structure of
the firm's administration. Louis was to charge later that
Franz had only been able to effect the change to a joint-stock
company because he too had been suffering from bad health
in 1920. Relegated in 1921 to the supervisory board, whose
chair Hans refused to vacate despite his incapacitating ill
health, Louis now felt hemmed in and bore a bitter grudge
against Franz.

Furthermore, in the management, Franz and Hermann,
who shared many of the same political and editorial interests,
competed for power. Franz looked after the daily papers,
Hermann the magazines and the book department. Franz
wished to centralize the management and was striving to
create and install himself in the position of general managing
director; Hermann backed the idea of decentralization. This
complex situation was complicated still further by the
presence of seven cousins and a number of in-laws who
competed for lucrative posts in the firm; naturally, each
brother backed his own family members. What could have
remained minor quarrels among the brothers became part of
a struggle of dynasties. The disagreements turned into
personal feuds. In early 1928 Hermann, frustrated by his
inability to advance his ideas, both political and managerial,
resigned from his post on the board of managing directors
and restricted his activities to the board of stockholders.
Henceforth he communicated with the other family members
mainly by letter. With the departure of Hermann, Franz
attained his goal; he became the general managing director of
the firm.[31]

[31] The Ullstein family, past and present, has deliberately attempted to conceal
the internal strife in the firm in the 1920s. Hermann and Heinz Ullstein, in their
respective memoirs, have only alluded to the disagreements and have played down
their significance in the firm's development. Peter de Mendelssohn's *Zeitungsstadt
Berlin*, a book commissioned by the Ullstein house in the 1950s, makes no
mention whatever of the fraternal quarrels. This account has been pieced together
largely from the briefs presented by the prosecuting and defence counsels in the
Ullstein *v.* Ullstein legal suit of 1930-1 (see Chapter VII) and from newspaper
articles covering these proceedings. The legal briefs, by Richard Frankfurter, 28
April 1930, and by Max Alsberg, Rudolf Dix, *et al.*, 18 June 1930, are to be
found in the NL Hermann, 11, pp. 105ff, and 12ff. respectively, Bundesarchiv
Koblenz. The Ullstein file in the Institut für Zeitungswissenschaft, Munich,
contains an extensive collection of articles on the legal suit.

The problematic nature of political developments in Germany after 1914, added to the rifts in the Ullstein family, produced an atmosphere of dissension and intrigue in the firm, which was hardly conducive to the smooth functioning of a freehanded owner-editor relationship. A major source of dispute in the house was Georg Bernhard, the editor of the *Vossische Zeitung* and, until 1920, the manager of the daily papers. Bernhard's patron when he rejoined the Ullstein firm in 1908 had been Louis Ullstein, but his duties put him into closest contact with Franz. There soon developed not only a mutual professional respect but also a firm personal friendship between the two men. They exchanged political views and the most confidential political information which one or the other happened to possess.[32] However, Bernhard's attitudes during the war, his subsequent advocacy of the acceptance of the Versailles treaty terms, and his obsessive preoccupation with his theory of *Kontinentalpolitik*, constantly tried the patience of the rest of the Ullstein family.[33] After 1918 the circulation of the *Vossische Zeitung* declined drastically; by 1923 it had sunk to 32,000; and voices inside and outside the firm asserted that Bernhard was destroying the paper.[34] Even Bernhard's assistant editors were unhappy. Carl Misch of the *Vossische Zeitung* told Ernst Feder in 1926 that he envied the *Tageblatt*'s journalists because they could pursue a consistent policy. 'We are tainted by our foreign-policy line and therefore have to dance on eggs.'[35] Franz Ullstein, nevertheless, faithfully and resolutely defended his friend and protégé against the complaints, attacks, and even the intrigues of the other brothers.

Bernhard was probably the most controversial editor in the whole of the German press. Plagued by personal ambition

---

[32] See the brief presented by Bernhard's lawyer Richard Frankfurter, 28 April 1930 (hereafter Frankfurter, Brief), pp. 16f.

[33] See Frankfurter, Brief, p. 16; Louis Ullstein to Maximilian Harden, 12 January 1916, NL Harden, 108, p. 9; and R.G., *Prelude*, pp. 275ff.

[34] See H. Ullstein, *Rise and Fall*, pp. 155f.; and the polemical article against Bernhard, 'Ein "courageux journaliste" ', *Deutsche Allgemeine Zeitung*, 7 July 1923.

[35] Feder diary, 11 May 1926 (*Heute*, p. 56).

that could not be satisfied, by an acute, almost paranoiac, feeling of insecurity, and by a sense of personal honour that belonged to an earlier century, he was not capable of cautiously steering his ideas; his ideas often steered him. He pushed theories to extremes, not because he was always convinced of their validity, but because he could not swallow the possibility of their being invalid. On the political left he aroused distrust because of his attitudes during the war, on the right passionate aversion because of his unyielding promotion of a pro-French, anti-English foreign policy after Versailles. Siegfried Jacobsohn of the *Weltbühne* classed him as a war criminal in the same category as Tirpitz, Reventlow, and Heydebrand. Stinnes's *Deutsche Allgemeine Zeitung* provoked Bernhard into taking legal action against it by calling the *Vossische Zeitung* the *Gazette de Foch*. Anti-Semites referred to Bernhard as the *Oberjude*.[36] The number of lawsuits in which Bernhard was involved, brought either against him or by him on grounds of character defamation, was surpassed perhaps only by Joseph Goebbels. In 1923 Bernhard was accorded permanent police protection. His aggressive nature did not manifest itself only in an intellectual manner. In an election campaign gathering in Halle in December 1924, he answered a right-wing heckler with a hefty punch; in a meeting a few days later, he in turn was assaulted by a member of the Stahlhelm.[37]

Ultimately, Bernhard hoped to gratify his intense craving for public recognition by a successful political career. Journalism was for him, in essence, a side-line activity, which he was forced to accept as his primary occupation for most of his life because his personal traits—his pride, his overbearing nature, his arrogance and lack of tact—repeatedly undermined his political aspirations. One means, he seemed to feel, of advancing his political ambitions was by accumulating public offices. In 1916 he became a lecturer on economics and finance at the Handelshochschule in Berlin; in

[36] See the DNVP paper *Pommersche Tagespost*, 137, 12 June 1924; clipping in NL Koch-Weser, 90.

[37] See *Nürnberger Zeitung*, 4 December 1924; *Deutsche Tageszeitung*, 21 December 1924; *Mitteldeutsche Presse*, 21 February 1925; clippings in the Bernhard file in the Institut für Zeitungswissenschaft, Munich.

1928 he was made an honorary full professor. He represented the journalistic profession on the Reich economic council. He was twice chairman of the Berlin Press Association, president from 1928 to 1930 of the Reich Association of the German Press, and a member of the executive committees of the Republican Press Union and the Berlin Association of the Provincial Press. His journalistic pursuits were crowned in November 1928 when the International Federation of Journalists elected him, at its congress in Dijon, to a two-year term as president.

'Qui trop embrasse, mal étreint' was an adage often cited to Bernhard. He was, in fact, so occupied by his countless offices that the actual editorial co-ordination of the *Vossische Zeitung* was performed by the deputy editor, Julius Elbau.[38] Nevertheless, even if he did not put as much work into his paper, Bernhard's ideas dominated the *Vossische* in the same way that Wolff's pervaded the *Berliner Tageblatt*. The bedrock of the paper's political crusades was always one of Bernhard's theories, which he personally presented in his regular Sunday front-page articles.

Wolff was a superb stylist. His artistic, literary background was evident in every leader which he wrote. Replete with literary references and poetic metaphors, interspersed with quotations from the classics, his articles were, in effect, scintillating political *feuilletons*, light yet forceful, witty yet serious, ironical and yet positive in tone. Bernhard, on the other hand, with his training in economics, wrote in a manner which frequently appeared pedestrian and inept, when compared to the grace and elegance of Wolff's prose. Bernhard could have simply accepted the difference; instead, he suffered under it. The business rivalry of the *Vossische Zeitung* and the *Berliner Tageblatt*, which catered to much the same reading public, Bernhard turned into a personal rivalry between himself and Wolff.

Bernhard's character was not without many positive and entertaining features. Louis Ullstein's son, Heinz, who on the

---

38 Heinz Pol in *Der Aufbau* (New York), 24 March 1961. See also Edgar Stern-Rubarth, . . .*Aus zuverlässiger Quelle verlautet*. . . (Stuttgart, 1964), p. 168.

whole had little respect for Bernhard and for years participated in intrigues to try and remove him as editor of the
Vossische Zeitung, could nevertheless describe him as 'exceptionally good-natured, obliging, and considerate'.[39] The
Young Democrats in the DDP appreciated both his *bonhomie*
and his leftist political inclinations and lobbied to find him a
promising constituency for the 1928 elections.[40] Anton
Erkelenz described him as 'a valuable man, whom I esteem
very highly on account of his temperament and his indefatigable diligence. I can pardon many a false move of his
because his open spirit delights me. In any case I find him
much more attractive than all the lawyers [in the DDP
ranks] who work merely with dexterity. Bernhard has
opinions and stands up for them, and such a man is far more
important to my mind than someone who cunningly weaves
through situations.'[41]

Socially, Bernhard displayed a striking amiability. At
intervals he ran a political salon, frequented by deputies,
cabinet ministers, and diplomats. The story is told that on
occasion Bernhard would be seen at a party making notes on
the cuff of his shirt and that afterwards he would immediately telephone his office to dictate a finished article
literally 'off the cuff'.[42] He was addicted to poker. Franz
Ullstein was continually bailing him out of debt. When he
was in Geneva, he could often be found playing cards until
the early morning hours.[43] French journalists respected and
admired him, not just because of his Francophilia but also
because of his Gallic vitality. In May 1930 in an article
devoted to Bernhard, the *Nouvelles Littéraires* called him
'one of the greatest, if not the greatest, journalist in Germany
today'. He was portrayed as a 'pilgrim of peace' who had
'prepared, by means of the written and spoken word, the
atmosphere in which the Locarno politics of Dr. Stresemann
could develop'.[44]

39 *Spielplatz meines Lebens* (Munich, 1961), p. 318.
40 Linke, *Restless Flags*, p. 287.
41 Erkelenz to Wilhelm Rexrodt, 28 June 1929, NL Erkelenz, 124.
42*Die Welt*, 8 February 1969.
43 W. Duesberg, *Le Soir* (Paris), 6 July 1930.
44 3 May 1930.

The year 1923, which witnessed the climax of both Poincaré's punitive policies against Germany and, internally, the monetary inflation, marked the nadir of the *Vossische Zeitung*'s fortunes as well. Stresemann's resolute and consistent propagation of a *détente* with France in the course of the next six years accorded a certain respectability to Bernhard's notions of *Kontinentalpolitik*. Former readers gradually returned to the paper. By October 1926 its circulation had risen to almost 60,000; two years later it stood at 71,370.[45] Nevertheless, the paper continued to represent a financial loss for the Ullsteins, as it was unable to attract sufficient advertising. Profitable advertising contracts from large business interests were not forthcoming. In addition to the low circulation, Bernhard's unwavering pro-French policy, his hostility to heavy industry, and his attachment to the idea of socialization, contributed to the reticence of business and industry to advertise in the paper.

The readership of the *Vossische Zeitung* was slightly more conservative in its thinking than that of the *Berliner Tageblatt*. Landed gentry, higher civil servants, the Protestant clergy, university officials, and members of the legal profession constituted a significant segment of the subscribers whom the Ullsteins had inherited when they bought the paper prior to the war. The political vagaries of the paper immediately after the war alienated much of this establishment-oriented, conservative-minded readership.

The Ullstein firm, as an entity, survived the inflation without suffering any irreparable damage, on account of printing contracts from the Reich government which paid in gold, the sales of its foreign-language publications, and the popularity of the other daily papers and the magazines. The financial success of the *Berliner Morgenpost* and *BZ am Mittag* led many observers into classifying these publications as purely profit-oriented, thereby implying that they were devoid of political opinion. To be sure, the two papers were popular in design and appeal and carried far less political commentary than the *Vossische*, but they had been founded

---

[45] See Appendix II, p. 314.

with an underlying political orientation and this was maintained in the 1920s. Both papers were devoid of intellectual
airs and consequently were able to present their editorial
views with a simplicity, a consistency, and a forcefulness
that their 'quality' sister paper often lacked.

On 11 September 1928 the Ullsteins began a new venture,
an evening paper called *Tempo*. Sensational to the hilt,
crammed full with pictures—which, as was pointed out in the
inaugural editorial, were to be regarded as 'news' rather than
'illustrations'—at times devoting several pages to advertisements for Berlin's more eccentric entertainments, and lacking
almost any political coverage, the paper set out to profit
from the culturally feverish mood of the German capital
city.[46] The name indicated the newspaper's aim, which was
to capture 'the verve of the young, self-asserting generation'.
'*Tempo*', the management claimed, 'is the total experience
of our time.'[47] The publication was the only indisputable
failure that the Ullsteins ever had to sustain in the newspaper
field, not from the point of view of circulation, which in
early 1931 had reached 145,450 and appeared about to rival
that of the *BZ am Mittag*, but because of the paper's inability to attract regular advertising. There was a bitter-sweet
irony in the singular lack of success of *Tempo*, a newspaper
claiming to offer 'the total experience' of its time. The
owners had obviously misinterpreted the real tempo of the
times.

On 23 December 1918 Therese Simon-Sonnemann, the
daughter and only child of Leopold Sonnemann, wrote
fretfully to Friedrich von Payer:

The blunders of our paper, which you decry, give me cause for
worry and concern as well. Naturally, one can understand why, after
the unprecedented experience of this war, the most radical views are
winning the upper hand for the moment, but presence of mind has
always prevailed in our firm; and this self-possession alone will assist us
in restoring good order. . . . Alas, if only united strength could succeed
in driving out the fateful radicalism of certain individuals from the
paper.[48]

46 *Tempo*, 1, 11 September 1928.
47 *Ullstein-Berichte*, October 1928.
48 NL Payer, 16, pp. 60ff.

The organizational traditions of the *Frankfurter Zeitung*, however, prevented the owners from interceding in editorial policy and in matters concerning editorial personnel without the agreement of the majority of the editorial board. To be hired by the paper was considered a significant achievement by the German world of journalism; to be dismissed was equally difficult. The advantage of this situation was the comfortable sense of security in which the editors worked; the major disadvantage was that disputes between the owners and individual editors or between the editors themselves could poison the atmosphere of the entire house without being resolved satisfactorily. In December 1918 Therese Simon longed for 'united strength' and 'presence of mind', without possessing any tangible means of encouraging their emergence. She sat on the supervisory board of directors of the Frankfurter Societäts-Druckerei (FSD), but she had no direct power to change the editorial policy of the *Frankfurter Zeitung*.

As a company of limited liability, the FSD was administered by a managing executive, which was chaired by Kurt Simon, one of the two grandsons of Leopold Sonnemann; its activity, in turn, was supervised by a board of directors. The functions of these two bodies were entirely separate from those of the editorial board, and the sole connecting link was the personage of Heinrich Simon, Sonnemann's other grandson, who chaired the meetings of the editorial conferences—if needed, he could cast the deciding vote—and also sat on the board of directors. Although one former editor, Benno Reifenberg, has described Heinrich Simon as having represented 'the nucleus of the intellectual impulses' in the offices of the *Frankfurter Zeitung*, [49] the authority which his personality carried was a far cry from that which Leopold Sonnemann had exercised in the same posts.

Neither Heinrich nor Kurt Simon had the forceful, imposing characters of their grandfather. They were the sons of the marriage between Therese Sonnemann and Felix Simon, the owner of the Ostdeutsche Bank in Königsberg. Both had attained doctorates in university, Heinrich in

[49] In the introduction to *Facsimile Querschnitt durch die Frankfurter Zeitung*, ed. Ingrid Gräfin Lynar (Stuttgart, 1964), p. 7.

literature and philosophy, with a dissertation on Novalis, and Kurt in law. Heinrich continued to dabble in literature and music for the rest of his life. He wrote two rather un-inspiring plays under the pseudonyms Alexander Gregory and Heinrich Anton, and when, in 1933, he applied for membership, unsuccessfully, in the Reich Union of German Writers, he listed Gerhart Hauptmann as one of his referees.[50] His mother, Therese Simon, had for years organized a private musical salon; Carl Fürstenberg, the banker, referred to the Simon home as 'a centre of Berlin music'.[51] In exile after 1934, Heinrich Simon first eked out a living as a piano teacher in Paris and later became the business manager of the Palestine Symphony Orchestra.

His congeniality in his role as mediator in the firm brought him friendship and esteem from all sides. At the end of the war he too was very anxious about the exuberance shown by certain of the editors for the revolutionary up-heavals, but he refused to try and apply any untoward pressures on his editors. In April 1928 Ludwig Cohnstaedt, a former financial editor and now a director, paid homage to his amicability: 'It really is admirable the way in which he has held the editorial board together until now; his co-operation has appeared and appears to me to represent a certain guarantee that the special nature of the Sonnemann paper will be maintained.'[52] However, albeit cordial in nature, Heinrich Simon did not enjoy his administrative duties, and his talents as a businessman were limited.[53] Often in the course of the financial ordeals which the *Frankfurter Zeitung* faced during the Weimar Republic, he left the impression that he was at heart an artist who un-willingly was forced to bear the burden of a family business and publishing tradition.

[50] The application is in the Kulturkammer file on Heinrich Simon in the Berlin Document Center.

[51] *Die Lebensgeschichte eines deutschen Bankiers*, ed. Hans Fürstenberg (Wiesbaden, n.d.), p. 512.

[52] In a letter to Payer, 26 April 1928, NL Payer, 17B, p. 85.

[53] See Rudolf Schwander to Payer, 8 May 1928, NL Payer, 17B, pp. 93f. Schwander was a member of the board of directors. Erich Welter, a former editor of the *FZ*, told the author in an interview, 25 March 1969, that the whole Simon family was 'far too good-natured' to be good businessmen.

Kurt Simon was a shy, retiring individual, by personality even less suited than his brother for the demanding responsibilities of managing a firm. He lacked the resoluteness and self-confidence needed to institute radical or unpopular reforms; and his most important contribution to German newspaper publishing lay instead in his activities in the Union of German Newspaper Publishers, where he was instrumental in organizing important social-security provisions for publishers and journalists.

During the 1920s, particularly after the inflation, dissatisfaction with the unprofessional, almost off-handed, manner in which the two brothers managed the business was voiced with growing frequency by some of the editors and directors of the *Frankfurter Zeitung*. Heinrich Simon's appearance at meetings of the editorial board became notably rare. In May 1928 the directors talked of finding a 'strong man' to manage the firm.[54] In June they decided to push Kurt Simon upstairs into the supervisory board.

The political economist Moritz Julius Bonn rated the *Frankfurter Zeitung* as 'Germany's greatest newspaper— perhaps the greatest newspaper on the Continent. . . . It did a great deal for my political education and for my education all round.'[55] Intellectually the *Frankfurter Zeitung* was the most demanding newspaper in Germany. Dr. Wilhelm Cohnstaedt, Dr. Robert Drill, both political editors, and Fritz Schotthöfer, a foreign-affairs editor, had studied with Lujo Brentano in Munich; Dr. Sally Goldschmidt, also a political editor, came from Max Weber's seminar in Heidelberg. Rudolf Kircher, London correspondent from 1920 to 1930, afterwards head of the Berlin bureau until 1939, and nominal chief editor (*Hauptschriftleiter*) of the paper from 1934 to 1943, was a doctor of law. Arthur Feiler, a political editor from 1910 to 1931, took his doctorate at Heidelberg in 1923, and completed his second, the inaugural, dissertation at Frankfurt in 1928 where he then lectured part-time until he was granted a full professorship in 1932 at the Handelshochschule in Königsberg. In the business

---

[54] Ludwig Cohnstaedt to Payer, 3 May 1928, NL Payer, 17B, p. 90.
[55] *Wandering Scholar*, pp. 40, 42.

section, Albert Oeser, its head from 1926 to 1938, and Erich Welter both had doctorates, as did Benno Reifenberg, who worked as Paris correspondent, then led the *feuilleton* section, became a political editor, and finally deputy chief editor after 1933.

A more extensive academic training was not the only attribute which distinguished the editorial board of the *Frankfurter Zeitung* from those of the *Berliner Tageblatt* and *Vossische Zeitung*. In political sympathies a more pronounced unity existed as well. The influence of the socio-economic and political thought of men like Lujo Brentano, Max Weber, and later Hugo Preuss on the paper was profound. At the turn of the century many of the leading editors had been enthusiastic supporters of Friedrich Naumann's National Social Union. Sonnemann, of course, had also taken care always to review the political ideas of prospective editors before they were hired. The *Frankfurter Zeitung*'s reputation, moreover, rested on the reliability of its news coverage. That its circulation would never soar upwards rapidly was a fact accepted by both editors and owners; therefore the paper did not feel the need to emphasize entertainment and variety to the same degree as the *Berliner Tageblatt* and *Vossische Zeitung*, whose publishers and contributors never relinquished the dream of spiralling circulations.

Politically the two most important posts on the *Frankfurter Zeitung* were the direction of the Berlin bureau, from which much of the paper's interpretation of Reich politics stemmed, and the chairmanship of the editorial board, which bore the onus of co-ordinating the views of the Berlin office with those of the editors in Frankfurt. The head of the Berlin bureau from 1883 to 1920 was August Stein. In the summer of 1920 he was replaced by Bernhard Guttmann who had been the London correspondent of the *Frankfurter Zeitung* before the war. In the twenties Guttmann exercised the most decisive influence in the political orientation of the paper. His supremely individual analyses of Reich politics would have conformed to all of Sonnemann's wishes for political coverage in his paper. His zeal for unmasking and reporting any irregularities in the democratic process, his unwavering opposition to the political pressures applied by industrial interest groups, to the army's involvement in politics, in short to all organizations bent upon deforming or debilitating constitutionalism and restricting the individual's freedom of choice in any way, were motivated by his conviction that the press shouldered immense social and political responsibilities in a democracy. '. . . [A] democracy which does not have an honest and able press at its disposal, has no chance of survival', he wrote; 'this is not a question of ideology but rather of existence. . . . The character of political life is determined everywhere for the most part by the character of the press; and for the character of the press, in turn, the prevailing spirit in the journalistic profession is most significant.'[56] The importance of ethical principles in journalism outweighed personal political sympathies and attachments as far as Guttmann was concerned, and consequently his own party, the DDP, was frequently subjected to criticism as severe as that accorded to other parties. The 'impetus of his conscience'[57] brought Guttmann under vicious attack from all sides, from Democrats as well as from ultra-nationalists.[58]

Another editor of the paper who aroused as much contention as Guttmann was the economics expert in the political section, Arthur Feiler. His articles on socialization in November and December 1918 attracted a great deal of attention. Before moving to the political staff of the paper in 1910, he had spent seven years in the business section. A member of the Reich economic council, the socialization commission, and the anti-trust board after the war, Feiler's articles made the German business community see red. Outspoken, intensely ambitious and energetic, he was in character the Georg Bernhard of the *Frankfurter Zeitung*; however, his political and economic ideas revealed considerably greater consistency and forethought than Bernhard's. First the drone and then the slumber into which the

[56] *Deutsche Presse*. XVII (28 May 1927), pp. 263f.

[57] Robert Haerdter, *Stuttgarter Zeitung*, 22 January 1959.

[58] Richard Bahr described Guttmann to the state secretary Hamm in 1922 as 'very evil and decidedly non-Aryan'; letter of 3 December 1922, Reichskanzlei files, R431/2475, p. 41.

economic council and the socialization commission fell
robbed Feiler of much of his authority by 1923, if not of his
combativeness. Heinrich Simon, in time, found his aggressive
nature aggravating. When Guttmann fell ill on one occasion,
Feiler plotted, unsuccessfully, personally to replace him; he
even aspired, so Heinrich Simon claimed, to installing himself
'as a kind of editor-in-chief' of the paper.[59]

The board of editors met every morning in Frankfurt, a
common view on the most important developments of the
previous twenty-four hours was hammered out, and one
editor was delegated to write the lead article for the next
morning on the basis of the discussion. The editorial then
appeared unsigned, simply under a dateline. Memoir literature on the *Frankfurter Zeitung* has left the impression that
an impregnable harmony and solidarity characterized the
relations of the editors on the paper and that there were no
insurmountable differences of opinion. A sense of fraternity
did exist but it should not be exaggerated. In fact a tension
verging on animosity prevailed between Feiler and the
business editors Albert Oeser and Erich Welter. In 1926
Fritz Naphtali, a business editor since 1921, left the paper
of his own accord because his ideas on 'economic democracy'[60]—corporatist notions springing from his involvement
with the trade-union movement—had lost all resonance
among his colleagues. Wilhelm Cohnstaedt, Walter Kamper,
and Sally Goldschmidt promoted highly controversial ideas
in their articles with a tone whose self-righteousness disturbed many of the other editors.[61] Unanimity did not exist
on the paper, and, of course, in view of the lack of regimentation and of the high intellectual calibre of the editors,
could not exist.

The *Frankfurter Zeitung*, like the *Times* of New York and
London and *Le Temps* of Paris, was a newspaper whose
appeal was directed exclusively at the intelligentsia and the

---

[59] See H. Simon to Payer, 5 July 1927, NL Payer, 17A, p. 50.

[60] Fritz Naphtali, *Wirtschaftsdemokratie* (Berlin, 1928). Naphtali later became a cabinet minister in Israel.

[61] Erich Welter, in an interview with the author, 25 March 1969.

business community. In 1927 the readership had the
following composition:[62]

	%
Businessmen, industrialists, firms	36·9
Banks, insurance companies, and their officials	14·5
Free professions: lawyers, doctors, architects, engineers, artists, students	13·2
Hotels, clubs, libraries, restaurants	9·5
Higher civil servants	9·3
Smaller merchants, white-collar workers	6·9
Pensioners, private individuals	4·7
Others	5·0

The predominance of the business community is striking.
Gustav Stolper, who edited the *Berliner Börsen-Courier* in
1925-6 and then founded the weekly *Der deutsche
Volkswirt*, patterned on *The Economist*, could write of the
Frankfurter Zeitung to his friend Joseph Schumpeter: 'I
know from wide experience that the *FZ* is respected but not
read. One always looks at it, has one thing or another
from it brought to one's attention, and one throws it
away. . . .'[63]

In 1915 the circulation of the *Frankfurter Zeitung* had
passed 100,000, an increase of over 60,000 from before the
war, due undeniably to the paper's established reputation
for independent and reliable coverage and to the thirst of
Germans during the war for just such coverage. By April
1920 the distribution had slipped to 87,000, and by 1924 to
under 50,000. In the next years a gradual upswing was
registered so that in 1928 the average circulation stood at
71,000.[64]

Aside from the general drop in circulation of all newspapers after the war, the sales of the *Frankfurter Zeitung*
suffered from the repeated French and Belgian occupations
of centres in the Rhineland and Palatinate and of the entire
Ruhr region in 1923; on these occasions the paper was

[62] This break-down is to be found in NL Payer, 17A, p. 127.

[63] Letter of 13 June 1926, NL Stolper, 31, Bundesarchiv Koblenz.

[64] See the report 'Frankfurter Zeitung 1925', NL Payer, 17, p. 148; and K.
Simon to H. Hummel, 22 December 1928, NL Payer, 17B, p. 325.

often banned from the occupied territory. Then, in addition, the indignation felt by many entrepreneurs and officials in business and industry at the *Frankfurter Zeitung*'s radical, economic and political, editorial policy in the immediate postwar period apparently led a substantial number of them to drop their subscriptions and to terminate their advertising contracts in protest. Before and during the war the *Frankfurter Zeitung* was taken by many people as a second paper, and since it was the most expensive newspaper in Germany, many families and individuals were forced by the inflation to give up this luxury; afterwards not all of them returned to the practice of supplementing a local publication with a national newspaper. In national sales, moreover, the *Frankfurter Zeitung* had to compete with the Berlin papers and was naturally at a disadvantage in that it was not published in the capital; not only because readers of a national newspaper instinctively preferred a paper which originated in the centre of government, business, and cultural activity, but also because the rail and air connections between Berlin and the provinces were superior to those between Frankfurt and the rest of the country, and delivery from Berlin was therefore more rapid.[65]

Also, an innate contradiction continued to exist between the appeal of the *Frankfurter Zeitung* and its political inclinations. The business community which constituted the bulk of its subscribers was, in most instances, unlikely to be converted to the socially conscious, liberal democracy and the enlightened, conciliatory foreign policy of *détente* and abnegation, preached by the paper. On the other hand, the *Frankfurter Zeitung* was too highbrow, too erudite to have any mass appeal and thus to contribute noticeably to the Democratic campaign of 'civic education' (*staatsbürgerliche Erziehung*).

---

[65] See the undated memorandum on the *FZ* of the Wirtschaftsstelle für das deutsche Zeitungsgewerbe, Reichskanzlei files, R431/2464, p. 249. Also 'Geschäftsbericht der Frankfurter Societäts-Druckerei G.m.b.H. für das Jahr 1926', p. 3, in the author's possession, kindly provided by Dr. H.G. Müller-Payer, Stuttgart. A regional break-down of subscribers to the *FZ* is available in the 'Erläuterungen zum Abschluss 1. Halbjahr 1927', NL Payer, 17A, p. 22. Only between one third and one half of the paper's subscribers lived in Hessen.

The inflation after the war was more damaging to the FSD than to either Ullstein or Mosse, because the Frankfurt firm was a small publishing house in comparison to the other two and had no well-developed publishing pursuits tangential to newspaper production. It did have a small book section, and produced an illustrated weekly and a daily paper of advertisements for local Frankfurt consumption, the *Stadtblatt der Frankfurter Zeitung*, but these were minuscule affairs compared to, for example, the Ullstein book output, the *Berliner Illustrirte*, the Mosse advertising agency, and the popular papers of both firms. The total assets of the FSD in 1927 amounted to 3·4 million marks; those of Ullstein in the same year to over 41 million.[66]

Quality newspapers with large staffs but with relatively small circulations depend on a steady advertising revenue to survive. Throughout the Weimar Republic the preoccupation of many branches of the German economy with recovery and reorganization, the rationalization process in industry, the general shortage of capital funds, depressed the advertising market. In addition, the high unemployment, even in the so-called years of prosperity between 1924 and 1929, and the reduced purchasing power of average citizens whose savings had evaporated in the inflation, drastically cut down the availability of the small personal advertisements and announcements, 'classified ads', which previously had constituted a significant part of the morning edition of the *Frankfurter Zeitung*. The *Frankfurter Zeitung* as a paper with a small circulation, with expensive rates for advertising, with a dispersed readership, with a split character as a national newspaper appearing in the provinces, and with its controversial editorial policies, had particular difficulty in attracting and retaining advertisers.

While the receipts of the FSD suffered badly in the 1920s, production costs were rising sharply: materials became more expensive, salaries and the living expenses of foreign correspondents rose, and the costs of publicity and of general improvements, necessitated by the competitiveness

66 'Geschäftsbericht der Frankfurter Societäts-Druckerei G.m.b.H. für das Jahr 1927', NL Payer, 17A, pp. 179, 193; and *Ullstein Geschäftsbericht*, 1927.

of the newspaper business, mounted. Trusting and praying that a turn for the better would eventually come, the owners of the FSD borrowed more and more credit from the Oppenheim and Dresdner Banks without instituting any major reforms in the newspaper; by November 1927 the firm's debts amounted to 800,000 marks.[67] 'That we can only count on a gradual recovery is clear to me', Therese Simon wrote to Payer in October 1927 in defence of her son's financial policies; 'but whatever happens, we must not lose our nerve.'[68] The other directors, however, were convinced that the simple policy of borrowing was suicidal. When they refused to agree to a further loan of 140,000 marks in 1927, a discordant tone crept into the relations between the Simon family on the one hand and, on the other, the former close friends of the family like Payer, Cohnstaedt, and Schwander, who all sat on the supervisory board of directors.[69] If they had agreed in the past to a business policy which they considered primitive and mistaken, Payer, the chairman of the board of directors, explained, 'this was because we believed that we constantly had to go along with Sonnemann's offspring to the furthermost limits of what was possible, and because the financial conditions of the firm still made such excesses appear relatively sufferable.' The time, however, for a thorough and realistic rethinking of the situation had come.[70] According to Payer, short-term bank loans were a form of escapism and could never cure the complex ailments of the *Frankfurter Zeitung*, perhaps indeed only multiply them. Some radical solution was necessary. 'What we need is long-term money, from the family or from a third party. . . .'[71] In simple terms, what Payer meant was that the Simon family, which owned four-fifths of the shares in the FSD, had to invest its private fortune in the firm or find a partner willing to con-

[67] Payer to T. Simon-Sonnemann, early November 1927, NL Payer, 17A, pp. 140f. [68] 5 October 1927, NL Payer, 16, p. 164.

[69] This tension is referred to by T. Simon-Sonnemann in her letter to Payer, 24 October 1927, NL Payer, 16, p. 165. See also the minutes of the board of directors meeting of 23 September 1927, NL Payer, 17A, pp. 96ff.

[70] Payer to T. Simon-Sonnemann, early November 1927, NL Payer, 17A, pp. 140f.

[71] Taken from the draft of a letter by Payer, whose recipient is not stated, dated 21 October 1927, NL Payer, 17A, p. 132.

tribute considerable funds to the teetering enterprise. The notes which Payer scribbled at the directors' meeting on 23 September 1927 contained the ominous words, 'who is to buy? bankers or industry?'[72]

The Ullstein, Mosse, and Sonnemann papers were often referred to, not only by the extremist right but also by many moderates, including Democrats, as the 'Jewish press'.[73] To what extent was this an accurate description?

The owners of all three firms were Jewish, as were most of the leading editors of their publications—Theodor Wolff, Ernst Feder, Rudolf Olden, Alfred Kerr, Georg Bernhard, Julius Elbau, Carl Misch, Max Osborn, Richard Lewinsohn, Bernhard Guttmann, Wilhelm Cohnstaedt, to name but a very few.[74] Georg Bernhard asserted in 1930 that non-Jews far outnumbered Jews in the democratic publishing houses, but he did not substantiate his claim with figures.[75] Arthur Koestler, on the other hand, has estimated that over one half of the editorial personnel in the Ullstein firm was Jewish.[76] Regardless of the exact number of Jews in the Berlin and Frankfurt democratic publishing houses, one can safely say that the Ullstein, Mosse, and Sonnemann firms did employ a far higher percentage of Jewish staff than any other newspaper concerns in Germany which were not producing specifically Jewish publications. The percentage of Jewish editors in the three firms was also well above the ratio, 7·29 per cent, which Jews constituted in the community of artists, independent scholars, and writers.[77] That a very large number of these Jewish editors and publishers were not

[72] NL Payer, 17A, p. 83.

[73] See, for example, Koch-Weser's diary for 5 July 1929, NL Koch-Weser, 39, pp. 59f.

[74] Lists, though not entirely accurate, of Jews in prominent positions in the firms are available in a number of publications supervised by the Nazis: *Die Juden in Deutschland*, ed. Institut zum Studium der Judenfrage (3rd edn., Munich, 1936), pp. 84ff.; the article by Joseph März, 'Judentum und Presse', in *Handbuch der Zeitungswissenschaft*, columns 2011ff. See also Siegmund Kaznelson (ed.), *Juden im deutschen Kulturbereich* (2nd edn., Berlin, 1959), pp. 134ff.; and E.G. Lowenthal, 'Die Juden im öffentlichen Leben', in *Entscheidungsjahr 1932*, ed. Werner E. Mosse (Tübingen, 1965), pp. 59ff.

[75] *Kölnische Volkszeitung*, 15 October 1930.   [76] *Arrow in the Blue*, p. 222.

[77] *Das Schwarzbuch, Tatsachen und Dokumente: Die Lage der Juden in Deutschland 1933*, ed. Comité des délégations juives (Paris, 1934), p. 83.

adherents to Judaism and that many—Bernhard Guttmann
and the five Ullstein brothers, for example—were Christians
did not diminish in any way the impressiveness of this
concentration of publicists of Jewish origin.

The Ullstein, Mosse, and Sonnemann newspapers—particularly the *Berliner Tageblatt* and *Frankfurter Zeitung*—were
also read widely by the Jewish community.[78] Frankfurt and
Berlin were the cities with the largest Jewish populations in
Germany, 6·3 and 4·29 per cent respectively.[79] The DDP,
moreover, prior to 1930, was the natural political home of
German Jews. A number of democratic editors were active in
the national association of German Jews and in the German
Pro-Palestine Committee. Consequently, the wide circulation
of the Ullstein, Mosse, and Sonnemann papers among the
Jewish population was to be expected.

How extensive was the political influence of the metropolitan
democratic press? In 1921 an anti-Semitic, *völkisch* pamphlet
called the *Berliner Tageblatt* 'the most influential paper in
Germany'. This democratic publication, the author asserted,
had led the campaign during the war for a compromise peace,
for eventual disarmament and demilitarization, and for
democracy. Other papers had joined in. 'The success of this
press campaign resulted in the disunity of the German nation
and in collapse from this stab in the back. Thus we see a new
great power accomplishing what several of the great powers
of the world were not able to effect by themselves: the
vanquishment of Germany by the great power press.'[80] The
polemicist was not merely trying to make a case for anti-
Semitism. He sincerely believed, as did Hitler,[81] that the
liberal-democratic 'Jewish' press had played a most significant role in the demoralization of the nation, in the subsequent military defeat, and in Germany's surrender to the
deleterious ideas of 'western democracy'. That the assassin-

---

[78] See S. Auerbach, 'History of the "Frankfurter Zeitung" ', *AJR Information*, XII (April 1957), p. 7; Ernst Kahn, 'The Frankfurter Zeitung', p. 228;
and the unpublished 'Aufzeichnungen Bernhard Falks', pp. 3f., NL Falk,
Bundesarchiv Koblenz.

[79] *Das Schwarzbuch*, p. 81.

[80] Theodor Fritsch, *Der jüdische Zeitungs-Polyp* (Leipzig, 1921), pp. 3, 6.

[81] *Mein Kampf* (Munich, 1943), pp. 205f., 264ff.

ation lists drawn up by extremist right-wing organizations often contained the names of Theodor Wolff, Rudolf Olden, Georg Bernhard, and Hellmut von Gerlach was evidence of the political importance attached by extreme nationalists to the activity of the leading democratic journalists.

However, this belief in the awesome political influence of the democratic press, especially of the papers of the Ullstein, Mosse, and Sonnemann firms, was not the exclusive property of the extreme right. Caustic attacks against these publishing houses and their journalists issued with regularity even from the more moderate parties. The publications of the three democratic firms, with their self-righteous criticism, their interminable negativism, their 'spiritual nihilism', had supposedly poisoned the political atmosphere in Germany.[82] In 1929 an SPD organ credited the Ullstein and Mosse press with having destroyed the Democratic Party, a claim which elicited considerable agreement from within the DDP.[83] Was the political influence of the metropolitan democratic press in fact as great as these polemical statements implied?

There are, of course, degrees of influence. A state of heightened political awareness, for instance, which may result from the reading of a highly political journal, is naturally still far removed from the distinct political act represented by the casting of a vote. That the leading German papers of democratic persuasion helped to arouse and intensify political interest among many of their readers can hardly be disputed. But so too did the press which backed parties other than the DDP. That the democratic newspapers, on the other hand, were directly instrumental in soliciting a large number of votes for the republican parties, votes which otherwise would have been given to parties opposed to republican democracy, is rendered doubtful by a glance at the social composition of the readership of the individual Ullstein, Mosse, and Sonnemann publications, at the various reasons why people

[82] See, for example, *Der Tag*, 171, 17 July 1932; and the letter of Professor O. Flamm to Gothein, 23 December 1921, NL Gothein, 20, p. 69, in which he called the *BT* and the *FZ* 'the grave-diggers of the German Reich'.

[83] *Leipziger Volkszeitung*, 269, 19 November 1929. See Koch-Weser's memorandum to Ludwig Haas, Oscar Meyer, and Ernst Lemmer, 23 November 1929, NL Koch-Weser, 39, p. 77.

subscribed to these publications, and at the character of these papers.

The *Berliner Tageblatt, Frankfurter Zeitung,* and *Vossische Zeitung* were purchased almost exclusively by the German intelligentsia. The readership of these papers was culturally, if not necessarily politically, liberal-minded and inherently resisted organization and regimentation. Many subscribers already shared the basic political outlook of these papers. Others were attracted primarily by certain sections of the three publications: for example, the extensive coverage of international news, the excellent and reliable financial reports, or the lively *feuilletons*. Still others, businessmen, government officials, and owners of public services, did not 'read' these papers but 'used' them, as one historian has remarked,[84] for information, for official files, and as reading-matter for clients. In point of fact, the kind of public at which the highly argumentative political appeal of the principal democratic dailies was directed—an intensely interested, politically open-minded public which was prepared to be won over by a rationally conducted *guerre de plume*—did not exist in any significant numbers. Individuals in a modern pluralistic society, as several Democratic intellectuals were well aware,[85] do not respond to ideas in the first instance but to direct social and economic pressures.

While the *Berliner Tageblatt, Frankfurter Zeitung,* and *Vossische Zeitung* aimed at promoting precise political decisions from an already politically interested audience, the other, more popular, Ullstein and Mosse publications were, in practice, less ambitious and less specific in their political purpose. Papers like the *Berliner Morgenpost* and *Berliner Volks-Zeitung* had a large working-class readership. Many, if not most, of their subscribers were traditionally SPD voters. These papers could not afford to follow a narrow propagandistic party line. The *BZ am Mittag* was famous for its 'up

---

[84] Wilhelm Mommsen, 'Die Zeitung als historische Quelle', in *Beiträge zur Zeitungswissenschaft: Festgabe für Karl d'Ester* (Münster, 1952), p. 167.

[85] See M.J. Bonn, *Die Auflösung des modernen Staates* (Berlin, 1921), pp. 24ff.; and his *Krisis der europäischen Demokratie* (Munich, 1925), pp. 15ff.; also Alfred Weber, *Die Krisis des modernen Staatsgedankens in Europa* (Stuttgart, 1925), pp. 134ff.

to the minute' news coverage and its elaborate reporting on sports. As a midday paper and, usually, a Berliner's second paper of the day, it was not purchased for its analyses of political events but for the sake of information. The publishers and editors of these papers felt, therefore, that the nature and appeal of their products precluded the adoption of a perpetually hortatory tone in political coverage; and although the support of these journals for a social and democratic liberalism was unmistakable, they did not attempt to prod or channel readers' opinions along one definite party line. Their primary political concern was to elicit a greater awareness of political issues among their readers, and in this limited aim they probably achieved a high degree of success. The task of mobilizing this awareness into political action was left to the politicians.

In general, the argument that the democratic press was an independent political power galvanizing and precipitating political action does not hold. At most, democratic newspapers could hope to induce contractions in the Republic's political institutions, which then might give birth to political action, but even for this to occur a latent predisposition for the particular ideas propounded in this press had to exist. During and immediately after the war such a predisposition, for peace, democracy, and social justice, had been present among a substantial section of German society, but in the course of the Weimar Republic it was steadily eroded, despite the efforts of the democratic press to counter this erosion.

In view of the very limited influence of the democratic press on the voting habits of its readers, attention in the remaining account is focused not on the insoluble question of whether and how the metropolitan democratic press could have rallied opinion to save the democracy of Weimar; but rather on the history of the three leading democratic publishing houses during the political and economic crisis at the end of the Weimar Republic; and on the manner in which the viruses which paralysed the other institutions of Weimar democracy also afflicted the democratic press and rendered it incapable of fulfilling the political role which it had assigned to itself.

PART TWO

V

THE ECLIPSE OF LIBERALISM

The elections of May 1928, following over a year of *Bürgerblock* government—a coalition of the Centre, its sister party, the Bavarian People's Party, the DVP, and the DNVP—brought once again an unexpected and thoroughly depressing setback to the Democratic Party. Its representation in the Reichstag declined from 32 seats to 25. 'Shortly before midnight [on election day], Koch-Weser, the party leader joined us', a Berlin Young Democrat remembered subsequently. 'His face was as white as chalk, his eyes sunk and nervous. . . . It was too painful to notice his effort at appearing composed.'[1] The party which triumphed in the election was the SPD. It increased its poll by more than a million votes over the December 1924 election and by more than three million over that of May 1924. The right-wing DNVP suffered the heaviest losses, surrendering close to two million votes and 30 seats. After negotiations lasting over a month the SPD agreed to lead a grand coalition government including the DDP, the DVP, the Centre, and the Bavarian People's Party. The socialist Hermann Müller became chancellor.

In view of the SPD gains and DNVP losses the Ullstein *BZ am Mittag* ran banner headlines on 21 May, the day after the elections, announcing 'Victory for the Republican Idea!' A day later the *Berliner Morgenpost* reflected in its editorial that 'while the democratic idea is marching along in a more sprightly and strapping manner than ever before, it long ago burst the confines of the Democratic Party.' Not all of the democratic papers would have accepted these particular postulations but they did for the most part agree that the impressive SPD recovery signified a consolidation of republicanism. The DDP losses, on the other hand, were attributed to the party's failure to define clearly its social and economic

---

[1] Linke, *Restless Flags*, p. 303.

programme and to align its political practice with its fundamental ideas; consequently, much existing republican, democratic support, whose natural home should have been the
DDP, had voted socialist.

In many liberal quarters these elections, as they approached, had been regarded as a final crucial test for the
DDP. Theodor Wolff, for instance, told Ernst Feder in mid-
April that this time he was not even going to vote for the
DDP; the campaign coverage for the party in the paper had
to be toned down and the party shown that it was hardly a
pied piper.[2] At the beginning of May, however, Wolff
relented and once again threw the support of his paper
behind the party. The disastrous outcome of the election for
the Democrats was subsequently interpreted by Wolff and
numerous other liberals as conclusive evidence that the party,
as it existed, no longer had a rationale. A soul-searching re-
examination of the purpose, the appeal, and the organization
of the DDP was imperative. On this point all Democrats
agreed. There was, however, little unanimity on the direction
that reforms should take. The situation was reminiscent of
that at the turn of the century. Some Democrats argued that
the party had to be swung more to the left and that greater
attention had to be given to social policy. Their opponents
within the party insisted that quite the reverse direction had
to be followed: the party had to stress its middle-class
character. Others suggested that the party's most telling
weakness was its organization and that every effort had to be
devoted to its renovation. Still others saw little hope for
German liberalism, whether of the left or the right, if it
remained divided into separate parties, and claimed that all
other issues were secondary to that of liberal unity. Indeed, it
was this last issue which became the dominant subject of
debate in liberalism between 1928 and 1930.

Although liberal unity had failed to materialize on the
national level in the autumn of 1918, certain members of
both the DDP and DVP had refused to abandon hope that
the two parties might be amalgamated at some time in the
future. In the DDP a number of former National Liberals,

[2] Feder diary, 16 April 1928 (*Heute*, p. 174).

several businessmen and industrialists, and a group of south-German Democrats subsequently led the effort to draw the parties closer together. The most active advocates of liberal unity in the ranks of the party were Eugen Schiffer, Otto Keinath, Hermann Fischer, August Weber, Willy Hellpach, and Carl Friedrich von Siemens. In the DVP the initiative was taken by left-wingers or moderates such as Wilhelm Kahl, Alexander Graf zu Dohna, and Stresemann's young protégé Rochus Freiherr von Rheinbaben. In October 1924 Schiffer, Keinath, and Heinrich Gerland, a professor at Jena and one of the active founders of the DDP, left their party on the grounds that it was wallowing in theoretical irrelevancies, moving too far left in domestic policy as far as Schiffer and Keinath were concerned and in foreign policy in the eyes of Gerland, and ignoring the interests of the middle class and of German liberalism as a whole.[3] In November of the same year they established the Liberal Association (*Liberale Vereinigung*) whose purpose was 'to revive that German liberalism which is founded on patriotism and social conscience and to prepare the way for the co-ordination of its forces in one united party'.[4]

However, this organization and its aims found little resonance in the ranks of either the DDP or the DVP. The Democrats looked upon Schiffer, Keinath, and Gerland as objectionable traitors, especially as the extensive publicity that their departure from the party received just prior to the December 1924 elections was felt to be highly damaging to the image of the DDP. The People's Party showed little interest either. After the devastating defeat suffered by the Democrats in the 1920 elections Stresemann was convinced that the DDP would eventually disintegrate because of the irreconcilable differences within its cadres. The right wing, he expected, would then naturally join the DVP; the

[3] The correspondence between Gerland and Koch-Weser on the subject of the departure of Gerland, Schiffer, and Keinath from the DDP was printed in '*Die Liberale Vereinigung*': *Materialien zur demokratischen Politik, Nr. 120*, dated 11 November 1924. The pamphlet is available in the Geheime Staatsarchiv, Berlin, in the excellent collection of printed DDP material there, XII Hauptabteilung, Teil III, 7.

[4] Manifesto of the Liberal Association, 27 November 1924, in NL Siemens, 4/Lf697.

left would either go over to the SPD or become an incon-
sequential splinter group. But in the mid-twenties a more
immediate reason for his opposition to a fusion of the two
liberal parties was his fear of losing his own party's right wing
to the Nationalists, and thus of surrendering support indispensable for his foreign policy. By 1928 he was in fact far
more interested in trying to detach from the DNVP those
elements in that party which were beginning to reject total
negativism as the basis of conservative policy in the parliamentary Republic.[5]

After the publicity accompanying its founding had subsided and the initial enthusiasm and momentum had tapered
off, the Liberal Association lapsed into an ineffectual dining
club. In early 1928, in view of the apparent economic recovery, the achievements in foreign policy in recent years, and
the relative political stability that had returned to the
country, both the DDP and DVP were hopeful that the 1928
national elections would mark an upturn in their individual
fortunes. The renewed rebuff suffered by the two liberal
parties in May 1928 revived the almost dormant idea of
liberal union. The Liberal Association sprang to life once
again, and there was a flurry of optimistic activity during the
summer of 1928.

The provincial liberal-democratic press, with few, admit-
tedly prominent, exceptions such as the *Königsberger
Hartungsche Zeitung*, the *General-Anzeiger* of Dortmund,
and the *Frankfurter Zeitung*, had always been sympathetic
to the notion of liberal unity. Such reputable provincial
papers as the *Hamburger Fremdenblatt*, the *Stuttgarter
Neues Tageblatt*, the *Dresdner Neueste Nachrichten*, and the
Kölnische Zeitung often spurred on the campaign for closer
co-operation between the DDP and DVP, and ideally their
fusion. In most cases these papers classified their political
orientation simply as 'liberal', even though they usually
stood closer to one party than the other, and concentrated
on emphasizing the numerous aims which the two parties had
in common. Of the Berlin papers the *Berliner Börsen-*

---

[5] See the letter of Stresemann to Rudolf Schneider, 11 July 1928, NL
Stresemann, 101, 174305f.

Courier consistently encouraged liberal consolidation. The Ullstein publications did so as well but in a cautious, often hypothetical, manner.

In the Ullstein house Georg Bernhard had been the political overlord since the war. He explained his dominant position in political matters in the firm as being due to the reluctance of the Ullstein brothers to step into the public eye on political issues.[6] As we have seen Bernhard had joined the DDP soon after its foundation, but ostensibly because of his attitudes during the war he had been treated as an outcast within the party in its early years. Stresemann, so Bernhard assumed, had established his own party to avoid a similar fate. The editor of the *Vossische Zeitung* regretted but fully understood Stresemann's reactions to the acrimony and insults hurled at him from the ranks of the DDP. Former differences of opinion among liberals on war aims and on the question of responsibility for the outbreak of the war Bernhard belittled as 'artificial reasons for division' in the liberal camp.[7]

Although Bernhard and his deputy editor Julius Elbau eventually adopted the official DDP explanation for the collapse of the negotiations on union in 1918—namely that Stresemann had sabotaged the effort by founding his own party—they none the less repeatedly expressed their desire to see greater responsiveness in the relations between the two parties. Support for the efforts to unify the liberal parties was rendered by the paper not because its editors sympathized with the domestic programme of the DVP, which was always subjected to relentless and disparaging criticism, but for the sake of rationalizing the unmanageable German party system and consequently for the sake of parliamentary stability and efficiency.[8]

One other consideration played an important part in developing the *Vossische Zeitung*'s policy towards the question of liberal unity. Stresemann's foreign policy of *détente*

[6] See Frankfurter, Brief, p. 29.

[7] *VZ*, 615, 2 December 1918. See also *VZ*, 617, 3 December 1918, and Bernhard's speech to the DDP Hauptvorstand on 13 April 1919, DDP files, R45III/15, p. 90.

[8] See Elbau, *VZ*, 240, 8 October 1929.

with France and economic and military collaboration with Soviet Russia corresponded closely to the *Kontinentalpolitik* advocated by Bernhard. In his own party and on the left in general, his concept of a continental alliance system, involving Germany, Russia, and France, and directed against English interference in European politics, met with repudiation and scorn.[9] By 1928-9, however, he felt that his ideas had been corroborated and vindicated by events; but only on account of the skill and persistence of one politician, Gustav Stresemann.[10] From 1923 on, after Stresemann, at the head of a great coalition government, had broken off passive resistance to the French occupation of the Ruhr, the *Vossische Zeitung* regarded him as Germany's only political leader of stature and promise.

At a session of the executive committee of the Liberal Association on 5 June 1928, amidst sharp, occasionally vicious, denunciations of the editorial policies of the *Berliner Tageblatt* and *Frankfurter Zeitung* from almost every member present, Professor Friedrich Meinecke expressed his confidence that Georg Bernhard could be counted upon to join the movement formally.[11] To the surprise of many, Bernhard nevertheless refused to commit himself personally or to provide more than moral support for liberal union in his paper. The DDP policy-makers still shunned the Liberal Association, and Bernhard, having at last been elected to the Reichstag in May as a deputy of the DDP, felt compelled to bridle his own independence. Late in June a manifesto of the Liberal Association, calling urgently for liberal consolidation, was published with 249 signatories—prominent personalities from politics, academic life, journalism, business, the arts, and the civil service, including names like Max Liebermann, Friedrich Meinecke, Count Johann Heinrich Bernstorff, Gerhard Anschütz, Otto Becker, Erich Brandenburg, and Alexander Dominicus.[12] The only name

[9] See Harry Graf Kessler's diary entries for 22 March 1919 and 17 April 1922, *Tagebücher 1918-1937* (Frankfurt a.M., 1961), pp. 160, 298.

[10] See the letters of Bernhard to Heuss, 3 June 1929, NL Heuss; and to Koch-Weser, 11 October 1929, NL Stolper, 44.

[11] The minutes of the session are in NL Siemens, 4/Lf697.

[12] The manifesto is in NL Siemens, 4/Lf697.

that could be associated with the Ullstein firm was that of Erich Eyck, who at that time was a lawyer at the Berlin Kammergericht and legal adviser to the *Vossische Zeitung*.

The political representation of the Ullstein house in public belonged to Bernhard's sphere of activity. The absence of an endorsement of the manifesto by any leading personality in the house was due to his insistence that the firm and its publications should not become directly involved. On this occasion, however, Franz Ullstein probably disagreed with Bernhard. A few days before the May elections Franz had sent birthday greetings to Stresemann, wishing him further success in his foreign policy and remarking in addition that 'nothing would be more desirable than our being able to support you even more than in the past in your work in domestic politics. This could be realized through the unification, under your leadership, of the middle-class parties which sponsor social and cultural progress.'[13] But Bernhard insisted that matters should not be rushed. and Franz Ullstein yielded to this decision.[14] The Liberal Association manifesto was not signed by the Ullsteins.

Family disagreements in the Ullstein house were accumulating. Hermann Ullstein had resigned from the board of managing directors early in the year because of the dissension. The other three brothers, Hans, Louis, and Rudolf, and the younger generation—the sons, nephews, and in-laws—resented the exclusive control on political decisions exercised by Bernhard and Franz Ullstein. Most of the family was convinced that Bernhard had to be removed. The continuing insolvency of the *Vossische Zeitung*; Bernhard's political involvement, intensified now as a result of his election to the Reichstag, and hence the inevitable association by the public of the paper, and perhaps of the entire firm, with the left wing of the DDP; all this the family considered detrimental to the firm's well-being. Moreover, as Franz Ullstein's second wife put it, 'the juniors considered it intolerable that the editor of the *Voss* put in no more than twenty minutes a day at the office, that he dictated his

---

13 10 May 1928, NL Stresemann, 320, n.p.
14 See Frankfurter, Brief, p. 29.

articles through the dictaphone, and that he lost at poker.'[15]
In 1928 a serious attempt was made to dislodge Bernhard;
however, his contract protected him and Franz Ullstein
remained unshakeably loyal to his controversial editor.[16]

In 1929 a club movement sprang up in Germany among
younger liberals. Societies were founded which aimed at
rejuvenating and regenerating liberalism as a political movement and as a philosophy of human behaviour.[17] Of these
clubs the two most active and important were the Rhineland-
based 'February Club' and the Berlin-based 'Front 1929'.
Both underlined the need for consolidating the politically
moderate parties of the German middle class if liberalism
was to survive the crush of extremist nationalism and revolutionary Marxism. The February Club was dominated by
DVP supporters who conceived of the People's Party as the
necessary focal point for assembling a liberal offensive. The
Front 1929 had no narrow party connotations and received
financial assistance and moral backing from members of the
DDP, DVP, and Economic Party.

The Front 1929 in Berlin regarded as its chief project for
the year the setting up of a joint DDP-DVP electoral list for
the city's municipal elections in November. One of the
leading organizers was Fritz Stein, head of the Berlin bureau
of the *Hamburger Fremdenblatt*. When Franz Ullstein was
approached, he showed avid interest. Bernhard was prepared
to, and actually did, support the effort in his paper; but he
also warned his employer not to become personally too
involved in the discussions since his participation would
naturally be interpreted as a commitment of the entire firm.
Franz Ullstein ignored the caveat and attended meetings to
which Bernhard, much to his chagrin, had not even been
invited. In September Fritz Stein wrote to Koch-Weser and
Stresemann urging them to give their consent to the effort,
for the local party leaders were unwilling to commit themselves without the approval of the national executives. In the

---

15 R.G., *Prelude*, p. 277; see also Heinz Ullstein, *Spielplatz*, pp. 317f.

16 See Frankfurter, Brief, p. 16; also Feder diary, 17 March 1928.

17 See Karl-Hermann Beeck, 'Die Gründung der Deutschen Staatspartei im
Jahre 1930 im Zusammenhang der Neuordnungsversuche des Liberalismus',
unpublished diss. (Cologne, 1957), pp. 18ff.

letter to Koch-Weser he added: 'You will be interested to learn that [at the meeting] yesterday as well as at the previous session Dr. Franz Ullstein backed the co-operation of the bourgeois parties with great determination. He declared that he would sponsor the idea in his firm and that, if our plans collapsed, the Democratic Party would no longer enjoy the support it had received in the past from his papers, because it would be beyond help.'[18]

According to Bernhard, Franz Ullstein had never before taken the initiative in a political matter as delicate as this without first consulting him.[19] The thin-skinned editor-in-chief of the *Vossische Zeitung* felt insulted and outraged that Franz Ullstein had taken this step towards emancipating himself from his political tutelage. When the negotiations in Berlin eventually failed, Ullstein in turn sought to find a scapegoat to burden with the responsibility for the failure. For his first independent sortie into politics he was subjected only to malicious ridicule from Bernhard, and so he turned upon his employee and blamed the latter's ill-will and that of his party, the DDP, for the breakdown. The relationship between the two men deteriorated rapidly. Bernhard underestimated Franz Ullstein's personal pride, and at the same time his own *amour propre* prevented him from trying to prop up the crumbling friendship on the basis of mutual concessions. Not only did his authority in the firm on political decisions suffer a fatal blow through the episode but, by allowing his only protector in the Ullstein family to slip out of his control, he placed his future in the firm in serious jeopardy as well. But why did Franz Ullstein suddenly decide to manifest a spirit of independence on political matters?

An important reason was undoubtedly Bernhard's more direct political involvement. As a DDP Reichstag deputy his room for manouevre within the party had been diminished appreciably. He now had a greater personal stake in the fate of the party, and the danger existed, in the eyes of the Ullstein family, that he would be tempted to use the

---

[18] 24 September 1929, NL Koch-Weser, 101, p. 81. Koch-Weser cabled his support to Stein. Stresemann died before he could reply to Stein's letter.

[19] See Frankfurter, Brief, p. 29.

Vossische Zeitung as a party organ. In 1903 when Bernhard
had participated in the heated debates on revisionism in the
SPD and had appeared to be destined for a prominent role in
the party, it was apparently Franz Ullstein who had insisted
that he be relieved of his duties in the firm.[20] Now, in 1929,
Franz Ullstein, as he himself wrote a year later, 'gradually
arrived at the opinion that a young, energetic person was
needed to head the *Vossische Zeitung* and not a tactician
enmeshed in every trivial political battle'.[21]

The Ullsteins espoused liberalism and democracy as their
political doctrines. Their liberalism, however, was never one
of sophisticated political programmes but based rather on a
straightforward belief in the need for human decency. The
character and intended appeal of Ullstein publications precluded a dogmatic party affiliation. In the past even the
Vossische Zeitung, though clearly sympathetic to the DDP,
took greater care than either the *Berliner Tageblatt* or
Frankfurter Zeitung to maintain its distance from the party.
The constant support of Ullstein papers for the idea of
liberal unity was in effect an expression of the Ullsteins'
spirit of catholicity; parochialism and dogmatism were alien
to this Ullstein *Geist*.[22]

It would perhaps be too crude a formulation to say that
commercial considerations dictated this latitudinarian mentality, but they certainly reinforced it. By the autumn of
1929 sections of the economy were already in an advanced
state of depression, and the forecasts for the economy as a
whole were not propitious. Although circulation figures for
Ullstein publications were climbing, production costs were
increasing even more rapidly and the advertising market was
contracting. The Ullstein's new daily, *Tempo*, had proved to
be a misadventure and had joined the *Vossische Zeitung* as
one of the firm's financial liabilities. In this situation any
tendency which might contribute to a drop in circulation had

[20] Ibid., p. 16; and Hellmut von Gerlach, *General-Anzieger* (Dortmund), 195,
18 July 1930.

[21] From Franz Ullstein's open letter to Leopold Schwarzschild, *Das Tage-
Buch*, XI (12 July 1930), p. 1112.

[22] See Sling [Paul Schlesinger], 'Und der Geist des Hauses', in *50 Jahre
Ullstein*, pp. 385ff.

to be checked. The DDP, with only 25 seats in the Reichstag, was no longer a party of great significance in the governing of the country; its immediate future, moreover, was totally bleak. Hence, it was natural that the Ullsteins now regarded any closer affiliation with the party as an inadmissible investment from a business viewpoint, as well as contradictory to their general political posture.

A novel and conspicuous influence on Franz Ullstein's pattern of life and thinking was exerted by a new circle of friends which he had acquired. At the centre of the circle stood an extraordinary woman, Dr. Rosie Gräfenberg, née Goldschmidt, a Berlin and Paris socialite who consorted with statesmen, diplomats, politicians, artists, and leading businessmen.[23] Born in 1898 she was the daughter of a prosperous Mannheim banker and one of the first and youngest women in Germany to complete a doctorate at university. In 1921 she married the fashionable Berlin gynaecologist Ernst Gräfenberg but the marriage lasted only three years. In 1924 she went to Paris where she was soon frequenting the most eminent salons. By profession she considered herself a free-lance journalist, writing for German papers on French affairs. She also travelled extensively, to Morocco in 1926, to Russia and West Africa in 1928, and wrote articles on her impressions. The last two trips were made under the auspices of Ullstein. She had met Franz socially for the first time in 1925; in 1927 she had shown him some of her work, and Franz, greatly enamoured of the petite, vivacious young woman, arranged her excursions the following year. In 1928 Franz's wife Lotte, the daughter of the businessman Lehmann, died suddenly. In November 1929 Rosie, more than twenty years Franz's junior, became Frau Dr. Ullstein.

That she had an enormous impact on Franz Ullstein's character, thinking, and style of life, the latter himself acknowledged.[24] Indeed, her forward, aggressive nature and

[23] See her autobiography, published under the initials R.G., *Prelude to the Past* (New York, 1934). The author also had an interview with her in New York, 31 May 1972. Curt Riess in his biography of Max Alsberg, *Der Mann in der schwarzen Robe* (Hamburg, 1965), gives a brief portrait of Rosie, based partly on a private interview with her. Riess's account, however, has inaccuracies.

[24] Franz Ullstein in *Das Tage-Buch*, XI (12 July 1930), p. 1113; and the brief presented by his lawyers Max Alsberg, Rudolf Dix, *et al.*, to the Landgericht I,

her insatiable appetite for public prominence prodded Franz
into dropping much of his reserve and his misanthropic
inclinations. She also encouraged him to utilize more directly the supposedly immense social and political influence
which he possessed as one of Europe's leading publishers.
'The first time I sat next to him at dinner', Rosie wrote in
her memoirs, 'I thought him incredibly shy for a newspaper
king. . . . He looked like a little schoolmaster: short, badly
dressed, with thin ashblond hair and extremely short-sighted
eyes behind thick glasses. . . . It never occurred to Franz
Ullstein and his wife to realize their power in the world.
They lived in a modest, frugal, retired way without making
any claim to social position.'[25] That a woman of Rosie's
calibre would have taken an active interest in the editorial
policies and the personnel matters of the publishing house
was inevitable. In the course of 1929 a number of minor staff
changes took place which appeared to have been inspired by
her. Bernhard developed an intense dislike for Rosie—
perhaps because their personalities were so similar—and he
began to see in her the principal threat to his authority in the
firm. By early 1930 he had assumed that she was intent on
removing him as chief editor of the *Vossische Zeitung* and
replacing him by her friend Friedrich Sieburg, the Paris
correspondent of the *Frankfurter Zeitung*. The differences
of opinion over the tactical approach to the question of
liberal union and Franz Ullstein's novel obstinacy Bernhard
attributed to Rosie's influence. Indeed, although her ac-
quaintances in politics included figures such as the Social
Democrats Paul Levi and Robert Weismann, her more
intimate friends generally stood on the right, and she was
instrumental in bringing Franz Ullstein into close, social and
inevitably political, contact with personalities and organizations attached to the DVP and DNVP.

These, then, were the circumstances that activated Franz
Ullstein politically in 1929 and led to the rupture of his
friendship with Georg Bernhard. The episode has considerable significance. Although the Ullstein papers were not

---

Berlin, 18 June 1930 (hereafter Alsberg, Brief), p. 72.
    25 *Prelude*, pp. 211f.

strictly party newspapers, they did belong to the ideologically oriented press which in its discussion of politics was forced to use the existing parties and their programmes as terms of reference. The events of 1929 in the Ullstein firm represented a step in the retreat from any party associations; the next years witnessed an intensification of this process. In itself the development was perhaps laudable. However, in view of the heavily pedagogic flavour and traditions of the German press, this disengagement from the party could be interpreted as, and more important, could inadvertently lead to, dissociation from political realities as a whole. Furthermore, the Ullstein-Bernhard rift together with the marriage of Franz Ullstein to Rosie Gräfenberg, were the two sparks which set off a devastating explosion in the electrified atmosphere of the Ullstein firm. They inaugurated a veritable time of troubles for the publishing house, a *Krankengeschichte*, as one contemporary journalist referred to it,[26] terminated only four years later by an operation which killed the patient.

The campaign for liberal unity, more specifically for the fusion of the DDP, DVP, and possibly the Economic Party, produced strange allies. Among those journalists in the left-democratic press who encouraged the campaign was Hellmut von Gerlach. His reasons for backing the idea of liberal union were entirely impersonal and intellectual. By 1928 he no longer had any sympathy for the DDP and, along with Carl von Ossietzky and Kurt Tucholsky of the *Weltbühne*, was numbered among its most persistent and caustic critics on the left. Ossietzky and Tucholsky ridiculed the idea of liberal consolidation. Gerlach, on the other hand, found liberal unity desirable because he was of the opinion that it would clarify the political picture and provide the politically naive German bourgeoisie with more understandable alternatives. The party structure would be simplified: reactionary conservatives and chauvinistic nationalists would flock to the DNVP; Catholics would continue to support the Centre Party; socialists would vote for the SPD; and the

26 Josef Bornstein in *Das Tage-Buch*, XI (28 June 1930), p. 1020.

interests of the liberal middle classes would be represented
by the new party. Gerlach, nevertheless, gave no indication
that he personally would support such a party.[27]

The reaction of Theodor Wolff and the *Berliner Tageblatt*
to the defeat of the DDP in 1928 was totally different from
that of Bernhard and the *Vossische Zeitung* or of Gerlach.
The first article that Wolff wrote on the election results and
on the fate of the DDP had the tone of an obituary notice for
the party. If we backed the Democratic Party in the recent
campaign 'in an exaggeration of our community spirit and
out of reverence for the party's past', Wolff said, we shall not
do so again under similar circumstances. According to Wolff
—who now seemed to have forgotten the exuberance and
expectations which had surrounded the launching of the
DDP—the party had fulfilled its original purpose: it had
helped to establish the constitutional Republic, had given the
German bourgeoisie a say in the creation of the new state,
and had assisted in paving the way for the present foreign
policy. But it was clear that the party no longer had any
impetus or appeal: superficiality, sentimentality, mediocrity
—*Bliemschenkaffeegeist*—had crippled it. Because energy and
imagination had been suffocated within the party, most
progressive elements had taken flight.[28] As far as Wolff was
concerned, a simple fusion of the DDP and DVP was a fool's
solution to the problems facing German liberalism. Most of
the DVP would, in this case, desert to the right-wing DNVP,
while the leftists in the DDP would either join the Social
Democrats or cease to participate in politics. Progressive
social liberalism would no longer have a forum for its
activity.[29]

At the end of May 1928 Wolff introduced into public
debate the idea of a completely new liberal party, to be
assembled around the leadership of Stresemann and the left-
wing Centrist and former Chancellor Joseph Wirth, and
around the rank-and-file membership and organization of the
DDP; a party to be based on ideological tolerance, unques-

[27] *Die Welt am Montag*, 23, 4 June 1928.
[28] *BT*, 248, 27 May 1928.
[29] *BT*, 271, 10 June 1928.

tionable loyalty to the Republic, a progressive policy of social reform, and a devotion to the principles of freedom and democracy. Beyond these very general remarks he did not expand.[30]

The reception accorded Wolff's vague proposal was varied. Two weeks after he had made it, he claimed that he had received numerous enthusiastic letters of support, particularly from young people.[31] But in political and journalistic circles the idea was not taken seriously. Wolff had weighed the idea for some time and had already approached Stresemann with the suggestion at the beginning of the year. However, the DVP leader had been sceptical.[32] The DDP executive committee dismissed the suggestion curtly.[33] Ossietzky and Gerlach told Wolff that he was a dreamer.[34] Where were the voters who would support the new party? What reasons were there to believe that this new party would have any more success than the Republican Party—that 'one-day fly' (Gerlach)—founded at the end of 1923 when, owing to the political and economic chaos, prospects for such a party were far brighter? 'It seems to me', Ossietzky wrote in an open letter to Wolff, 'that your estimation of the spiritual disposition of our bourgeoisie is too innocent.' Despite the rebuffs Wolff continued to propagate his idea even after Stresemann's death in October 1929.[35]

That the Republic was in dire need of a strong liberal-republican party of the centre, which would co-operate with the SPD, was evident to all the defenders of the Weimar state. Wolff saw in Wirth and Stresemann the only capable and experienced politicians who carried sufficient authority and respect to launch such a party successfully. None the less, the criticisms levelled by Ossietzky and Gerlach were not unjustified. A new party could not be founded overnight and only on the basis of a few imprecise ideas. This was one

[30] *BT*, 248, 27 May 1928.
[31] *BT*, 271, 10 June 1928.
[32] Feder diary, 13 February 1928 (*Heute*, p. 157).
[33] Koch-Weser's diary for 22 June 1928, NL Koch-Weser, 37, p. 139.
[34] *Die Weltbühne*, XXIV (19 June 1928), pp. 927ff.; and *Die Welt am Montag*, 23, 4 June 1928.
[35] See *BT*, 472, 6 October 1929.

lesson which Wolff should have learned from his venture into active politics in 1918. He, like Gerlach, like Rathenau, had recognized that the DDP, shortly after its founding, was in reality little more than a continuation of the Progressive People's Party under a new name and not the strikingly new political creation which he and many other left democrats had envisaged. The DDP, moreover, had been a party that relied almost entirely on its ideological appeal—an appeal to moderation, reason, justice—to attract support, but its steady decline revealed that political liberalism would not survive if it relied solely on an appeal to intellect and public morality. Wolff did not discuss what in fact the party he visualized would have to offer that was new, apart from a perhaps more inspiring leadership. The idea that he rejected, that of consolidating the existing liberal parties into one, had the advantage, at least, of proposing to work with existing party organizations. Wolff's proposal was more ambitious, perhaps more attractive, but also less practical.

The *Frankfurter Zeitung* joined Wolff in disparaging a mere combination of the DDP and DVP. That the fusion of the two parties would cure the ills of liberalism, as many of the activists in the Liberal Association maintained, the *Frankfurter Zeitung* derided as simple-minded thinking. Union of the liberal parties could only be sanctioned if the strengthening of liberalism would be the certain outcome of the step. The editors of the paper, however, had little confidence that a combination between the national liberalism of the People's Party and the democratic liberalism of the DDP could further the political aspirations of either group of liberals.[36] The paper had for years propounded the view, at times even more resolutely than the *Berliner Tageblatt*, that the DDP's decline was a result, not of the abandonment of liberalism by the voting public, but of the betrayal of social liberalism by Democratic politicians who had failed to draw a sufficiently sharp line between the DDP and DVP. During June 1928 the *Frankfurter Zeitung* printed endless motions from Democratic organizations throughout the country, which rejected the idea of any formal tie with the DVP,[37]

36 See the lead article in the *FZ*, 421, 7 June 1928.
37 For example *FZ*, 438, 14 June; 439, 14 June; and 467, 24 June 1928.

and itself responded to these declarations by urging the leaders of the Democratic Party to take courage and to re-define the intentions of the party in truly social and demo-cratic terms.[38]

Owing to difficulties which he was having with the industrial right wing of his own party, and having also decided that the potential rebels around Lambach and Treviranus in the DNVP were not prepared to join the People's Party if they broke with their own party, Stresemann concluded by the summer of 1929 that steps did indeed have to be taken to consolidate the liberal centre if German liberalism was not to fade into oblivion. He finally took up serious consultations with Koch-Weser, which aimed at co-ordinating the programmes of their parties. However, his death on 3 October 1929 interrupted the discussions and cast a wrench into the spokes of liberal *rapprochement*.

The idea of liberal unity did not die with Stresemann; it was simply emasculated. The left wing of the DVP was rendered leaderless, and under the chairmanship of Ernst Scholz the party drifted gradually but steadily to the right until it became in effect a hanger-on of Hugenberg's DNVP. The latter party, in turn, manifested itself as the political play-thing of Hitler.

In the communal elections of November 1929 the liberal parties suffered further losses. In the *Vossische Zeitung* Julius Elbau wrote: 'All depends on the activation of the liberal centre if at this eleventh hour the German people are to be spared a fateful polarization of the political situation. The individual parties of the centre cannot do justice to the task incumbent upon them.' These parties must unite; there were no other alternatives, Elbau asserted.[39] Theodor Wolff once again returned to his theme of a brand new party. Merely throwing the present parties together would produce a 'useless, static lump'. The old parties had to dissolve them-selves, and out of the then fluid situation a new 'State Party' could be formed.[40] But again Wolff did not elaborate on his

---

[38] Lead article, *FZ*, 421, 7 June 1928.
[39] *VZ*, 276, 19 November 1929.
[40] *BT*, 555, 24 November 1929.

idea. The *Frankfurter Zeitung* remained cautious. It warned against hasty and artificial constructions, but by early 1930 it too admitted that a 'real reorganization of the German party system' was necessary.[41] For the democratic press the DDP was, to all intents and purposes, dead by 1930.[42]

It was the Democratic Party which, in spite of its inadequacies and shortcomings, had tied the democratic press to the Republic, and had given this press a political *raison d'être* in real rather than just theoretical terms. As the DDP declined in significance as a factor in the politics of the Republic, the *Berliner Tageblatt, Frankfurter Zeitung*, and *Vossische Zeitung* were correspondingly less able to relate to the imperfect realities of the Republic. Cast increasingly in the role of outsiders by events, by their political opponents, and even by their own political colleagues, most editors of the left-democratic press were prepared, by 1928-9, to acknowledge this role themselves.

While liberals fumbled for answers to the political riddles confronting them, Hugenberg launched his offensive against the Republic in the form of his 'freedom law', calling on the nation to repudiate in a referendum what he considered to be the hallmarks of the republican system, reparations and the war-guilt clause of the Versailles treaty; the stock-market crashed on Wall Street and foreign capital remaining in Germany took flight; and the National Socialists and Communists registered their first substantial electoral gains in local elections. The grand coalition government, which had been formed in June 1928, stumbled along. It was led by a party, the SPD, which had grown tired of the ideological compromises demanded of it by governmental responsibility, and by a chancellor, Müller, who did not possess the full confidence of his own party. The coalition held together only as long as the Young Plan on reparations was an outstanding issue on the government's agenda. As soon as the Plan was

[41] Lead article, *FZ*, 109, 10 February 1930; see also 169, 4 March 1930.

[42] See Ernst Feder, *BT*, 194, 25 April 1930. The article concluded with a line from a German song: 'Sie waren längst gestorben und wussten es selber kaum.' Feder wrote in his diary, 25 April, that he struggled with his conscience for a long time before deciding to let the line stand (*Heute*, pp. 257f.).

ratified by the Reichstag in March 1930 the coalition crumbled, and the *Staatskrise*, which had been latent in the Republic since its early years, finally gained an irrepressible immediacy.

In the meantime a momentous change took place in one democratic publishing firm, and a disastrous public scandal rocked another.

VI

ODD BEDFELLOWS:
THE *FRANKFURTER ZEITUNG* AND I.G. FARBEN

The growing ideological crisis which pervaded German liberalism in the second half of the 1920s was an intrinsic precondition for the particular course which events followed in the Mosse, Ullstein, and Sonnemann firms at the end of the decade and at the beginning of the thirties. In politics, the depression which gradually enveloped the country by 1929 did not cause but merely helped to accentuate the state of disarray and confusion in which the parties and their ideologues and tacticians found themselves, and on which Hitler and National Socialism were eventually able to capitalize. Similarly, the economic recession, on the national level, did not introduce but only aggravated the diverse difficulties facing the press.

Because of the decentralization and consequent low circulations of German papers, economic insecurity had always been an ineradicable feature of newspaper publishing in Germany. Not merely small local news-sheets had to struggle to survive but much of the quality press as well. In the entire newspaper trade a fierce sense of competition, for readers and for advertising, prevailed. The generally unsettled state of the economy in the Weimar years only served to intensify the spirit of rivalry among papers.

By the end of 1927 the publishers of the *Frankfurter Zeitung* had, according to one of the directors, 'almost reached the dangerous point where debts devour all the yields' because of the interest repayable on borrowed capital.[1] The firm's deficit for the business year 1927 exceeded a quarter of a million marks, the second year in succession that enormous losses had been registered. The total deficit now amounted to over RM 700,000.[2] Most of

---

[1] Schwander to Payer, 24 January 1928, NL Payer, 17B, pp. 39f.
[2] FSD 'Geschäftsbericht' for 1927, NL Payer, 17A, p. 184.

the firm's directors were agreed that a continuation of the present financial methods was out of the question, for there was absolutely no indication that the foreseeable future would bring any substantial change in economic, political, or social conditions which would promote an upswing in either the *Frankfurter Zeitung*'s individual fortunes or those of the press as a whole. Only a chasm of bankruptcy and disintegration lay at the end of the path which the owners of the paper were following. Such was the stern assessment of the situation by Friedrich von Payer, Ludwig Cohnstaedt, and Rudolf Schwander.

The search for a course of action which might alleviate the *Frankfurter Zeitung*'s financial difficulties unearthed a variety of possibilities. The most pessimistic was that the paper should cease to be a national journal and should revert to being simply an ordinary provincial newspaper, serving primarily Frankfurt. Another, almost equally desperate view was that the paper should restrict its attention to business news, in other words should readopt Sonnemann's original aim when he had founded the paper. These conceptions, though aired, were never seriously debated. Kurt Simon, as business manager, wished to pursue several other ideas first.

One, that of some form of arrangement with Wolfgang Huck, 'the Generalanzeiger king', who owned papers in Dresden, Breslau, Munich, Stettin, Halle, Cassel, Mannheim, and Wiesbaden, and with whom Kurt Simon was on friendly terms, did not pass beyond the stage of vague feelers. Far more serious were the deliberations concerning some agreement with either the owners of the moderate, liberal *Frankfurter Generalanzeiger*, the largest Frankfurt daily (approximate circulation 155,000), or with the Berlin firm of H.S. Hermann, the publishers of the *Berliner Börsen-Courier*, a very small but respected liberal financial paper (circulation in 1928 25,000) which normally stood close to the entrepreneurial right wing of the DDP.[3]

---

[3] In 1925 when the Stinnes empire was dissolved, Hermann bought the Reimar Hobbing and Büxenstein printing firms for 11·5 million marks cash. It was rumoured that his private fortune was greater than even that of the Ullsteins. See Gustav Stolper's letters to Karl Schlesinger, 1 November 1925, and Josef Schumpeter, 7 July 1926, NL Stolper, 30 and 31.

Kurt Simon became 'hypnotized' by the latter idea and, disregarding protests and objections from Payer and Ludwig Cohnstaedt that the project of fusion with the *Börsen-Courier* was impractical, initiated extensive negotiations with Fritz Hermann.[4] Theodor Vogelstein, one of the founders of the DDP in 1918 and now a banker with the Bankhaus Dreyfus in Berlin, gave particular encouragement to the idea of uniting the two papers. The Hermann family, suddenly presented with the prospect of perhaps being able to compete seriously with the Mosse and Ullstein papers, displayed an irrepressible enthusiasm for a deal with the FSD. Kurt Simon, however, could persuade neither the directors of the FSD—Payer, for example, felt that the firm had to bring order to its finances, by cutting spending radically, before it could negotiate properly[5]—nor his colleagues in the management that the union of the two papers or even merely a merger of their reporting staffs would improve the lot of the Frankfurt house. Especially strong was the feeling that any arrangement with the small *Börsen-Courier* was beneath the dignity of the time-honoured and august institution that the *Frankfurter Zeitung* was considered to be.[6]

After the idea had already been buried by the firm's directors and financial advisers, Kurt Simon stubbornly refused to break off discussions with the Hermann concern. By August 1928 rumours about the negotiations were circulating through newspaper head offices and had excited a number of publishers. Mosse and Ullstein were naturally not eager to face competition in Berlin from a combined *Frankfurter Zeitung-Berliner Börsen-Courier*; Martin Carbe of Mosse and Ernst Kahn of Ullstein were sent scurrying to the Simon brothers with, according to Ludwig Cohnstaedt, 'vague statements about assistance' for the *Frankfurter*

---

[4] L. Cohnstaedt to Payer, 26 April 1928 and 1 February 1928; also the report entitled 'Betr. evtl. I.G. der FSD mit BC', NL Payer, 17B, pp. 88, 48ff., 111ff.

[5] See the draft of a letter by Payer, dated 14 January 1928, NL Payer, 17B, pp. 11ff.

[6] L. Cohnstaedt called the *Börsen-Courier* 'the little BBC which for decades has been able neither to live nor die'; in a letter to Payer, 28/9 March 1928, NL Payer, 17B, p. 56.

Zeitung.[7] Even Kurt Broschek, co-owner of the *Hamburger Fremdenblatt*, approached Kurt Simon for consultations. What was actually discussed in these various meetings is not clear, but Kurt Simon did tell Ludwig Cohnstaedt that he had not been impressed by these approaches. As Cohnstaedt wrote to Payer: 'To him [Kurt Simon] Hermann is preferable to Mosse or Ullstein or anyone else; they all want to exert some kind of influence, thus possibly imperilling the character of the Sonnemann paper. Only Hermann does not, and he alone is prepared to cover the . . . debts without charging interest.'[8]

Meanwhile, as these negotiations dragged on without any sign of progress, the economic predicament of the FSD worsened. By October 1928 the firm was 1·75 million marks in the red. The rumours in August, however, had caused more ears to prick up than only those of publishers. In the middle of that month an encounter took place in Berlin between Fritz Sabersky, a lawyer and close friend of the Simon family, who in May 1927 had been appointed a director of the FSD, and Hermann Hummel, a former deputy chairman of the south-German People's Party to which Sonnemann and Payer had belonged, in 1922 state president of Baden, and now a DDP Reichstag deputy for Magdeburg. Initially Hummel had been a prominent Democrat. In 1924 he ran against Koch-Weser for the chairmanship of the DDP. Although he sided with the left wing of the party on certain issues, his over-all concept of liberalism placed him on the right of the DDP. Immediately after the revolution he had decided that the notions harboured by the left democrats about the feasibility of a synthesis between capitalism and socialism were unrealistic and inappropriate, and could only result in the permanent debilitation of the German economy. Only an unequivocal endorsement of free enterprise would sponsor and assist the country's recovery. In November 1918 Hummel worked actively and successfully in Baden for the unification of the liberal parties there. An unpublished

---

[7] In a letter to Payer, 10 August 1928, NL Payer, 17B, p. 178; see also Feder diary, 12 July 1928 (*Heute*, p. 187).

[8] 25 September 1928, NL Payer, 17B, p. 220.

biographical sketch of his career, written either by himself or
someone who was very close to him, asserted, revealingly,
that the democratic liberalism espoused in Baden 'had
nothing of the proselytizing fanaticism and pseudo-
proletarian weakness of mind which emanated from the
German north and ever after rendered the taste of democracy
more and more loathsome to the nation'.[9] In the mid-
twenties a personal clash with the patriarch of Baden
liberalism, Ludwig Haas, frequent verbal attacks on his
person by the left wing of the DDP, and censures from the
leadership about his lack of commitment to the party, led
Hummel to withdraw from conspicuous political activity.[10]

During the inflation Hummel began to take an active
interest in newspapers as a means of influencing public
opinion. Impressed by the inroads that Hugenberg and heavy
industry were making into the press after the war, Hummel
took up contact with the Ullsteins in 1923 and persuaded
them to participate in the founding, the following year, of
the Imprimatur G.m.b.H., an investment-loan organization—
modelled after Hugenberg's Mutuum Darlehens and Alterum
Kredit companies—which, through financial assistance to
provincial papers, hoped to exercise an influence on their
editorial policies. Hummel's motives in this enterprise were
based first on economic, and only indirectly on political
considerations: he wished above all to influence public
attitudes, and to lessen public hostility, towards the owners
of capital and industry, the generators of the economy in his
opinion. He was convinced that economic stability was a
prerequisite for political stability.

Hummel's undertaking never flourished as he had hoped.
One impediment was the launching in February 1925 by the
DDP of its similar venture, the Verlag Neuer Staat, with
the financial aid of Ullstein, Mosse, and the FSD. The

[9] Manuscript entitled 'Hermann Hummel', in the Zentralarchiv of the
Frankfurter Allgemeine Zeitung, Frankfurt a.M.

[10] Erkelenz to Hummel, 12 April 1924, and Erkelenz to Robert Bosch, 2
February 1929, NL Erkelenz, 31 and 51. Feder diary, 29 June 1928. In 1927
Hummel's private secretary wrote to Erkelenz: 'I am permitted to inform you
that Hummel has an outstanding idiosyncratic desire to avoid any public concern
with his person . . . .' Letter of 29 September 1927, NL Erkelenz, 45.

Ullsteins, not wishing to involve themselves in too many commercially unpredictable outside activities, withdrew from Hummel's project.[11] The Imprimatur company, though it subsequently showed signs of life only sporadically, did nevertheless continue to exist. In 1925, when the Stinnes industrial empire was broken up, Hummel expanded his interests in the press by acquiring three small provincial news services, Arens, Wiemann, and Frankfurt am Main, which together supplied about one hundred local papers with syndicated columns. He also purchased shares in the *Nürnberg-Fürther-Morgenpresse* and bought the *Dessauer Zeitung* outright. In August 1928 Hummel dealt with the FSD in his official capacity as head of the Imprimatur investment-loan organization, but the company was merely a convenient agency and Hummel an intermediary for more important and powerful interests.

In 1922 Hummel became friends with Carl Bosch, then the chairman of the managing board of the chemical concern Badische Anilin- und Soda-Fabrik. In 1925 Bosch was the driving force behind the merger of the major chemical firms in Germany and the creation of the mammoth chemical trust I.G. Farbenindustrie. As chairman of its managing board and foremost decision-maker, he soon persuaded Hummel, who himself had a university education in physics, mathematics, and chemistry, to join the ranks of the directors. Hummel became the representative of the DDP on a fifty-man board of directors which included members of all the major non-socialist parties.

Carl Bosch, a nephew of the Stuttgart industrialist Robert Bosch, was, unlike his uncle, not instinctively interested in politics. He considered himself above all a scientist, and an entrepreneur only incidentally. Together with Fritz Haber he had developed the fixation process for nitrogen; both men had been awarded the Nobel Prize for their achievement. Nevertheless, Bosch's prominence in the industrial world forced him to confront political problems. In 1919, for example, he belonged to the German peace delegation in

---

11 'Hermann Hummel', Zentralarchiv of the *FAZ*; and W. Stephan to Erkelenz, 22 September 1925, NL Erkelenz, 130.

Paris as an economic adviser. Thereafter he took an interest in promoting Franco-German understanding and was responsible for eliciting a contribution from I.G. Farben to Coudenhove-Kalergi's Pan-European movement.[12] His political sympathies were essentially a by-product of his professional standing and interests. He favoured reasoned discussion, political moderation, international co-operation, and cosmopolitan attitudes; but he also believed, like Hummel, in the blessings of a strictly capitalist economic structure.

Bosch, as an educated and enlightened scientist and industrialist, appreciated the informative, cultural, educational, and, not least, political value of a paper like the *Frankfurter Zeitung*. To him personally the prospect of the disappearance or radical transformation of this paper was perturbing. However, at the same time, the distrustful and basically inimical attitudes of the journal to heavy industry and other capital interests were irritating to the chairman of the management of the largest German industrial corporation. The possibility of sharing in the ownership of the internationally respected Frankfurt publishing house and thereby exerting some influence on the editorial policies of the *Frankfurter Zeitung* was thoroughly appealing to Bosch.

But considerations wider than just Bosch's personal interest in the *Frankfurter Zeitung* were in play in 1928. Two years earlier I.G. Farben had taken the decision to embark on the production of synthetic gasoline. Construction and research costs for the development of the process of coal hydrogenation were enormous. In 1928 the capital of the chemical trust had to be increased by 250 million marks.[13] Between 1926 and 1932 an estimated 100 million marks were invested in the project. But progress was slow. In 1927 Farben admitted publicly that it was having difficulties; unexpected costs and technological problems hampered production. Pressure built up on the chemists and engineers

---

[12] Louis Lochner, *Tycoons and Tyrant* (Chicago, Ill., 1954), p. 44.

[13] Thomas Parke Hughes, 'Technological Momentum in History: Hydrogenation in Germany 1918-1933', *Past & Present*, No. 44 (1969), p. 118. In 1929 Farben had a share capital of 1,100 million marks; the stock-market value of these shares stood at 3,000 million.

engaged in the research, but particularly on Bosch, the other members of the management, and on the directors. In 1927-8 the whole project was subjected to growing public criticism, particularly from the political left. The enterprise was attacked as a waste of funds at a time when capital was short in Germany. In December 1927 Hummel, enraged by an article in the *Berliner Tageblatt* on Farben's Leuna works, called up Carbe and damned the piece as 'thoroughly communist'.[14] A sense of urgency gripped Bosch and his advisers. They not only were faced by technological difficulties, but they had to try, at the same time, to persuade political and economic interests of the feasibility and practicability of their product.

In 1927 Carl Duisberg, the chairman of the board of directors of Farben, had urged German industry to become more involved in political matters.[15] He addressed his exhortation especially to the electrical and chemical industries, which, in comparison to coal and steel interests, had shown reluctance to become directly implicated in party politics. In 1927 Farben had added reason to concern itself with political opinion. With its enormous investment in the production of synthetic gasoline, the chemical firm naturally wanted a protective tariff on oil imports; it therefore needed a sympathetic ear in the media and in the political parties. When the Hugenberg complex acquired the majority shares in UFA that year, Farben bought in as well. The interest in UFA was twofold: on the one hand it was an important customer for Farben, and on the other UFA's weekly news films were seen by millions of German cinema-goers, and it was essential from Farben's point of view that it and its projects be treated sympathetically. In the following years contributions were made to the coffers of all the non-socialist parties, including by 1932 at the latest, the NSDAP.[16] The interest in the *Frankfurter Zeitung* shown by

---

14 Feder diary, 5 December 1927.

15 Hughes, 'Technological Momentum', p. 128.

16 Lochner, *Tycoons and Tyrant*, p. 113; see also Richard Sasuly, *I.G. Farben* (New York, 1947), pp. 66ff.; and Henry Ashby Turner, Jr., 'Big Business and the Rise of Hitler', *American Historical Review*, LXXV (1969), pp. 56ff., especially p. 63.

Bosch in 1928 must be seen in this context, that is as part of
the attempt to create a climate of opinion favourable to the
products of Farben, especially to synthetic gasoline. The
Frankfurt paper had always been among the most severe
critics of Farben.

Hummel was the middleman whom Fritz Sabersky contacted in August 1928. Distinct interest in further discussions
was displayed immediately by both parties. On 11 October
1928 Rudolf Schwander wrote to Payer:

Dr. Heinrich Simon has informed me of the Berlin negotiations. This
time the matter is truly serious; it goes in the direction that I have
considered all along as the only way out of the hopeless situation
which we are in. The same sources of capital are also involved of which
I knew that they wished to exert an influence on the Fr[ankfurter]
Z[eitung]. For the newspaper a very serious matter indeed, but, with
certain assumptions, the only thing that can really help.[17]

On the 'certain assumptions' to which he alluded,
Schwander did not have to elaborate. How severe were the
terms to be on which Bosch was prepared to invest capital in
a less than sound business proposition? To what extent
would the prospective shareholders insist on changes in
editorial policy? Would they perhaps even insist on controlling editorial policy?

For the Simon brothers the ghost of Leopold Sonnemann
haunted the negotiations. Their correspondence at the time
was filled with remarks which betrayed their uneasiness,
their state of depression and feelings of guilt. 'In the past
weeks I have constantly looked for the cloven hoof in this
whole business,' Heinrich Simon confessed in February 1929,
'but I must now admit that I was perhaps too nervous and
uneasy.'[18] The FSD needed two million marks; Carl Bosch
appeared prepared to provide it.

Hummel was an astute negotiator. He managed to persuade
the Simons—although it must be said that they clearly
wished to be persuaded—that the motives of Bosch were
largely benevolent and charitable and not political or
commercial; that Bosch was interested in the *Frankfurter
Zeitung* as a *Kulturfaktor* rather than as a business prop-

---

[17] NL Payer, 17B, p. 241.
[18] In a letter, 13 February 1929, NL Payer, 17C, p. 53.

osition.[19] Of the directors, Schwander and Sabersky encouraged the discussions; Payer and Ludwig Cohnstaedt showed occasional moments of scepticism, but never protested strenuously. Everyone who knew of the negotiations tended to underplay the significance of Bosch's terms, and no one objected with arguments of principle. By March 1929 Heinrich Simon was referring to Bosch as a 'democratic friend'.[20]

What then were the conditions? Were they in fact non-political? They were outlined by Hummel in a letter to Kurt Simon on 6 December 1928.[21] In his will Leopold Sonnemann had insisted that the political orientation of the *Frankfurter Zeitung* always remain 'liberal, in social-political matters always just and friendly to reform'. As a foundation for editorial policy he had suggested the 'Munich programme of the [prewar] German People's Party'. He had, however, added an important qualifying phrase: 'This foundation would, of course, always have to be adapted to new conditions.'[22] Here was the important hook on which Hummel was able to hang his arguments. He told the Simons that as a former member of this party he regarded himself as the 'personification' (*lebende Versuch*) of Sonnemann's intentions. What he and Bosch wanted was 'to develop the paper technically and in its organization and to bring its policies into harmony with the political dynamics of today's age'.

Hummel was implying, of course, that the attitudes of the *Frankfurter Zeitung* were anachronistic and out of touch with the contemporary situation in Germany, and that Sonnemann would have been pleased to see some of them modified. One means of putting Sonnemann's testament into effect, said Hummel, was 'to emphasize, with calm objectivity, the significance and activity of industrial, commercial, and agricultural concerns'. In other words, the scarcely concealed antagonism of the paper towards free enterprise as an

19 See L. Cohnstaedt to Payer, 15 November 1928, NL Payer, 17B, p. 272.

20 H. Simon to the board of directors of the FSD, 5 March 1929, NL Payer, 17C, p. 91.

21 NL Payer, 17B, pp. 286ff.

22 *Geschichte der Frankfurter Zeitung*, p. 1056.

economic system and towards this system's most successful
and obvious representatives was considered unjust and ill
founded. Here was a clear reference to I.G. Farben's interests.
Consequently, Hummel announced, it was 'necessary to
expand and improve the editorial board'. 'If the personnel
situation in the editorial board in Frankfurt is difficult to
alter,' he told Kurt Simon, 'you yourself have hinted at the
possibility of effecting a change, along these lines of thought,
in the political section by reorganizing the Berlin office and
in the economic section by bringing back an economic editor
from Berlin.' Hummel had in mind the replacement of the
Berlin correspondent, Bernhard Guttmann, and the introduction of more conservative thinking into the economic
staff in Frankfurt, to counter the ideas and influence of men
like Arthur Feiler and Albert Oeser. Finally, Hummel
mentioned that if agreement was to be reached in the
negotiations 'the rights of supervision of the board of
directors over the general policies of the newspaper' had to
be enhanced. He himself would become a member of the
board to represent the new interests. Hummel was demanding
that the 'collegiate system' of determining editorial policy
be altered in practice if not in theory. In sum, the letter
demanded certain changes in the editorial staff, a general
reconsideration of editorial policy, particularly towards
sections of the economy, and the extension of the supervisory powers of the directors of the firm to include
editorial policy.

In view of the amount of capital that Bosch was prepared
to invest in the FSD, the demands were not thought to be
unreasonable. As a matter of fact, they were considered
unusually and unexpectedly moderate in comparison with
the terms normally attached by industrial circles to extensive
capital investments in the press. 'That we have been given
this opportunity, which will involve so little change, if any at
all, in our fundamental orientation, must indeed be regarded
as a great stroke of luck', Heinrich Simon wrote.[23] Obviously, since the financial situation of the firm was so
appalling, the Simon brothers had braced themselves for

[23] In a letter to Payer, 13 February 1929, NL Payer, 17C, p. 54.

more radical and thoroughgoing alterations and concessions prior to the appearance on the scene of Hummel and Bosch. Only in this light can the unlikely partnership be understood, a partnership between the gargantuan I.G. Farbenindustrie, Germany's largest business corporation, and the Simon-Sonnemann family whose newspaper Leopold Sonnemann had hoped would 'always [be] inclined to support the economically weak'.[24]

None the less, one may ask whether other possibilities were sufficiently explored, whether sources of capital, whose ideological tendencies were more closely related to those of the *Frankfurter Zeitung*, did not, in fact, exist. The response of Payer to a suggestion that Robert Bosch, Carl Bosch's uncle, be somehow involved in the deal was indicative of the predominant frame of mind at the time among the owners and directors. 'How you have hit upon Robert B. I cannot comprehend. There you have a Social Democrat with violent tendencies; he would be a severe burden to the firm', Payer replied to Cohnstaedt.[25] Robert Bosch was an industrialist with an acute social conscience. He was in fact not a Social Democrat but a member of the DDP. He shared many of Walther Rathenau's ideas on economic and political questions and many of the views which had been expressed on labour and social problems in the pages of the *Frankfurter Zeitung* in the past ten years.[26] His association with the FSD would have been far more natural in view of the past history of the paper than that of his nephew Carl Bosch.

The conditions stipulated by Bosch and Hummel were accepted, and on 26 February 1929 a formal contract was signed by the FSD management and by Hermann Hummel.[27]

---

[24] From Sonnemann's will; see above, pp. 27-28.

[25] From Payer's notes for a letter to L. Cohnstaedt, 17 January 1929, NL Payer, 17C, p. 19.

[26] See the letter of Robert Bosch to Rathenau's Demokratischer Volksbund, 21 November 1918, NL Haussmann, 114, in which he urged that plans be drawn up immediately for the socialization of the German economy. Bosch owned the Deutsche Verlags-Anstalt in Stuttgart which published the moderate liberal *Stuttgarter Neues Tageblatt*. He contributed considerable funds to the DDP and some to the SPD. For a massive but often disappointing study of Bosch, see Theodor Heuss, *Robert Bosch: Leben und Leistung* (Stuttgart and Tübingen, 1946).

[27] Copy in NL Payer, 17C, p. 62.

Neither Carl Bosch nor I.G. Farbenindustrie was mentioned in the document. The Imprimatur company acquired shares worth RM 700,000 or 35 per cent ownership in the FSD. These shares were bought at twice their par value, that is for 1·4 million marks. Included in the agreement was also a loan of 1·5 million marks, at the extremely low interest rate of 5 per cent. Each party agreed to the other's right of pre-emption in case further shares were sold. On 12 March 1929 the transaction was ratified by the directors of the FSD, and Hermann Hummel was elected to the supervisory board. A new era began for the *Frankfurter Zeitung*.

At the Nuremberg trials after the Second World War, one of the leading members of the managing board of Farben, Georg von Schnitzler, mentioned in an affidavit that Carl Bosch, together with the treasurer of Farben, Hermann Schmitz, 'reserved exclusively for themselves the handling of distribution of money to political parties, the press, etc.'[28] Bosch, as chairman of the managing board, had a substantial fund of Farben capital at his disposal, which he could administer without consulting the rest of the management or the directors. It was from this source that he drew the capital used to purchase the FSD shares and to provide the loan.[29] How much was known to the other members of the managing and supervisory boards about the details of the transaction is not clear. Hermann Schmitz was drawn into the discussions soon after they began.[30] Presumably at least the central committee of the managing board (*Personalaus-schuss*), consisting of seven members and the chairman of the supervisory board, was informed in detail by Bosch.[31] The

[28] *Trials of War Criminals before the Nuernberg Military Tribunals*, vol. VII ('The Farben Case') (Washington, 1953), p. 556. Schmitz was offered the economics ministry by Brüning in October 1931; he turned the invitation down because he apparently did not wish to be associated with Brüning's middle-of-the-road cabinet. See Andreas Dorpalen, *Hindenburg and the Weimar Republic* (Princeton, N.J., 1964), p. 237. In November 1933 he became a Reichstag deputy for the NSDAP.

[29] Benno Reifenberg, in an interview with the author, 25 March 1969.

[30] See K. Simon to Payer, 12 December 1928, NL Payer, 17B, p. 293; and also C.F. von Siemens to H. Schmitz, 14 December 1931, NL Siemens, 4/Lf514.

[31] According to the by-laws of the managing board of Farben, which are printed in *Trials of War Criminals*, VII, pp. 386ff., the central committee, by itself, could take care of 'matters requiring particularly confidential treatment'.

most important point here, however, is that the FSD people were perfectly aware that they were dealing with Farben funds and not with the private capital of Bosch or Hummel.[32]

Despite the intricate arrangements made to obscure the facts of the deal from probing eyes, by April 1929 rumours were already circulating that I.G. Farben had bought into the FSD. The publishing firm was compelled to make a statement. In an article in the *Frankfurter Zeitung* on 29 April it stressed that the majority of shares in the FSD was still in the hands of the Simon-Sonnemann family. Ever since the founding of the firm shares had also been owned by a number of individuals who were close to the family, and recently Professor Hummel, an executive member of the DDP and a Reichstag deputy, had joined this circle: 'Conjectures,' the statement continued, 'which are founded on the fact that Professor Hummel is also a director of the I.G. Farbenindustrie, are feeble. The allegations purporting an interest, even a minority interest, of the I.G. Farbenindustrie or any other business enterprise in the Frankfurter Societäts-Druckerei, in any form whatsoever, are untrue.' The denial did not dispel suspicions.

The editors of the *Frankfurter Zeitung* remained unaware of the exact details of the transaction at first. As a result, the change in ownership did not bring any sudden volte-face in the editorial policy of the paper. Bosch did not think this desirable, nor did the collegiate system of formulating editorial policy permit it. However, gradual changes in personnel were made, and editorial policy began slowly to shift. More than a year elapsed before Bernhard Guttmann, the Berlin correspondent, was replaced. As he was already sixty years old, his departure could be presented as voluntary retirement. In June 1930 he withdrew quietly with his pension to the Black Forest where he lived for another thirty active years; he continued to write articles for the *Frankfurter Zeitung*, but on exclusively non-political topics. When Ernst Feder asked one of the Simons in November

---

See also Fritz ter Meer, *Die I.G. Farben Industrie Aktiengesellschaft* (Düsseldorf, 1953), pp. 56f.

32 This is clear from the correspondence in the NL Payer.

1929 why Guttmann was going to be leaving the paper, he received an evasive reply.[33]

Guttmann's place in Berlin was taken by Rudolf Kircher, who since October 1920 had been the paper's political correspondent in London. Kircher's job in London was given to Friedrich Sieburg, formerly Paris correspondent; Benno Reifenberg in turn replaced Sieburg in Paris. Kircher was a great admirer of British democracy and parliamentary practice and was the most prolific German interpreter of British life in the Weimar years.[34] He believed that politics had to be the pursuit of the possible. 'There exists no higher political art than the art of compromise', he wrote. 'Political realism', 'constructive criticism', 'self-confidence', and the ability to reach and accept compromise were features of parliamentary practice that were indispensable if democratic government was to function properly.[35] When he returned to Germany in June 1930 to head the Berlin office of the *Frankfurter Zeitung*, he had been out of the country, except for brief visits, for over ten years. He moved into the most important political post on the *Frankfurter Zeitung* at a time when pragmatism was hardly fashionable and when the chances of observing in Germany the standards of political procedure which had pleased him in England were more remote than ever.

Compared to Guttmann's spirited and pungent reporting, Kircher's political pieces were restrained and calculating. In London he had developed a style of journalism which he brought with him to Berlin. The reports from the Berlin office became more factual and reserved in tone, less polemical than hitherto. Sharp criticism did not disappear

[33] Feder diary, 15 and 18 November 1929. After the Second World War Guttmann was one of the founders of *Die Gegenwart*, a weekly journal of political commentary.

[34] See his books, *Engländer* (Frankfurt a.M., 1926), in translation as *Powers and Pillars: Intimate Portraits of British Personalities*, trans. C. Vesey (London, 1928); *Fair Play: Sport, Spiel und Geist in England* (Frankfurt a.M., 1927), in translation as *Fair Play: The Games of Merrie England*, trans. R.N. Bradley (London, 1928); *Wie's die Engländer machen: Politik, Gesellschaft und Literatur im demokratischen England* (Frankfurt a.M., 1929), in translation as *How they do it in England*, trans. Frances, Countess of Warwick (London, 1930).

[35] *How they do it in England*, pp. 45ff., 62.

altogether, but the intention was constructive, for Kircher believed that political and social realities had to be faced and that problems had to be tackled, piecemeal if need be, on the basis of facts and not some fanciful theories and ideals.

Another of Hummel and Bosch's victims was Arthur Feiler, an economic expert in the political section. For many years Heinrich Simon had been less than happy with Feiler, and when the prospective new shareholders had expressed their dissatisfaction with Feiler, the Simons had acquiesced to his removal. Once again, as in Guttmann's case, the dismissal was not hurried, and Feiler was not dropped from the paper's pay-roll until early 1931; however, in the interval comparatively few articles of his appeared in the paper. Feiler was replaced by Erich Welter from the economic staff, a man who had always been at loggerheads with him because of his impassioned and radical views on economic matters, particularly on socialization. Both Guttmann and Feiler were members of the DDP. Kircher and Welter did not belong to any party. It may not have been pure coincidence that the two new appointees were Gentiles whereas their predecessors were both Jews. In each case, Guttmann's and Feiler's, a personal settlement was reached between the owners and the journalist without involving the whole editorial board directly. Consequently, the departure of the two men did not appear as a dismissal. Feiler subsequently devoted himself to university teaching; in 1932 he was appointed full professor at Königsberg. In the summer of 1933 he emigrated and joined the faculty of the New School for Social Research in New York.

One other important change took place in June 1929. Friedrich von Payer retired as chairman of the board of directors. Because of the rotation system used by the board, his term as chairman had elapsed. One of the more enthusiastic proponents of the link with Bosch took his place, Rudolf Schwander.

Despite the injection of almost three million marks in capital into the FSD, its economic outlook did not improve. The circulation of the *Frankfurter Zeitung* continued to rise slightly, but with the onset of the general economic depression advertising fell off drastically. Within eighteen

months of the deal with Bosch the FSD had exhausted its
new capital resources. In 1930 a further 14·5 per cent of the
firm's shares—these had previously belonged to the so-called
small shareholders, friends of the Simon family—were purchased by Bosch through Hummel, so that now Farben
capital owned 49·5 per cent of the FSD.

If the new co-owners did not, and could not, openly
dictate editorial policy, the staff changes after 1929—simply
the difference in character and views of Kircher, Welter,
Schwander, and Hummel on the one hand, compared to
Guttmann, Feiler, and Payer on the other—made modifications in policy inevitable. Kircher's voice from Berlin soon
gave the keynote for the political attitudes enunciated in the
paper.[36] Kircher was an intimate friend of Heinrich Simon
and provided a channel for the discreet implementation of
the general political directives from Bosch and Hummel.
Following the tone he set, the editorial pronouncements of
the *Frankfurter Zeitung* assumed a new elasticity. The
paper's hitherto often noticeable tendency to make doctrinaire judgements grew weaker; 'political realism' now characterized its editorial stance. For example, the former basically
negative attitude towards reform and reconstruction of the
liberal centre gave way to an appeal for wholesale political
reorganization, for the creation of broad political groupings
which would be representative of the major streams of
political opinion in Germany. Oskar Stark, the Reichstag
correspondent, described the political reorientation as a new
class consciousness on the part of the paper. In the summer
of 1930 he told Ernst Feder that the *bürgerliche* tendency
which had recently been introduced by Heinrich Simon and
Kircher was not to his liking and added that he was considering taking a job in industry as a result.[37]

For some readers the modifications in policy were too
subtle to be noticed. Others considered the shift in editorial
policy as simply a sober reaction on the part of the paper's
owners and editors to the intense economic and political
crisis afflicting Germany. Nevertheless, some did recognize

[36] Benno Reifenberg in *Die Gegenwart*, XI/special issue (31 October 1956),
pp. 44f.
[37] Feder diary, 22 August 1930 (*Heute*, p. 263).

that the new tone was connected with the changes in the administration and structure of the FSD, news of which inevitably leaked out in part. 'I like the paper very much since the changes', a member of the executive of the State Party wrote to the former Reichswehr minister Gessler, making special reference to Schwander's influence as chairman of the board of directors.[38] Anton Erkelenz felt differently. '. . . on the whole I still think highly of the *Frankfurter Zeitung*', he wrote in a letter in August 1930. 'But the new political orientation is taking the paper considerably further to the right than the true [political] inclinations of the leading gentlemen should permit.'[39] The editors of *Das Tage-Buch* were more acerbic. They had got wind of the changes in ownership and in January 1931 disclosed them in broad outline, lamenting the surrender of the *Frankfurter Zeitung*, 'this classic organ of democracy', to 'those very forces against which it had battled for 84 [*sic*] years'. Regardless of the form of the arrangement with Farben, the article continued, the fact that the chemical trust had bought into the Frankfurt publishing house could no longer be concealed. First there had been personnel changes—the departure of 'the most notable publicists in this school of German journalism'—and gradually the new regime was also making its influence felt in the content of the paper.

That this highly cultured editorial board, educated in such honourable traditions, could sink to the same level as that of the *Deutsche Allgemeine Zeitung*—a base, malicious, and banal representative of group interests—is hardly the question. The chemical industry is, of course, basically different from the cannibalistic prototype of our heavy industrialists. However, in more refined, more intelligent ways . . . the *Frankfurter Zeitung* is already revealing a growing sympathy for those political and economic ideas whose perniciousness it accepted as beyond question recently; and the paper has begun, with its gentle reproaches, a process of distancing itself from its former friends.[40]

On the following day the *Frankfurter Zeitung* published an immediate *démenti*:[41] ownership of the majority interest in

---

[38] Rosa Kempf, a member of the executive of the State Party, in a letter to Gessler, 24 May 1932, NL Gessler, 19, p. 27, Bundesarchiv Koblenz.

[39] Erkelenz to Ludwig Bothas, 2 August 1930, NL Erkelenz, 128; see also Erkelenz to W. Cohnstaedt, 20 July 1931, NL Erkelenz, 61.

[40] *Das Tage-Buch*, XII (24 January 1931), pp. 125f.

[41] *FZ*, 66, 25 January 1931.

the FSD by the Simon-Sonnemann family, and the complete independence of editorial policy, were unaltered; nor was one single share in the hands of I.G. Farben or any other industrial corporation. 'However,' the statement went on, 'it is of course only natural that the storms of the present day, the struggle of opinions and generations, have not roared by without leaving some mark on us as well. No community, no matter how close it might be, is protected in this turbulent period from disputes and their consequences in staff relations.' The editors of *Das Tage-Buch* scoffed at this response, pointing out that the *Frankfurter Zeitung* had neither denied nor adequately countered the charge that it was being subjected to pressure from I.G. Farben; direct ownership was not the only way to assure influence.[42] The *Frankfurter Zeitung* did not bother to continue the exchange.

Cutbacks in spending and other efforts at retrenchment were of little avail; the FSD continued to lose money at a breathtaking rate. In September 1931 the three daily editions of the paper were cut to two. The seventy-fifth anniversary of the *Frankfurter Zeitung* was celebrated quietly on 29 October 1931 with only a sixteen-page commemorative issue and the publication of a short treatise by Heinrich Simon about the youth of Leopold Sonnemann. Already in 1928 the decision had been made that the firm could not afford the expense of hiring a historian to bring the *Frankfurter Zeitung*'s history up to date, from 1911 to the present. In 1931 circulation continued to creep upwards and by the end of the year accounted for 60 per cent of the paper's income[43]—in relation to advertising income, which now stood at 40 per cent, the exact reverse from earlier years. At the end of 1931 losses for that year were estimated at 1·2 million marks. The prospects for 1932 looked very bleak indeed.[44]

Towards the end of 1931 the Simon brothers finally gave up the idea of tenaciously maintaining a majority interest in

[42] *Das Tage-Buch*, XII (31 January 1931), p. 166.

[43] *FZ*, 967, 30 December 1931.

[44] See C.F. von Siemens to H. Schmitz, 14 December 1931, NL Siemens 4/Lf514.

the FSD. Further capital was again required, and as Bosch was reluctant to sink more money into the enterprise, Carl Friedrich von Siemens, the electrical magnate and president of the German railroads, was offered 25 per cent of the family shares. Had Siemens accepted the offer the family would have been left with only one-quarter ownership. However, he refused, partly because of the unfavourable terms of the offer and partly because of the disquieting economic situation in general, which in his opinion forbade any unpromising investments.[45]

In 1929 the FSD concluded a transaction with I.G. Farben which ran counter to the spiritual legacy of Leopold Sonnemann. In 1931 his heirs were prepared to turn over the firm, almost entirely, to industrial interests. Long-standing beliefs and cherished traditions were in a state of flux on all fronts in Germany at the end of the 1920s: in the arts, in politics, in social behaviour, in morality, in values. The developments in the Frankfurter Societäts-Druckerei were only symptomatic of the turmoil and fluidity of the situation. The depression was not responsible for the firm's difficulties; it only exacerbated them.

[45] Ibidem; and also Siemens to Dr. Simon, 14 December 1931, NL Siemens, 4/Lf514.

VII

ULLSTEIN *v.* ULLSTEIN

In mid-December 1929, shortly after his marriage to Rosie Gräfenberg, Franz Ullstein received a letter from Paris from a Bureau International de Presse.[1] Enclosed was an article in manuscript form entitled 'Journalism, Espionage and Love'. The subject of the article was Frau Dr. Rosie Gräfenberg; she was described as a secret agent of the German ambassador in Paris, Leopold von Hoesch. The accompanying letter, which went even further by suggesting that Rosie was also spying for France and was therefore a double-agent, advised an immediate denial if Franz Ullstein considered the allegations false. The letter was signed by a Joseph Matthes.

Matthes was a notorious political charlatan. From 1909 to 1915 he had been an editor of the liberal *Aschaffenburger Zeitung*. Lawsuits for slander had been brought against him repeatedly. After the war he had been a leader of the Rhenish separatist movement, and since 1924 had been living in exile in Paris. His Bureau International de Presse was a small disreputable undertaking, scorned by all except the most unscrupulous scandal-mongering tabloids. In fact the main purpose of this news syndicate was to serve as a front for Matthes's blackmail operations.

When Franz Ullstein did cable an emphatic denial and warning to Matthes, the latter replied that the whole matter would now be delved into thoroughly. At the same time he sent copies of his correspondence with Franz Ullstein to Leo Stahl, the Paris correspondent of the *Vossische Zeitung*. Stahl, out of curiosity, contacted Matthes and was shown several photocopied pages of documents, supposedly from the political section of the police archives. The documents seemed to substantiate the charges that Rosie Ullstein had at least been suspected of spying. Stahl reported his discovery

[1] The following account is based on the briefs presented in the Ullstein *v.* Ullstein lawsuit; see above, p. 116, n. 31; and on articles in the press covering the case.

to Berlin and was instructed by the other Ullstein brothers to pay Matthes the money he demanded as compensation for the fees which he and the author of the article had lost. Thereupon the Paris correspondent paid Matthes 3,000 francs.

On 15 January 1930 Franz Ullstein, unaware of the developments of the past month, returned to Berlin from a rest cure in a sanatorium in Dresden. Three days later he was informed by his brothers that he would be wise to divorce Rosie and withdraw from his post as managing director of the firm. On 20 January Franz's lawyers, Max Alsberg and Paul Levi, requested of the supervisory board of Ullstein that some form of proof for the charges against Rosie be provided. The plea was in vain. On 28 January, by a majority vote of the shareholders, that is by vote of the rest of the family, Franz Ullstein was discharged of all his duties in the firm and banished. He was not permitted to come to the firm, and even the private telephone line between his home and the Ullstein offices on the Kochstrasse was cut.

The most active conspirators against Franz were his brother Louis, Louis's son Heinz and son-in-law Fritz Ross. Hans, the eldest brother, was too incapacitated to take sides. Both Rudolf and Hermann backed the ousting of Franz, although Hermann laboured under pangs of guilt and soon made his peace with Franz.[2]

Georg Bernhard sided with the anti-Franz camp as soon as he got wind of the Paris affair. Without bothering personally to verify the fantastic accusations levelled against Rosie Ullstein, Bernhard adopted the line that the accuracy or the inaccuracy of the allegations was not really important. What was important was the reputation and honour of the Ullstein house. The mere possibility that the accusations might be true, Bernhard tried to explain in a letter to Franz on 21 January 1930,[3] was justification enough for the steps being taken. Because of Bernhard's prominence as a

---

[2] See the interview which Hermann Ullstein gave to the *Neue Wiener Journal*, 27 May 1930.

[3] Reprinted in Frankfurter, Brief, pp. 12f. By 21 January the two men were no longer on speaking terms.

public figure and also because he gradually became the most aggressive of Franz's opponents, one camp in the Ullstein house came to be called the 'Bernadines', the other the 'Franciscans'.[4]

Bernhard was spurred to action by two lines of thought—one idealistic and one self-seeking—which often blended and became indistinguishable. First, he was truly anxious about the future of the *Vossische Zeitung*. Were one iota of the rumours about Rosie being a spy—whether for Germany or France or both—true, then in Bernhard's opinion the *Vossische Zeitung* was finished. A newspaper which for over a decade had fought for Franco-German reconciliation and European understanding could never survive the public scandal which would be touched off by the disclosure that the wife of one of the owners and administrators had in some way been connected with secret intelligence work. Therefore, as far as Bernhard was concerned, immediate precautions had to be taken: Franz had to divorce Rosie and, into the bargain, withdraw from his executive station in the firm. In other words, Bernhard decided that Rosie was to be considered guilty until proved innocent.[5]

Even Bernhard, with all his inconstancy and excitability, would not have swallowed this line of argument under normal circumstances. Ironically, just a few months earlier he had warned his readers to guard against informers; Germany was full of them. 'When informers notice that documents are desired, documents are forged', he wrote. 'Those who pay for documents must realize that they are stimulating the market for forgeries.'[6] But now growing uncertainty about his future in the Ullstein firm and the alarming sensation of witnessing his authority slowly suffocating in the executive offices turned Bernhard into a highly nervous and vindictive

---

[4] Koestler, *Arrow in the Blue*, p. 212, remembers that the whole firm, 'from editor to office boy', split into two hostile camps.

[5] Bernhard had heard that some kind of document mentioning Rosie was also on file in the Reichswehr ministry. 'Whether the allegations are true or not is irrelevant', he wrote to Franz on 21 January. 'The danger for the house rests in what the documents say and in the fact that we cannot disprove the accuracy, but that on the other hand a third party can prove the existence, of the documents.' Printed in Frankfurter, Brief, p. 13.

[6] *VZ*, 161, 7 July 1929.

man. Anger and hatred sapped his reasoning powers. Rosie Ullstein he saw as the personification of deceit, disease, and destruction. A normal code of values and behaviour could not be applied to her. She embodied evil and hence could be fought with all means imaginable. Evidence against her could be accepted from disreputable characters with whom Bernhard otherwise would have had no truck. Stories about the sexual activities of Rosie Ullstein at the age of twelve could be fabricated and related, supposedly as proof that she was perfect material for espionage work. But most remarkable of all, Bernhard could league himself with his most inveterate enemies—Louis Ullstein, Fritz Ross, and Heinz Ullstein, men who for years had been trying to remove him from his post—and with complete insensitivity and disregard for the personal feelings of Franz Ullstein, could turn brutally on his former friend and patron.

Franz contested the right of the family, the other shareholders that is, to depose him from his executive office. He took the matter to a commercial court for arbitration. Franz's lawyers argued that neither the shareholders nor the supervisory board of directors could remove the general managing director from his post without officially stating a reason. However, in June the court decided against Franz, purely on the basis of the theoretical division of authority, responsibility, and control in a joint-stock company.[7] Enraged by the decision, Franz began to seek a way of withdrawing his share of capital in the firm.

In the meantime Franz and Rosie Ullstein had begun legal proceedings against Louis and Rudolf Ullstein, Fritz Ross, Georg Bernhard, and Leo Stahl because of the insinuations that Rosie had been a spy. A disclaimer was demanded. Certain junior members of the family then permitted some information about the fraternal feud to be printed in two Berlin scandal sheets. Statements from both sides followed. On 22 February a Dortmund paper wrote: 'For the last fortnight the conflict which has broken out among the Ullstein brothers has been the sensation of the capital city. What at first was treated only as rumour in

7 *FZ*, 446, 18 June 1930.

political circles became the topic of discussion for the public at large owing to the publication by a number of papers of some of the facts of the case.'[8] In April, May and June preliminary hearings were held at which the counsels for the plaintiffs and the defendants presented their briefs. These hearings were open and were covered by the press. By and large the press handled the affair gingerly. The reports on the hearings were generally restrained and usually appeared on an inside page. Although the actual court case did not take place until March 1931, the most important details were public knowledge by the early summer of 1930.

Already at the start of the preliminary hearings it was quite clear that the evidence for the defence, which tried to show that Rosie Ullstein had been suspected of being a spy, did not stand up to examination. The police documents which Stahl claimed he had seen initially in Paris never re-appeared and had presumably been forgeries. Léon Blum, who was Rosie's attorney in Paris and had access to police reports, vouchsafed to assert that no incriminating material existed in the records of the Sûreté Générale. A note on Rosie Ullstein in the Reichswehr files in Berlin turned out to be completely meaningless, and the public prosecutor declared that the state had no cause whatever to proceed against Rosie.

From April onwards Bernhard's world came crashing in around him. At the end of the month he himself visited Paris and met Matthes on two occasions. He later said that he had spent three hours examining documents which dealt with the activities of Rosie Ullstein between 1925 and 1929 and whose authenticity could not be doubted.[9] By contacting Matthes personally, he, the editor of a national newspaper, a Reichstag deputy, and president of the International Federation of Journalists, had laid himself open to the charge of consorting with a separatist and traitor. Moreover, the documents, like the ones Stahl claimed to have seen, were never produced, only constantly mentioned.

8 *General-Anzeiger* (Dortmund), 53, 22 February 1930.
9 Bernhard statement in *VZ*, 320, 10 July 1930.

In April the other Ullstein brothers decided to part with Bernhard at the end of the year, even if this would cost the firm 600,000 marks, the amount Bernhard demanded as severance pay in view of the firm's breach of contract. [10] In January he had sided with his adversaries of long standing in the hope of prolonging his career in the Ullstein firm. The desperate gamble had backfired. The public was told that the forthcoming departure of Bernhard had nothing to do with the present disagreements in the family and had been under negotiation for some time. Hermann Ullstein ascribed the decision to 'political differences'. [11] Since the four brothers and some of the junior partners had for years been trying to remove Bernhard and since Franz had been his sole adamant protector, Hermann Ullstein's account was not incorrect. On the other hand, without the personal animosities that had poisoned the atmosphere in the Ullstein house, Bernhard might still have remained with the firm for a good number of years, if only because of the enormous settlement which he was prepared to exact.

If commentators in the press happened to reveal sympathies for one side or the other, they always favoured Franz and Rosie Ullstein on grounds of the unbecoming methods—the dealings with Matthes, the vulgar elaborations on Rosie's sexual life—employed by their opponents. In June and July the journal *Das Tage-Buch* opened its pages to the cause of Franz Ullstein and his wife. [12] Encouraged by the attitude of the press, Franz became more confident and increasingly convinced that the other side did not in fact have any concrete evidence against Rosie. In mid-May Hermann Ullstein announced that he was withdrawing from the anti-Franz camp. As Franz grew more confident, he grew more aggressive as well.

---

[10] *Neues Wiener Journal*, 25 May 1930. The exact terms of Bernhard's contract with Ullstein could not be ascertained. See also Feder diary, 26 April 1930.

[11] See the interview of Georg Bernhard in *Neues Wiener Journal*, 25 May 1930, and that of Hermann Ullstein two days later.

[12] *Die Weltbühne* then, presumably on account of its rivalry with *Das Tage-Buch* rather than because of any intention or desire to identify itself with Bernhard's cause, printed an article by Bernhard, Nr. 29 (15 July 1930), pp. 82ff.

He became obsessed with destroying the public career of
Georg Bernhard, to whom he attached the greatest guilt in
the germination of the whole squalid affair. His attack
began indirectly, with an article in *Das Tage-Buch* written
by a regular contributor to the journal, Josef Bornstein.[13]
The article was a combination of brilliantly argued refutation
of the spy charges and counterattack. Material and opinions
had been made available to Bornstein by Franz Ullstein and
his wife. Bernhard was censured incisively for having 'over-
reacted' to certain indications that Rosie Ullstein wished to
have some influence on policy in the firm. Bernhard viewed
the remarks as libellous and immediately filed a suit for
defamation against Bornstein and Franz Ullstein.[14]

Several days later Franz Ullstein himself published an
article in *Das Tage-Buch* which spat venom.[15] 'My case is of
burning interest to the public', he wrote, 'only because it
has gradually become an eminently *political* one. . . .' And
it was Georg Bernhard and Leo Stahl who had made it such
by consorting with 'one of the most evil political adventurers'
of the day, the Esterhazy of the Ullstein case, Joseph
Matthes. Matthes, Franz Ullstein continued, had indeed
become the *régisseur* of the present drama, with Bernhard
and Stahl in the lead roles and the other Ullstein brothers
with walk-on parts. A challenge was then issued to both the
Democratic Party and the Reich Association of the German
Press to investigate thoroughly this 'continuing co-operation'
between Bernhard, the DDP deputy and chairman of the
journalists' national organization, and Matthes, 'the salaried
separatist and French policy spy'.

The DDP did take action. On 18 July the Reichstag was
dissolved and new elections were set for September. Because
of the public scandal surrounding the Ullstein firm, the
party leadership was reluctant to agree to Bernhard's candidacy. A three-man committee was set up to look specifically
into Bernhard's behaviour in the whole Ullstein affair. The
lawyer and *Oberpräsident* of Pomerania, Julius Lippmann,

13 *Das Tage-Buch*, XI (28 June 1930), pp. 1020ff.
14 Bernhard, *VZ*, 320, 10 July 1930.
15 *Das Tage-Buch*, XI (28 June 1930), pp. 1109ff.

chaired the committee; Otto Nuschke, the chief editor of the *Berliner Volks-Zeitung*, was appointed by the party; and Theodor Heuss was chosen by Bernhard as the party member most likely to understand his position and actions.[16] The committee held hearings and deliberated for two days, 26-7 July, and then reached a unanimous decision. It appreciated, it said in its report, Bernhard's intense concern for the editorial independence of the *Vossische Zeitung* and realized that Bernhard had considered the danger of intrusion and interference great. 'Nevertheless, we must reproach him for the form which the defence used. Errors were committed in this respect which must be regarded as incompatible with his position as a leader in German public life. This judgement applies particularly to his relations with the separatist Matthes.'[17] In the next days all regular party work was interrupted by the startling and, for most Democrats, unexpected news of the founding of the German State Party, which envisaged, to begin with, an amalgamation of the DDP with the Young German Order, one of the earliest and also more moderate *bündisch* organizations; and with the DVP, if it wished to join. When the excitement and commotion had settled somewhat, the DDP executive noticed to its surprise that Bernhard's renomination was being rapidly pushed through by his supporters in the Potsdam I constituency.[18] On 14 August Franz Ullstein wrote to Hermann Dietrich, the Democratic vice-chancellor and economic minister in Brüning's government, that he found it incredible that Bernhard could even be considered for nomination again after the judgement passed on him by the DDP's 'court of honour'. His candidacy would be 'a catastrophe for the State Party'.[19] The leadership of the DDP and of the *Jung-deutschen* exerted pressure on the party caucus which had to

[16] According to Heuss, Bernhard chose him because he was not a deputy at the time—he had failed to be re-elected in 1928—and occupied himself principally with journalism. Heuss, *Die Machtergreifung und das Ermächtigungsgesetz*, ed. E. Pikart (Tübingen, 1967), pp. 42f.

[17] A draft copy of the report of the committee is in NL Heuss.

[18] 'Is it really true that Georg Bernhard is to be put up again?', Koch-Weser asked the general secretary of the DDP, Werner Stephan, in a letter on 6 August 1930. 'Then I'd suggest that we pack it in.' NL Koch-Weser, 105, p. 213.

[19] NL Dietrich, 126, p. 57.

ratify nominations, and on 16 August Dietrich could reply with relief to Franz Ullstein: 'The Bernhard matter is settled. I'll not give up the State Party.'[20] A week later, August Weber, an unwavering proponent of liberal unity and a chairman of the Liberal Association, was nominated lead candidate in Potsdam I. Bernhard claimed that the DDP organization in Potsdam I and even the DDP's central nominations' committee (*Aktionsausschuss*) backed his nomination almost unanimously; only executive wire-pulling in the party destroyed his candidacy.[21]

In the meantime Bernhard had found his existence in the Ullstein offices bearable no longer. At the end of July he decided that he could not wait out the year and resigned all his duties. On 8 August his name appeared for the last time as that of the chief editor of the *Vossische Zeitung*. He proceeded, almost immediately, to take up a post that had been waiting for him since May, a managing directorship in the Association of German Department Stores.

Now, without direct ties with the press, Bernhard's chairmanship of the national press association became incongruous. Moreover, since early July prominent voices in the nation's press had come out in favour of an investigation of Bernhard's role in the Ullstein affair. Most press people regarded Bernhard's dealings with Matthes as outrageous and many echoed Franz Ullstein's assertion that Bernhard was doing harm to the entire journalistic profession as long as he was permitted to remain head of the press organization.[22] On 4 July 1930 Bernhard actually did offer to resign, but the Berlin branch of the press association, feeling that the situation did not as yet call for urgent action, hushed up the offer. The events of the rest of the summer, however, strengthened feeling against Bernhard, and at the annual conference in October he resigned the chair without oppo-

[20] NL Dietrich, 126, p. 55.

[21] Bernhard to A. Günther, 8 September 1930, NL Herrmann, 11, pp. 185f. See also Feder's report of his conversation with Bernhard, diary, 7 August 1930.

[22] See for example the remarks of the conservative journalist Rudolf Pechel to Fritz Büchner, chief editor of the *MNN*, 5 July 1930, NL Pechel, 52, Bundesarchiv Koblenz. Both men were executive members of the press association.

sition.[23] His political and journalistic career in Germany was at an end.

The Bernhard story, as Hellmut von Gerlach suggested,[24] was an almost perfect classical tragedy—'quem deus perdere vult, dementat prius.' A man of intelligence, of professional and public standing, of influence, was destroyed by hubris. Bernhard claimed that he was acting only with the interests of the *Vossische Zeitung* at heart. He no doubt believed this himself. But his innumerable involvements outside publishing—from politics to teaching, to, for example, active work in the Pro-Palestine Committee—allowed him precious little time to learn what the exact interests of the paper were and to look after them with care. He became enmeshed in the sordid accusations against Rosie Ullstein not because he had any evil intentions but because his injured pride clouded his vision and thinking. Bernhard was at no time completely convinced that Rosie Ullstein was actually a spy, and he was well aware that his case rested on the suspect reports of informers. He should have realized that the *Vossische Zeitung* was in no way endangered by the existence of these reports. If published by scandal sheets, they should have been ignored; if repeated by reputable journals, these could have been taken to court. The *Vossische Zeitung* would not have been affected adversely. After all, the nationalist right had for years slandered Bernhard with allegations that he was in the pay of the French, and it never crossed his mind that he might be a liability to the paper which he edited. Bernhard, however, felt threatened by Rosie; he suspected her of intrigues against him and was therefore prepared to believe that other people had suspected her of greater iniquities. Once engaged in battle, Bernhard's self-esteem did not permit him to throw in the towel ever. Such was his character. In the war he had supported the

[23] See Bernhard's exchange of letters with A. Günther, a leading member of the Leipzig branch of the press association; letters of 3 and 8 September 1930, NL Herrmann, 11, pp. 181ff. See also the protocol of the meeting of the executive committee of the Reich Association of the German Press, 12 October 1930, available in the documents of Pressestelle II Hamburg (AII 2a), Hauptstaatsarchiv Hamburg.

[24] *General-Anzeiger* (Dortmund), 195, 18 July 1930; printed also in *Das Tage-Buch*, XI (19 July 1930), pp. 1149ff.

general staff to the very end, not out of conviction but because he could not admit personal error. In 1930 he allowed himself to be crucified by his ambition and his *amour propre.*

The outcome of the affair when it finally reached the courts in March 1931 was easily predictable. The suit by Franz and Rosie against the other brothers, Bernhard, and Stahl, began final hearings on 12 March but was recessed to await the verdict in Bernhard's suit against Franz and the journalist Bornstein which began a week later. The same witnesses appeared, the same stories were told, and the same newspaper articles were written as a year earlier. Only this time Bernhard and his lawyer Richard Frankfurter admitted finally, to the amazement of the Moabit courtroom, that their side had no official documents, either French or German, to present as evidence other than a summons to Rosie in 1925 from the prefecture in Paris to apply for an extension of her visa. The journalists who had covered the affair for over a year groaned at the unequivocal admission of defeat. However, when the judge pronounced his decision in the early hours of a Sunday morning, 29 March, Franz and Rosie Ullstein had little reason to celebrate; theirs was only a Pyrrhic victory, for their marriage had not been able to withstand the strain of the events of the past year. They had been divorced in December. The irony was great. In the *Berliner Tageblatt* Rudolf Olden poignantly described Franz Ullstein as the truly tragic figure of the whole case. 'When he had the group of well-wishers and the door of the courtroom behind him, he hurried, head down, his coat collar up, through the empty, almost dark corridors of the criminal court, to the steps, and out into the cold winter night.'[25]

The other Ullsteins accepted the decision and decided to reach a private settlement with Franz in their case. On 31 March in the *Vossische Zeitung* Hans, Louis, and Rudolf Ullstein publicly expressed their apologies about the whole affair, acknowledging that the allegations against Rosie had never been justified. In June the reconciliation of the five brothers was announced.[26] Franz and Hermann had rejoined the firm. Franz and Louis were now to be the co-chairmen of the supervisory board, Hermann and Rudolf deputy co-chairmen. Hans became the honorary head.

This was a stiff, artificial solution that solved few problems. It did not remove and was in fact the result of the rancour and ill feeling that had become deeply embedded in the brothers' attitudes towards each other. The greatly vaunted Ullstein family spirit, the devotion of individual members of the family, which reputedly had motivated so much of the firm's expansion in the twenties, had been sapped completely by the feud and was never revitalized. Co-operation among the brothers became formal and awkward. The elasticity in management that was purported to be the major advantage of family businesses was no longer present in the Ullstein house. Moreover, the tension of the ceasefire arrangement at the top pervaded the entire establishment. The journalists in the Ullstein firm were depressed by the whole affair. The brothers were so preoccupied with their personal quarrels that supervision of editorial policy came to rest in the hands of two political *blancs-becs*, Heinz Ullstein and Richard Müller.[27] Both men wished to swing the Ullstein papers more to the right.

The series of legal battles and settlements not only destroyed morale but dug deeply into the capital assets of the firm as well. Court costs were considerable. Germany's most brilliant and expensive lawyers were employed by both sides—Max Alsberg, Paul Levi, Rudolf Dix, Richard Frankfurter, Otto Landsberg, to mention but a few. Alsberg demanded an advance of RM 50,000 before he would even agree to take up the case for Franz and Rosie Ullstein.[28] The severance pay to Bernhard was also not a pittance. This strain on the house of Ullstein's liquidity came just when the depression was beginning to have its first serious effects on the firm.

---

[26] See the notice in the *Zeitungs-Verlag*, XXXII (13 June 1931), p. 466.
[27] Feder diary, 22 August 1930 (*Heute*, p. 263), and 30 September 1930.
[28] Riess, *Max Alsberg*, p. 234.

The Ullstein affair was interpreted in various ways by various sections of the public. Those commentators who sought to remain dispassionate in their judgements usually treated the whole case in terms of personalities; the framework for their generalizations did not extend beyond the Ullstein house. Those writing with a political purpose argued that more was at stake than merely the fate of one publishing enterprise: the Ullstein scandal symbolized, in the opinion of the political left and right, the decline and dissolution of liberalism and, for the left in addition, the decadence of capitalism.[29] The affair provided sufficient ammunition for many an extreme attack on the Weimar Republic and on Weimar society, from individuals and groups opposed to plutocracy and to an openly capitalist economy, from anti-Semites who revelled in this Jewish family feud, and from social conservatives who feared and despised the cosmopolitanism and the progressive attitudes of Ullstein.

The name Ullstein, like Rothschild, Carnegie, Hearst, Krupp, implied more than just a commercial concern. The size, the success, the resplendence of the business made the name representative in the minds of Germans of an entire way of life, of an entire social and political outlook. Ullstein, like the constitution, like Stresemann, like the Reichstag, like the Bauhaus, like Emil Ludwig, came to be regarded as a pillar of the Weimar state. The climax of the family struggle came at a time when the Weimar state could ill afford the weakening of any of its remaining supports. The constitution was being stretched out of all recognizable shape; Stresemann was dead; Brüning's 'constitutional authoritarianism' was rendering the Reichstag a passive onlooker in the legislative process; the Bauhaus was being attacked for 'art bolshevism'; Emil Ludwig had already emigrated to Switzerland. In one year the Ullstein scandal undid much of the political work of the firm during the past decade.

In the final analysis, the battle which flared among the Ullsteins in December 1929 and continued for over a year settled little. The roots of the feud lay well in the past but the explosion was touched off in large part by the course of

[29] See *Leipziger Volkszeitung*, 183, 8 August 1930.

events and the mood in the country at large. The Ullstein firm reflected the crisis of political belief that had infected most of the nation. The family disagreements could never have taken their virulent and vicious form had not bewilderment, perplexity, and insecurity become characteristic of the political mood of the Ullsteins and of their editors and correspondents. Leopold Schwarzschild, editor of *Das Tage-Buch*, was to look back on the affair surrounding Rosie Ullstein and to call it that 'extraordinary manifestation of the general decay in Germany'.[30]

---

[30] In his review of Hermann Ullstein's book, *Nation*, CLVI (10 April 1943), pp. 529f.

VIII

THE ADVENT OF STOICISM

The great coalition government which ruled Germany from June 1928 to the end of March 1930 was the coalition prescribed by the democratic press. All republican elements were well aware that if this government fell a power vacuum would result which might not allow itself to be filled in accordance with the procedure followed hitherto in the formation of governments. The democratic press therefore appealed for sanity on the part of the coalition parties and their leaders. Ernst Feder remarked: 'The national government is not in danger because of the strength of its opponents; it can only be threatened by its own weakness.'[1]

When the government did fall on 27 March 1930 because of its inability, or rather its unwillingness, to agree on a detail of the unemployment-benefit system, democrats were startled and dumbfounded by the apparent abandonment of reason. Although it was clear that the crisis which led to the resignation of the government had been instigated by the People's Party—its leaders were called *Krisenmacher*, crisis-mongers, and its policies *Katastrophenpolitik*—the immediate reaction of the leading democratic press was to condemn the SPD for its irresponsibility and lack of judgement in not bending slightly in order to save the coalition. The intransigence of the socialists had played into the hands of industry, capital, the military, the bourgeois right, and the east-Elbian Junkers, all forces which wished to remove the SPD from the government. Theodor Wolff said of the Social Democrats that 'they clubbed themselves on the head with a cudgel because they were being bothered by a fly.'[2] The *Frankfurter Zeitung* blamed them for pushing political opinion to the right. 'Parliamentary democracy suffered a great setback yesterday. . .', the paper concluded in its main editorial

---

[1] *BT*, 33, 20 January 1930.
[2] *BT*, 152, 30 March 1930.

article on 28 March. 'Everything has become dark and uncertain', it declared in an earlier edition on the same day.
'Fiscal measures by Article 48? A cabinet of civil servants
without a clear majority? Government by the right? We are
facing portentous developments.'[3]

The Centrist Heinrich Brüning was given the task of
forming a new government. On instructions from the Reich
president, Hindenburg, it was to be a government of political
personalities rather than of party spokesmen and was not to
include any representatives of the socialist left. By accepting
these conditions Brüning severely restricted his room for
manoeuvre in his search for parliamentary support; his only
hope of avoiding a vote of censure lay either in eliciting the
sufferance of the SPD or in gaining the confidence of the
nationalist right while of course maintaining the backing of
the smaller middle-class parties. However, for the eventuality
that he could not find sufficient parliamentary support, he
was equipped by the Reich president with the right to invoke
the emergency powers of the constitution, article 48, to
promulgate any necessary fiscal measures which the
Reichstag refused to sanction. Still under the Müller government the *Frankfurter Zeitung* had warned that the use of
article 48 for anything but an obvious emergency, in which
life, property, law and order were visibly endangered, would
undermine the whole concept of legality in the state. Indeed,
illegality would be encouraged and tendencies and developments in Reich politics sponsored which could conceivably
result in 'the complete suspension of constitutional liberties
and in actual dictatorship'. Since the overthrow and elimination of the present constitutional order were precisely the
goals of the radical right, any intentional manipulation, and
hence weakening, of the constitution would only assist the
enemies of the Republic.[4]

When Brüning took office the democratic press, in a
chorus, urged him not to abuse the constitution. He was
advised to make every effort to re-establish the great coalition by drawing the SPD into the government again. But

[3] *FZ*, 234, 28 March 1930.
[4] Lead article, *FZ*, 185, 10 March 1930.

beyond this caveat and this one concrete suggestion, editorial policy was characterized by anger, bewilderment, and frustration. The *Berliner Tageblatt* did state unequivocally that the use of article 48 to promulgate any normal legislation would represent a breach of the constitution; article 48 could never be a surrogate for a missing parliamentary majority.[5] On 14 July Günther Stein cautioned Brüning: 'A man who uses article 48 as a cover for his own inadequacy, who concentrates his energy on creating a state of emergency instead of solving the problem of finances, is breaking the constitution not only from a legal but also from a moral point of view. . . .'[6] However, when two days later both the political left and right decided on a test of strength in the Reichstag and when, consequently, the emergency machinery of the constitution was actually applied, the paper, while remaining intensely hostile to Brüning, retreated from its advance position and declined to repeat openly and without qualification its assertion that the use of article 48 for the present purposes was unconstitutional. Stein, from whose pen the most vehement attacks on Brüning had originated, was in turn soon sent on a six-month tour around Europe. In September 1931 he was given an Asian assignment and in late 1932 became Moscow correspondent. According to Erwin Topf, the agricultural correspondent of the *Tageblatt*, Stein's 'leftist tendencies' were no longer appreciated in the Mosse house. In 1931 his place in Berlin was taken by a more reserved commentator, the former Reichstag correspondent of the *Frankfurter Zeitung*, Oskar Stark.[7]

The *Frankfurter Zeitung* and the *Vossische Zeitung*, in contrast to the *Tageblatt*, never took as doctrinaire a position on article 48 initially. Once Brüning had had the Reichstag dissolved by Hindenburg and had invoked the emergency powers, these papers tended to turn a blind eye to the constitutional question. The Frankfurt paper now revealed the new elasticity that its editorial policy was beginning to assume since the link with I.G. Farben. Without ignoring or

5 Anonymous lead article, *BT*, 158, 3 April 1930.
6 *BT*, 327, 14 July 1930.
7 Erwin Topf, cited in Schwarz, *Theodor Wolff*, p. 241.

underestimating the worrying ramifications of Brüning's action, the *Frankfurter Zeitung* none the less declared on 22 July that the question of constitutionality in the application of the emergency powers was now only 'a subject for academic debate' (*Doktorfrage*), and the use of article 48 had to be accepted as a *fait accompli*. Moreover, the editorial added, now that the Reichstag was dissolved the continued use of article 48 to pass bills into law was justified. Principle and ideology were taking a back seat in the *Frankfurter Zeitung* to what Hermann Hummel had called 'calm objectivity' and 'political dynamics'.

Elections were set for 14 September. Throughout the summer the Ullstein, Mosse, and Sonnemann papers emphasized the awesome significance of the forthcoming election: the fate of German democracy was at stake. The choice confronting the nation was democracy or some form of authoritarian government; 'the crossroads' had been reached, in Theodor Wolff's words.[8] To prevent a 'disguised dictatorship' from becoming an 'open' one, an operable parliament had to be elected.[9]

Brüning and his cabinet were naturally subjected to sharp opposition on specific issues such as the *Osthilfe*, the aid programme organized for agriculture in the east; the cutbacks threatened in certain areas of social welfare; the wage reductions which were becoming increasingly common in industry; and the allotment of credit for the building of another pocket battleship. But these issues were, in the final analysis, completely swallowed by the overriding question of democracy or authoritarian experimentation. That only democratic government could extricate the country from the critical economic slump which it was experiencing and that authoritarian government would, on the other hand, lead to chaos, anarchy, and conceivably civil war, were the *a priori* foundations of the case presented by the democratic press.[10]

---

[8] *BT*, 338, 20 July 1930.

[9] The quotations are from the lead article in the *FZ*, 675, 10 September 1930; see also RK [Rudolf Kircher] in *FZ*, 632, 26 August 1930.

[10] See J.E.'s [Elbau's] articles, *VZ*, 190, 10 August 1930, and 214, 7 September 1930. In the first article he stated that democracy had liberated

The republican parties, the parties of the Weimar Coalition, had to be strengthened. Theodor Wolff enjoined his readers to 'buttress up the political left'.[11] The *Berliner Morgenpost* prescribed 'only the parties of healthy progress' for voters.[12] 'Vote republican!', the *Vossische Zeitung* trumpeted in enormous headlines on election day. Intensive propaganda and support for one particular party exclusively, most of the democratic press recognized, would have been incongruent with the type of campaign that was being conducted, that is with the sweeping issues being disputed, issues which crossed party lines. Yet, despite this awareness, one party did receive preferential treatment in the democratic press. No longer, however, was it the DDP.

By May 1930 even the *Frankfurter Zeitung* had finally given up hope in the DDP. Of the three major democratic newspapers, the Frankfurt paper, despite its frequently vehement criticism, had always been the DDP's most faithful supporter. The party was now seen to be in rapid dissolution, 'absolutely leaderless', relying on totally inappropriate 'pre-war methods and ideas'.[13] When the Reichstag was dissolved and the election campaign of August loomed near, it seemed doubtful whether the DDP would receive any positive treatment whatsoever from the Ullstein, Mosse, or Sonnemann papers.

The DDP chairman Erich Koch-Weser sensed that his party would be completely decimated in the elections and organized German liberalism virtually extinguished if radical precautionary measures were not taken immediately. After the May 1928 elections he had concluded that unification of the liberal parties of the centre was indispensable if liberalism was to be in a position to compete seriously with 'nationalist fantasies and Marxist utopias'.[14] Both he and Stresemann, in

---

Germany from chaos and implied that chaos would return if democracy disappeared. See also RK in *FZ*, 632, 26 August 1930.

[11] *BT*, 410, 31 August 1930.

[12] *BM*, 219, 13 September 1930.

[13] Lead article, *FZ*, 335, 6 May 1930.

[14] From an article by Koch-Weser in the *Demokratische Zeitungsdienst*, the party news service, 13 June 1928; NL Koch-Weser, 37, p. 157.

their subsequent conversations on liberal unity, had decided to encourage the Young German Order to participate in any eventual amalgamation of their parties.

On 27 July the establishment of a new party, the German State Party, was suddenly announced. Victor Hahn of the *8-Uhr-Abendblatt* commented: 'One morning we democratic newspaper publishers woke up, and there was no Democratic Party left.'[15] The State Party was founded by a number of DDP leaders in co-operation with Artur Mahraun, the 'grand master' of the Young German Order, with some Young Liberals including Josef Winschuh and Theodor Eschenburg, and with several representatives of the Christian trade-union organization. The DVP was also urged to join. The new party stressed that it hoped to consolidate all those elements which loyally supported the Republic, desired a stable European order based on Franco-German friendship, and wished to provide a certain minimum of social and economic security to citizens of the German state.[16]

For a week after its founding the State Party was the centre of political discussion and speculation in the press of all political colours. The combination of the demure and sedate Democratic Party and the extravagantly fanciful para-military Young German Order with its medieval, romantic trappings aroused wide interest. Much of the liberal press was exuberant about the new party, regarding its creation as possibly the overture to the complete reorganization and reform of the party-political structure in Germany.[17] Some of the most enthusiastic support for the State Party came from the *Kölnische Zeitung*, a highly respected paper of national liberal convictions which had always stood close to Stresemann but had consistently backed the efforts to bring about liberal unity. The arguments which this paper presented at the end of July to explain its position closely resembled, as they often had in the past, those of the

15 Cited in R.G., *Prelude*, p. 346.

16 For a short history of the State Party, see Erich Matthias and Rudolf Morsey, 'Die Deutsche Staatspartei', in *Das Ende der Parteien 1933*, ed. Matthias and Morsey (Düsseldorf, 1960), pp. 31ff.

17 A summary of press reactions is given in *Demokratischer Zeitungsdienst*, 30 July 1930; NL Dietrich, 222, p. 11.

Vossische Zeitung on the question of a liberal merger. The
political views of the latter publication were now being co-
ordinated by Julius Elbau. Both papers insisted that the
political situation demanded broad-mindedness. A return to
democracy was essential, and this was feasible only if the
republican parties won a majority in the elections; such a
majority, in turn, was only conceivable if a liberal party
which was prepared to co-operate with the SPD could assert
itself. The two papers pleaded with the DVP and its leader
Scholz to show a willingness to compromise and to join the
new party.[18] The Ullsteins donated RM 10,000 to it at the
beginning of August.[19] 'Something is in motion', wrote Elbau
on 1 August; 'everyone can sense that.'[20]

The *Frankfurter Zeitung* agreed with Elbau and, much to
the surprise of many observers, reacted very positively to the
new party. Since the beginning of the year the paper had
harped on the need for rejuvenating the old political parties,
to give them some appeal to youth which was showing
increasing hostility to the present political system. According
to the *Frankfurter Zeitung*, the inclusion of the Young
Germans gave the State Party this appeal. The party provided
'the young generation. . ., the most important element in
contemporary German politics', with 'scope for activity'
within the framework of constitutionalism and republicanism, wrote Rudolf Kircher.[21] Eighteen months earlier the
paper, which had always opposed any opportunistic alliance
between the DDP and liberal, let alone conservative, groups
to the right, would have been appalled and incensed by the
political marriage that Koch-Weser and Mahraun arranged. Of
all the leading Democrats Anton Erkelenz and Ludwig
Quidde had been treated most sympathetically by the
Frankfurt paper in the past; these two were among those who

[18] See the issues of the *Kölnische Zeitung* for the last days of July and the
first week of August 1930; the paper's position at the time is summarized in Kurt
Weinhold's *Verlag M. DuMont Schauberg, Köln* (Cologne, 1969), pp. 266ff. The
basic arguments of the *VZ* are presented in J.E.'s articles, 179, 29 July 1930, and
182, 1 August 1930.

[19] A memorandum dated 7 August 1930 in NL Koch-Weser, 105, p. 239.

[20] *VZ*, 182, 1 August 1930.

[21] *FZ*, 632, 26 August 1930; 654, 3 September 1930; see also the lead
articles in 555, 28 July; 559, 30 July; 625, 23 August 1930.

now refused to transfer their allegiance to the new party, because they were unable to reconcile their 'social-republican' ideas with the undisguised anti-Semitism and irrational, cult-oriented observances of the Young Germans. Erkelenz immediately joined the SPD; Quidde helped to found a Union of Independent Democrats, which in November constituted itself as the Radical Democratic Party.[22] The *Frankfurter Zeitung* of course felt uncomfortable about the anti-Semitic practices of the Young German Order—Jews were excluded from membership—but nevertheless the paper took great care to clothe its rebuke to Mahraun on this one point in very restrained, polite language.[23] Of the major democratic papers the *Frankfurter Zeitung* alone told its readers categorically that only one party was worthy of their votes, the State Party.[24] The virtually uncritical support for the new party in the election campaign was another important indication that fundamental changes had taken place in the FSD.

The *Berliner Tageblatt* was somewhat ambivalent and confused in its approach to the new party. Two days after its founding Helmut Sarwey wrote that the paper sympathized with the attempt to counter 'the atomization of the bourgeois centre and left' but that the measure of support which the paper could give the party depended entirely on its development. 'Our political position is firm,' he maintained, 'unaffected by the collapse and rebirth of parties. Everyone is familiar with it: it is republican, democratic, and social.'[25] Developments, however, did not please the editors and administration of the *Tageblatt*. Ernst Feder noted in his diary on 16 August: 'Democratic Party is dead, State Party is stillborn.' Martin Carbe and Rudolf Olden thought the party reactionary and privately advocated support of the SPD. Wolff himself, although dejected by many aspects of the State Party, apparently found the type of person who belonged to the Young Germans very attractive in character,

[22] See Erkelenz's letter to Koch-Weser, 29 July 1930, NL Erkelenz, 132; and Ludwig Quidde's statement in *Das Tage-Buch*, XI (9 August 1930), pp. 1255ff.

[23] Lead article, *FZ*, 583, 7 August 1930.

[24] *FZ*, 666, 7 September; 685, 14 September 1930.

[25] *BT*, 352, 29 July 1930.

and commended Mahraun for tying them to the Republic. [26] In the end both he and Feder came out in favour of the party, 'for reasons of expediency' according to Feder.[27]

When in the spring of 1930 Brüning threatened the Reichstag with article 48 and dissolution if it did not pass his financial bills, the democratic press entreated him to negotiate with the SPD and to bring the socialists back into the government. The *Vossische Zeitung* and *Frankfurter Zeitung* warned the chancellor explicitly against calling a national election. '. . . the inescapable consequence', the Frankfurt paper commented in a leader, 'would be a tremendous growth of the extremist parties and hence a fateful radicalization of political life with all the attendant dangers for the development of our constitutional and economic life.'[28] 'Tremendous growth' by a party was conceived by the *Frankfurter Zeitung* as a trebling of its strength. In June 1930 Hitler's National Socialist German Workers' Party (NSDAP) increased its representation in the Saxon Landtag from 5 to 14 seats, and the paper remarked that a comparable increase on the national level would be a miracle because economic and political conditions in Saxony were much worse than in the Reich as a whole.[29] In May 1928 the NSDAP had sent 12 deputies to the national parliament. Thirty-six seats were therefore the limit forecast by the *Frankfurter Zeitung*. Ernst Feder of the *Berliner Tageblatt* was prepared to give the Nazis the benefit of a few more seats: he estimated their next parliamentary delegation at between 40 and 45 members.[30] Ullstein's *BZ am Mittag* generously predicted 50 seats for the NSDAP.[31] Several days before the elections, Kurt Grossmann, Hellmut von Gerlach, Ernst Toller, Robert

[26] Feder diary, 16 August, 10 and 12 September 1930 (*Heute*, pp. 263, 266).

[27] *BT*, 410, 31 August 1930; Feder diary, 10 September 1930 (*Heute*, p. 266). In a letter on 13 September 1930 Wolff mentioned to Stolper the personal struggle which he had gone through before deciding to support the party; NL Stolper, 44.

[28] *FZ*, 444, 17 June 1930. See Bernhard's articles, *VZ*, 89, 13 April, and 172, 20 July 1930.

[29] Lead article, *FZ*, 460, 23 June 1930.

[30] Diary, 13 August 1930 (*Heute*, p. 262).

[31] *BZ am Mittag*, 247, 10 September 1930.

Kuczynski, and Carl von Ossietzky, all from the *Weltbühne* circle, were bandying about prognostications over coffee on Unter den Linden. Gerlach was willing to concede at most 25 seats to Hitler; Toller thought this to be far too high an estimate; Kuczynski forecast not more than 30 Nazis in the Reichstag; Ossietzky speculated on 36; and Grossmann was thought to be suffering from manic depression when he predicted 50 to 60 seats.[32] Opinions about the probable strength of the German Communist Party were not as divergent: its prospects were placed at between 50 and 60 deputies. On 14 September Germans elected 107 National Socialists and 77 Communists to the Reichstag.

There is no better illustration of the degree to which the political phenomenon of National Socialism was misunderstood than the discrepancy between the election predictions and the actual outcome of the voting on 14 September 1930. It was in fact not so much the nature of National Socialism that was misconstrued by German republicans, liberals, and democrats as the extent to which the German public was susceptible to its ideas and manifestations. The democratic press emphasized from the very beginning of its coverage of the movement that Nazism in itself presented no danger; the danger lay rather in the frame of mind of the nation as a whole and in the weakness of the republican state; the strength of the NSDAP was only a reflection of the fragility, inefficiency, and confusion of ideas displayed by the bourgeois parties. In view of this interpretation of Nazi successes, the underestimation of the vulnerability of the Weimar state is even more striking.

Prior to the 1930 elections, Hitler's party, despite its gains in local elections throughout the Reich in the past year, was still looked upon essentially as a lunatic fringe, a collection of 'petty bourgeois gone mad',[33] a haven for the politically homeless, the perennially dissatisfied, the ideological vagrants of politics. The Nazi leaders were called putschists, traitors, and criminals. Hitler was looked upon as a misfit, a casualty of the advance of history, a deranged

[32] Kurt R. Grossmann, *Ossietzky: Ein deutscher Patriot* (Munich, 1963), pp. 248f.

[33] J.E., *VZ*, 159, 5 July 1929.

demagogue not worthy of detailed attention. Nazi claims to legality were pronounced irrelevant. Violence and terror were described as the basis of Nazi political tactics, anti-Semitism as the core of the domestic programme. The *Frankfurter Zeitung* asserted that in his proposals for foreign policy 'Hitler means war.'[34] The NSDAP was in general belittled; it was dismissed as a product of economic instability; a party which would disappear, as it indeed almost had between 1924 and 1929, as soon as the country's economic difficulties were resolved. The only respect accorded to the party by the democratic press was prompted by the remarkable propaganda feats, the pageantry, the unrelenting activism of Hitler and his followers.

The National Socialists were occasionally called the Communists of the right, since both parties, the NSDAP and KPD, were supposed to be bent on the violent overthrow of the republican government. However, the NSDAP was regarded as by far the more dangerous of the two parties, because it cleverly knew how to disguise its treachery in the garb of nationalism and because it, in addition, was more sophisticated in its organization and propaganda techniques. The KPD was thought to be in an advanced state of decline despite recent increases in electoral support.[35]

Although the democratic press warned the public and its political leaders not to take Hitler and his party lightly, the confrontation with National Socialism in this press before the September elections of 1930 remained on a polemical level. No serious sustained attempt was made to analyse Nazi ideas, the social basis of the party's membership and support, the reasons for its strength in Thuringia, Saxony, and Schleswig-Holstein. Some members of the democratic press complained in fact that too many polemics were being written against the Nazis,[36] and that these served only as additional propaganda for the party. Liberal and democratic journalists constantly stated that reasoned discussion

[34] Lead article, *FZ*, 623, 2 September 1930.

[35] See Elbau, *VZ*, 68, 20 March 1930; lead article, *FZ*, 297, 22 April 1930.

[36] Feder for one; see his diary, 6 September and 16 December 1930 (*Heute*, pp. 266, 279).

of National Socialist ideas was not possible. Since Nazism was interpreted to be essentially an 'emotional outlet'[37] for all the contemporary negative social impulses of Germans, the only cure against it was said to be inspired, energetic government. In other words, the electorate had to give the republican parties a majority in parliament; these parties had to devote more attention to the aims which they had in common than those that separated them; and Brüning had to provide imaginative and responsible leadership.

Hermann Ullstein, the youngest of the five Ullstein brothers, was one leading member of the liberal press who felt particularly strongly that the liberal and democratic forces in the Republic were defaulting to their opponents instead of resolutely meeting the challenge extended. Like the other Ullsteins he was a man without very precise political ideas, but he was convinced that his political inclinations carried responsibilities with them. The decline of the DDP and of liberalism as a whole disturbed him deeply. He searched for explanations, and having, according to Vicki Baum 'a keen sense for sales propaganda, packaging and slogans',[38] he instinctively placed great stress on the mistakes committed and the omissions made by the democratic forces in the realm of publicity. A major portion of the blame for the decline of liberalism had to be attributed, he thought, to the press of liberal persuasion which had ignored its duties of inculcating attachment and commitment to the republican state amongst the public. In his view, the political influence of the moderate, liberal press on its readers was negligible compared to that of the nationalist papers of the right. Hugenberg, in Hermann Ullstein's opinion, 'made use of his power to the same extent that we [the liberal press] failed to employ ours. . . . While that section of the press remaining loyal to the Republic fought shy of taking a strong stand, the Hugenberg press drove home its advantages and took care to coddle Hitler's interests.'[39]

37 Lead article, *FZ*, 460, 23 June 1930.
38 *I Know What I'm Worth*, p. 238.
39 *Rise and Fall*, pp. 236ff.

In early 1928 Hermann Ullstein had resigned from his managerial position in the family business owing to the disputes which he was having with his brothers. Next to differences of opinion on how the firm should be administered, one of the subjects of contention was the degree to which Ullstein publications should be involved politically. Hermann wished to enhance the political commitment of such popular journals as the *BZ am Mittag* and the *Berliner Illustrirte Zeitung*, but he was outvoted on this matter by his brothers and the other directors, who already in 1928 were beginning to argue that for commercial reasons the house had to become not more outspoken but more thrifty in its political commentary.[40] According to Franz Ullstein the press was not meant to lead public opinion but to mirror it.[41] After his departure from the firm Hermann Ullstein was able to devote more attention to his political interests.

In October 1929 he attended the Democratic Party's national conference in Mannheim and there heard a speech on economic policy by Gustav Stolper, the widely respected editor of the *Deutsche Volkswirt*, a former Vienna economic correspondent for the *Vossische Zeitung*, and since 1926 a member of the DDP executive committee. Stolper's speech was an articulate affirmation of capitalism as the economic system capable of providing the 'greatest well-being of the individual' but it was also an elegant appeal to social justice within a free-enterprise economy.[42] Hermann Ullstein was captivated by the way Stolper formulated his ideas and by his presentation. *'What a leader he would be!'*, he wrote enthusiastically to his niece and her husband several days later. Stolper, he felt, was a man with ideas, style, and appeal; he deserved avid support, which should have been forthcoming from the liberal-democratic press, but was not. 'Our press', he continued in his letter, is short on praise; it

[40] Ibid., pp. 233ff.; also Hermann Ullstein, 'We Blundered Hitler into Power', *Saturday Evening Post*, Nr. 213 (13 July 1940), pp. 12ff.

[41] Franz Ullstein to Margaret T. Edelheim, 14 August 1944, Ullstein file, Leo Baeck Institute, New York.

[42] The speech is summarized in Toni Stolper, *Ein Leben in Brennpunkten unserer Zeit* (Tübingen, 1960), pp. 233ff. It was published as a pamphlet; a subsidy for this printing was provided by Hermann Hummel.

does not make potential leaders popular, and consequently actually acts as a handcuff on democracy, which could otherwise be victorious. . . . Practically the entire press is ignoring the acclamation which greeted the speech. And Elbau [the deputy editor of the *Vossische Zeitung*], who was present, is reserved and even caustic in his account, because he fears his lord and master [Georg] Bernhard. Bernhard, of course, has entirely different ideas [from Stolper] about everything and wishes to hear nothing of free individuals in a free economic system. He is an antipode. Direct taxes can never be high enough for him; the state can never be too involved in economic affairs as far as he is concerned; expenditure and wages can never be driven high enough. He is a harmful pest, because the *Vossische Zeitung* was surrendered to him, the Marxist. The party [the DDP] groans under the same burden. And the eleventh hour, when a reversal would still be possible, is slipping away. . . . A change must come, because Germany is crying out for it.[43]

This was a remarkable confession for an Ullstein to make, even privately. The youngest brother was siding with those members of the DDP who were sharply critical of the left-democratic press and was accepting as valid the charge that this press had failed to fulfil the responsibilities incumbent upon it. The letter also evidenced that there was no love lost between Hermann Ullstein and Georg Bernhard.

Hermann Ullstein saw in Gustav Stolper a potential leader around whom German democracy could rally, and he decided to use his influence and contacts to try and organize press support for Stolper and his economic ideas. He would attempt to form 'a phalanx in the German press', he informed Stolper, 'which fights for your goals'.[44] Not only would the political press of obvious liberal-democratic inclination be approached, but it was to be hoped that some 'non-political' papers would also participate. Hermann Ullstein felt that, for example, those owned by the General-anzeiger magnate Wolfgang Huck[45] should not be averse to promoting at least Stolper's economic ideas. 'I think that if the press is won,' he wrote, 'a great deal would be won, for

[43] Letter to Herbert and Nelly Peiser, 10 October 1929, NL Stolper, 44. The emphasis is in the original.

[44] In a letter, 7 December 1929, NL Stolper, 46A.

[45] According to the Nazi Kulturkammer file on Wolfgang Huck, he was a member of the DDP prior to 1933; see the letter of the Gau-Personalamt, Berlin, to the Kreisleitung Berchtesgaden-Laufen, 5 December 1942, in this file in the Berlin Document Center.

after all how did Hugenberg do it? Hardly by the force of his personality but with the strength of the press which backed him.' Hugenberg had been elected chairman of the DNVP the previous year. Hermann Ullstein envisaged that, given adequate and proper publicity, Stolper could become an important and powerful figure in German politics.

The reorganization of the moderate middle-class parties was central to Hermann Ullstein's plans for Stolper. He was delighted when Stolper informed him that the *Kölnische Zeitung*, which stood close to the DVP, had approached him independently, urging him to consider taking the leadership of a prospective new party which would encompass all the current moderate parties of the centre, from Democrats on the left to rebellious Nationalists on the right. Stolper agreed with Hermann Ullstein that a well-coordinated press could be a powerful political instrument, and he encouraged him to proceed with his plans. However, he also pointed out that if the campaign was to be effective the papers involved in the proposed arrangement would have to accept direction from a central source. Hermann Ullstein acknowledged this as the ideal, and he admitted that its realization was still virtually unimaginable, but he urged that a start be made none the less. 'What I really have in mind at the moment', he told Stolper, 'is above all the persistent pressure that those papers which we have won over to our cause would exert on the parties, so that they feel obligated to reorganize themselves.'[46]

In his memoirs Hermann Ullstein remembered that letters were sent out to 'about twenty great publishing houses, whose political policies in the main reflected those of the centre parties'.[47] These included Mosse; the Cologne firm of DuMont Schauberg which published the *Kölnische Zeitung*; the Huck-owned *Dresdner Neueste Nachrichten*, managed and edited by a leader of the movement for liberal unity, Julius Ferdinand Wollf; the publishers of two Königsberg papers, the venerable *Königsberger Hartungsche Zeitung* and the *Königsberger Allgemeine Zeitung*, the former inclined to

[46] See the letters of Stolper to Hermann Ullstein, 14 December 1929, and of Ullstein to Stolper, 17 December 1929, NL Stolper, 46A.

[47] *Rise and Fall*, p. 212.

support the DDP, the latter the DVP; the owners of the *Hannover Anzeiger*; and the Hamburg firm of Broschek & Co. which published the *Hamburger Fremdenblatt*. Manager and part owner of the latter was Max Wiessner, who had resigned from the *Frankfurter Zeitung* in 1920 and had then become head of the Berlin bureau of the *Hamburger Fremdenblatt*. In September 1921 he had become managing director of the Broschek firm and in 1924 co-owner. Wiessner, according to Hermann Ullstein, was the most ardent champion of this proposed 'press circle' (*Pressekreis*). Wolfgang Huck displayed a personal interest as well.

Hermann Ullstein's efforts to arrange a general meeting prior to the September elections of 1930 were in vain. The founding of the State Party also cast a wrench in his plans for Stolper, who, because of his economic ideas, was subjected to some vitriolic attacks from the Young Germans.[48] The outcome of the elections was catastrophic for German liberalism. The State Party won only 20 seats, a loss of five from the previous DDP representation. Of these 20, only 14 belonged to former Democrats. The DVP's decline was just as decisive. Its parliamentary party shrank in size from 45 to 30 members. On the other hand, the remarkable leap in strength of the Nazi party from 12 to 107 seats had no precedent in German party history.

Hermann Ullstein did not renounce his plans. On the contrary, they had gained a new dimension and a new immediacy as a result of the elections. In November he personally purchased the *Neue Leipziger Zeitung*, with its circulation of over 100,000, to serve as a mouthpiece for his political intentions, and announced publicly that he was interested in acquiring other publishing concerns outside Berlin.[49] In the late autumn of 1930 the 'press circle' was finally assembled for its first session. Representatives came from Hamburg, Frankfurt, Munich, Stuttgart, Düsseldorf, Hanover, Mannheim, Dresden, Breslau, Bremen, and Stettin. However, according to Hermann Ullstein's later account, 'the fear of

---

[48] See the letters of Stolper to the editors of *Der Jungdeutsche*, 19 October 1929, and to Dietrich Mende, 5 September 1930, NL Stolper, 44.

[49] *Neues Wiener Journal*, 26 November 1930.

Hitler lay already too deep in the bones of many of these people' to allow them to co-operate in a republican-democratic front against the enemies of the Republic. 'The greatest fear of all . . . was that of losing their readers. One representative from Hanover calculated that at least one half of all his readers were Hitlerites. The result was that he had to refrain from any criticism.' Wolfgang Huck, who attended the meeting with the general manager of his papers, apparently also now expressed his doubt about the ideas Hermann Ullstein voiced. In a second session some time later opinions clashed sharply again and 'after two or three further conferences the press circle broke up and its idea was abandoned.'[50]

Hermann Ullstein's stillborn 'press circle' can easily be dismissed as a naively idealistic project. For an administrator and successful businessman he did, in fact, reveal a startling innocence about the mechanics of politics and about the behaviour patterns and survival instincts of publishers. Unable to mobilize his own brothers and the Ullstein firm into a more effective unit for political propaganda, he assumed for some reason that he might be more successful in organizing his competitors and in persuading them to support his political projects. Still, if somewhat ingenuous, Hermann Ullstein's plans were well intentioned. When first approached by the publisher, Gustav Stolper replied: 'Your kind letter truly moved me, for the number of people in Germany who take an interest in something without any selfish motivations, is terribly small.'[51] Hermann Ullstein was, indeed, one of the few members of the liberal press, and of the liberal camp as a whole, who was prepared to see and admit how desperate the political situation was in Germany as early as 1928. After the collapse of his plans for reorganizing the moderate press, he continued to remain involved in efforts to co-ordinate propaganda for the republican state.

German liberals were thunderstruck by the results of the September elections. Ernst Feder recorded in his diary that

[50] *Rise and Fall*, pp. 212f.
[51] 14 December 1929, NL Stolper, 46A.

on the evening of 14 September a 'mood of catastrophe' hung over the editorial offices of the *Berliner Tageblatt*.[52] Arthur Koestler remembers that in the Ullstein house 'everybody there was . . . dazed.'[53] For a few days panic gripped sections of the German bourgeoisie, including, according to Feder, even Theodor Wolff. 'Yesterday evening T.W. rang me up and asked me to throw out an editorial piece of Olden's against the Reichswehr, a piece which had been in the express edition', Feder noted in his diary on 16 September. 'Today T.W. instructed Kirchhofer to go and observe the Reichswehr manoeuvres. He is fleeing before the swastika into the arms of the Reichwehr.'[54]

At the beginning of October Artur Mahraun severed his compact with the Democrats and withdrew the Young German Order from the State Party, which then was left with a mere 14 seats in the Reichstag. The Young Germans sat separately in parliament as the *Volksnationale Reichsvereinigung* and even requested that in the Reichstag they be accorded places between the DVP and DNVP deputies rather than next to the Democrats. The liberal press deplored 'this distressing and shameful event' which, it was felt, further underlined the political immaturity and irresponsibility of the German bourgeoisie. Felix Hirsch likened the fate of German liberalism to the Austrian case where 'now only a few Viennese newspapers testify to the vanished splendour' of the liberal age.[55] The bitterly satirical journal *Die Weltbühne*, however, had only scorn for most of the democrats of the Berlin and Frankfurt press who, it charged, had contributed to the destruction of German social liberalism. Heinz Pol, the regular film critic for the *Vossische Zeitung* commented under a pseudonym in *Die Weltbühne*: 'An ideology of liberalism does not exist any longer since liberalism itself no longer exists, except in the large democratic press—and there no longer as a moral example and challenge but only in lead articles. The great days of this press will

[52] Diary, 14 September 1930 (*Heute*, p. 267).
[53] *Arrow in the Blue*, p. 221.
[54] *Heute*, p. 267.
[55] Felix Hirsch in *8-Uhr-Abendblatt*, 235, 8 October 1930.

soon be over as well, for it bears part of the responsibility for the founding of the State Party and therefore for the fiasco of democracy.' He wondered, he said, how much longer the readers of this press would 'swallow its stupid twaddle'.[56] Anton Erkelenz remarked that Germany's desperate situation was above all the result of the 'ineptness, the mistakes, and the blindness of the governing parties of the last years, their organizations and their press. . .',[57] and writing in the SPD organ *Vorwärts* he announced that 'Social Democracy must, whether it wants to or not, take over the heritage of German liberalism; otherwise there will soon be only black gloom in Germany.'[58]

The decimation of the old liberal parties, the huge electoral gains registered by the National Socialists and Communists, and the break-up of the State Party, threw the editors of the democratic press into new depths of depression. Editorial comments of course had to remain optimistic and positive on the surface, but they now lacked any conviction. The slogans about *staatspolitische Sammlung*, amalgamation of all politically responsible elements in the bourgeoisie, were still mouthed and appeals for a great coalition government constantly repeated, but it seemed that even the democratic press no longer took them seriously. In an article which appeared in the *Frankfurter Zeitung* on Christmas Day 1930, Bernhard Guttmann declared: 'It is true: the era of liberalism is dead.' In the same issue Heinrich Simon began his reflections with the words: 'Darkness covers Germany. Darkness covers the world.' And in plaintive language he referred to the hope of all true democrats that their god, Reason, would one day return to Germany triumphant. 'That is the light, the only light in this darkness: the stoical, imperturbable faith of man in himself.'

56 Jacob Links, *Die Weltbühne*, XXVI (14 October 1930), p. 573.
57 Erkelenz, *Deutsche Republik*, V (8 November 1930), pp. 164ff.
58 *Vorwärts*, 501, 25 October 1930.

IX

THE NEW RELATIVISM

The September elections of 1930, instead of introducing a new flexibility into the political situation as Brüning had hoped, solidified the political alternatives which had existed in the spring. These were government based either on the passive co-operation of the socialist left or on the active collaboration of the nationalist and extreme right. The one significant difference now was that the DNVP had surrendered its commanding position on the right to the NSDAP. This difference was significant enough, however, to make the SPD recognize that Brüning, as long as he was not prepared to co-operate with Hugenberg and Hitler, represented the last barrier to a reactionary regime of the right, which, were it to come to power, would certainly attempt to establish a dictatorship. From September 1930 until his dismissal at the end of May 1932, Brüning governed as 'Hindenburg's chancellor' with a conservative cabinet of 'experts' and with the aid of article 48. This 'primacy of the government to parliament'[1] was 'tolerated' by a heterogeneous parliamentary majority consisting of the centre parties and the SPD. Parliament was called upon less and less to discuss the nation's business and to exercise its function as a legislative assembly, and increasingly only to ratify the decrees of the executive. When it met, it sat only for a few weeks, later only for days, and then was recessed again for months. In 1930 five emergency decrees were promulgated, in 1931 forty-three, and by the end of May in 1932 nineteen. Parliamentary activity declined correspondingly: in 1930 the Reichstag held ninety-four sessions, in 1931 forty-one, and in all of 1932 only thirteen.[2]

[1] Friedrich Meinecke in the *Kölnische Zeitung*, 696, 21 December 1930, reprinted in Meinecke's *Politische Schriften und Reden*, p. 442.

[2] Karl Dietrich Bracher, *Die Auflösung der Weimarer Republik* (4th edn., Villingen, 1964), p. 422; Helmut Heiber, *Die Republik von Weimar* (Munich, 1966), p. 230.

Brüning governed by the grace of the president who had the authority to dismiss the chancellor and to dissolve the Reichstag. However, the constellation of power in the Reich also made him dependent on the favour of the political arm of the Reichswehr. Brüning's competence was therefore defined directly by the president and by the army and not, as the constitution implied, by the configuration of political forces in the Reichstag. He remained in office only as long as he possessed the confidence of Hindenburg and of the military whose political spokesman was General Kurt von Schleicher.

The economic situation in the country continued to deteriorate rapidly after September 1930. Brüning's sharp deflationary measures—wage reductions, price controls, increases in indirect taxation, cuts in government spending—lowered real wages considerably and, to the public at large, appeared only to aggravate the economic misery. The local and state elections of 1931 and early 1932 evidenced the enormous growth of political radicalism, both on the right and left. In the spring of 1932 the strength and appeal of Hitler were such that the octogenarian Hindenburg was seen to be the only figure capable of defeating him in the presidential elections. The state elections of April 1932 corroborated the impression that the NSDAP was the most popular political party in the Reich. The polarization of political opinion was accompanied by the spread of violence and terror, so that the spectre of civil war began to loom ominously.

How to cope with National Socialism without, on the one hand, provoking civil war and, on the other, surrendering to the demands of Hitler became in the eyes of Schleicher and Hindenburg the most pressing political problem facing the country. Brüning tried to skirt the domestic political crisis by concentrating on scoring diplomatic successes which he hoped would accord his government greater legitimacy in the public eye and hence weaken some of the dissatisfaction which nourished radicalism. Schleicher, on the other hand, became obsessed with negotiating a *modus vivendi* with the Nazis. Brüning claimed later that he would have succeeded had his policies been given sufficient time to take effect.[3] However, when he was felled in May 1932, he was far from his goal; and his failure to deal with National Socialism was the most important reason for his dismissal. Schleicher had concluded that Brüning was incapable of solving the Nazi riddle in any way which was 'acceptable' to the Reichswehr and persuaded Hindenburg to drop him.[4]

With few exceptions the press on the democratic left, like the politicians of the centre and moderate left-wing parties, recognized after September 1930 that the fall of Brüning could lead only to a so-called government of 'nationalist concentration', in other words to an undeniably anti-democratic government of the right, presumably including and possibly dominated by the Nazis. The left-liberal press generally viewed Brüning and his government as by far the lesser evil. Yet the response to Brüning of progressive journalists and publishers was not determined entirely by negative considerations. The chancellor's quiet intellectual air, his aloofness, his apparent composure and confidence eventually gave him a certain measure of appeal in the eyes of many left-liberal publicists. At a time when demagoguery seemed to be in fashion in politics, Brüning's unassuming temperament, his asceticism, and his almost prosaic political style came to be appreciated by many disoriented democrats who saw in the taciturn chancellor an island of sanity, strength, and hope in a mad world. But while evoking a qualified respect Brüning never won the trust of left-liberal journalists.

On the extreme bourgeois left the journals *Die Weltbühne* and *Das Tage-Buch* displayed an uncompromising hostility towards Brüning's government and called incessantly for its resignation. The Ullstein, Mosse, and Sonnemann papers considered this attitude irresponsible and dangerous and refused to endorse such unbridled sentiments in national politics, but none the less a strong distrust and latent animosity towards Brüning always existed in this press as well.

---

[3] 'Ein Brief', *Deutsche Rundschau*, LXX (1947), pp. 1ff.

[4] See Dorpalen, *Hindenburg*, pp. 311, 324; and Bracher, *Auflösung*, p. 520.

Simply because Hindenburg had armed Brüning with the right to invoke article 48 to promulgate any legislation which he regarded as indispensable and had refused this backing to Brüning's Social Democratic precursor, Müller, many democratic editors were inclined to suspect Brüning as a fifth columnist in the pay of the right, as a clever saboteur of the democratic constitutionalism of Weimar. Later as an *émigré* Brüning had harsh and bitter words for the democratic press, especially the Ullstein and Mosse papers which he accused of having accentuated the rifts in the nation.[5]

The ambivalence towards Brüning manifested itself in fluctuating editorial attitudes which switched from fierce criticism prior to the September elections in 1930 to acceptance and encouragement in the wake of the startling election results; to sharp reprimands again in December 1930 when the government permitted the American film version of Remarque's novel *All Quiet on the Western Front* to be banned throughout the country because its showing was thought to be an unnecessary threat to public order; to approval and optimism again when the national budget for 1931 was accepted by the Reichstag in March; to growing anxiety and impatience with Brüning through the summer, autumn, and early winter of that year as the depression deepened, as unemployment figures rose to over six million, and as the extremist parties continued to gain new support; to renewed acclaim in December 1932 for the vigour and determination which Brüning displayed in the emergency measures which were decreed that month; to dejection and rebukes against the government once more when the ban on Nazis in the Reichswehr was lifted in January 1932; and finally, to increasing optimism as a result of Hindenburg's victory over Hitler in the presidential elections in March and April, the proscription of the SA and SS, and the promising prospects for a positive outcome of the forthcoming international discussions on the reparations question.

Generally, the democratic press admitted that if the SPD was unwilling to co-operate in the government, there was no

[5] Heinrich Brüning, *Memoiren 1918-1934* (Stuttgart, 1970), pp. 53, 72f., 75, 175; and Kessler's diary, 20 July 1935, *Tagebücher*, pp. 737f.

alternative to rule by article 48. The *Vossische Zeitung* often invoked the image of Brüning's government as the indispensable dam which had been erected against the flood tide of radicalism.[6] According to the *Frankfurter Zeitung*, 'a certain elasticity in the interpretation' of the emergency powers was imperative;[7] and the *Berliner Tageblatt* now called the emergency decrees of the government 'a necessary evil'.[8] Germany's politicians and parties had discredited themselves, the left-liberal press acknowledged, and the power vacuum created by this distressing renunciation of responsibility had to be filled by the president and his appointed chancellor, the 'trustees of the nation', as they were described now.

But what did the future hold in store as far as the constitution was concerned? On this point the *Frankfurter Zeitung* and *Vossische Zeitung* gradually became more outspoken as Brüning's chancellorship drew on, as the emergency decrees accumulated, and as the country sank ever deeper into economic misery. Rudolf Kircher, in his reports from Berlin, edged the *Frankfurter Zeitung* to a position where it was advocating substantial amendment of the constitution. There could be no return, he said, to the abject dictatorship of individual party interests; the machinery of government had to be reformed to ensure 'a suitable distance between government and parties'.[9] Kircher often reflected between September 1930 and May 1932 that the presidential government being practised had its beneficial aspects: it was teaching the Reichstag and the parties a vital lesson by showing them that they could not dictate policy to the government, and was emphasizing the authority that the office of chancellor should possess.[10]

The *Vossische Zeitung* advanced comparable arguments and in May 1932 even went a step further when it printed, in its front-page editorial column, an article by the former chairman of the DDP, Erich Koch-Weser, which expressed the

[6] M.R., *VZ*, 29, 3 February 1931; J.E., *VZ*, 32, 6 February 1931.

[7] Lead article, *FZ*, 592, 11 August 1931.

[8] Oskar Stark, *BT*, 2, 2 January 1932; see also Ernst Feder, *BT*, 567, 2 December 1931.

[9] RK, *FZ*, 595, 12 August 1931; RK, *FZ*, 122, 15 February 1931.

[10] See for example RK, *FZ*, 2, 1 January 1931.

view that government by a popularly elected president and
his adjutant, the chancellor, was no less 'democratic' than
parliamentary government. German society, Koch-Weser had
decided on the basis of his own frustrating political experience, did not possess sufficient solidarity or singleness of
interest to be able to sponsor a viable parliament. The
president alone could represent a 'unified popular will'
(*Einheit des Volkswillens*).[11]

The *Berliner Tageblatt* was far more cautious. It still
talked of 'the road back'[12] to a normal parliamentary
government based on mature and responsible leadership
emanating from the parties; but it agreed with the
Frankfurter Zeitung and *Vossische Zeitung* that if authority
was to be successfully reinvested in parliament many reforms
would have to be undertaken, above all in the electoral
system and in the party structure. Public respect for the
parties as legislators, in so far as it had existed previously, had
disappeared and reviving it would be a formidable task.
Exasperated outrage was the reaction among most left-liberal
journalists in November 1930 when yet another party was
founded, the Radical Democratic Party, of renegades from
the State Party and of former Democrats who could not
accept the *mariage de convenance* with the Young German
Order. Of the democratic press only the *General-Anzeiger* of
Dortmund was sympathetic to the new party. Georg
Bernhard and Hellmut von Gerlach were two of the party's
leading members. Bernhard had just lost both his place in the
Ullstein firm and his candidacy for the State Party; Gerlach
had just been removed as chief editor of *Die Welt am Montag*.
Of the purpose of the new party Bernhard said: 'We must
collect all those people whose genuine political participation
is stifled by the unprincipled State Party and the completely
bureaucratized Social Democratic Party.'[13]

---

[11] *VZ*, 215/16, 5 May 1932. In a letter to Otto Gessler in March Koch-Weser
expressed his support for the formal revision of the constitution in order to
strengthen the president's powers: 'Power must reach the Reich president not
through a back door but through the main door.' 26 March 1932, NL Gessler, 19,
p. 16.

[12] Helmut Sarwey, *BT*, 341, 22 July 1931.

[13] From a speech on 1 March 1931, printed in *Radikaldemokratische
Briefe*, Nr. 3 (March 1931), NSDAP Hauptarchiv, 42/861.

Unable to place much confidence in the parties for the time being, the leading Berlin and Frankfurt democratic papers saw themselves forced to put their trust in the sagacity of the chancellor and especially in the discretion of the Reich president. Since Hindenburg possessed ultimate executive competence to dismiss and appoint the chancellor, to dissolve the Reichstag, and to authorize emergency legislation, the fate of the Weimar state was clearly in his hands. The response of virtually all republican elements to this realization was blatantly to curry favour with Hindenburg, to try circuitously by their support to bind him to the republican constitutional state. In the summer of 1930 a campaign of adulation for the field marshal was begun which peaked during the preparations for the presidential election in the spring of 1932. With rarely a note of criticism the republican camp prostrated itself before its former inveterate enemy, a man who previously had been denounced as the incarnation of imperial Germany, the *Obrigkeitsstaat*, of militarism, monarchism, and élitist authoritarianism. If Hindenburg had been embraced as an *Ersatzkaiser* by that conservative section of the population which had elected him in 1925, after 1930 he was accepted as a *de facto Ersatzkaiser* by most of his former opponents. Because he appeared to represent the last non-violent defence available to republicans against the onslaught of the anti-democratic forces, he was exalted as a mystical, omniscient patriarch of almost superhuman stature who would protect his distraught nation from harm. Hindenburg was Germany, past, present, and future; he embodied Germany's strength, her glory, her resilience; he was the custodian of the nation and of the constitution. The public was told to have complete trust in him, in his devotion and fidelity to the constitution. The *Frankfurter Zeitung* even furnished apologies for the doubts which it had expressed about his competence in 1925.[14] Given the hypothesis that Brüning was felled by the rightist parties in the Reichstag and that a right-wing government was formed, Max Reiner of the *Vossische Zeitung* wrote in February 1932, 'would Hindenburg then act differently? Would he be

---

[14] See the lead article, *FZ*, 87, 2 February 1932.

less faithful to the constitution, would he pay less attention to his own perceptive judgement?' No, he answered; a right-wing government would still have to abide by the constitution. In the *Berliner Tageblatt* Helmut Sarwey announced: 'We are voting for Hindenburg because he has remained true to his oath of office and will always remain true to it.' Julius Elbau now called Hindenburg the 'peace Marshal'.[15]

Many democratic journalists were not blind to the paradox inherent in their attitude to the president. This awareness occasionally surfaced in a brief conditional phrase which was otherwise drowned in bouquets of flattery. 'In ideology a great deal separates him from us,' remarked Theodor Wolff, 'but we must honour and admire him, for he is truly an extraordinary creation, in his gnarled tenacity, his genuineness, his gallantry, a wonderful patriotic figure, from Tannenberg till today a reliable support amidst the dangers and confusion of the times.'[16]

The left had, at various stages, momentarily entertained the candidacy for president of several other public figures. Carl Petersen, the mayor of Hamburg and chairman of the DDP from 1919 to 1924 had been mentioned as a possibility, as had the novelist Heinrich Mann. But with the rise of Hitler, the socialist and democratic left, emphasizing as it did that political realism and forbearing open-mindedness were the only way of salvaging the republican-democratic state, saw the candidacy of Hindenburg as the only possible defence against the challenge of Nazism. In the democratic press the almost totally uncritical campaign for Hindenburg was unprecedented. The Democratic Party had never received such unconditional support, and even Georg Bernhard and the *Vossische Zeitung* had shown more initiative and independence of spirit while supporting the general staff during the war. The policy of the leading democratic papers towards Hindenburg was an excellent illustration of the extent to which this press had felt forced to relinquish its cherished ideal of independent criticism and outspoken intellectual

---

[15] M.R., *VZ*, 62, 6 February 1932; Helmut Sarwey, *BT*, 120, 11 March 1932; J.E., *VZ*, 125, 14 March 1932.
[16] *BT*, 124, 13 March 1932.

honesty; freedom of opinion had been suppressed by *raison d'état*.

The near deification of Hindenburg was a mistaken if well-intentioned policy. That sector of the population which was still sympathetic to the Republic and which might have been prepared to defend actively the ideals and accomplishments of Weimar was told by its leaders and its press to place complete trust in Hindenburg: he would defend the Republic for them. The nation was left entirely unprepared for the eventuality that the president might not live up to expectations, despite clear indications already that he was inclined to listen to the exhortations of a *camarilla* of ultra-conservative confidants. The rationale for a militant, pro-democratic organization like the Reichsbanner was undermined by the totally uncritical nature of the intensive publicity for Hindenburg, and potential active opposition to the Republic's enemies was eviscerated.

Hindenburg did defeat Hitler by a substantial margin, but he was not happy with his victory. When Walter Zechlin congratulated him on his election to a second term of office, Hindenburg remarked: '. . . who elected me then? The Socialists elected me, the Catholics elected me, and the *Berliner Tageblatt* elected me. My people did not elect me.'[17]

The gradual but certainly perceptible shifts in editorial policy that took place in the democratic press on such questions as the use of article 48, the constitutional authority of the Reich president, and the tolerance and leeway that should be granted to the Brüning government, were interpreted in some quarters as an 'ideological retreat'. Extremely caustic criticism was directed at the Ullstein, Mosse, and Sonnemann houses particularly from the *Weltbühne* and *Tage-Buch* circles and from the Münzenberg Communist press, where the leniency which the democratic papers were showing towards Brüning was denounced as an ideological trimming of sails and as a betrayal of principles. The leading left-liberal journalists of course refused to acknowledge that any renunciation of fundamental precepts was involved. Their policy, they claimed, was steered by a sense of

[17] Walter Zechlin, *Pressechef bei Ebert, Hindenburg und Kopf* (Hanover, 1956), p. 119.

responsibility and by a devotion to realistic and constructive, as opposed to wishful, commentary. In the life-and-death struggle facing the state and liberal democracy, the republican forces could not afford the luxury of dogmatism and *prima-donna* journalistic performances. In explaining its support of the Brüning government, the democratic press echoed, by implication if not openly in editorial pronouncements, the words of Hermann Dietrich, the Democratic vice-chancellor, when he told the Reichstag: 'What matters today is not how we reach the goal but that we reach it.'[18] By 1932 success and not methods had become the measuring-rod applied to government policy: as long as the economic crisis was weathered and National Socialism was prevented from attaining any significant executive power, virtually any means adopted by the government to achieve these ends was tolerated, if not always appreciated.

A newspaper as an economic unit has been described as 'a very sensitive barometer of the general economic situation'.[19] Any cramps in the economy are normally felt immediately in the press, in the first instance in the advertising section which from the economic point of view is the life-giving heart of a newspaper. In 1928 900 million marks were spent on advertising in the German press. By late 1931 there had been a decline of 50 per cent from this figure. Between April and September 1931 alone, during the bank crashes in Germany, a drop in advertising of 18·4 per cent was registered in the metropolitan press and 22 per cent in the press in the smaller cities and towns.[20] If a paper survived these drastic reductions in income, the shortage of capital necessitated radical steps at retrenchment. The number and size of editions were cut, staff was reduced in numbers, and salaries were scaled down. Publishers, anxious not to offend advertisers or readers in any way for fear that they might take their business elsewhere, constricted editorial independence

[18] Cited in Adelheid von Saldern, *Hermann Dietrich* (Boppard am Rhein, 1966), p. 105.

[19] Max Grünbeck, 'Die deutsche Presse in der Wirtschaftskrise', *Zeitungswissenschaft*, VI (11 December 1931), p. 392.

[20] Ibid., pp. 388, 392f.

increasingly, passing on instructions to editors that any criticism or views which might offend advertising clients or sections of the readership be avoided. Most journalists who were out of work or were threatened by the prospect of un-employment would write anything so as to please their employers.

Exceedingly few newspapers which were still financially independent at the end of the twenties managed to escape contracting debts during the depression. Because money was tight, credit or mortgages could be obtained only from big business concerns, from the larger banks, and from heavy industry; and these rarely provided funds in the first place to newspapers which opposed their political interests and secondly without seeking at the same time to align the editorial policy of a paper with their own political and economic priorities. The political tendencies of industrial and financial groups stood in the main distinctly on the right in the political spectrum, more and more obviously so as the depression deepened.

With their financial investments menaced, German news-paper publishers tended to become the pliant servants of interest groups and of public opinion. In 1931 at the annual conference of the Union of German Newspaper Publishers Heinrich Krumbhaar, the chairman, stated: 'In general the influence of a newspaper on those segments of the public which support it is greater than, conversely, the influence of public opinion on the paper.'[21] He was musing about a by-gone era, for contemporary facts blatantly refuted the statement.[22] The Ullstein, Mosse, and Sonnemann papers provided no exception. If their leading editors publicly

[21] Cited in Walter, *Zeitung als Aufgabe*, p. 122.

[22] The best documentation for these general remarks is available in the private papers of Hermann Dietrich. He was involved financially in a large number of pro-vincial papers, mainly in Baden, which usually supported the DDP/State Party but in some cases stood closer to the DVP. In addition, being independently wealthy, he was constantly approached by publishers seeking capital and explain-ing their difficulties. There is consequently a wealth of material in these papers illustrating the drift to the right of the liberal press, always under the pretext of depoliticization. The political biography of Dietrich during the Weimar period by Saldern does not touch upon this area of Dietrich's activity.

denied that editorial policy was moving right, events within these firms belied their assertions.

The injudicious nature of Hans Lachmann-Mosse's speculative activities in the 1920s became fully obvious at the turn of the decade. Enormous sums of money had been swallowed by various unsound projects. At first, existing assets had been mortgaged to furnish new capital; then open debts were contracted. When the depression struck, the owners of the Mosse firm found themselves in a financial quagmire. To cover debts elsewhere Lachmann-Mosse began to play with the finances of his newspapers and other publishing interests. He dug into the pension fund for his employees—according to one report 3·6 million marks were appropriated from this fund by 1933;[23] to economize he reduced salaries and contributors' fees, both of which were already low—the former were cut by up to one half, the latter, for regular free-lance contributors, by two-thirds;[24] and he trimmed the staff on his newspapers to skeleton proportions. Often he simply refused to pay his debts.[25] The business practices of the Mosse advertising agency became notorious: other publishers did not receive payment for the advertisements which they accepted through the agency, and the money from clients was misappropriated for other purposes. Vast sums were sunk into the foreign branches of the agency: in a few years the New York branch, for example, absorbed close to two million marks. Carbe speculated that the owners were making contingency preparations for flight abroad in the future.[26] By 1933 the uncovered debts alone of the entire business amounted to 8·8 million marks.[27]

Lachmann-Mosse had always looked upon his publishing and advertising concern as primarily a commercial enterprise.

[23] *VZ*, 14 July 1933. Social-security provisions belonged to the prewar era anyway, Lachmann-Mosse told Carbe on one occasion. Feder diary, 12 December 1930 (*Heute*, p. 277).

[24] Feder diary, 15 November 1931; Boveri, *Wir lügen alle*, p. 35.

[25] Kessler diary, 7 April 1932, *Tagebücher*, p. 658.

[26] Feder diary, 5 September 1932.

[27] *VZ*, 14 July 1933; see also the letter of Arthur Rawitzki to Paul von Schwabach, 20 February 1932, Reichskanzlei files, R431/2527, p. 204, which notes the desperate financial plight of Mosse.

Political or ideological considerations never received much attention from him, and any political involvement on his part—his nominal membership in the Democratic Club for example—stemmed purely from business interests. A newspaper was for him above all an article of sale; if any feature of his papers impeded, in the slightest, their marketability, it was undesirable. As political opinion in Germany polarized, as the political sympathies of the bourgeoisie shifted strikingly to the right after the death of Stresemann and the onset of the depression, and as liberal democracy as a tangible political movement was almost eliminated, Lachmann-Mosse, the businessman, could no longer justify to himself the continued rigid association of his papers with an unmarketable political ideology. The startling election results of September 1930, and especially the Nazi gains, jolted him into a concerted effort to try and co-ordinate the policies of his papers more directly with the political mood of the day.

Since Rudolf Mosse's death he had often attempted to exercise a more personal influence on the management of his newspapers, but the irremovability of Theodor Wolff and Martin Carbe from their posts, which Rudolf Mosse had stipulated in his will, had blocked any schemes of his which went beyond more or less minor administrative matters. By 1930, however, Wolff and Carbe were tiring of their incessant disputes with the owner. In late September 1930, for instance, Wolff complained bitterly to Ernst Feder about Lachmann-Mosse: Hitler could be dealt with, he said; this was only a professional problem, but the eternal battles with Lachmann-Mosse were gradually destroying him.[28] The owner's plans for his two leading newspapers, the *Berliner Tageblatt* and the *Berliner Volks-Zeitung*, revolved around making them non-political journals of the Generalanzeiger type.[29] These plans naturally necessitated the removal of the politically most opinionated and committed editors.

Lachmann-Mosse initiated his project in December 1930 by firing Otto Nuschke, the chief editor of the *Volks-*

---

28 Feder diary, 29 September 1930 (*Heute*, p. 270).

29 See Heuss to Dietrich, 27 October 1930, NL Dietrich, 255, pp. 123f.; Heinrich Rumpf to Dietrich, 2 December 1930, NL Dietrich, 123, pp. 14f.; and Feder diary, 13 and 16 December 1930 (*Heute*, pp. 278ff.).

Zeitung, who had worked for the firm for twenty-two years, and with him Alfred Müller-Hepp, the deputy editor. Nuschke, still an active member of the DDP/State Party, was now considered a liability by Lachmann-Mosse. Upon his dismissal from the Mosse firm Nuschke became general secretary of the State Party and later editor of the party journal *Deutscher Aufstieg*. Wolff and Carbe were incensed by this treatment of long-standing members of the firm. For Carbe, who had been general manager of the firm since 1907 and was the son of Emil Cohn, the founder of the *Volks-Zeitung*, these events were in fact the last straw. Of late he had found the atmosphere in the firm unbearable and Lachmann-Mosse's conduct and policies far too objectionable for him to continue. He condemned in particular the 'incredibly brutal' treatment of employees by the owner; recent attempts to influence editorial policy so as to attract, or not to offend, advertising clients; and the increasing space allotted in the Mosse papers to so-called *Schmutzinserate*, classified advertisements with sexual overtones.[30] Lachmann-Mosse evidently found these advertisements a lucrative business. Many people, however, besides Carbe took offence at them. Feder recorded in his diary that his dentist was circulating a list for people to sign who were prepared to give up their subscriptions to the *Tageblatt* on these grounds, and even the Brüning government was looking into whether the press which printed these advertisements could be prosecuted for aiding and abetting illicit practices.[31] In mid-December Carbe reached a financial settlement with Lachmann-Mosse—for his life-long contract and his shares in the *Volks-Zeitung* he received 1·5 million marks[32]—and left the firm at the end of the year. When the news was made official, a Düsseldorf paper commented that in its significance for the German newspaper world the departure of Carbe from Mosse was as if someone like Jakob Goldschmidt had resigned from his bank.[33] Bernhard Weiss, the vice-president of the Berlin police, on being informed by Feder of

---

30 Feder diary, 12 December 1930 (*Heute*, pp. 277f.).
31 16 December 1930 (*Heute*, pp. 279f.).
32 *Der Mittag* (Düsseldorf), 25, 30 January 1931.
33 *Der Mittag*, 294, 17 December 1930.

Carbe's decision and what led to it, remarked: 'Then we can pack it in, we republicans.'[34] Carbe had recently been advising the Ullstein brothers who were locked in the suit brought against them by Franz Ullstein. In January 1931 Louis Ullstein offered him a post in the firm and Carbe accepted. However, he was not happy in the new surroundings, and when the dispute between the brothers was technically settled, his position, which was never clearly defined in terms of responsibilities, became precarious. In June he was thrown out. He looked about for other employment but without success. A year later in a fit of depression he committed suicide.

Carbe's place as general manager was taken by Karl Vetter, a man in whom intense ambition and opportunism repeatedly overwhelmed basically progressive political inclinations. Vetter's career had been a checkered one. Having spent his younger years in the German youth movement, he became an ardent pacifist during the war and in 1919 helped found the Peace League of War Veterans. Unable to attract any party support, especially after the Independent Social Democratic Party dissolved itself in 1922, the Peace League was no match for either the nationalist or Social Democratic veterans' associations. Vetter tried to appeal to both nationalist and socialist instincts by calling for a *grossdeutsch* socialist state—one of his manifestos envisaged a 'German unitary state from the Meuse to the Memel, and from the Adige to the [Great] Belt'[35]—but without success. Until 1924 Vetter was an assistant editor on the *Berliner Volks-Zeitung*, and together with Carl von Ossietzky the inspiration behind the radical and aggressive character of this paper. That year, however, because of his prominent role in the short-lived Republican Party of Germany, which the Mosse papers refused to support, he was forced to leave the firm. He then suddenly retired from politics, changed professions, and as publicity co-ordinator for the Berlin Fair and Exhibition Office acquired a formidable reputation for his talents in the field of advertising.

[34] Feder diary, 14 December 1930 (*Heute*, p. 279).
[35] Cited in Istvan Deak, *Weimar Germany's Left-Wing Intellectuals* (Berkeley and Los Angeles, Calif., 1968), pp. 55f.

At the end of the decade Lachmann-Mosse fetched him back to have him apply his publicity skills in the firm, and upon Carbe's resignation Vetter assumed the position of general manager. Together the two men planned ways of cutting expenses and reshaping the character of the Mosse papers to give them greater popular appeal. They decided that a salient tendency could be dispensed with and that the political staff could consequently be greatly reduced: it would be sufficient if Theodor Wolff wrote a lead article in the *Tageblatt* once a week. 'After all we support the Brüning cabinet', said Lachmann-Mosse; 'and if we say this in two lines, then that's enough.' Why so much about Hugenberg and Wilhelm Frick (the Nazi minister of the interior in Thuringia), he asked.[36]

Vetter appeared to have renounced his previous political sympathies entirely. The editors of the *Tageblatt* attempted to organize a defence: an editorial committee was formed which tried to negotiate with Vetter and Lachmann-Mosse. Wolff refused to belong to it. With Carbe gone, his will to resist the persistent harassment of the owner seemed to be broken. Still in December 1930 he told Feder that he could not be bothered fighting Lachmann-Mosse any longer and would leave as soon as he had found another position.[37] By 1932 he communicated with Lachmann-Mosse only by letter. Wolff's colleagues noted that he was ageing rapidly; he often looked jaded and uninterested and suffered increasingly from spells of forgetfulness; the passionate interest in his paper was no longer there.

Ernst Feder, the deputy editor of the *Tageblatt*, was the next prominent victim of Lachmann-Mosse's axe, without warning and only with the explanation that the action was necessitated by economic considerations. However, Lachmann-Mosse regarded Feder as a 'party politician' who did not fit his plans for the *Tageblatt*.[38] Wolff was not even informed directly that his right-hand man was being removed. When he learned of the dismissal he rushed to Lachmann-

---

36 Feder diary, 13 and 16 December 1930 (*Heute*, pp. 278f.).
37 Feder diary, 13 December 1930 (*Heute*, p. 279).
38 Feder diary, 8 December 1930.

Mosse in the most excited state that Carbe had ever seen him in and forced the owner to revoke his decision.[39] But a few days later Feder sent in his letter of resignation, to be effective 30 June 1931:

It is terribly difficult for me to give up my activity on the *Berliner Tageblatt* at a time when more than ever before the co-ordination of all republican-social forces in a defence against political adventurers, against the incitement of the masses, against anti-Semitism, is indispensable. But I find it impossible to give my services, longer than my contract obliges me, to an enterprise whose owner is not able to appreciate my work and who is giving me notice after more than eleven years of devoted activity. This is happening without any cause or previous intimation, albeit the most competent judge, the editor-in-chief, has informed him that he sees in me the pillar of the political staff.[40]

Feder intended to return to his law practice. The news of the dismissals in the Mosse firm aroused great interest in newspaper circles. At the end of December Feder remarked in his diary that the Ullstein affair had been superseded by the Mosse affair.[41]

The decimation of the editorial staff was accelerated in 1931. If editorial opinion in the Mosse papers was to be minimized, Vetter and Lachmann-Mosse did not see any need for more than one political, one foreign-affairs, and one local-news editor on each paper. By the end of 1931 about fifty editors and correspondents had been dismissed, among them the influential political commentators Rudolf Olden and Paul Steinborn, and Fritz Engel, the theatre critic who had been a close friend of Rudolf Mosse and had served the house religiously for forty-one years. Steinborn had a nervous breakdown when he learned of his fate.[42] Even the Washington office of the *Tageblatt* was closed. When Feder wished Theodor Wolff a happy Easter in 1931, the latter replied that there could be no talk of happy days, and Günther Stein remarked: 'We shan't survive long.'[43]

From the large number of Jews among those sacked some historians have deduced that Lachmann-Mosse was trying

[39] Feder diary, 13 December 1930 (*Heute*, p. 278).
[40] Feder diary, 19 December 1930 (*Heute*, p. 280).
[41] Feder diary, 27 December 1930.
[42] Feder diary, 13 April 1931.
[43] Feder diary, 2 April 1931.

intentionally to remove the evidence for the right-wing assertions that the Mosse papers belonged to the *Judenpresse*.[44] What is clear is that Lachmann-Mosse did not wish to identify openly with the Jewish cause. The issue of anti-Semitism was treated with an increasingly marked reserve in Mosse publications. A kind of internal censorship was even introduced into the *Tageblatt*. When on one occasion Alfred Kerr, the paper's theatre critic, used the term 'lift-goy', this was altered to 'lift-boy'.[45]

The effect of the measures taken by the owners was not as noticeable in the editorial policy of the Mosse newspapers as perhaps could have been expected or even indeed as Lachmann-Mosse intended. Some readers did discern a 'shift to the right'. Alfred Wiener, syndic of the Jewish Central Association, commented on the deterioration in quality of the *Tageblatt* and said that this view was shared by many other readers.[46] There was, however, too much tradition embedded especially in the *Tageblatt* and *Volks-Zeitung* for these papers to change policies overnight. Besides, Theodor Wolff's personal authority guaranteed a certain continuity in the editorial policy of the *Tageblatt* as long as he remained its chief editor. In 1932 these papers still described them-selves as 'democratic without party affiliations'. In the eightieth anniversary issue of the *Volks-Zeitung* Kurt Caro, the new editor-in-chief, referred constantly to the 'radical' tradition of the paper.[47] The other two Mosse dailies, the *Berliner Morgen-Zeitung* and the *8-Uhr-Abendblatt*, con-tinued to classify themselves as 'progressive'.

Nevertheless, the staff changes—the removal of many of the more outspoken editors—and the generally downcast mood of the publishing house choked both the urge and scope for militancy among Mosse journalists. They were all afraid for their jobs. The edge on political commentary was blunted. Delicate political questions were handled with

[44] See Boveri, *Wir lügen alle*, p. 40; and A. Paucker's introduction to the selection of Feder diaries which appeared in *Year Book XIII* of the Leo Baeck Institute (London, 1968), p. 169.

[45] Boveri, *Wir lügen alle*, p. 40.

[46] Feder diary, 21 August 1931 (*Heute*, p. 305).

[47] *Berliner Volks-Zeitung*, 1, 1 January 1932.

greater restraint and with less obvious conviction that
solutions were available. Vetter and Lachmann-Mosse also
began to intervene frequently in the text of the papers on
behalf of advertisers.[48] Even Theodor Wolff's leaders had
lost much of their former pungency and liveliness.

That the circulation of the Mosse papers declined after
1930 was due in the main to the economic depression rather
than to editorial policy. Almost all papers suffered a decline
in sales, regardless of their political orientation, in virtually
direct relation to the unemployment figures in the country.

In the Ullstein house events took a more subtle turn. Here,
since the departure of Bernhard, there was no festering feud
between owners and editors, no threatening economic
débâcle. The firm was larger, more heterogeneous in its
interests, and therefore the various constituent units—the
newspapers, the magazines, the book section—functioned
with somewhat greater independence than in the Mosse concern. Furthermore, the disputes within the Ullstein family
contributed to the tendency to decentralize, to distribute and
define authority. This apportionment of competence made
sharp reversals in policy and any kind of thoroughgoing reorganization a more difficult process. Nevertheless, Arthur
Koestler, who moved from his correspondent's post in Paris
to the Ullstein offices in Berlin in September 1930 and
worked as a science editor for the *Vossische Zeitung* and
assistant editor of the *BZ am Mittag* until early 1932,
remembers that developments in the Ullstein house paral-
leled and exemplified the 'steady descent into the abyss' of
the Republic. He recalls the 'half-conscious shift of emphasis'
in editorial policy, the increasing nationalism, the replacement of 'balanced criticism' by 'pompous self-righteousness'.[49]

Because the firm was in a financially healthy and prosperous state when the depression struck, it did not begin to
feel the economic pinch until late 1930. Even then it did not
suffer in any way like the Mosse concern or the Frankfurter

48 Feder diary, 7 March and 4 May 1931.
49 *Arrow in the Blue*, pp. 222ff.

Societäts-Druckerei, where already in the relatively encouraging middle years of the Weimar Republic resources had been overstretched. The business year 1930 was ended still with substantial gains, although these were by no means comparable to the grandiose profits of 1927-8. In 1931 extensive retrenchment was necessary but it was not until 1932 that the Ullsteins recorded an over-all financial loss in the year's business.[50] Nor was there any wholesale dismissal of staff members as was the case with Mosse. In fact, the number of editors and correspondents employed by the firm's papers and news service remained almost steady between 1928 and 1932; the staff reductions were limited to technical and unskilled personnel, and even here there was still only a cutback of less than 5 per cent between October 1930 and July 1932.[51] In September 1931 the Ullsteins could emphatically deny the rumour that parts of the firm were to be liquidated: there was simply no substance to these assertions.[52]

However, despite the relative financial stability recorded in the firm's business reports, there was an atmosphere of anxiety and gloom in the concern. Little *rapport* now existed among the brothers or between the older and younger generations in the family. In 1931 Franz and Hermann Ullstein insisted that the deed of partnership drawn up in 1921 be altered so as to make it easier for any member of the family to withdraw from the company with his share of the family fortune. Agreement could not be reached. First Richard A. Müller, the general manager, was called upon to act as mediator in yet another family dispute. When he failed to make headway, the state secretary in the finance ministry, Hans Schäffer, was approached and asked to become the director general in the firm.[53] In the spring of 1932 he accepted the post along with the task of arbitration and

50 *Ullstein Geschäftsberichte*, 1926-32.

51 In 1928 the firm employed 212 editors and correspondents, in July 1932 217. The relevant data is available in the *Ullstein-Berichte*, 1928 through 1933.

52 See *Dresdner Neueste Nachrichten*, 218, 18 September 1931.

53 Schäffer diary, 20 November 1931, Institut für Zeitgeschichte, Munich. See also Dr. Meinhardt and Prof. Geiler to Schäffer, 19 February 1932, NL Dietrich, 140, p. 13.

succeeded in persuading the brothers to agree once more on a truce. 'External unity', to use Hermann Ullstein's words, was achieved albeit 'internal estrangement' remained.[54]

The journal *Tempo* continued to lose money, and recriminations flew in all directions in the house. In addition, the *Vossische Zeitung* kept registering its 'unceasing losses' and by 1932 the brothers 'began to wonder whether such a luxury could be justified'.[55] In 1931 the paper lost RM 500,000; by the beginning of 1933 it was costing the firm RM 200,000 a month to keep alive.[56] Hermann Ullstein has hinted in his memoirs that the 'prestige' of the firm was the primary consideration in maintaining this enormous financial burden.[57]

Hans Schäffer was not the only outsider who joined the formerly inbred directorial ranks of the Ullstein publishing house. In the autumn of 1930 Peter Reinhold, the former Reich finance minister, and three men with experience in banking and industry, Ferdinand Bausback, Eduard Benfey, and Otto Krüger, were engaged so as to provide competent executive judgement which was unaffected by the family quarrels. These four men were all respected members of the German business establishment, but with the exception of Reinhold[58] they had little practical knowledge of publishing. The effect of all these appointments was to emphasize further the business interests of the Ullstein house and to provide a new channel for pressures on the firm from outside. This situation led naturally to a more cautious, controlled, ultimately more conservative political outlook on the part of the firm and its publications. Reinhold was contacted by the Brüning government in October 1930 and asked to exert his

54 *Rise and Fall*, pp. 218ff.

55 Ibid., pp. 245, 247.

56 See the eclectic notes on the Ullstein concern by Carl Jödicke, a former employee, 'Dokumente und Aufzeichnungen betr. Ullstein-Verlag 1933-45', p. 60, Institut für Zeitgeschichte, Munich. The inspiration for these assorted reminiscences was Mendelssohn's book *Zeitungsstadt Berlin*, which Jödicke regarded as inaccurate and too apologetic towards the Ullsteins.

57 *Rise and Fall*, p. 247.

58 Between 1913 and 1921 Reinhold had owned and directed the democratic *Leipziger Tageblatt* and the publishing company Der neue Geist which produced some pacifist material. See K.F. Reichel, *Die pazifistische Presse* (Würzburg, 1938), p. 49.

influence in the firm to bring the Ullstein papers behind government policy. On 8 January 1931 Pünder noted with satisfaction in a letter to Reichswehr minister Groener that the approach had been successful and that the Ullstein publications had adjusted their attitudes to a position of 'extensive support for the policies of the Reich government'.[59] Again in November 1931 Schäffer, then still state secretary in the finance ministry, was asked by Brüning to contact the chief editors of the daily papers in the Ullstein firm and to discuss with them the policy of their papers towards the government. Brüning had been upset recently by a number of reports in these papers on economic matters, reports which he felt were either incorrect or disclosed confidential information. In his memorandum to Brüning on his meeting with Elbau and four other editors, Schäffer remarked on the reticence of some of the Ullstein journalists to commit themselves to any agreement. Nevertheless they had finally acceded to the request that any information of a secret nature on government economic and financial policies would not be published without Schäffer's knowledge. 'I consider this arrangement', Schäffer closed, 'as an attempt to achieve something of the unity in the press that we always notice with the French. . . .'[60]

Ullstein, like Mosse, became very sensitive to any criticism or objections from advertising clients or readers. Carl Jödicke recalls that towards the end of the Republic the guiding principle of the *Berliner Morgenpost* had become 'the consumer's viewpoint'.[61] In 1931 the film reviews of Heinz Pol, the reviewer for the *Vossische Zeitung*, began to be censored by his editorial superiors because of their negative remarks about UFA films. UFA had complained about Pol to the chief editor of the *Vossische*, Julius Elbau, and threatened to withdraw its advertising from the paper. Pol was also a regular contributor on political affairs to the *Weltbühne*

---

[59] Reichskanzlei files, R43I/2480, p. 4.

[60] Schäffer diary, 11 and 12 November 1931, and Schäffer to Brüning, 14 November 1931.

[61] 'Dokumente und Aufzeichnungen', p. 57.

and was known by the Ullsteins to have Communist sympathies.[62] When he confronted Elbau he was told that the
polemical tone of his articles was irritating UFA and the
publishers. 'You must take the general political and economic
situation into account, as the Voss does', said Elbau. 'That
you still attack certain trends in your reviews, with which we
have to reckon today, is intolerable.'[63] Pol remained un-
repentant and, unaware that his dismissal was on its way in
any case, resigned on the spot. He then joined the
Münzenberg organization full-time, first as editor of the *Neue
Montags-Zeitung* and, when this paper was suppressed by the
Papen government in June 1932, as assistant editor of the
more influential *Welt am Abend*.

That the Pol incident was not an isolated case resulting
from misunderstandings was illustrated by events in
December 1931. In the middle of that month Franz
Höllering, the editor-in-chief of the *BZ am Mittag*, was
suddenly relieved of his duties and a few weeks later sent off
to Washington as the U.S. correspondent of the paper.
Höllering, like Pol, had connections with the Münzenberg
press, but these lay in the past. Largely because of his ties
with the intellectual left, particularly with promising young
authors, he had been hired by Ullstein to serve as an editor in
the book section. But having rapidly impressed the management with his editorial acumen, he was appointed chief
editor of the *BZ am Mittag* in 1929 at the age of thirty-
three. In the autumn of 1930, however, the *BZ* aroused the
anger of Brüning, Groener, Schleicher, and other political
and army leaders by printing a sensational and frightening
report about Nazi preparations for a putsch and by charging
that official circles were perfectly well aware of these
preparations. According to the report the Berlin SA, led by
Walter Stennes, was organizing the putsch. Every member of
the SA supposedly possessed a list of fifteen names and telephone numbers which he was to ring as soon as he himself

[62] Pol frequently wrote for the *Weltbühne* under the pseudonym Jacob Links.
See his obituary on Elbau in *Der Aufbau* (New York), 24 March 1961. Pol's most
severe attack on UFA came in a *Weltbühne* article, XXVII (7 April 1931), pp.
506ff., in which he charged that the German board of film censors was dominated by UFA people.

[63] Pol, *Die Weltbühne*, XXVII (29 September 1931), p. 482.

was called. In this manner the entire SA could apparently be mobilized in thirty minutes. Information had also been collected, the article alleged, on where the possible opposition lived, how well it and the police were armed, and where arms were stored. These facts, the report concluded, 'prove once again that the systematic preparations for a putsch cannot be denied'.[64] At the time a ban of the *BZ* was considered but the legal means for this did not exist as yet.[65] None the less the Ullsteins were informed of the displeasure of the cabinet and of the Reichswehr authorities. Then, when Ossietzky was put on trial for treason in November 1931, the *BZ* damned what it called the prostitution of justice to reactionary political ends. And when finally in early December 1931 the *BZ* published an article about Hitler's private air force and the threat that this posed, Groener and Schleicher insisted that Höllering be dismissed.[66] The owners complied. Höllering left and his place was taken by Fritz Stein, a Berlin correspondent for the *Hamburger Fremdenblatt*, but not before Groener, the Reichswehr minister, Hermann Dietrich, the finance minister, Otto Meissner, the president's secretary, and Hermann Pünder, the state secretary in the chancellery, were consulted and had approved the appointment.[67] In a letter which he wrote to Brüning, Stein indicated that his editorship of the *BZ* was intended as only the first phase of his work in the Ullstein house: in view of the 'very definite political reasons' for his appointment, he explained his task as that of 'giving first the *BZ am Mittag* and later the *Vossische Zeitung* a new political form and redirecting them on to the path of responsible political thought and action, a path which I and my political friends have followed for ten years'.[68]

[64] *BZ am Mittag*, 256, 19 September 1930. When Feder telephoned Wilhelm Abegg, the state secretary in the Prussian ministry of the interior, and Bernhard Weiss, the vice-president of the Berlin police, both these men emphatically denounced the rumours. Feder diary, 20 September 1930 (*Heute*, p. 268).

[65] See Hermann Pünder to Josef Wirth, the Reich minister of the interior, 27 January 1931, Reichskanzlei files, R431/2480, p. 5.

[66] See Walter Kiaulehn's remarks in *Die Zeit ohne Eigenschaften*, ed. L. Reinisch (Stuttgart, 1961), p. 232.

[67] Fritz Stein to Brüning, 19 December 1931, Reichskanzlei files, R431/2480, p. 106.

[68] Ibidem; see also Max Wiessner to Brüning, 15 January 1932, R431/2480, p. 137.

Ossietzky commented with bitter sarcasm on the developments:

The Ullstein firm may deny that Höllering has been sacrificed to the seething Acheron in the Bendler-Strasse. But it cannot deny the growing laxity of all its papers. It cannot deny the tendencies which are reflected by the choice of Höllering's successor. . . . This is Herr Fritz Stein. . . , a journalist who can neither write nor impress with his talents as a reporter or thinker. [He is] a corridor type, an effeminate Mr. It, who always lurks where two ministers are conversing; a complaisant gramophone record of the Wilhelm-Strasse, without knowledge, opinions, conviction; a man with connections, borne by the favour of ministers, state secretaries, and press directors.

The *BZ*, Ossietzky continued, would now probably look like 'the bastard son of Goebbels and old lady Voss'. He then turned to some general remarks on the decay of the bourgeois liberal press. Everywhere editorial freedom of opinion was being suppressed by publishers who feared repercussions if anything disquieting for the ruling authorities was uttered in their journals. The Berlin press set the tone for the entire provincial press. On the basis of the events in the Ullstein house a democratic editor in the provinces would now ask himself if he dared publish any report which would displease the Nazis and possibly evoke a frown from the military, and his publisher would certainly decide that if his Berlin colleagues were so cautious, he had no reason to take risks. The next time some Nazi arms cache or document revealing putschist intentions would be discovered, one would be able to count on one's fingers the number of papers which took notice. And he closed: 'Those are the shocking and far-reaching consequences of the Höllering case, and therefore the behaviour of the Ullstein house in this affair is more than just the mistake of misguided businessmen. It marks the most scandalous capitulation yet to National Socialism. It represents a crime against German press freedom in the midst of its most difficult crisis.'[69]

When Höllering was sacked, Arthur Koestler, his deputy and also foreign-affairs editor, attempted to organize a collective protest. Although Höllering was liked and admired

69 *Die Weltbühne*, XXVIII (5 January 1932), pp. 3ff.

by his colleagues, none of them was prepared to sign 'the quite moderate letter' which Koestler claims he had drafted. 'Some shrugged and muttered: "You are a young man, but I have my family to consider"; others talked of "Communist methods".'[70] Shortly afterwards Koestler himself was dismissed. He had recently become a member of the KPD and religiously had set about organizing sympathizers in the firm and passing on any pertinent information to the party *apparat*. His activities were disclosed to the management by a conscience-stricken young trainee, and in May 1932 he was served notice on the pretext that the economic difficulties necessitated staff reductions.[71]

Of the three major democratic publishing houses, the FSD was the most successful in hiding its inner workings from public scrutiny. At any rate, as Heinrich Simon remarked to Ernst Feder, Sonnemann's testament prevented the owners of the FSD from acting as 'brutally' as the Ullsteins or Lachmann-Mosse.[72] Nevertheless the link with I.G. Farben had precipitated changes in personnel and policy on the *Frankfurter Zeitung*. The paper did not become a crude propaganda organ for Farben and its interests. On occasion the economic staff still wrote critically of the chemical trust and its activities. The shift was more sophisticated and was to be seen in the support which the paper gave to the strict deflationary policies of Brüning, who in October 1931 appointed a director of Farben, Hermann Warmbold, as economic minister, and who also worked closely with Hermann Schmitz, treasurer of Farben, on international financial matters. The Brüning cabinet put the protective tariff on oil imports, so desired by Farben, into effect.

The outcome of the national elections in 1930 awakened German liberals with a fright, first to the condition of extensive decay in which the political fibre of the state found itself and secondly to the appeal which National Socialism

---

[70] Koestler, *The Invisible Writing* (London, 1969), p. 47.

[71] Ibid., pp. 22ff.; and Koestler's contribution in Koestler *et al.*, *The God that Failed* (London, 1950), pp. 49f.

[72] Feder diary, 4 October 1931.

had for the masses. The presidential elections of March and April 1932, in which Hitler was the only serious challenger to Hindenburg, indicated to them how near the nation was to experiencing the Third Reich about which Hitler and his followers ranted.

The Ullstein firm witnessed the 'swing to the right' of political sentiments at first hand when two of its prominent editors, Hans Zehrer and Friedrich Zimmermann, took charge of the almost defunct journal *Die Tat* and transformed it into a widely read organ of revolutionary social conservatism. The periodical hoped to mobilize a 'third front', led by intellectuals, which would provide a uniquely German answer to the problems of modern industrial society.[73] Zehrer, who wrote weekly foreign-affairs articles for the *Vossische Zeitung*, was, under the pseudonym Hans Thomas, the anonymous editor of *Die Tat* for two years before he finally left the Ullstein firm in October 1931. In September 1932 he also became chief editor of the *Tägliche Rundschau* which was now backed financially by Schleicher. Zimmermann, whose penname was Ferdinand Fried, was economic editor of *Tempo* before he left Ullstein.

Theodor Wolff discovered the Nazi terror personally when he learned that his name was third, following Generals Schleicher and Stülpnagel, on a list of public figures whom the Nazis planned to eliminate after their seizure of power.[74] This threat induced him and Lachmann-Mosse to arrange for security precautions: the owner's private home was equipped with five emergency alarms and guarded by two police detectives, the publishing house patrolled by three plainclothes men and four uniformed guards. Some Mosse editors even demanded that they be supplied with revolvers.[75]

But although political events and disagreeable personal experiences had a sobering influence on the attitudes of most

[73] See Kurt Sontheimer, 'Der Tatkreis', *Vierteljahrshefte für Zeitgeschichte*, VII (1959), pp. 229ff.; also Hermann Lebovics, *Social Conservatism and the Middle Classes in Germany, 1914-1933* (Princeton, N.J., 1969), pp. 178ff.

[74] Feder diary, 6 October 1930 (*Heute*, p. 272). Wolff had been on an extremist list for assassination earlier in the Republic; Ernst von Salomon, *Der Fragebogen* (Hamburg, 1951), p. 128.

[75] Feder diary, 14 October 1930 (*Heute*, p. 274).

democratic journalists towards National Socialism, and led them to delve more deeply into the origins and character of this political phenomenon, they could not elicit any unanimity on how the Nazi threat could best be countered. After September 1930 there was no shortage of articles in the democratic papers trying to explain Nazism and its appeal: the *Berliner Tageblatt, Frankfurter Zeitung*, and *Vossische Zeitung* often carried long analytical contributions which set out to account, with sociological, economic, and political arguments, for the successes of the NSDAP in certain areas of the country. Nor was there any shortage of polemical pieces against the Nazi party, deriding and attacking its arguments and propaganda. Yet, thinking in this press on possible ways and means of dealing with National Socialism meandered: it was full of contradictions, innocent speculations, unrealistic hypotheses. Because German liberals, or for that matter any other political grouping opposed to Hitler, could not come to grips with what it was exactly that Nazism meant; because essentially they could not take Hitler seriously, that is at his word; and because they simply could not envisage the destruction of the *Rechtsstaat*—the elimination of civil liberties, and the establishment of a primitive and barbaric dictatorship; liberals were unable to decide on the means by which Nazism might be thwarted. This inability to find a clear policy towards a political party whose fundamental ideas were diametrically opposed to all the tenets of liberalism reflected not only the protean, catch-all nature of National Socialism, but also the disorientation within the liberal-democratic camp; the lack of confidence of German liberalism; the state of doubt and confusion in which it found itself; and, perhaps most important of all, the inherent weakness of a political movement which was without a firmly anchored base in institutions, social groups, and political traditions, and whose essence was compromise, negotiation, and an optimistic faith in the rationality of human behaviour.

In the leading democratic newspapers the success of Hitler and his movement within the German bourgeoisie was still diagnosed in negative terms. The Nazi gains were seen first and foremost as the product of a general malaise born of economic insecurity and frustrated national aspirations. Most of the party's votes, claimed the *Berliner Tageblatt*, came from 'fellow travellers' who had absolutely 'no inkling' of what National Socialism stood for.[76] The opportunism of the right-wing bourgeois parties—especially the DVP and DNVP which hoped to capitalize on the growing nationalism and conservatism of the population—was alone responsible for the air of respectability in which Hitler could parade about, and for his being able to present his party as a legitimate political alternative. But for the democratic press it was no such thing. Nazism was interpreted as a disease: '[It] is in fact not a party. Nor is it an ideology. National Socialism is the expression of a mood of despair. It is an illness. National Socialism is the revolutionary eruption of the despair of the proletarianized middle classes.'[77] Distracted by their inability to discern a consistent and precise programme in National Socialism, and struck primarily by the total challenge of the movement to traditional values and motivations, most liberal-democratic editors tended to regard Nazism mainly as a moral problem, an outgrowth not so much of tangible grievances which the public sought to correct by voting National Socialist but rather of a more general 'crisis of values'. The Nazi vote was a protest vote in the eyes of the democratic camp: it was not inspired by confidence in Hitler but by dissatisfaction with the traditional parties.

The portrayal of Hitler and his party was patronizing to the extreme. The party's core, with only a few exceptions— Gregor Strasser was the only Nazi treated with any semblance of respect—was described as an assemblage of mental pygmies, of the most abhorrent elements of German society, of social failures and criminal types. The continuing strife between the party's leadership and the SA was always taken as an indication that the party would not hold together if it encountered any setbacks. The place of Hitler in the party received conflicting interpretations. Genuine, unquestioning, and fanatical devotion to a leader was incomprehensible to the left-liberal editors, and hence they seized on any sign that

[76] Wolfgang Bretholz, *BT*, 19, 12 January 1932.
[77] Lead article, *FZ*, 109, 10 February 1931; see also *BM*, 60, 10 March 1932.

Hitler's command in the movement might be failing. In April 1932 the *Vossische Zeitung* printed an anonymous full-page article by 'an especially well-informed politician' who declared that Hitler was not in control of his party. 'Behind the mask of the dictator is hidden a soft, pliable, indecisive Austrian disposition with the occasional inclination to excess and violence.'[78] Many observers saw the greatest danger not in the *Trommler* Hitler but in the growing impatience of his revolutionary army, the SA.

It was largely this paramilitary legion of unemployed and the threat to the security of the state which it appeared to pose that provided the most persuasive arguments for the case that Hitler's intentions were illegal. On the surface there seemed to be no doubt in the democratic press that the whole issue of legality was a veil cleverly used by Hitler to confuse the public. The Boxheim revelations in November 1931, which uncovered Nazi plans for action after the seizure of power, the discovery in March 1932 that the SA had been put on alert for the eventuality that Hitler won the presidential elections, the endless remarks of Goebbels that legality was only a tactic to be used until the day of victory and that then heads would roll, all this appeared to convince democratic editors that *Adolf Légalité* was directing a grand *Komödie der Legalität*.[79] Rudolf Heberle wrote in the *Vossische Zeitung* that as long as illegality was even contemplated by the NSDAP, it could not be regarded as a legal party.[80]

And yet there were nagging doubts about whether these arguments were watertight, for the logical conclusion was not drawn, namely that in view of the illegal intentions and illegal political methods of the NSDAP the party should be banned. Ernst Feder asked the government in November 1930 whether it was going to 'stick its head in the sand' in the face of the illegal putschist character of National

---

[78] *VZ*, 161, 3 April 1932; see also the lead article, *FZ*, 248, 2 April 1931; J.E., *VZ*, 79, 2 April 1931; and *BM*, 262, 3 November 1931.

[79] Bretholz, *BT*, 135, 19 March 1932; and *BM*, 68, 19 March 1932.

[80] *VZ*, 140, 23 March 1932.

Socialism and thereby legalize illegality. But his own recommendations did not go beyond curtailing the allotment of federal funds for financing the police of Braunschweig and Thuringia where Nazi ministers were politicizing the police forces.[81] In December 1931 Rudolf Kircher did call for the prohibition of the SA,[82] but no campaign to this effect was begun either in his paper, the *Frankfurter Zeitung*, or any other democratic paper. After the discovery that the SA had marching orders for 13 March 1932 in case Hitler managed to defeat Hindenburg, a number of democratic journals urged that a ban be placed on the Nazi stormtroopers. But the suggestion that the entire party be proscribed was never uttered publicly.

This refusal to carry the arguments on legality to their logical conclusion had several causes. To begin with, the idea of a general ban raised the whole issue of civil liberties, and on this point German liberals were too aware of their own precarious position to wish to recommend what they feared would be a dangerous precedent. Secondly, the prospect of civil war if the Nazi party as a whole were banned seemed very real. And finally, the democrats were still convinced that the state possessed sufficient safeguards to deal with Hitler without resorting to the extreme solution of a ban on his party. If Hitler tried to seize power by force he would be committing political suicide. Furthermore, National Socialism could never win a majority in national elections, for to achieve this it would have to cut deeply into the faithful supporters of the SPD, KPD, and Centre Party. If, when he realized that he was in a political cul-de-sac, Hitler turned to co-operation in a government, Hindenburg and the Centre Party would check any unconstitutional projects which he might have in mind.

There was no doubt in the minds of the democratic journalists that public disillusionment with National Socialism was inevitable. That Germans could continue to be duped for very long by a movement based only on hate, resentment, and violence, and lacking any coherent positive

---

[81] *BT*, 517, 1 November 1930.
[82] *FZ*, 947, 20 December 1931.

programme, was totally inconceivable to these rationalists. The belief that this process of disintegration would be accelerated if Hitler was somehow lured into accepting some of the responsibilities of government gained increasing adherence on the left after the elections of September 1930. Robert Weismann told Feder on 29 September that prominent elements in the SPD were not averse to entertaining this view.[83] In the *Frankfurter Zeitung* Rudolf Kircher interpreted Hitler's participation in the Harzburg gathering of right-wing parties in October 1931 as a sign that he was considering joining a government of 'national concentration'; Hitler had obviously realized the limitations on his popular support and therefore was preparing his party for co-operation in a right-wing coalition.[84] Without wishing Germany a reactionary government, Kircher now felt that a government including Hitler was neither an unrealistic nor an intolerable idea so long as the Centre Party held the reins; for by drawing Hitler directly into the legislative process of the state the revolutionary impetus of his movement would be undermined.

The *Frankfurter Zeitung* was the first of the leading democratic papers to take up this position, which it consistently maintained until Hitler's appointment as chancellor. Part of Kircher's campaign in the paper for realistic and constructive thinking, it annoyed many of his younger fellow editors and supplied fuel for the charges of the more uncompromising radical left that the *Frankfurter Zeitung* was selling out to the forces of reaction. The *Berliner Tageblatt* toyed vaguely with the idea of thrusting responsibility on the right in October 1931,[85] but shortly thereafter rejected the idea again categorically.[86] The *Berliner Morgenpost* took the position that marked changes in the attitudes and policy of the National Socialist leadership had to become visible before the party could be allowed into a national govern-

[83] Feder diary, 29 September 1930 (*Heute*, p. 270).

[84] *FZ*, 761/762, 13 October 1931; 823, 4 November 1931; and 81/82, 31 January 1932.

[85] See Rudolf Olden, *BT*, 491, 17 October 1931.

[86] See Bretholz, *BT*, 127, 15 March 1932.

ment.[87] And the *Vossische Zeitung* was still adamant for the time being that there be no compromises whatsoever with the National Socialists. Peter Reinhold, who wrote regular Sunday articles for the paper, took the popular quip 'qui mange du pape en meurt'—a reference to a possible coalition including the Catholic Centre and the Nazis—and reversed it: 'To sup of National Socialism means death.'[88]

In the democratic press the editorial thinking on the political situation after September 1930 was based on assumptions: that Hindenburg would resolutely keep his oath to the Weimar constitution; that Brüning would not be replaced by a man of the right; that enough residual opposition against National Socialism existed within the population to guarantee that Hitler could never institute his dreams of dictatorship; and that the NSDAP as a party was too heterogeneous in ideas and in social composition to stand the stress of governmental responsibility. Although National Socialism was attacked vehemently by the democratic press, the public was prepared in no way for the eventuality that one or more of the safety valves of the republican-democratic state might fail: that Hindenburg might unwittingly betray his oath of office, that the Centre Party might become too obsessed with the problem of law and order to stand up unflinchingly to Nazi demands, and that the army leadership might accede to the dictatorial aspirations of a 'Bohemian corporal'. Instead of endeavouring to mobilize that section of the population still loyal to the Republic, democratic editors, either voluntarily or under pressure, sought to calm their readers' political emotions; they thought it safer, on the whole, to play down rather than to overstate the threats to the republican system. On the one occasion when a democratic paper, the *BZ am Mittag*, warned of Nazi putsch preparations—perhaps on the basis of unreliable evidence—it received a stern rebuke from the government, the army leaders, its owners, and even from its fellow democratic papers,[89] and was instructed not to excite public opinion. Eventually the

87 *BM*, 261, 1 November 1931.
88 *VZ*, 98, 27 February 1932.
89 Feder diary, 20 September 1930 (*Heute*, p. 268).

chief editor of the paper was removed. Hermann Ullstein's subsequent accusation that the public 'was lulled into a false sense of security' by its press was not without substance.[90]

In one of its infrequent editorial articles the Ullstein daily *Tempo* repined in August 1931 in a mood of inarticulate despondency: 'Things must finally change—so many emergency decrees, taxes which are too heavy, no work; things must finally change, something else must come.'[91] The lament reflected the feeling of impotence that had overcome the press of the republican left.

[90] *Rise and Fall*, p. 232.
[91] *Tempo*, 179, 4 August 1931.

X

'PRELUDE TO SILENCE':
THE LIQUIDATION OF DEMOCRACY

On 30 May 1932 Heinrich Brüning and his cabinet submitted their resignations to Hindenburg. The fall of the government had been engineered by General Kurt von Schleicher who had convinced the Reich president that only a government detached entirely from the parties and unambiguously nationalist and conservative in composition had any chance of being able to deal with Hitler and of defusing the explosive political situation. From 1 June, when the hitherto almost unknown Franz von Papen was appointed chancellor, to 30 January 1933 when Adolf Hitler's *Kampfzeit* terminated, the political fate of Germany was decided in endless, often secretive tête-à-têtes in the chambers of the presidential palace in Berlin, in the reception rooms of the president's estate in East Prussia, and behind other eminent doors locked by conspirators. Plots and counterplots, injured pride and private resentments, personal ambitions and naive assessments and plans, swirled about Hindenburg in the second half of 1932 and the first month of 1933. Old and weary he yearned to escape from his onerous, thankless, and confusing duties. At the end of January 1933 he was persuaded by his *camarilla* of confidants that the appointment of Hitler as chancellor offered the best hope for a stabilization of the political situation and thus for just such an escape.

From June 1932 until the advent of Hitler's government parliament played no active role in the politics of the country. Papen had the Reichstag dissolved twice and elections set both times for the latest possible date permitted by the constitution. In December, when Schleicher himself became chancellor, the Reichstag convened and adjourned itself again three days later *sine die* without even calling on the head of the government to face it. Under Papen and Schleicher the country was governed entirely by presidential decrees. If the sentiments of the Reichstag—which contained 230 National Socialists and 89 Communists after the July elections and 196 Nazis and 100 Communists after those of November—could be and were ignored, the mood of the populace, for which the elections acted as a barometer, could not be brushed aside as easily by the ruling conservative military-industrial coterie. The approach to elections, however, was plebiscitary. The strength of the vote for the extremist parties was taken as an indication of the dissatisfaction present in the country rather than as an expression of any positive wishes.

In this context it was natural that the press was not treated with any deference by the government. The ruling authorities looked upon newspapers not as independent voices but as solely the instruments of pressure groups. Criticism was equated with opposition, and opposition, particularly in the eyes of Papen, was equivalent to 'unnational' behaviour, especially if it emanated from the left. Already under Brüning press freedom had been severely curbed by various intricate restrictions and stipulations decreed to control incitement, slander, and falsification in newspapers. The limitations on the free expression of opinion were extended further by Papen. The extremist press suffered most but increasingly more sedate publications came under attack. In June a moderate Catholic paper like the *Kölnische Volkszeitung* was suppressed briefly, as was the SPD organ *Vorwärts*. On 22 July Mosse's *8-Uhr-Abendblatt* was proscribed for four days; on 25 July and again on 15 September the *Berliner Volks-Zeitung* suffered the same penalty. On each occasion the authorities had taken exception to remarks or, in one case, a cartoon which showed Papen in a bad light.[1] The *Berliner Tageblatt*, commenting on the ban of *Vorwärts*, declared that the freedom of the press was at an end in Germany.[2]

Prior to the depression the political parties had been convinced that a direct relation existed between the amount of press support that a party received and its electoral

[1] See the Reichskanzlei file on newspaper bans, R43I/2533, pp. 202ff.
[2] *BT*, 310, 2 July 1932.

strength. The remarkable growth of the extremist parties, the NSDAP and KPD, after 1929 appeared to refute this connection conclusively. The press of the National Socialists had a total circulation of less than one million in 1932, and yet the party attracted over 13 million votes; Communist newspapers had a printing of 0·6 million, but the KPD vote exceeded 5 million. On the other hand, while the electoral support of the nationalist right and of the liberal left dropped substantially after 1928, the sales of newspapers identified with these political tendencies declined only slightly by comparison.[3] However, Emil Dovifat, the professor of journalism at the Berlin Institute for the Study of the Press, was not prepared to draw from these statistics the conclusion that the German newspaper reader had liberated himself entirely from the political influence of his paper. Although the reader no longer necessarily accepted the specific editorial interpretations or suggestions of his paper, said Dovifat, his political opinions and decisions were still invariably based on the politically biased news coverage of the paper which he read. The Nazis, for example, were capitalizing on the nationalist, anti-socialist, anti-Semitic emotions which had been nurtured by the right-wing conservative press, Dovifat argued.[4]

This analysis was not wrong, merely incomplete. Evidence exists that many readers of liberal papers which were strongly opposed to National Socialism in their editorial policy none the less voted for Hitler. For instance, the chairman of the supervisory board of the *Oberländer Zeitung* in Singen in Baden, a publication which supported the State Party, wrote to Hermann Dietrich in June 1932 that the paper could no longer afford to back the liberal party without financial support from it, 'because a large part of our readers. . . are National Socialists.'[5] Robert Schlegel, the editor of the *Seebote* in Überlingen in Baden and a former chairman of the DDP in the local constituency, expressed similar views in August when he informed the

[3] See Appendix I, p. 313.

[4] 'Neue Aufgaben der deutschen Publizistik', in *Krisis: Ein politisches Manifest* (Weimar, 1932), pp. 256ff.

[5] Adolf Harder to Dietrich, 18 June 1932, NL Dietrich, 268, p. 15.

Demokratische Zeitungsdienst that his paper was curtailing its subscription to this news service of the State Party.

The political shift among our readers [he wrote] forces us to formulate our political attitudes in such a way that we continue to follow our traditionally progressive and patriotic line but that we avoid a pronounced democratic policy. The fact that 80% of our readers support National Socialism and that if we were to lose these readers the economic foundations of our concern would be undermined does not permit us to treat this movement only critically any longer. Since the *Demokratische Zeitungsdienst* with its thoroughly aggressive attitude towards the NSDAP is no longer of use to us, we are forced to give up this service. . . . We regret this development; we feel that we are free of any responsibility though. We have not renounced our democratic sentiments but have been abandoned by our voters, that is our readers.[6]

That Nazi voters read liberal papers is not as surprising as it might seem. First, Nazi news coverage and journalistic writing were on the whole notoriously bad; even Goebbels admitted that National Socialism was devoid of 'writers of experience and skill'.[7] Simply for the sake of information Nazi sympathizers continued to read their former papers. Secondly, a part of the Nazi vote was inherently a protest vote against the other parties. These voters did not take Nazi statements or even the party at their face value and continued to subscribe faithfully to anti-Nazi publications. And finally, the NSDAP leadership did not hand down directives to its followers to boycott the opposition's press until September 1932 when Goebbels initiated a campaign to this effect.[8] Until then Nazi voters felt no particular onus to renounce the 'bourgeois-national' or even the 'Jewish press'.

If the editorial opinions of the press were being disregarded by the government and by much of the public, Rudolf Kircher of the *Frankfurter Zeitung* still felt that the press had a vital political significance. With parliament not functioning, one of the important controls of the government

[6] Robert Schlegel to the *Demokratische Zeitungsdienst*, 17 August 1932, NL Dietrich, 267, p. 226. Heinrich Mann, *Ein Zeitalter wird besichtigt* (Berlin, 1947), p. 329, also noted that Nazi voters had often read democratic newspapers.

[7] Goebbels's diary entry, 4 January 1932, *Vom Kaiserhof zur Reichskanzlei* (Munich, 1934), p. 17.

[8] *Der Angriff*, 24 September 1932; Goebbels, *Vom Kaiserhof*, pp. 164ff.; and *Zeitungs-Verlag*, XXXIII (1 October 1932), p. 672.

had been removed, he argued. 'Public opinion, not least the leading press, has taken over the role which parliament is not capable of playing at the moment.'[9] Kircher was being idealistic; he was assuming that the press was functioning correctly as an independent channel of communication between the state and society and was respected simultaneously by the state and society as a purveyor of its own opinion. In the mind of the public, however, as well as among the government authorities newspapers were inextricably bound up with special-interest groups and therefore entitled to no special respect outside the corporate body of interests with which they were associated—the parties, business groups, church organizations, professional unions, as the case may have been.

Kircher, in his remarks on the role of the press, ignored or suppressed the reality of the situation. Even the large democratic papers which for so long had advertised the independence of their editorial opinion were now shackled by a variety of tangible and intangible fetters. Economic and ideological insecurity, the government's prodding and intimidation, the pressures exerted by powerful economic interests, had undermined and led to the imposition of restrictions on the free initiative of editors. Moreover, the course of political events—the disappearance of an operative Reichstag along with the growth of radicalism, the step-by-step suspension of parliamentary government, and the institution of presidential rule—removed much of the basis for constructive criticism. The democratic press could easily regret past developments, but when faced with the enigmatic practical problems of the day, it often admitted that no alternatives to current policy existed. The debate on the use of article 48 followed this path as did that on the advisability of trying to draw the National Socialists into the government. In September 1932 the *Vossische Zeitung* remarked: 'Today not even the defenders of the Weimar Republic will deny that the prospect of mastering the present political situation strictly according to the dictates of the constitution is hopeless.'[10]

---

9 *FZ*, 1/2, 1 January 1933.
10 Erich Krämer, *VZ*, 444, 15 September 1932.

And in the same vein, in October 1932 the *Frankfurter Zeitung* could say that it did not blame Hindenburg for the dismissal of Brüning and the Papen experiment since it had been necessary to attempt to lure Hitler into a government and since Brüning had clearly been an obstacle to such an attempt.[11] Rudolf Kircher referred to the law which governed his political thinking in the crisis and which he implied should govern that of his republican colleagues as 'the law of the lesser evil'.[12] Furthermore, the relentless decline of the Democratic Party and the ensuing confusion within the party had eroded the commitment of especially the more radical editors in the left-liberal press to the party and by corollary to the imperfect Republic. The almost total decimation of organized left liberalism in 1932—in the July elections the State Party won only four seats, in November a mere two—destroyed the foothold of democratic publishers and editors in the politics of the state. After September 1930 Ernst Feder, for example, felt that he could no longer vote in elections, and Wilhelm Cohnstaedt withdrew from an active role in party politics.[13] With the fate of the Republic apparently in the hands of a few individuals, and with the ceaseless appeals of the democratic press to sanity and reason seemingly falling on deaf ears, a feeling of ineffectualness and an air of resignation were often evident in the democratic publishing houses.

The first reaction of the democratic press to the dismissal of Brüning and the appointment of Papen was one of stupefaction and dismay. Brüning was not loved by liberals of the left but he had on the whole succeeded in the last two years in winning a certain measure of respect. A majority of the Reichstag tolerated the Brüning government; the prospects for a successful solution to the reparations question at the forthcoming Lausanne conference looked bright; and the economy could not fail to improve since any further deterioration was unimaginable. The change in government was therefore considered not only unnecessary but most

---

[11] Lead article, *FZ*, 736/738, 2 October 1932.

[12] *FZ*, 472, 26 June 1932.

[13] Erna Feder, the widow of Ernst Feder, in an interview with the author, 28 February 1969.

untimely. The *Berliner Tageblatt* called the Papen appointment 'a joke'; the *Vossische Zeitung* termed it 'most
unfortunate'.[14] The *Frankfurter Zeitung* was more cautious;
it regretted the fall of Brüning but was prepared to await
developments before judging the Papen experiment; the
dangers inherent in the situation, however, were immense,
it pointed out.[15] There was no difference of opinion about
the principal purpose of the Papen government: Hindenburg
clearly hoped that the National Socialists and the Centre
Party would tolerate an expressly right-wing cabinet without
party ties. Nor was there any disagreement that Schleicher
was the strong man behind the government and that Papen
was merely his stooge. When it became obvious that the
'government of national concentration' was set on openly
wooing the NSDAP, Wolfgang Bretholz commented that
Hitler was in fact 'the secret chancellor' and Peter Reinhold
described the new regime as a 'government by the grace of
Hitler'.[16]

The change in chancellors elicited serious doubts in the
democratic press, for the first time since 1930, about the
reliability of Hindenburg as a guardian of the Weimar
state. His own intentions were not called into question, but
the events surrounding the switch in governments revealed
the aged president's susceptibility to the one-sided advice of
the ultra-conservative inner circle around him. If the new
political leaders were proved wrong in their assessment of
Hitler, that is of his readiness to tolerate the government or
to join in a coalition, would Hindenburg remain master of
the situation, Kircher asked.[17]

The subsequent steps which were taken to try and placate
Hitler in order to entice him into co-operating with the new
regime—the lifting of the ban on the SA and SS, the removal
by presidential decree of restrictions imposed by various
state governments on the wearing of private uniforms and the
holding of open-air demonstrations, the eviction on 20 July

[14] Lead article, *BT*, 256, 1 June 1932; M.R., *VZ*, 261, 1 June 1932.
[15] RK, *FZ*, 403, 1 June 1932; and 406, 2 June 1932.
[16] *BT*, 267, 7 June 1932; *VZ*, 281, 12 June 1932.
[17] *FZ*, 406, 2 June 1932; see also Bretholz, *BT*, 257, 1 June 1932; and J.E.,
VZ, 262, 1 June 1932.

of the caretaker government led by the Social Democrats in
Prussia and its replacement by a Reich commissioner—these
steps caused great consternation among all democrats, not
necessarily because all democrats opposed the attempt to
make the NSDAP *regierungsfähig*, disposed to participation
in a government, but because the approach adopted by Papen
and Schleicher was seen to be undermining the constitution,
impairing the authority of the Reich president, and legalizing
political terrorism. The *Frankfurter Zeitung*, for example,
was a staunch supporter of negotiations with the National
Socialists to see if there was any way of bringing Hitler to
assume some responsibility, and consequently was prepared
to grant the Papen government a certain leeway in its
actions; but Papen's policies, the paper admitted after the
July *coup* in Prussia, amounted to no less than a surrender to
Nazi demands without any guarantee of concessions in
return. Hans Schäffer, who held great political sway in the
Ullstein firm after his appointment, told the Social Democrat
Rudolf Hilferding on 21 July that he supported Papen's
intentions but did not think that the cabinet had the strength
to achieve its goals.[18]

In the immediate aftermath of 20 July, when the Prussian
government was deposed, the opposition of the democratic
press to Papen's domestic policies was unequivocal. However,
as the summer wore on, this opposition became less and less
aggressive. When in August Hindenburg rejected Hitler's
demand that he be appointed chancellor since after the
elections of 31 July his party, with 230 seats, was by far the
strongest in the Reichstag, the democratic papers felt that
Hindenburg had earned their confidence again. 13 August,
the date of the Hitler-Hindenburg meeting, was regarded as a
watershed; Hitler would now have to recognize the limits of
his power. On the assumption that he could hardly fail to do
so, the *Vossische Zeitung* now finally joined the *Frankfurter
Zeitung* in urging that, if it was at all possible, a government
based on a Reichstag majority should be formed.[19] Both
these journals and the other Ullstein papers welcomed the

---

[18] Lead article, *FZ*, 539, 21 July 1932; Schäffer diary, 21 July 1932.
[19] See Elbau, *VZ*, 389, 14 August 1932.

discussions that took place between the leaders of the Centre Party and the NSDAP in August and at intervals afterwards. Kircher wrote on 17 September that the attempts to draw Hitler into a government had to be continued until the populace saw for itself that the Nazi Führer was not interested in responsible government.[20]

Already during the summer of 1932 opinion in the Centre Party seemed to favour a coalition government with Hitler over 'toleration' of Papen and his regime.[21] By the end of January 1933 the Catholic political leaders, Brüning and Kaas, had decided definitely that a Centre-NSDAP coalition had to be tried as long as certain 'guarantees' were written into the agreement. Of the leading Berlin and Frankfurt democratic papers the *Berliner Tageblatt* alone sensed the perils of this arrangement. Theodor Wolff wrote on 29 January that the Centre's assumption that it would be in a position to fell a government including Hitler if the Nazis became too unruly in their antics rested perhaps 'on grave illusions'. 'Certainly they [the Centre] could defeat a Hitler government in parliament, but who would guarantee that they [the NSDAP] would then have to disappear from the scene?' The Reich president might be pressured into leaving Hitler in office supplied with emergency powers. 'And Hindenburg would then be eighty-six years old.'[22]

When it was clear, after the second national elections in November and after a further meeting between Hindenburg and Hitler that month, that Papen's plans had boomeranged, Schleicher became the obvious candidate to form a new government. The reactions of the democratic press to the chancellorship of Schleicher were a mixture of relief, optimism, and *Schadenfreude*: relief, because the general was considered a man of action and a solid opponent of Hitler's pompous claims to complete control of any government which he might join; optimism, because the Nazi tidal wave appeared to have reached its maximum strength and the

[20] *FZ*, 698/699, 18 September 1932.

[21] Detlef Junker, *Die deutsche Zentrumspartei und Hitler 1932/33* (Stuttgart, 1969), pp. 86ff.

[22] *BT*, 49, 29 January 1933.

national as well as local elections since early November indicated clearly that it was receding, and also because the economy was finally showing definite signs of improvement;[23] and *Schadenfreude*, because it seemed appropriate that Schleicher should have to assume responsibility for leading the country out of the political impasse into which he, more than any other individual, had helped to manoeuvre it since May. In retrospect it is ironical that in the last two months prior to Hitler's appointment the mood among German liberal-democrats was one of growing confidence that the economic and political crisis was at last abating. Faith in Hindenburg had returned, accompanied by renewed accolades and homage. The Nazi movement itself seemed to be falling apart owing to the restlessness of its activists, an evident shortage of funds, its fear of another election, and the widely publicized rift between Gregor Strasser and Hitler. In an anonymous editorial on 11 January the *Berliner Tageblatt* asserted that Hitler was no longer the unassailable Führer of the Nazi party and that in his decisions he was no longer free from pressures within the movement.[24] The entire democratic press took every conceivable opportunity to trumpet the decline of National Socialism.[25]

This belief that the fortunes of the Nazi movement were on the wane elicited a noticeable nonchalance in the treatment of National Socialism by many democratic publicists in the last half of 1932. In August Franz Ullstein happened to be in the same railway carriage as Hitler on an overnight journey and was able to observe him closely. He concluded that Hitler was 'a poor fanatic, a pitiable man', and in talking to Schäffer about the experience left the latter with the impression that he, Franz, could no longer take the Nazi movement seriously.[26] When Hitler, a few days later, sent a

[23] Paul Elsberg, the co-ordinator of all the economic editorial staffs in the Ullstein concern, noted that formerly when one asked someone how business was, people quipped: 'Thanks, better than next year'; but that now this resignation was disappearing. *Ullstein-Berichte*, October 1932.

[24] *BT*, 18, 11 January 1933.

[25] On 11 October 1932, for example, the *FZ* carried a long front-page article on the results of the communal elections in Gerdauen in East Prussia, where fewer than two thousand people had voted; the NSDAP had suffered a decline of over 50 per cent in this small community.

[26] Schäffer diary, 8 August 1932.

telegram of sympathy to the Nazi stormtroopers who had just been condemned for the savage murder of a Communist worker in Silesia, the so-called Potempa murder, the *Berliner Tageblatt* and *Vossische Zeitung* surprisingly ignored the matter almost totally. Then in December Rudolf Kircher could write: 'We do not hesitate to recognize even from our standpoint that the National Socialist movement, despite all the evils that it has brought with it, has rendered a service in that it has contributed considerably to the invigoration of German politics which had become rather inflexible and sterile.'[27] In this statement Kircher was echoing the widespread view that Hitler and the NSDAP had exposed many of the deficiencies and errors, programmatic and purely psychological, of the other parties, which had failed to pay respect to many of the deeper, more basic needs of the German people. Many liberals felt that the most significant mistake of Weimar liberal-democrats had been their disregard for the nationalist feelings of the population. Max Warburg, the Jewish banker, voiced the following opinion in a letter to Georg Gothein in August:

Probably few people react to the Nazi movement as sharply as I do, but nevertheless I look at it without any bitterness. It is the natural outcome of the mad policies of Germany's enemies. In one sense one has to be pleased that after all the years of suffering such strong and energetic forces have survived among the German nation and have joined together in this movement. That so much hate is being sown, which will not disappear for many years, is to be deeply regretted. But this is surely an inescapable reaction.[28]

The attitude that many good intentions and well-meaning patriotic instincts were embedded in the Nazi party became widely accepted currency among the opponents of the party once it was felt that Hitler, on his Icarus flight, had singed his wings.

The *coup de grâce* which Hitler was administering to the middle-class liberal parties was also not without its advantages, the *Vossische Zeitung* mused. A 'new liberalism' would be able to emerge after the destruction of the old parties, one that would no longer take liberal freedoms for granted

[27] *FZ*, 924/925, 11 December 1932.
[28] 21 August 1932, NL Gothein, 33, p. 134.

and on the basis of its experience would approach its tasks more seriously.[29] In the meantime, however, the *Vossische Zeitung*, along with the other leading democratic papers, still felt that the State Party, despite its numerical weakness and many mistaken policies, fulfilled a need in the political life of the nation in that it was the only party which stood for the ideals of democracy.[30]

But propaganda for the State Party had become very scarce in the pages of the Ullstein, Mosse, and Sonnemann papers. Only the occasional article appeared at election time explaining the ideas of the party, and although a complete break with it was never effected, readers were now simply urged to vote for one of the republican parties of the former Weimar coalitions, that is either the SPD, Centre, or State Party.

In the autumn of 1932 rumours flew about in Germany that the Berlin and Frankfurt democratic press was on the brink of economic collapse and about to undergo sweeping changes. Unsubstantiated reports appeared in the social-conservative *Tägliche Rundschau* and in Goebbels's *Der Angriff* in early October that Theodor Wolff was to be replaced as editor-in-chief of the *Berliner Tageblatt* by a triumvirate consisting of Felix Pinner, the economic editor, Oskar Stark, a political editor, and Josef Räuscher, a foreign-affairs editor of the paper. Such rumours about the pending departure of Wolff had become almost commonplace. In June 1928 Koch-Weser had noted in his diary that Wolff was about to make way for Erich Dombrowski, the former deputy editor of the *Tageblatt* who in 1926 had taken over the editorship for the *Frankfurter Generalanzeiger*; and in January 1931 when Carbe left Mosse, the *General-Anzeiger* of Dortmund repeated the usual story that Wolff was about to leave as well.[31] However, this time in 1932 the suggestion seemed more credible. Lachmann-Mosse was said to be

---

29 Elbau, *VZ*, 367, 2 August 1932; see also E. Krämer, *VZ*, 203, 28 April 1932.

30 See Hans von Eyntern, *VZ*, 187, 19 April 1932.

31 Diary, 22 June 1928, NL Koch-Weser, 37, p. 139; and *General-Anzeiger* (Dortmund), 10, 10 January 1931.

negotiating with the Reich for financial assistance for some of his building enterprises, and it was conceivable that the government was attaching conditions about staff and policy changes on the *Tageblatt* to any prospective financial aid for any of Lachmann-Mosse's ventures. On 7 October a *démenti* on the reports to this effect which had appeared in the right-wing press was published in the *Tageblatt*, but a member of the paper's staff did indicate to Ernst Feder that Mosse had become dependent on the Dresdner Bank.[32] In March 1932 the Dresdner Bank and the Darmstädter und Nationalbank had been merged by presidential decree, and the Reich owned two-thirds of the share capital in the new Dresdner.[33] A few days after the denial in the *Tageblatt*, the *Berliner Börsen-Zeitung*, which had particularly good relations with Reich finance ministry officials, took up the matter again and suggested that pressure was being exerted indirectly by the Reich government on the political tendencies of Mosse publications and that this was possible because of the firm's dependence on financial institutions which in turn were dependent on the Reich.[34] In November Friedrich Zimmermann of the *Tat* circle alleged that the Reich had passed on close to 2·5 million marks to Mosse via the Dresdner Bank.[35] What in fact had happened was that a partner of Lachmann-Mosse in a land development company, the Woga A.-G., had withdrawn, and Lachmann-Mosse had negotiated successfully to take over his debts with the Dresdner Bank. Beginning in October outside observers remarked on the noticeable change in attitude, the pronounced and uncharacteristic civility of the *Berliner Tageblatt* towards Papen and later towards the Schleicher government.[36] Theodor Wolff did not leave; as his contract

[32] Diary, 6 October 1932 (*Heute*, p. 318).

[33] Karl Erich Born, *Die deutsche Bankenkrise* (Munich, 1967), p. 169.

[34] See *Der Jungdeutsche*, 238, 9 October 1932. When the vice-consul in Posen, von Campe, wrote to the state secretary Erwin Planck suggesting that the government buy the *Berliner Tageblatt* outright, the latter replied: 'that would cost too much money.' Letters of 10 October and 19 October 1932, Reichskanzlei files, R431/2480, pp. 258ff.

[35] See the mimeographed manuscript entitled 'Pressebeeinflussung durch Wirtschaft', n.d., NL Dietrich, 140, p. 39; and Dietrich to H. Bornhöft, 10 October 1932, NL Dietrich, 256, p. 12.

[36] Feder diary, 1 October and 18 December 1932 (*Heute*, pp. 315, 326).

was for life, he may have demanded too high a settlement from the owners. On the other hand, some arrangement for the future may have been reached, for Wolff was already sixty-four years old and quite likely was thinking of retiring shortly.

Meanwhile, the Frankfurter Societäts-Druckerei continued to lose money on a grand scale. In late 1932 reports leaked out that the owners were negotiating with the publishers of the right-wing liberal *Kölnische Zeitung*, who also were in serious financial straits, to see whether some degree of co-operation between the *Frankfurter Zeitung* and the Cologne paper could be agreed upon. Similar talks took place between representatives of the *Kölnische Zeitung* and the Ullstein firm, and then also between Ullstein and the *Frankfurter Zeitung*, but in none of these discussions was any positive accord reached.[37] The Frankfurt paper, while often critical of Papen's political tactics, did not condemn his goals and revealed general sympathy and approval for his economic policies. Warmbold of I.G. Farben remained economic minister in Papen's cabinet, and the tariff on oil imports which Brüning had introduced was retained.

In the Ullstein firm the future of the *Vossische Zeitung* looked dark. The financial burden which the paper represented was beginning to outweigh the prestige considerations on the other side of the scale. In January 1933 a suggestion that the paper be turned into a weekly was debated,[38] but no decision had been reached when Hitler took office. Hermann Ullstein remembered also that changes in the mood of the house were perceptible after the fall of Brüning. 'The atmosphere became oppressive', he wrote during the war, 'and the party of those weaklings who in their hearts were prepared to surrender to the "victor", Adolf Hitler, grew larger and larger. Was he not, after all, perhaps the man of the hour? Was there not possibly something good in the Hitler movement? . . . Couldn't one give it the benefit

---

[37] See H. Bornhöft to Dietrich, 6 October 1932, and Dietrich's reply, 10 October 1932, NL Dietrich, 256, pp. 12f.; and the manuscript 'Pressebeeinflussung durch Wirtschaft', NL Dietrich, 140, p. 40.

[38] See Carl Jödicke's proposals for the *VZ*, 23 January 1933, in 'Dokumente und Aufzeichnungen', pp. 6ff.

of the doubt?'[39] The most important political voice in the firm now, the recently appointed director general Hans Schäffer, was relatively sympathetic towards the Papen experiment. He agreed that Hitler should be drawn into the government if possible, although he was in fact sceptical whether Hitler would allow himself to be trapped in this way.[40] A Nazi-Centre coalition with Hitler as chancellor Schäffer considered the 'ideal solution' to the political crisis. Brüning was surprised how positively his former colleague, and the Ullstein papers generally, treated the Papen government.[41] It was on Schäffer's initiative that the *Vossische Zeitung* received a new editor-in-chief in October 1932. This was Erich Welter, until then the economics expert in the political section of the *Frankfurter Zeitung*. Welter had the reputation of being a conservative liberal;[42] he had replaced Arthur Feiler after the 'purge' in the Frankfurt paper in 1929-30. Under the direction of Schäffer and Welter the *Vossische Zeitung* dropped its resistance to the idea of National Socialist participation in a coalition government and repeatedly urged that a parliamentary solution to the political crisis be tried, despite the obvious risks involved.[43]

In May 1932 Carl Jödicke, an assistant to Richard A. Müller, the manager of the daily newspapers in the Ullstein firm, produced a list of editorial guidelines, which he suggested the Ullstein papers should follow. The main proposals are worth summarizing because as the year 1932 drew to a close most of them had been implemented not only by Ullstein publications but by the democratic press as a whole.

While optimism should be maintained as a principle in the attitudes of liberals to human behaviour, Jödicke began, the present emergency in Germany demanded that 'many of

---

[39] *Rise and Fall*, p. 241.

[40] Ibid., pp. 231f.; also Schäffer diary, June to October 1932.

[41] Schäffer diary, 9 September 1932.

[42] Koestler called him a 'stalwart nationalist', *Arrow in the Blue*, p. 224.

[43] See Schäffer diary, 19 November 1932; and Schäffer's remarks on the political alternatives in 1932 in his contribution to *Carl Melchior: Ein Buch des Gedenkens und der Freundschaft* (Tübingen, 1967), pp. 97f. Reinhold had been advocating this position since Brüning's fall.

the old methods of liberalism, democracy, and capitalism. . . be modified or suspended'. *Weltanschauung* should not blind liberal-democrats to practical problems and ways of overcoming them. For example, it was essential, he continued, that the concept of leadership (*Führung*) be emphasized and strengthened for the time being, regardless of the temporarily detrimental effects of this concept to traditional political and economic theories of liberalism and democracy. When the crisis was over there would be a renaissance of democracy and the anti-liberal emergency measures could then be disassembled. Then, concern with the welfare of the entire nation had to be stressed. Scepticism and ivory-tower rationalism, with which the democratic press was associated by the public, had to make room for more of an emotional commitment and more impassioned appeals. Trivialities were to be avoided, said Jödicke, and to illustrate his point he suggested that the democratic press should not bring one-sided reports about the 'attacks of the evil Nazis on the peace-loving Reichsbanner people'. And finally, the opposition to the extremist parties, he remarked, should be based on fundamental questions and not be characterized by polemics.[44]

In short, Jödicke was saying that despite the emergency situation in the state—to meet which special steps inimical to liberalism had to be taken and accepted by liberals—the one party, which more than any other had aggravated the emergency and whose political intentions and methods were constantly described as illegal, was to be treated like any normal political organization. Many of its ideas were also to be accorded respect. While Papen and Schleicher and the conservative right in general tried to outflank National Socialism in the party-political arena, Weimar liberals as a whole hoped to parry the ideological thrust of Hitler and his movement not by any bold counterattack but by a tactical retreat. A kind of ideological appeasement of the right, which had appeared already at the end of the 1920s, finally gained considerable momentum in 1932. Theoretically

[44] 'Taktische Skizze', dated 9 May 1932, in 'Dokumente und Aufzeichnungen', pp. 2ff.

this strategy was not without its attractions and possibilities, but for success it depended on strength; on a well-fortified position and on other strategical alternatives which could still be applied if events did not follow the hoped-for pattern. Weimar liberals were in no such position to say the least, nor was the opposition to Hitler as a whole. Therefore this policy was a gamble, a total leap in the dark. If it misfired it could only benefit Hitler.

XI

GLEICHSCHALTUNG, PHASE ONE:
THE ELIMINATION OF OPPOSITION

When Hitler became chancellor of Germany on 30 January 1933, he possessed no precise blueprint for the establishment of a National Socialist dictatorship. Yet the course which events followed in the first 'hundred days' of the new government, during which the foundations for the dictatorship were laid, was not merely the result of spontaneous and ingenious improvisation either. In general, the theoretical side of the take-over of complete power in the state was clear to Hitler and his closer associates: the political opposition had to be emasculated; the administrative organization of the Reich revamped; and the institutional apparatus of the democratic, republican order demolished or appropriated. The emergency powers available to the president would be the principal weapon used, thus preserving the semblance of legality; and the argument that the state was on the brink of total disaster and a Communist *coup d'état* would be presented as the justification for the government's measures.

The success of the general scheme required control of the ministries of the interior of the Reich and of Prussia. The only other Nazis in the Hitler cabinet, Wilhelm Frick and Hermann Göring, assumed these posts. The first hurdle that Hitler faced after his appointment was obtaining a dissolution order for the Reichstag; on 1 February Hindenburg complied with the request. The dissolution permitted a five-week election campaign in which Nazi ideas could be hammered relentlessly into German heads. Goebbels, whom Hitler called his 'commander-in-chief in the war of the mind',[1] was

---

[1] In conversation with Richard Breiting, 4 May 1931; Edouard Calic, *Ohne Maske: Hitler-Breiting Geheimgespräche 1931* (Frankfurt a.M., 1968), p. 34. It must be stated that certain scholars regard the Breiting documents with scepticism because their origin is shrouded in some mystery. Neither the occurrence nor the general tenor of the interviews is suspect, only the complete accuracy of Breiting's notes and the subsequent fate of those notes. In view of this, the

jubilant: 'Now the fight will be easy,' he wrote ecstatically in his diary, 'for we can employ all the apparatus of the state. Radio and press are at our disposal. We shall achieve a master-piece of propaganda. Of course we are not lacking funds this time either.'[2] The over-all plan was to harass, intimidate, and disembody adverse opinion.

Among the institutions to be dealt with first was the oppositional press. In *Mein Kampf* Hitler had written that the political power of the press was 'truly immense' and could 'not be overestimated'.[3] By 1931, however, in the wake of more extensive political experience, he had modified this view. In May of that year he apparently told Richard Breiting, the editor-in-chief of the right-wing nationalist *Leipziger Neueste Nachrichten*, that he was not at all interested in 'what the bourgeois press writes about me and my movement. I don't believe in the almighty power of the press. We have grown large without a press, and so I place my trust solely in the spoken word.'[4] But if Hitler had only scorn for the 'bourgeois press' and belittled its power to influence public opinion, he still recognized that newspapers were an essential channel of communication in the state and potentially a powerful organ for propaganda. In his view the press in the Weimar Republic was powerless because as a whole it was governed by selfish individualism, private interests, and commercial considerations. Together with the Reichstag, the *Schwatzbude*, as Hitler referred to it, the Weimar press symbolized the anarchy, the disorderliness, the insalubrity of the liberal state. In the Third Reich, Hitler told Breiting, the press 'will serve the community and no longer private interests. We want to have a decent press. . . .'[5] In short, although the press was not a power at the moment, Hitler intended to make it a power.

---

passages which I have cited or referred to never represent purported parenthetical sentiments of Hitler but always general views which were reiterated time and again in the interviews.

[2] Diary, 3 February 1933, *Vom Kaiserhof*, p. 256.

[3] p. 262.

[4] Calic, *Ohne Maske*, p. 38.

[5] Conversation with Breiting in June 1931, ibid., p. 57.

In the interviews which Hitler gave Breiting in 1931 he disclosed that he was supremely confident that the German middle class would present him with no problem whatever during his take-over of power and his construction of a state based on National Socialist principles. As a matter of fact it would fall over backwards to align itself with the new order. 'With the German bourgeoisie we shall do exactly what we want', he predicted, and then added that he expected much more difficulty from 'Marxism'.[6] When in the cabinet meeting on 1 February 1933 he announced that the government's election propaganda would focus on 'the battle against Marxism', he was not merely issuing a successful campaign slogan but was acting according to personal conviction. The Reich government and Prussian administration then proceeded to unleash a Draconic assault on the Communist and Social Democratic parties and their press, based in the first instance on presidential decrees of the previous year issued under Papen and Schleicher and after 4 February on the regime's own emergency legislation. The campaign of repression—raids, confiscations, newspaper bans, arrests of editors and party functionaries—reached its climax in the days immediately following the Reichstag fire and the promulgation of the 'Reichstag fire emergency decree' on 28 February, which indefinitely suspended all personal liberties, including the free expression of opinion, and became the legal corner-stone of the National Socialist dictatorship. Between the beginning of March and election day, 5 March, 108 newspapers, mostly on the left, were banned and the proscriptions on 26 others were extended. In the week before the elections the campaign of the socialist and communist left was silenced almost completely.[7]

Since the Catholic Centre was another party where potential active opposition was thought to lie and from whose ranks Hitler could expect few deserters, its leaders

---

[6] Ibid., pp. 37f., 42, 62.

[7] Gerhard Schulz's contribution in Karl Dietrich Bracher *et al.*, *Die national-sozialistische Machtergreifung* (Cologne and Opladen, 1962), pp. 548f. See also Kurt Koszyk, *Das Ende des Rechtsstaates und die deutsche Presse 1933-1934* (Düsseldorf, 1960), pp. 9ff.; and his *Zwischen Kaiserreich und Diktatur*, pp. 202ff.

and press were also subjected to intimidation, violence, and repression. About twenty papers which backed the Centre were banned for varying periods, including the principal organ of the party, *Germania*.[8]

On the surface it was surprising that the press of the liberal left fared tolerably well in the period prior to the elections. The Nazi command, particularly Goebbels, had, after all, an inveterate hatred for this 'Jewish gutter press'. On 15 February, for example, the Berlin *Gauleiter* and editor Goebbels exulted in the legal powers provided in the decree of 4 February: 'Now we have . . . a real grip on the press, and the bans are going to burst like bullets in rapid succession. *Vorwärts* and *8-Uhr-Abendblatt*, all those Jewish organs which have caused us so much trouble, will disappear all at once from the streets of Berlin. That thought is a comfort; it soothes the soul.'[9] The *8-Uhr-Abendblatt* was subjected to a week's ban on 15 February. It was banned again on 1 March but this time, it seems, as the result of a mistake; the police president of Berlin had assumed that it was an SPD organ. The paper reappeared on the following day.[10] But aside from *Tempo*, which disappeared for a week on 17 February, and the *8-Uhr-Abendblatt*, the Ullstein and Mosse papers were not touched. The mild treatment, by comparison, of the left-liberal press was due to a combination of factors: partially to the relative insignificance of the political forces with which this press was most closely associated; to the fact that Hitler planned to take active steps to remove Jews from public life only after his political control was established; and, perhaps most important, to the total lack of any virulent and articulate opposition to the new government in the democratic press.

Indeed, the reactions of the metropolitan democratic news-papers to the first month of National Socialist government consisted of shock, extreme depression, and intellectual

---

[8] Rudolf Morsey, 'Die Deutsche Zentrumspartei', in *Das Ende der Parteien*, p. 348.

[9] *Vom Kaiserhof*, p. 263.

[10] See Joseph Wulf, *Presse und Funk im Dritten Reich* (Gütersloh, 1964), p. 25.

paralysis. Events moved so rapidly and the spirit of the new government was so alien to all liberal conceptions that not even a feeling of outrage could be mustered. Only amazement, sorrow, and finally a mood of resignation prevailed among left-liberal editors.

To the news of Hitler's investiture as chancellor the Ullstein, Mosse, and Sonnemann papers had varying responses, albeit all expressed profound disappointment that the new government did not include the Centre and therefore was not based on a Reichstag majority. 'Government had to be turned over eventually to Hitler, and the German people had to pass through such a period. Even those who were most reluctant to accept this idea had gradually reconciled themselves to it', wrote Theodor Wolff on 31 January. 'But the way in which, and the conditions under which, this experiment could be tried were the decisive points.' Wolff for one did not have any illusions about what the immediate future held in store. The Nazi leadership would do all in its power 'to intimidate and throttle the opposition, to appease the SS and the SA, and to give the party faithful their just reward. . . .' The police in Prussia, Wolff predicted, would be purged and adapted to serve Nazi goals; the prohibition of the KPD was inevitable; and the press would suffer severe restriction of its freedom.[11] The *Vossische Zeitung*, too, admitted its 'discomfort, doubts, and anxiety' about the new government, without however specifying its fears. The paper concluded its main news article on 30 January with the terse remark: 'Hindenburg has appointed Hitler. The storm warnings are up.'[12] In the *Frankfurter Zeitung* Rudolf Kircher's first article after the formation of the new cabinet remained remarkably relaxed and optimistic. In his opening sentence he asked rhetorically whether the rejoicing of the National Socialists would last long. The tasks facing the government were formidable, he continued, and Hitler's coalition partners were no puppets. Kircher assured his readers that Blomberg, the new Reichswehr minister, would never permit a dictatorship to

[11] *BT*, 51, 31 January 1933.
[12] *VZ*, 50, 30 January 1933.

be established. By joining this cabinet as chancellor, Hitler had proved that he could be 'tamed'.[13] What prompted Kircher to write such a confident report cannot be determined exactly. His opinions may have been sincere. He may, on the other hand, have hoped to gain the attention both of the Nazi leaders to try and dampen their elation and of the Reichswehr command to remind it of its responsibilities. And undoubtedly he had an interest in maintaining composure and calm among the opposition to Hitler so as not to provide the Nazis with an excuse for taking drastic retaliatory measures.

This last concern preoccupied the entire leadership of the liberal and socialist left. Directives went out to members of the Social Democratic Party to withhold counter-demonstrations and not to allow Nazi intimidation to provoke them.[14] Ullstein's *Berliner Morgenpost*, the newspaper with the highest circulation in Germany and with a large working-class readership, headlined its edition on 31 January with the plea: 'Keep cool and calm!' 'We shall not allow ourselves to be provoked,' it went on to say, 'and we recommend that everyone who is not exactly inspired by this change in government should do likewise.' And even Wolff, his grim and accurate forecast notwithstanding, wrote in a mood of stoical resignation which intimated that for the time being active opposition would be futile and therefore senseless.[15]

Faced by the constant threat of bans and confiscation, the democratic press became increasingly reluctant to voice frank opinions. On 26 February Theodor Wolff spoke of the 'necessary economy of language' and of the 'subdued campaign vocabulary' in evidence in the press of the liberal left. He explained that since these papers did not have the backing of any appreciable political strength, as was still the case with the Centre press, they could 'only register facts and bring their own points of view in a very restrained form'.[16]

[13] *FZ*, 81/82, 31 January 1933.
[14] Erich Matthias, 'Die Sozialdemokratische Partei Deutschlands', in *Das Ende der Parteien*, pp. 158ff.
[15] *BT*, 51, 31 January 1933.
[16] *BT*, 97, 26 February 1933.

But even the reporting of facts reflected the fear and in-security prevalent among the owners and editors of demo-cratic journals. On 17 February Göring issued the so-called *Schiessbefehl*, the order to shoot, whereby he instructed the Prussian police to take forceful action against all opposition elements on the slightest provocation and to avoid clashes with the SA, SS, and Stahlhelm; and on 22 February he created the *Hilfspolizei* and enlisted 50,000 'auxiliary police' from the ranks of the Nazi and right-wing nationalist para-military organizations. Both these developments were news-worthy, but they received very scant coverage, in some cases none at all, in the leading left-liberal papers. No discussion appeared on the political implications of Göring's measures. Nor was any attempt made to interpret for readers the momentous significance of the emergency decree which followed the Reichstag fire and which in fact completed the destruction of the German *Rechtsstaat*. Editorial criticism of government policy became lame and gentle. In the *Vossische Zeitung* lead articles were suddenly no longer signed. Demo-cratic editors had always despised the non-partisan General-anzeiger press which they considered colourless and inferior and accused of neglecting the educative duties incumbent upon the press. Ironically, between 30 January and 5 March 1933 left-liberal journals moved distinctly in the direction of similar non-partisanship.

The psychological effect on the democratic press of the dragoon tactics of the Nazis against opposition newspapers cannot be underestimated, but nevertheless, aside from imposing greater restraint on the actual tone of editorial remarks and limiting their frequency, Nazi intimidation did not, and could not, significantly alter the substance of editorial comment prior to the elections. Ultimately, editors in the left-liberal press felt more tightly handcuffed by their own political tenets than by their fear of Nazi strong-arm methods. As democrats they felt compelled in their pub-lished statements to honour public opinion and thus to await the decision of the electorate on 5 March. They never con-templated advocating 'illegal' violent resistance to Hitler. All that they considered themselves capable of doing politically was to advise their readers on how to vote; but then in

February and early March events largely spoke for themselves, they contended. The *Berliner Morgenpost* declared:
'Words are of little value in making clear the momentous
decision to be made. Recent events speak eloquently for
themselves. Everyone must have realized in these weeks
what is at stake.'[17]

However, the homage that left-liberal publicists continued
to pay to democracy in the five weeks between Hitler's
appointment and the elections of 5 March was as artifical
as that paid by the National Socialists. Both camps were well
aware that the Weimar constitution was in ruins. In an
editorial conference several months earlier Schäffer had told
Ullstein editors that they should not admit publicly that the
constitution had not survived the assaults on it.[18] Hitler,
Goebbels, and Göring themselves asserted that the national
elections were a mere formality; their outcome, if negative
for the 'national revolution', would not be respected by the
National Socialists. Moreover, that Hitler had established
extensive dictatorial control before the elections was perfectly clear. Nevertheless, the campaign appeals of the democratic press concentrated almost solely on the need to
respect the constitution, the equality of citizens, and the
code of justice which it prescribed. Intellectual argument,
reason, and quiet persuasion were the only weapons which
democrats thought they were in a position to use. The
arguments were timeworn, outdated, and inapplicable;[19] they
were hollow and meaningless to the mass of the population
which was informed by other non-Nazi sources that Hitler's
actions were all based on the constitution and therefore
entirely legal. How helpless and how isolated the democratic
press felt was illustrated by the prosaic editorial appeal of the
Berliner Morgenpost one week before the national elections.
The reader was reminded that there would, in fact, be two
elections in the following fortnight, one for the Reichstag
and one for the Prussian Landtag. 'Please do not confuse the

---

[17] *BM*, 55, 5 March 1933.

[18] Schäffer diary, 4 October 1932.

[19] Benno Reifenberg later admitted that the campaign of the *FZ* had been
based on 'old vocabulary'; in his introduction to *Facsimile Querschnitt durch die
Frankfurter Zeitung*, pp. 7f.

two! And our most emphatic plea: please do not confuse the
parties; give your vote only to those parties which offer a
happy future for a Germany protected by the constitution.'[20] None of the Ullstein, Mosse, or Sonnemann papers
looked beyond the elections in their editorial comments, for
on serious and honest reflection democrats saw nothing but
a gaping void. The reliance on the tattered constitution in
their political arguments was a form of escapism from the
monstrous dilemma that they faced: what was a democrat to
do in the situation at hand? In reality, Hitler's dictatorship
was acknowledged and accepted as a *de facto* state of affairs
almost immediately after his appointment, and the appeals
of the democratic press to honour the spirit of the constitution were directed more at the National Socialist leadership
than at the middle-class voter in whom the left-liberal press
had long since become disillusioned.[21] A number of current
and former democratic journalists left Berlin immediately
after the Reichstag fire, among them Theodor Wolff,
Hellmut von Gerlach, Rudolf Olden, and Georg Bernhard,
without even awaiting the results of the elections.

The aggressive and pointed editorial criticism which had
been a hallmark of the metropolitan democratic press
during most of its existence had weakened into at most meek
and unassertive protest, and on occasion even compliant acceptance of Nazi measures. Such compliance was the
essence of the editorial which the *Frankfurter Zeitung*
printed on 2 March. The paper stated that it was prepared to
approve the elimination of civil rights in the wake of the
Reichstag fire if the Communist Party alone were affected.
That the KPD aimed to overthrow the state by violent means,
not even its leaders denied, and therefore, said the Frankfurt
paper, its present fate could elicit no sympathy. The
editorial then continued with a plea to the Nazi authorities
to make a distinction between Communists and Social
Democrats. The two parties were of a completely different
stripe. Formerly the *Frankfurter Zeitung* had often classed
the KPD and NSDAP together, namely as violent, extremist

[20] *BM*, 49, 26 February 1933.
[21] 'The bourgeoisie . . . will be ashamed of itself when it looks back on this
period', Hans Schäffer noted; diary, 4 October 1932.

groups bent on destroying the Republic. That the paper should now publicly acquiesce in the brutal repression of one by the other was certainly nothing less than hypocrisy. Presumably many of those out of sympathy with the paper relished the irony contained in the title of its editorial piece on 4 March, the day before the elections: 'Nicht aus Angst mitrennen!' (Don't follow the crowd from fear!).

In the national elections on 5 March 1933 the Hitler government won a majority of 51·9 per cent of the votes (NSDAP 43·9 per cent, DNVP 8 per cent). The Prussian elections one week later confirmed the victory. The consolidation and extension of the dictatorship began. One by one the *Länder* which as yet had not been 'co-ordinated' received Reich commissioners. Police powers throughout the Reich were placed in the hands of SA and SS leaders. The secret police and concentration camps, 'rehabilitation centres' as Frick called them, appeared; and terrorism mounted. On 23 March the Reichstag put its official seal on the dictatorship by approving with the necessary two-thirds majority an 'enabling law' which turned over legislative and executive powers to the cabinet for four years and which, in its second article, explicitly stated that government measures could deviate from the constitution.

On 13 March a new national ministry for 'public enlightenment and propaganda' was created by presidential decree, tailored for Hitler's propaganda expert, Goebbels. The 'cleansing' and reorganization of the German press was placed within the sphere of his portfolio. In a speech to the press a few days later, on 15 March, Goebbels outlined his conception of the role of the press in the National Socialist state. Beginning with the customary Nazi assertion that fourteen years of socialist-liberal rule in Germany had left the country in a condition of total chaos and decay, he declared that 'the new government of national revolution' had to make clear to the nation the reasons for the 'horrifying' decomposition of public life. Here would lie the initial task of the press. Newspapers, he emphasized, were meant 'not only to inform but also to instruct'. His ideal, he continued, was 'to see that the press be so artfully organized that it is so to speak like a

piano in the hands of the government, on which the government can play. . . . The achievement of this I see as one of
my principal duties.'[22] In short, Joseph Goebbels aimed at
becoming the editor-in-chief of the entire German press.

In National Socialist theories of the press the journalist
was regarded as no more than a civil servant, individual newspapers as branches of an official national information service,
and publishers as merely the business managers of these
branches. In October 1933 the *Schriftleitergesetz*, the
editors' law, formalized these views of the journalistic and
publishing profession.[23] By that date National Socialists were
already in full control of all journalists' and publishers'
organizations still in existence.[24] Freedom of the press had
not been abolished, argued the Nazis; on the contrary,
article 118 of the Weimar constitution had been only a
phrase and National Socialist rule had realized true freedom
for the press by liberating it from its enslavement to its three
former masters, moneyed interests, the parties, and the Jews,
and by giving it only one master in return, the German
nation.[25]

The outcome of the Reichstag elections in March extinguished the last flickering hopes in the democratic press
for some form of 'legal' political opposition to Hitler's
schemes for extending his power. Despite the unfair practices
of the Nazis in the election campaign, the actual elections
had been free, the nation had expressed its will, and consequently had no alternative to accepting the popular verdict
and saluting the National Socialist victory. These were the
lines along which editorials in the left-liberal papers reasoned

[22] Excerpts from the speech are printed in Wulf, *Presse und Funk*, p. 63.
Hitler repeated these arguments almost verbatim in a speech to journalists and
publishers on 6 April; see the report in *VZ*, 165, 7 April 1933.

[23] On Nazi press theories see Eugen Hadamovsky, *Propaganda und nationale
Macht* (Oldenburg, 1933); and Theodor Lüddecke, *Die Tageszeitung als Mittel der
Staatsführung* (Hamburg, 1933). For the application of these theories see Walter
Hagemann, *Publizistik im Dritten Reich* (Hamburg, 1948); Karl-Dietrich Abel,
Presselenkung im N-S Staat (Berlin, 1968); and Hale, *The Captive Press*.

[24] Ibid., *pp. 76ff.*

[25] See Walter Schubert, *Freie Meinungsäusserung, freie Presse* (Würzburg,
1939), pp. 101ff.; and Hitler's later remarks on the subject of press freedom,
Hitler's Table Talk 1941-1944, trans. N. Cameron and R.H. Stevens (London,
1953), p. 480.

in the first days following the elections. The mood was one of resignation: the battle was over; it had been lost.[26] 'The National Socialist revolution has become a fact', wrote Rudolf Kircher. 'We are nearer its beginning than its end.'[27] And in the same issue of the *Frankfurter Zeitung* the lead article declared that 'any form of opposition would be powerless'.

The predicament facing papers whose owners and editors were fundamentally opposed to the government was whether for the sake of principles they should express this opposition unambiguously and, as they thought, inevitably be banned as a result, or whether they should endeavour to survive by adopting a noticeably propitiatory attitude towards National Socialism. The latter approach was embraced by the 'bourgeois' press without exception. The *Frankfurter Zeitung*, which for years had argued that the goals and political devices of the National Socialists were illegal in the constitutional context of the Weimar state, but from late 1931 on had none the less advocated the acceptance of the NSDAP in a national government, with certain guarantees of course, completed the final phase of an about-face in policy on 7 March by declaring that: 'The political tactics practised hitherto by National Socialism have borne fruit; the movement has won power by legal democratic means.'[28] A fortnight later the *Vossische Zeitung* endorsed this view by saying that the National Socialist 'revolution' had occurred 'without a breach of the laws'.[29] Thus the notion of the legality of the Nazi take-over of power was disseminated among those same circles which previously had been told repeatedly that the aim of destroying the republican-democratic state was an illegal aim.

Goebbels's masterfully staged propaganda spectacle at the garrison church in Potsdam on 21 March—'the day of the national revolution'—to mark the official opening of the new Reichstag session was totally dependent on the press for success. And an enormous success it was. Extra editions of

---

26 *BT*, 110, 6 March 1933; *VZ*, 111, 7 March 1933; *FZ*, 178, 7 March 1933.
27 *FZ*, 193, 12 March 1933.
28 Lead article, *FZ*, 178, 7 March 1933.
29 *VZ*, 135, 21 March 1933.

newspapers were put out, and Ullstein's *Tempo* devoted four whole pages full of pictures and reports to the ceremony.[30] This paper seemed at least to have come into its own. By the same token, no trace of opposition was voiced to the enabling law, before or after its passage. The deputies of the moderate parties were not encouraged to vote against the law, and on the day prior to the decisive vote the *Frankfurter Zeitung* even thought it necessary to predict its passage.[31] By endorsing the enabling law, the liberal and Centre parties wrote a rude finis to the frustrations and troubles of the Weimar state. Hitler's speech on the day of the vote, 23 March, was described in the *Vossische Zeitung* as original and 'musical', and the *Berliner Morgenpost* felt that it was 'decidedly statesmanlike in format' and that as it progressed 'it grew to greatness'.[32] The *Gleichschaltung* of the *Länder*, the complete centralization of administration in the Reich, was greeted as a positive step and acknowledged as having been one of the most cherished aims of democratic liberalism since the war.[33] 'And parliamentarianism?', asked Rudolf Kircher: 'We are the last to regret that others are illustrating its limitations, which we ourselves tried in vain to make clear to the party politicians. The tighter organization of all public life was unavoidable; it was more than that: it was a vital necessity.' A week later he urged that 'a final line be drawn through the past'.[34]

On 27 March Goebbels remarked in his diary: 'The Jewish press is whimpering in horror and fear. Numerous Jewish organizations are proclaiming their loyalty to the government.' On 1 April, with delight: 'The press is already working in complete harmony.' A week later, ecstatically: 'We have a splendid press.'[35]

A variety of interacting, though not always consistent, arguments were involved in the 'decision' of the press of democratic persuasion to follow a distinctly conciliatory

30 *Tempo*, 62, 21 March 1933, Extra-Ausgabe.
31 Lead article, *FZ*, 219, 22 March 1933.
32 *VZ*, 141, 24 March 1933; *BM*, 71, 24 March 1933.
33 *FZ*, 187, 10 March 1933; *VZ*, 157, 2 April 1933.
34 *FZ*, 269, 9 April 1933; 284/5, 16 April 1933.
35 *Vom Kaiserhof*, pp. 289, 291, 296.

policy towards the Nazi regime. In the first place few non-Nazis in Germany could conceive that Hitler's government might survive for longer than a few months despite his dictatorship; the advent of disillusion and sobriety among Hitler's currently enchanted followers was considered inevitable once the Führer was forced to tackle concrete problems of government. Karl Vetter, the general manager in the Mosse firm, is said to have remarked in February: 'If you ask me, in six weeks two hospital orderlies will come to fetch Hitler from the Wilhelmstrasse.'[36] If, on the other hand, Hitler did manage to stay in power, publishers and editors entertained the hope that they might be able to exert a restraining influence on Nazi schemes and that National Socialist policy and tactics would soon take on a more respectable, that is conventional character. It was better to speak with a muffled voice for the time being than not at all. Many editors felt, in addition, that the older left-liberal papers had a responsibility to their faithful subscribers who undoubtedly would refuse to read Nazi publications and would always prefer their traditional paper, certain modifications in its editorial attitudes notwithstanding. Furthermore, a very basic concern about their personal safety and the prospects of livelihood in a National Socialist state was, of course, of utmost importance in determining the political behaviour of press people. Some democratic journalists received threats on their lives; on 11 March the offices of the *Frankfurter Zeitung* were invaded by a squad of armed Nazis; subscription canvassers and subscribers were terrorized by Nazi block wardens.[37] To the fear of physical violence was added the fear of unemployment if a paper was proscribed 'indefinitely'. On 10 March the *Berliner Tageblatt* was banned, and only after the Mosse firm had given the Berlin police president 'guarantees' that the paper would not step out of line in the future was it allowed to appear again two days later.[38] Owner-publishers assumed that as long as

36 Cited in Boveri, *Wir lügen alle*, pp. 45ff.

37 Jameson, *Wenn ich mich recht erinnere*, pp. 283f.; also the diarial memoirs of the Ullstein social columnist Bella Fromm, *Blood and Banquets* (New York, 1942), p. 112; and *FZ*, 193, 12 March 1933.

38 *BT*, 118, 12 March 1933; Boveri, *Wir lügen alle*, pp. 76ff.

Hitler remained in office the only alternatives that existed for them were either the arrangement of some form of *modus vivendi* on the basis of extensive political concessions to the new rulers or sale under pressure, and possibly even expropriation.[39]

These were the subjective considerations involved in the 'decision' to continue publishing on the terms imposed by the regime. However, the 'decision' that the journalists and publishers felt they were making was in fact purely nominal. In the offices of the *Frankfurter Zeitung* the possibility was mentioned of moving the paper to Switzerland, as it had been transferred to Stuttgart in 1866 when Bismarck occupied Frankfurt,[40] but the proposal never received serious attention. The resolution to accept the Nazi dictatorship without any call for open resistance or even a gesture of defiance was a natural conclusion to the political, economic, and administrative developments in the liberal-democratic press in the Weimar Republic. Opposition newspapers would not have surrendered their integrity as blatantly and as readily as they did had not their foundations, both ideological and structural, been in a state of advanced decay, had not their integrity already been compromised. Certainly, opportunism, hopes, and fears played an important part in events in February and March 1933, but they alone cannot account for the speed and smoothness of the Nazi take-over of power. An American journalist who witnessed the developments noted that 'before the state had applied its full pressure', most newspapers 'were already lined up', and a Swiss commentator observed that the German press succumbed only too willingly to the prevailing winds.[41] The accommodation with National Socialism, so rapidly arranged by the democratic press, was determined more by the obvious

[39] See Walther Jänecke, 'Der Übergang der Presse von der Weimarer Republik zum Dritten Reich', *Zeitungs-Verlag und Zeitschriften-Verlag,* Nr. 13 (1 May 1963), pp. 592ff. Jänecke was a leading member of the national publishers' association.

[40] Helmuth Diel, 'Grenzen der Presselenkung und Pressefreiheit im Dritten Reich untersucht am Beispiel der "Frankfurter Zeitung" ', unpublished diss. (Freiburg, 1960), p. 107.

[41] J. Emlyn Williams, the German correspondent of the *Christian Science Monitor,* in *Journalism Quarterly,* X (December 1933), p. 285; and Max Rychner in the *Neue Zürcher Zeitung,* 1830, 10 October 1933.

political and ideological disorientation and the related economic and administrative problems of this press than by subjective hopes and fears. The political tenets, the moral values, and the institutional basis of democracy had been steadily corroded and corrupted in recent years and ultimately rejected by a clear majority of the German public. The journalists of the democratic press had become correspondingly disaffected with the political system as it functioned, and their readiness to defend the Weimar state had been simultaneously eroded. In the end they responded to National Socialism either by emigrating or adjusting to the new regime. Publishers had undergone a similar process of disenchantment and alienation, for political but even more emphatically for commercial reasons. The Weimar state, with its incessant political and economic instability, could not offer them the prospect of economic security. In 1931 Hitler shrewdly foresaw how the liberal middle class would react to his take-over of state control. 'Today's bourgeoisie', he told Breiting, 'is rotten at its core. It has no idealistic momentum any longer and is only concerned with earning money. . . .' Once he took office, he predicted, the middle classes would soon accept his revolution as a *fait accompli*. [42] Franz Ullstein was later to sum up the feelings of liberal publishers in 1933 when he wrote: 'To swim against the stream continually is suicide. To say that it is better to lose half of one's readers today than all of them tomorrow is nonsense. . . . Whoever loses half of his readers today is sure to lose the rest tomorrow.'[43]

Of course, in February and March 1933 there were those among the staff of the Ullstein, Mosse, and Sonnemann firms who were less hesitant than others to accept the National Socialist regime and to emphasize its positive features. They came almost invariably from the ranks of the more recent appointees and from the middle and lower echelons of the staff, and in most cases personal gain was the prime motivation for their actions after the accession of Hitler. Of the post-1928 appointees very few emigrated during the

[42] Calic, *Ohne Maske*, pp. 37f., 42.

[43] Franz Ullstein to Margaret T. Edelheim, 14 August 1944, Ullstein file, Leo Baeck Institute, New York.

Third Reich, whereas of those who were dismissed after 1928 scarcely one remained in Germany through the whole Hitler era. After 30 January even a number of genuine NSDAP members suddenly appeared.[44] The manoeuvring and machinations of these people after Hitler took office naturally assisted in the *Gleichschaltung* of the press.

On 12 March Hindenburg signed a decree which made the swastika and the black-white-red the state flags. In an editorial entitled 'Goodbye' on the same day the *Frankfurter Zeitung* paid its last respects to the black-red-gold colours and to the Weimar Republic. The moving final sentence of this article spoke not only for the editors of the Sonnemann paper but for Theodor Wolff, Georg Bernhard, Rudolf Olden, Hellmut von Gerlach, and others who had already fled Germany in fear for their personal safety. 'We would lose all self-respect were we not to bear witness publicly to the black-red-gold flag, to the dream which this flag represented, and to the goodwill of those who loved it.' When the editorial conference earlier that morning had unanimously accepted the draft of the article, Wilhelm Cohnstaedt rose and abruptly left the room, his face covered in tears.[45]

---

[44] For the Ullstein firm Jödicke, 'Dokumente und Aufzeichnungen', pp. 44ff., estimated the number at only 'a few dozen'; he rejected Hermann Ullstein's claim in *Rise and Fall*, p. 12, that about a third of Ullstein's employees turned out to be Nazi supporters. Deak, *Left-Wing Intellectuals*, pp. 286f., does not document his assertion that 'by the early 1930's Ullstein's was . . . thoroughly infiltrated by National Socialists.' See also Boveri, *Wir lügen alle*, p. 79, who says that in the Mosse firm 'a few' employees turned out to be Nazis. On the Nazi tactics of infiltration in general see Dietrich Orlow, *The History of the Nazi Party: 1919-1933* (Pittsburgh, Pa., 1969), pp. 195ff., 241.

[45] *FZ*, 193, 12 March 1933; Reifenberg in *Facsimile Querschnitt*, p. 7.

XII

GLEICHSCHALTUNG, PHASE TWO:
THE END OF ULLSTEIN, MOSSE, AND SONNEMANN

In 1932 the Berlin Institute for the Study of the Press calculated that there were 4,703 newspapers in Germany. In 1934 the Institute counted 3,097 papers.[1] Thus in two years the number of German newspapers declined by more than one third. Of the 1,606 publications which disappeared, fewer than 200 were papers attached to the Communist and Social Democratic parties, whose property and assets were confiscated in the course of 1933.[2] The vast majority consisted of small privately run newspapers in the provinces, where during the Nazi take-over of power many local Gauleiters organized vicious campaigns to destroy the 'bourgeois' press which competed with party organs. Subscribers and advertisers were often coerced into transferring their business to Nazi papers; slander and threats of boycott and violence were levelled at private publishers and their employees; official notices were printed only in party journals. The resulting drop in circulation and advertising income often dealt a mortal blow to small papers which were already in a highly precarious economic position. Either closure or merger with the local party paper was the common upshot of these developments.[3] As the number of newspapers declined steadily, one journalist coined the motto: 'One nation, one Reich, one newspaper.'[4]

However, in spite of these events, rationalization and concentration in the press were not adopted as an official

---

[1] *Handbuch der deutschen Tagespresse* (1932), p. 27; and the 1934 edition of the same publication, p. 23. By 1937 the number had declined to 2,208, and by 1945, finally, to 977. See Hale, *The Captive Press*, p. 215; and [Fritz Schmidt,] *Presse in Fesseln: Eine Schilderung des NS-Pressetrusts* (Berlin, 1947), p. 7.

[2] See Hale, *The Captive Press*, pp. 63ff.

[3] See ibid., pp. 102ff.

[4] Cited in Werner Stephan, *Joseph Goebbels: Dämon einer Diktatur* (Stuttgart, 1949), p. 156.

policy of the Nazi leadership until 1935, when in April Max Amann, president of the Reich Press Chamber, issued his press ordinances, the second of which was entitled 'On the closing of newspaper enterprises to eliminate unhealthy competitive conditions'.[5] Hence, although the process of concentration in the press had taken a great leap forward in 1933, this was not accomplished at the behest of the central authorities in the NSDAP. In fact, the ruthless tactics employed by excited local officials and the subsequent collapse of innumerable provincial papers ran counter to the wishes which the party leaders responsible for the press gradually enunciated in 1933. At the end of March and the beginning of April Hitler and Goebbels assured representatives of the national publishers' association that as long as newspapers independent of the party accepted and supported the new state their future was not in danger.[6] On several occasions Max Amann voiced his dismay at the harassment of small private newspaper firms by local party placemen. On 13 July 1933 Otto Dietrich, the Nazi press chief, issued directives to all party personnel connected with the press, instructing them in the name of the Führer to desist from 'unfair methods of competition'.

The collapse of newspaper concerns, in so far as such collapse is not the result of natural economic developments and of the attraction of our own burgeoning press, deprives. . . thousands of workers and office employees, to no small extent National Socialists, of their livelihood. The economic plans and intentions of the Führer are thereby severely disrupted. The complaints to the party leadership, specifically from National Socialist cells in the firms affected, are accumulating from day to day. Consequently, we expect that in future party officials will refrain from any aggressive acts in press matters which contradict the orders of the party leadership and especially those of the Führer.[7]

Germany was beginning to emerge from the depths of the depression, and Dietrich's instructions to the Nazi press revealed that National Socialist policy makers wished to avoid any unnecessary obstruction of the recovery and of the gradual reduction of unemployment. By April 1933 all

5 See Hale, *The Captive Press*, pp. 148f.
6 See Jänecke, 'Der Übergang der Presse', pp. 594f.
7 In NL Herrmann, 13, pp. 3ff.

traces of unambiguous opposition to the government had disappeared from the press, and therefore the elimination of the 'bourgeois' press, simply out of vengeance and local resentments, was not considered to be worth the negative economic repercussions of such action.

The economic argument played an important part in the decision of the government to allow the Ullstein, Mosse, and Sonnemann papers to continue publication. In January 1933 the Ullstein firm alone employed 9,608 people, and Mosse over three thousand.[8] That the administrators of these firms recognized that the economic argument represented a ledge to which they might be able to cling was evidenced already in March in the negotiations which the Mosse firm conducted to secure the retraction of the ban imposed on the *Berliner Tageblatt*.[9] Hjalmar Schacht, the former Democrat, whom Hitler installed as president of the Reichsbank and who was consulted repeatedly for advice on the economics of the newspaper trade, was an adamant apologist for the maintenance of these firms after their policies, staffing, and organization had been co-ordinated with Nazi ideas.[10]

Another consideration which weighed heavily in the balance was Germany's image abroad. The *Frankfurter Zeitung*, *Berliner Tageblatt*, and *Vossische Zeitung*, along with the *Kölnische Zeitung* and the conservative-industrialist *Deutsche Allgemeine Zeitung*, were the most frequently read German newspapers in foreign capitals.[11] As long as Hitler was bent on alleviating the nervous apprehension of foreign governments about his intentions, he could not afford to eliminate this press; he needed it and actually admitted as much, as early as 6 April, to the publishers whom he met on

[8] *Ullstein-Berichte*, January 1933; *VZ*, 14 July 1933.

[9] Boveri, *Wir lügen alle*, p. 79. The argument was also used by the management of the *Deutsche Allgemeine Zeitung* after this paper was banned in May; see the letter of Fritz Wolters and Fritz Klein to the state secretary in the Reich chancellery, Lammers, 12 June 1933, Neue Reichskanzlei files, R43II/482, Bundesarchiv Koblenz.

[10] See the Reichsbank proposals 'Gleichschaltung der Ullstein-Betriebe', submitted to state secretary Lammers, 29 September 1933, Neue Reichskanzlei files, R43II/471.

[11] In 1936 the *FZ*, *BT*, and *Kölnische Zeitung*, in that order, had the highest circulations abroad; see the note in the Reichsfinanzministerium files, R2/4926, pp. 479ff., Bundesarchiv Koblenz.

that occasion.[12] After he, in a fit of rage over a particular article, had had the *Deutsche Allgemeine Zeitung* proscribed for three months in May, the ban was lifted prematurely in June largely owing to the protestations of Neurath, the foreign minister. In London for the world economic conference Neurath cabled Hitler on 15 June:

In my conversations about the situation in Germany I am constantly confronted with the objection that the right to free expression of opinion is totally paralysed in Germany. The ban of the *DAZ* is referred to in particular, and the point is made that no independent press opinion is reaching foreign countries any longer and that information about the mood in Germany can only be gathered from the foreign press.

And in conclusion he remarked: 'On the basis of my impressions and observations here, I feel that the preservation of this important organ [the *DAZ*], which is regarded as independent in its views, is absolutely necessary because of the effective support which it can give our foreign policy. By virtue of its reputation it can render a service to our foreign-policy goals.'[13] Both Hitler and Goebbels accepted this reasoning as valid, and the *Deutsche Allgemeine Zeitung* reappeared. In September in Geneva the propaganda minister repeated these views to representatives of the *Frankfurter Zeitung* and *Berliner Tageblatt*, informing them that the measure of independence in editorial policy still accorded to them was permissible only because of the foreign audience of their papers.[14]

Linked with these considerations was also a less precise motivation for maintaining these papers. The continued appearance of journals which formerly had been vehemently opposed to National Socialism but now obviously paid more than just lip-service to the government was a source of pride and prestige for the regime. When a man like Friedrich Sieburg, recently the London correspondent of the *Frankfurter Zeitung*, told English readers that National Socialism represented the essence of Germany, the resulting smiles of Nazi leaders were prompted not only by sardonic

---

[12] Jänecke, 'Der Übergang der Presse', p. 594.
[13] Neue Reichskanzlei files, R43II/482.
[14] Boveri, *Wir lügen alle*, p. 162f.

pleasure but also by genuine delight. In his 'prefatory letter' to the English version of his book *Es wurde Deutschland* Sieburg wrote:

It would. . . convey an erroneous idea of the situation if one were to maintain that Germany is subject to the dictatorship of a party. Certainly the regime established in Germany still retains a good deal of its party origin—in particular, all those phenomena and excesses which have excited such head-shakings and protests in foreign countries—but, on the whole, it must be said that the bulk of the German people has recognized National Socialism as the expression of Germany. Why? Because this movement incorporates an inner truth which consorts with our character.

Of the Nazi 'revolution' Sieburg remarked: 'True, the victors were often cruel, and many submitted only grudgingly, but it would be untrue to maintain that the Third Reich secured its sway by dint of sheer violence. It was raised to supremacy by the force of a few great ideas, from which not a single German could dissociate himself.' It was only natural, according to Sieburg, that 'liberalism abandoned its positions in Germany almost without a struggle.'[15]

Finally, Hitler and Goebbels's latent respect for the cultivated literary skills of journalists employed on the old democratic papers must be mentioned. In the early 1920s Goebbels had repeatedly tried to have articles accepted in the *Berliner Tageblatt*. The bitter memory of rejection stayed with him, and in 1933 Goebbels alone of the leading Nazis seemed prepared at times to give vent to all his hatred for the democratic press and to be inclined to destroy it completely. Yet beneath this rancour there remained a profound admiration for the brilliant style of a Theodor Wolff. One of his associates in the propaganda ministry has recorded that Goebbels read no other paper with such concentration and thoroughness as he did the *Berliner Tageblatt* and that he often would complain that no one in the party press could write an editorial to rival those of the *Frankfurter Zeitung* and *Berliner Tageblatt*.[16] In the Nazi press school which was later established students were apparently told to read the

---

[15] *Germany: My Country*, trans. W. Ray (London, 1933), pp. 13f., 17, 20. The book was dedicated to Heinrich Simon, publisher of the *FZ*.

[16] Friedrich Christian zu Schaumburg-Lippe, *Zwischen Krone und Kerker* (Wiesbaden, 1952), p. 147.

old lead articles of Wolff for pointers on style.[17] Hitler, too, often expressed his dissatisfaction with the party's press, its colourlessness and mediocrity. In October 1933 he is reported to have said that National Socialist journalists would be wise to take a lesson from the 'bourgeois' press, and that as long as the party's organs could not compete honestly with the independent newspapers they should refrain from attacking them.[18]

A great deal has been written about the sophisticated 'between-the-lines' opposition of newspapers and periodicals in the Third Reich. Undeniably, considerable courage was demanded of journalists who wrote critically about Genghis Khan, Tamerlane, Robespierre, and Frederick the Great, while in fact referring to Hitler, and who tried to encase the truth of a particular matter in provocative headlines which on the surface denounced this very truth as a lie.[19] However, there is no question that the audience which was able to appreciate this intellectual craftsmanship was limited to a very small and select group and that an effect on society as a whole was a pipe dream. Balanced against the reasons why National Socialism permitted papers like the *Frankfurter Zeitung* and *Berliner Tageblatt* to continue and the purposes which these papers served, this opposition was weightless. The mere survival of formerly democratic publications paid far greater dividends to the regime than to the cause of German liberalism. The *Berliner Tageblatt, Frankfurter Zeitung*, and *Vossische Zeitung*, the latter until it ceased publication at the end of March 1934, became the Abigails and Cinderellas of the Third Reich.

The adjustments in the editorial policies of the Mosse, Ullstein, and Sonnemann papers obviously necessitated cer-

[17] Boveri, *Wir lügen alle*, p. 161.

[18] See the letter of Dertinger to Dyrssen, Breslau, 20 October 1933, in the Brammer collection, 1, pp. 132ff., Bundesarchiv Koblenz.

[19] See, for example, Rudolf Pechel, *Deutscher Widerstand* (Erlenbach-Zürich, 1947), and his *Zwischen den Zeilen* (Wiesentheid, 1948); Fred Hepp, 'Der geistige Widerstand im Kulturteil der "Frankfurter Zeitung" gegen die Diktatur des totalen Staates, 1933-34', unpublished diss. (Munich, 1949); Helmuth Diel, 'Grenzen der Presselenkung und Pressefreiheit im Dritten Reich'; and the interesting debate in the *Neue Zürcher Zeitung*, 12 January and 19 January 1947.

tain corresponding personnel changes in these firms. Long before Goebbels's law of October 1933, removing Jews and other undesirable elements from the journalistic profession, was implemented, and even before he first mentioned publicly, on 6 April, the imminent introduction of such a law,[20] the three firms had begun reorganizing their staff.

In the Mosse house changes were promised to the Nazi authorities in early March in order to secure the lifting of the ban on the *Berliner Tageblatt*.[21] Karl Vetter directed the purge which followed. Wolfgang Bertholz, who had written the article which led to the ban, was forced to go into hiding and then was the first of the Mosse journalists to follow Wolff into exile. On 21 March, the day of the Potsdam ceremony, Theodor Wolff's name finally disappeared from the paper, and Oskar Stark, section editor for domestic politics, was dismissed. On the next day Wilhelm Ohst, an SA man and a lottery organizer by profession, was appointed National Socialist 'commissioner' for the firm. At the beginning of April, 118 Jewish office workers in the house were relieved of their duties; and then in two stages, in mid-April and in early May, the editorial boards of the *Tageblatt* and the other Mosse papers were completely restructured and the remaining Jews sacked.[22] The *Berliner Volks-Zeitung* received an SS man as chief editor, Franz Wynands. Kurt Caro, the former editor, fled to Paris. No obvious trace was now left in the Mosse papers, either in policy or personnel, of the social liberalism which they had formerly advocated. On 9 April in an article adjoining an announcement of editorial changes, Erich Haeuber, the acting chief editor of the *Tageblatt* and previously a staff member of the decidedly right-wing nationalist *Leipziger Neueste Nachrichten*, declared appropriately that Hitler had brought an end to a liberalism polluted by Marxism, a liberalism which had disintegrated into anarchy.[23] Anton Erkelenz, in a letter to

20 This speech to the press is contained in a collection of Goebbels's speeches, *Signale der neuen Zeit* (Munich, 1937), pp. 127ff.

21 *BT*, 118, 12 March 1933.

22 Boveri, *Wir lügen alle*, pp. 80ff.; *Völkischer Beobachter*, 5 April 1933; and Pem [Paul E. Marcus], *Heimweh nach dem Kurfürstendamm* (Berlin, 1952), pp. 68ff.

23 *BT*, 166, 9 April 1933.

the editors announcing the cancellation of his subscription, described the *Tageblatt* now as 'a bad version of the *Völkischer Beobachter*'.[24]

In the Ullstein and Sonnemann firms personnel alterations were not effected with quite the same speed. Among the technical staff in Ullstein a sizeable National Socialist cell formed itself soon after Hitler's accession to office and subsequently organized demonstrations of strength with increasing regularity, producing even a complete stoppage on 12 May which prevented the firm's evening papers from appearing. The reason for this particular show of force was reported to be the slow progress in the ejection of Jews from the firm. The May events accelerated changes.

The two men who then played the leading roles in the *Gleichschaltung* of Ullstein were Ferdinand Bausback and Eduard Stadtler. Bausback, who became a managing director of Ullstein in 1930, was a Catholic, a banker by profession, co-owner of the Hugo Oppenheim & Son bank in Berlin, a director of UFA and of several industrial concerns in Württemberg. He was a hardened financier and businessman who had close personal relations with the Reichswehr minister Blomberg and the foreign minister Neurath. On 11 March 1933 Hans Schäffer, a Jew, was asked by the Ullsteins to resign from his position as chairman of the managing directors, and his place was taken by Bausback and Richard A. Müller.[25] Thereafter Bausback emerged as the Ullstein family's principal negotiator with the regime in power. Eduard Stadtler, on the other hand, was very much a political opportunist with a romantic nationalist background. An Alsatian by birth, a student of Martin Spahn in Strasbourg, active before the war in the youth movement of the Centre Party, he had experienced Russian captivity during the war and in late 1918 had been instrumental in founding an Anti-Bolshevik League in Germany with financial assistance from Hugo Stinnes and moral support initially from Friedrich Naumann. A close associate of

---

[24] 3 April 1933, NL Erkelenz, 136.
[25] Schäffer diary, 11 March 1933; Jödicke, 'Dokumente und Aufzeichnungen', p. 58, remembers that Müller was very enthusiastic about the Nazis at first. See also Schäffer's reminiscences in *Carl Melchior*, p. 99.

Moeller van den Bruck he joined first the DVP and then later went over to the DNVP. In July 1932 he was elected to the Reichstag as a deputy of Hugenberg's party. In that year he called Hitler a 'dreamer' in a journal, *Das Gross-Deutsche Reich*, with which he was connected. After the elections in March 1933 he informed Hitler personally that he regretted his political past and joined the NSDAP parliamentary party in the Reichstag. Although now a Nazi deputy, his application for membership in the party was nevertheless rejected.[26] Without a secure footing in the party, Stadtler was forced to look about for a new political role for himself. In June 1933 he approached the Ullstein firm, requested a meeting, and was obliged by Hermann Ullstein and two of his nephews. At their encounter Stadtler informed the Ullstein representatives that he was on excellent terms with Hitler, had constant access to the chancellery, and that if the publishing enterprise were to take him on as its 'political adviser' it would have nothing to fear from the National Socialists.[27] That Stadtler was hired almost immediately illustrated the desperation of the firm's owners. In his first speech to the assembled editorial staff of all Ullstein publications Stadtler announced that if the firm was to survive the editors must display not only a willingness to co-operate with the new rulers but obvious enthusiasm for their new political role.[28] That he did have access to Hitler Stadtler proved by obtaining a meeting with the chancellor on 12 July. However, that he possessed the confidence of the Nazis was a personal illusion if not an outright fabrication. He was refused membership in the party; the Berlin Gauleitung regarded him with suspicion; and Goebbels recognized that he had been hired by the Ullsteins only in a desperate effort to protect their firm.[29]

[26] See the Kulturkammer file on Stadtler in the Berlin Document Center; also Fritz Stern, *The Politics of Cultural Despair* (New York, 1965), pp. 279ff.; Heuss, *Naumann*, pp. 453f. and 500.

[27] H. Ullstein, *Rise and Fall*, pp. 24f.

[28] Ibid., p. 25.

[29] Gauleitung Gross-Berlin to the president of the Reichsschrifttumskammer, 13 December 1935, in the Kulturkammer file on Stadtler, Berlin Document Center. Also Jödicke, 'Dokumente und Aufzeichnungen', p. 74.

During the summer of 1933 Bausback and Stadtler went
to work to preen the firm so that it would meet National
Socialist requirements. In the second week of October both
reported to the chancellery on their progress.[30] Over seventy
editors in the newspaper and magazine departments had
been removed and replacements found who, as Stadtler said,
'support the new course with intense personal conviction'.
'For the future I can guarantee', he wrote to Hitler, 'that the
newspaper, magazine, and book sections will make every
effort to put into action, selflessly, enthusiastically, and in
the spirit of the new state, the very considerable weapons and
power which the Ullstein firm has built up in years of work.'
As in the Mosse house, all the older editors who had accompanied the Ullstein concern in its rise to international
renown were dismissed. Julius Elbau, Carl Misch, Max
Osborn, Kurt Korff, Richard Lewinsohn, to name but a few,
all departed, and most, deprived of a livelihood by the
editors' law, went into exile.

In the Sonnemann firm, perhaps out of respect for the
part-ownership of the concern by I.G. Farben, no outright
National Socialist was forced on the management or on the
board of editors. Nevertheless, the staff of the *Frankfurter
Zeitung* was also reorganized. In March three editors of long
standing in the section responsible for domestic politics left
the paper; in the next few months they were followed by
four others from the same section, as well as two correspondents and three financial editors.[31] In the Frankfurt publishing house certain efforts were made to protect the Jewish
members of the staff but with only nominal success. At the
end of 1936 there were two 'half-Jews' and two men married
to Jewesses still on the staff of the paper.[32]

Goebbels had once said that he could think of no greater
pleasure than 'to see the gentlemen in the Eschenheimer

---

[30] Bausback to state secretary Lammers, 12 October 1933; and Stadtler to
Hitler, 13 October 1933, Neue Reichskanzlei files, R43II/471.

[31] Benno Reifenberg in his contribution to the special issue of *Die Gegenwart*,
31 October 1956, p. 44.

[32] See Albert Oeser to Alfred Herrmann, 29 December 1933, NL Herrmann,
11a, pp. 30ff.; and Reifenberg in *Die Gegenwart*, 31 October 1956, p. 44.

Gasse dancing to my tune'.[33] In 1933 they began to dance and danced for ten years—until the *Frankfurter Zeitung* ceased publication in 1943. Occasionally, for a split moment, they grimaced or made disrespectful signs behind their backs, but in the audience very few noticed, for attention was focused on the highly accurate dance steps. A British journalist was one of the audience: in August 1933 Henry Wickham Steed remarked bitterly that the formerly proud *Frankfurter Zeitung* had become 'an almost *gleichgeschaltetes* tool of unfreedom'.[34]

Throughout the Weimar Republic the Reich and state governments subsidized and in some cases even bought newspapers which were in financial distress and were thought to be important and desirable contributors to German public life. Particular attention was paid to the maintenance of German newspapers, as well as other cultural institutions, in border territories, in lands separated from Germany as a result of the Versailles treaty, and in other areas outside Germany where Germans constituted a substantial ethnic group. Already in the early years of the Republic one man emerged as the chief organizer and executor of government aid to the press. To the public he was unknown, to the press itself he remained a mystery figure, but no individual in Germany possessed more confidential knowledge about the entire German publishing business than Max Winkler.[35]

Born in 1875 in West Prussia, Winkler began his career as a minor civil servant in the postal service. By the end of the war he had become deputy mayor of Graudenz and in January 1919 was elected as a Democratic representative to the Prussian constituent assembly. When Graudenz was incorporated into Poland, Winkler began lobbying in Berlin,

[33] Cited ibid., p. 42.

[34] In a letter to Leopold Schwarzschild in Paris, printed in *Das neue Tagebuch*, I (19 August 1933), pp. 180f.

[35] Information on Winkler is available in Hale, *The Captive Press*, pp. 127ff.; Mendelssohn, *Zeitungsstadt Berlin*, pp. 324ff.; Boveri, *Wir lügen alle*, pp. 227ff. The following account is also based on the files of Winkler's denazification proceedings in the Institut für Zeitgeschichte, Munich, and in the Bundesarchiv Koblenz; and on Winkler's own memorandum 'Wirtschaftliche Betreuung deutscher Minderheiten', NL Dietrich, 210, pp. 1ff.

among his own party associates and within various government ministries, for the official organization of economic
and cultural support for Germans outside the national
frontiers. To assist the extra-territorial German press an
organization called the Concordia Literarische Anstalt was
founded in early 1920 with Winkler as its managing director
and with an advisory committee composed of representatives
of the five major political parties, later chaired by Hermann
Dietrich. The Reich and Prussian governments each provided
half of the initial capital and future funds for Concordia.
This was only a beginning for Winkler. As the operations of
Concordia grew in number and size, he parcelled up its
various functions and launched separate companies, each to
look after a particular sector of duties and interests. The
Zeitungsbedarf G.m.b.H., to administer capital investment in
the press, was founded in 1923; the auditing company Cura
in 1926; and a covering organization for the administration
of the whole effort, Cautio, was established in 1929. As the
activities of these concerns expanded in turn, their functions
often overlapped, so that eventually Winkler's financial web
became a highly complicated, to the uninitiated totally
confusing and impenetrable operation. On the inside, however, it was run with astonishing efficiency by a remarkably
small staff of employees in Berlin who were sworn to
secrecy.

By 1933 Winkler was a trustee for nineteen enterprises
answerable in practice ultimately only to the Reich central
accounting office. His dominion in the press stretched from
Denmark to Zürich, Vienna, and South Tyrol; and from the
Saar to Riga. But it was no longer limited, as at its inception,
only to papers outside the Reich and in border areas. The
inflation, the occupation of the Ruhr, and Hugenberg's
penetration of the provincial press had given him a pretext
for extending his sphere of operations increasingly to papers
within the country. In 1922-3 alone, 294 newspapers in the
Rhineland, the Palatinate, Hessen, and Westphalia received
financial assistance from Winkler's organizations.[36] In 1925

---

[36] Foreign minister Stresemann to the state secretary in the Reich chancellery, 10 May 1928, Büro des Reichministers RM28, 1, Politisches Archiv des
Auswärtigen Amtes, Bonn.

he arranged the purchase of the *Deutsche Allgemeine Zeitung* from the Stinnes concern by the Prussian government and in 1926 the transference of its ownership to the Reich.[37] The *Frankfurter Nachrichten*, another Stinnes paper, and *Neuer Tag* of Cologne were also bought by Winkler for the Reich.

Although Winkler was initially a member of the DDP, his political interests were shallow. He was above all a manager and financial wizard who revelled in his own success and expertise. In 1921 he lost his seat in the Prussian Landtag and thereafter devoted all his time to his duties as a trustee of the Reich. Newspapers which came into his fold were never influenced politically, a feature which distinguished his press empire from that of Hugenberg. Nor was he out for personal profit. Rather, he indulged in a kind of innocent paternal attachment and devotion to his creations and projects. He felt, probably justifiably, that no one else could replace him and carry on with his activities without bringing immense disorder to his operations. The numerous changes of government in the Reich did not affect Winkler; he knew that he was indispensable.

When Hitler came to power Winkler's attitude, as he himself stated, was that if he had served under eighteen governments already he could just as easily serve under a nineteenth. In February 1933 his offices in the Brückenallee in Berlin were searched twice. Then in mid-February Hitler's secretary Lammers summoned him to report on his activities as a trustee of the Reich. Present at the meeting was Hitler's press chief Walther Funk, a former editor of the right-wing financial daily, the *Berliner Börsen-Zeitung*. Winkler's account of his operations evidently left a highly favourable impression on Lammers and Funk, for shortly after the March elections he was asked by Funk on behalf of Goebbels to carry on with his functions.

If Winkler had reason to be proud of his managerial skill and his financial manipulations during the Weimar

---

37 See Winkler's memorandum, 'Wirtschaftliche Betreuung', NL Dietrich, 210, pp. 22f.; and the correspondence between Winkler and Dietrich in NL Dietrich, 275, *passim.*

Republic, in the Third Reich he spun a web through the publishing and film industries the size of which even Alfred Hugenberg would have envied. He in fact dismantled Hugenberg's empire and incorporated it into his own; for Amann's Eher Verlag he purchased much of the provincial press; and he regrouped a large number of other dailies under holding and managing companies which he directed. He merged the Wolff Telegraph Bureau with the Telegraph Union to form the official DNB news agency. In 1935 he also took on the title of 'Reich plenipotentiary for the German film industry'. It was no accident that in lighter moments Winkler was called the 'Reich trustee for everything'.

That a former Democrat was instrumental in delivering the two great democratic publishing houses of Ullstein and Mosse into the possession of Hitler's Third Reich was ironic, symbolic, and perhaps fitting.

In the spring of 1931 the circulation of all Ullstein publications had begun to decline. Advertising revenue had already decreased noticeably in the previous year. Throughout 1931 and 1932 the drop in business continued. Between January 1931 and January 1933 the circulation of the *Vossische Zeitung* declined from 81,000 to 53,000, that of the *Berliner Morgenpost* from 591,940 to 449,710, that of the *BZ am Mittag* from 175,170 to 139,390, that of *Tempo* from 145,450 to 96,920, and that of the firm's greatest money-maker, the *Berliner Illustrirte Zeitung*, from 1,753,580 to 1,502,090.[38] The advent of Hitler and the initial measures of the government against the press were, of course, viewed as a very serious threat to the existence of the firm, but all hope was not immediately discarded. In the first months of 1933 circulations picked up slightly. It was felt, moreover, that Hitler's government could not last. As for the economic depression, this would be weathered easily, even if some capital had to be borrowed temporarily to prop up the firm. However, the optimism was short-lived. After April circulation figures began to dip once again, now clearly

[38] See Appendic II, p. 314.

because of the political pressures on the public. Advertising contracts suffered a similar fate.

On 20 March Louis Ullstein died, aged sixty-nine. One of his last remarks to Carl Jödicke was that National Socialism had been completely misunderstood.[39] His place as chairman of the board of directors was taken, not, as would have been natural, by one of the other brothers, but by a brother-in-law, Fritz Ross, an 'Aryan'—a step clearly meant as a concession to the new state. In April the literary review *Querschnitt* was sold to the Kurt Wolff Verlag (which Peter Reinhold had bought from Kurt Wolff in 1930); on 5 August *Tempo* ceased publication; in September the humorous monthly magazine *Uhu* appeared for the last time; and after 31 October the *Vossische Zeitung* was issued only once a day. In the course of the year a four-million-mark loan had to be negotiated with the Deutsche Bank and Berliner Handelsgesellschaft. Finally, on 31 March 1934 the last issue of the *Vossische Zeitung* was printed. By then its circulation had declined to under 50,000. These publications were dropped not because, as members of the family later insisted,[40] the Ullsteins did not want to publish National Socialist propaganda, but simply because they represented too great a financial drain on a firm which was now in considerable distress. The idea of closing down *Tempo* and the *Vossische Zeitung* predated Hitler's take-over of power. In its last year of business under the Ullstein family the firm suffered a loss of 2·1 million marks.[41] Eduard Stadtler's promise to protect the Ullsteins' interests when he joined the firm in June 1933 turned out shortly to be pure sham. In a meeting which he had with Hitler on 12 July he was informed that the editorial *Gleichschaltung* of the firm would not suffice and that changes also had to be undertaken in matters of ownership and management. Stadtler was instructed to consult Hjalmar Schacht, the Reichsbank

---

[39] Jödicke to Johannes Weyl, 22 September 1964, contained in 'Dokumente und Aufzeichnungen', pp. 118f.

[40] Franz Ullstein to Margaret T. Edelheim, 14 August 1944, Ullstein file, Leo Baeck Institute, New York; and Heinz Ullstein in a letter to the editor, *Welt am Sonntag*, 45, 5 November 1967.

[41] *Ullstein Geschäftsbericht* for 1933.

president, on these questions.[42] Bausback then contacted Schacht and by late September a formula had been drawn up for 'Aryanizing' the Ullstein A.G.[43]

The Ullstein family was to surrender the majority of its shares in the company to a cross-section of non-Jewish bankers and industrialists acceptable to the National Socialist regime. The terms of sale were to be extremely favourable to the new shareholders. The minority of shares left in the possession of the family would be administered in trust by Fritz Ross, the one non-Jewish member of the family. Possible shareholders were then sought out by Bausback; the proposals were submitted to Goebbels and Hitler; and on 2 November the reorganization of ownership and management was ratified in a general meeting of shareholders and directors.[44] The Ullsteins obviously had little choice in the matter, but the arrangements were made more palatable in that among the new shareholders were a number of people who were favourably disposed to the Ullstein family despite political differences. They included Professor Karl Haushofer, an acquaintance of Fritz Ross from the war, Professor Martin Spahn, with whom Stadtler had studied, and three men whom Bausback knew personally, Hugo Debach, director of a Württemberg metal factory, Heinrich Pferdemenges, owner of a textile concern, and the large landowner Günther von Wulffen. Bausback became the chairman of the ten-member board of directors, which now included only two representatives of the Ullstein family, Fritz Ross and Franz Ullstein.

Hitler had approved the prospective changes in October without making further demands.[45] What the exact attitude of Goebbels was is not clear. In a deposition during his denazification proceedings Winkler declared that Goebbels was set on destroying the Ullstein firm entirely—a firm

[42] Stadtler to Lammers, 21 August 1933, Neue Reichskanzlei files, R43II/471.

[43] 'Gleichschaltung der Ullstein-Betriebe', memorandum from the Reichsbank-Direktorium to state secretary Lammers, 29 September 1933, Neue Reichskanzlei files, R43II/471.

[44] See the correspondence between Bausback and Stadtler, and Bausback and Lammers in October, Neue Reichskanzlei files, R43II/471.

[45] Lammers to Stadtler, 24 October 1933, Neue Reichskanzlei files, R43II/471.

which had once refused to publish his novel *Michael*—and that it was only his, Winkler's, arguments which persuaded Goebbels that a purchase of the firm might be feasible instead.[46] Winkler's later account was obviously biased; moreover factually it was confused, and therefore it must be treated with care.[47] Goebbels naturally wished to weaken the Ullstein firm as long as the family still held executive control. That he was intent on destroying the firm itself as a publishing enterprise is on the other hand highly unlikely. The idea of pressuring the Ullsteins into selling their remaining share in the concern was far too obvious a solution for Goebbels not to have considered it before Winkler made the suggestion. Winkler probably merely persuaded Goebbels that the negotiation of the sale would not be as difficult a task as Goebbels might have expected.

Winkler's assurance to Goebbels that the Ullsteins would sell was based on information which he had gathered from the Ullstein family directly and from his friend and former associate Hermann Dietrich. In early 1934 Winkler attended a dinner party at Dietrich's home. At table he sat beside Franz Ullstein's wife who conveyed to him her husband's anxiety about the future of the firm. A few weeks later Dietrich informed Winkler that Franz Ullstein wished to speak to him.[48] Early in 1934 Hjalmar Schacht apparently advised Franz Ullstein to sell and leave Germany; the Hitler regime would not last more than three or four years; when it fell, the family could return and reclaim their firm.[49] Both Franz and Heinz Ullstein later acknowledged the willingness of the family to sell.[50] Hence, the idea of a sale had advanced beyond the stage of speculation by the end of April 1934. On

[46] Deposition entitled 'Ullstein A.G.', 12 September 1947, in Winkler file, Institut für Zeitgeschichte, Munich.

[47] Hale's account, *The Captive Press*, pp. 132ff., relies too heavily on Winkler; Mendelssohn's account, *Zeitungsstadt Berlin*, pp. 371ff., is too one-sided in favour of the Ullsteins.

[48] Winkler deposition, 12 September 1947, p. 42.

[49] Jödicke, 'Dokumente und Aufzeichnungen', p. 44.

[50] Franz Ullstein in a statement given to New York City authorities, 3 July 1942, and in a letter to Margaret T. Edelheim, 14 August 1944, Ullstein file, Leo Baeck Institute, New York; and Heinz Ullstein in a letter to the editor, *Welt am Sonntag*, 45, 5 November 1967.

29 April Goebbels accelerated events by suddenly banning the *Grüne Post*; the suspension was to be mercilessly long, three months.

Goebbels's truculent action against the non-political journal devoted to country life was occasioned by an article entitled 'Mr. Reich minister—a word please!'[51] written by its chief editor Ehm Welk. On 19 April Goebbels had spoken to a conference of the national journalists' association and had bemoaned the monotonous uniformity and lack of inspiration in the German press. Welk, writing under the pseudonym Thomas Trimm, responded with a lightly ironical, gently critical appeal to Goebbels to seek the reasons for this monotony within the system of controls applied to the press by the National Socialist state. Goebbels was infuriated by Welk's impertinence and effrontery, but he also saw in the article a welcome excuse to deal an injurious blow to the Ullstein firm. Next to the *Berliner Illustrirte*, the *Grüne Post*, with its circulation of over 700,000, was Ullstein's leading source of income, and at a time when the firm was already in a desperate financial plight, to lose this major source of revenue would spell complete disaster for the concern. The Ullsteins would either sell or face eventual bankruptcy. Goebbels had every reason to believe that the former would be the case.

When the article appeared he rang up Himmler personally, who just a few days earlier had replaced Diels as head of the Prussian Gestapo, and demanded immediate suspension of the *Grüne Post* for three months and the arrest of its chief editor, Welk.[52] On 30 April Goebbels explained his action in a letter. Welk's derisive article was a 'direct slap in the face' for Hitler and himself, he claimed.

Since the journal *Grüne Post* has a very wide circulation and since it is read especially by simple citizens, the ban must serve as an example that the National Socialist government will not stand for attacks on its authority. The publishers of the *Grüne Post* share responsibility for the article because they still have the duty, even after the promulgation of

---

[51] *Grüne Post*, 17, 29 April 1934.

[52] Memorandum dated 30 April 1934 in the files of the Reichssicherheitshauptamt, R58/1011, Bundesarchiv Koblenz.

the editors' law, to look after the general attitude of their publications by proper selection of personnel.[53]

The Ullsteins soon recognized that the end had finally come. Through Karl Haushofer Fritz Ross managed to arrange a meeting with Rudolf Hess but was told in the most uncompromising fashion by Hess that Jewish ownership in the Ullstein firm had to be eliminated entirely.[54] A delegation which visited Goebbels—consisting of Bausback, Jödicke, and a Nazi member of the management, Theodor Martens—met with similar cold treatment and intransigence. If the firm continued to remain in Jewish hands, said Goebbels, 'we'll ban another, even larger publication.'[55]

Franz Ullstein, on the advice of Hermann Dietrich, then immediately contacted Winkler again, and serious negotiations began in mid-May between Winkler, whom Goebbels had instructed to proceed with the purchase, and representatives of the Ullsteins—Bausback, Ross, and a team of lawyers. On 7 June the deal was closed. The family and directors had estimated the total value of the enterprise at close to sixty million marks.[56] The ultimate sale price amounted in all to twelve million: six million for the shares—of which only 2·5 million were still in the hands of the family after the changes of the previous November; four million for the non-voting stock, a sum which was transferred into bonds; and two million for publishing and title rights. When both the transactions of November 1933 and June 1934 were taken into account, along with the various deductions imposed—such as capital transfer tax, settlement of publishing and title rights with the former, pre-1914, owners of the *Vossische Zeitung*, the Lessing family—the Ullsteins received in the end approximately six million marks for their business.[57] Towards Winkler, however, the family had no hard feelings.[58] The Ullsteins were grateful that they

[53] Goebbels to the Geheime Polizeiamt, 30 April 1934, Reichssicherheitshauptamt files, R58/1011.

[54] Mendelssohn, *Zeitungsstadt Berlin*, pp. 377f.

[55] Jödicke, 'Dokumente und Aufzeichnungen', p. 75.

[56] H. Ullstein, *Rise and Fall*, p. 271.

[57] Winkler deposition, 12 September 1947, p. 43; Mendelssohn, *Zeitungsstadt Berlin*, pp. 380f.; H. Ullstein, *Rise and Fall*, p. 271.

[58] Heinz Ullstein in a letter to the editor, *Welt am Sonntag*, 45, 5 November 1967; Winkler deposition, 12 September 1947, p. 43.

received as much as they did. For a time they had feared the possibility of outright expropriation.[59]

The shares of the Ullstein firm, which retained its name until 15 November 1937 when it became the Deutscher Verlag, were taken over by Winkler's Cautio enterprise. However, much to Winkler's surprise, payment for the purchase eventually came from Max Amann and the Eher Verlag rather than from either the propaganda ministry or the ministry of finance. On the evening of the day that Winkler concluded the negotiations for the purchase, on behalf of the propaganda ministry as he thought, Hitler met with Amann, Funk, and Goebbels to discuss the purchase. Amann trumped Goebbels with the argument that a government ministry could not properly own and operate a large publishing business and that the Ullstein concern should therefore come under the aegis of the party publishing house. On consideration Hitler accepted Amann's view, and consequently Ullstein was consigned to the fold of the Eher Verlag. At the same meeting it was decided, naturally, to lift the ban on the *Grüne Post*.[60]

All the Ullsteins departed from the firm, and the board of directors and the management were reorganized once again. Bausback remained chairman of the directors; Stadtler was ejected as political director; and the editorial staff underwent yet another purge. The new general manager and political policy co-ordinator was Max Wiessner, the former Berlin correspondent of the *Frankfurter Zeitung* who had assisted Theodor Wolff in the founding of the Democratic Party in November 1918 and had been an enthusiastic worker for this party in its early years. However, Wiessner had subsequently become so disillusioned with the DDP and with republican politics that his thinking became fraught with cultural pessimism and political despair.[61] Carl Jödicke has

59 Jödicke, 'Dokumente und Aufzeichnungen', p. 75.

60 Memorandum dated 8 June 1934, Reichssicherheitshauptamt files, R58/1011; and Hale, *The Captive Press*, pp. 133f.

61 For an indication of the development of Wiessner's ideas, see his letters, to Payer, 25 October 1921, NL Payer, 14, pp. 87ff.; to Gessler, 20 January 1928, NL Gessler, 18, pp. 180f.; and to Koch-Weser, 11 October 1930, NL Koch-Weser, 110, pp. 171ff.

described Wiessner as a heavy drinker and a basically primitive man. He apparently often said of himself: 'I see everything in simple terms; I'm a farmer's son from the Erzgebirge.' His appointment to the Ullstein firm, arranged by his friend Walther Funk, was but another of the bitter and symbolic ironies that accompanied the death and interment of the former democratic press.[62]

In contrast to the Ullstein concern, which in January 1933, despite recent financial losses, was on paper still a stable business enterprise, the Mosse firm was on the verge of bankruptcy when Hitler came to power. The uncovered debts of the business ran to 8·85 million marks and over eight thousand creditors clamoured for a settlement. Hans Lachmann-Mosse and his wife now spent most of their time abroad, and rumours flourished that the sale of the publishing house was imminent. On 26 March, however, the *Berliner Tageblatt* still rejected these speculations in a front-page statement. Then within a fortnight the position changed abruptly. On 9 April the *Tageblatt* announced that the owners were relinquishing their control of the firm and transforming the business into the Rudolf Mosse Foundation, the profits of which would be donated for the next fifteen years to victims of the war. The former management would continue to run the firm.

This gesture was totally specious for any profits which the business realized in the foreseeable future would undoubtedly be swallowed by its creditors. It was designed actually to give the owners a further short respite during which they hoped to transfer some more of their private wealth abroad. The creditors, sensing yet another attempt to deprive them of their claims, quickly organized themselves and demanded a court settlement.

The first section of the business to be dismantled was the advertising agency. In July the various German branches were allocated to receivers.[63] Then in September bankruptcy court

---

62 Wiessner joined the SA but an application of his in 1944 for membership in the NSDAP was rejected on grounds that he had once been an active Freemason in Hamburg. See the Party Correspondence file on Wiessner in the Berlin Document Center. See also Jödicke, 'Dokumente und Aufzeichnungen', p. 76.

63 *Zeitungs-Verlag*, XXXIV (29 July 1933), p. 489.

proceedings were opened to deal with the rest of the Mosse firm's assets. The tangible private wealth which the Lachmann-Mosses had to leave behind in Germany when they emigrated—the considerable art collection, real estate, building and entertainment investments, and other property— was eventually expropriated. In early 1934 Lachmann-Mosse signed over, in Paris, the family's shares in the publishing house to receivers.[64]

Since the publishing house appeared to be in a hopeless financial quagmire, the creditors tried to find a buyer. In February 1934 Walter Haupt, their spokesman, approached Winkler, informing him that the Mosse business would have to fold unless a buyer was found. Thousands of workers, Haupt told Winkler, would be thrown out of work; the government surely was interested in preventing this. Winkler considered the matter and reported to Goebbels. However, a few days later he notified Haupt that he was not in a position to negotiate.[65] The reason for the negative reply may have been that at that particular moment he and Goebbels were occupied with the problems of Ullstein. The creditors then tried different approaches: they attempted to find money from other government sources, and some endeavoured to sell their shares individually, but without success.

Then in the autumn of 1934 Goebbels had a change of mind. Max Amann had succeeded in snatching the Ullstein concern from his grasp, and Goebbels may have been titillated by the idea of bringing the traditional rival of Ullstein, the Mosse firm, into his domain. Another contributing factor to his decision may have been his hearing that the directors of the firm were in contact with a Swiss bank consortium which had revealed an interest in buying the firm.[66] At any rate, one day he suddenly instructed Winkler to negotiate the purchase.[67]

[64] *Zeitungs-Verlag*, XXXIV (16 September 1933), p. 602; (7 October 1933), p. 653; (18 November 1933), p. 755. Also Boveri, *Wir lügen alle*, pp. 219ff.; and the recapitulatory memorandum by Schwarzrat for the finance ministry, 26 August 1942, Reichsfinanzministerium files, R2/4957, pp. 269ff.; and that by Dahlgrün, 20 March 1943, in the same file, pp. 428ff.

[65] Boveri, *Wir lügen alle*, pp. 220, 233f.

[66] Ibid., pp. 222f.

[67] See Winkler to Funk, 31 March 1939, Reichsfinanzministerium files, R2/4957, p. 97.

Winkler's offer of just over four million marks was accepted greedily by the creditors. The finance ministry supplied three million marks and the Dresdner Bank the rest.[68] The Mosse publishing house was then incorporated into the Berliner Druck- und Zeitungsbetriebe A.G. which Winkler had founded and which he controlled through his Cautio company.[69] The name of Mosse thus finally disappeared from the German newspaper scene.

The fate of the Frankfurter Societäts-Druckerei was less complicated. Its financial prospects did not improve in 1933. Since 1930 the sale of the rest of the Simon-Sonnemann family shares in the firm to the spokesmen of I.G. Farben had been considered and discussed at intervals.[70] In view of the political events of 1933, the Simon brothers and their mother Therese Simon-Sonnemann, decided at last to dispose of their majority shares. On 1 June 1934 the *Frankfurter Zeitung* published a short notice which stated that the family had sold its holdings to the former owners of the minority shares in the firm, the Imprimatur G.m.b.H. As a result of the sale Farben possessed indirectly all but 2·04 per cent of the FSD. This nominal percentage of shares was bought by a friend of Hermann Hummel, Wendelin Hecht, who became the general director of the firm.

Protected by Farben, a chemical trust whose co-operation was essential to Hitler's rearmament programme, the *Frankfurter Zeitung* enjoyed a degree of liberty unavailable to any other German newspaper in the Third Reich. The circulation of the paper gradually picked up as a result, as did its advertising income. By 1938, however, the considerations which had led to Carl Bosch's original interest in the FSD were no longer present, and at the end of that year the firm was sold, in the greatest secrecy—unbeknown even to

[68] Memorandum dated 20 May 1939, Reichsfinanzministerium files, R2/4957, p. 103; Winkler's statement in the restitution case of Felicia Lachmann-Mosse against Cautio-Treuhand G.m.b.H., 1954, reprinted in Boveri, *Wir lügen alle*, pp. 233f. and 242ff.

[69] Under its new owners the old Mosse firm continued to lose money and needed repeated subsidies, which it received from the propaganda ministry. See the financial reports of Cautio in the Reichsfinanzministerium files, R2/4959, pp. 135ff.

[70] Werner Wirthle, chairman of the Verlagshaus Frankfurter Societäts-Druckerei, in a letter to the author, 16 December 1968.

the editors of the *Frankfurter Zeitung*—to the Herold company, a subsidiary of the Nazi party's Eher Verlag.[71] On 20 April 1939 the ultimate paradox was enacted: at a birthday party arranged for Hitler, Max Amann presented the *Frankfurter Zeitung* to the Führer as a birthday present.[72]

---

[71] See Mendelssohn, *Zeitungsstadt Berlin*, pp. 390f.; and Hale, *The Captive Press*, p. 290.

[72] Hans Dieter Müller in his introduction to *Facsimile Querschnitt durch das Reich* (Munich, Berne, Vienna, 1964), p. 9.

CONCLUSION

It is not laziness, ill-will or clumsiness that makes me
fail in everything, but the lack of ground under my feet,
the lack of air, the lack of law. My task is to create
these things.
—Franz Kafka

The Weimar Republic was an idea which never became a
reality.[1] That idea foresaw a humane and just society, in
which bigotry, cruelty, and unwarranted privilege were at a
minimum; it envisaged responsible and rational government
based on the leadership and co-operation of responsible and
rational men. The Weimar Republic was to be a democracy
devoted to social justice within and a peaceful international
order without. The idea had a long, although hardly prolific
or rich, intellectual ancestry in Germany; liberalism was its
main, albeit often inhospitable, political home. From the
perspective of 1918, the idea had taken its most recent shape
gradually since the early 1890s, in the wake of rapid industrialization and social change, first as the progeny of a few
intellectuals and a handful of politicians who were dis-
enchanted with the mainstream of German liberalism, and
then haltingly as the vision of a wider segment of the
population. An advance of particular significance had come
in the years since the turn of the century in that the idea had
burst the confines of political liberalism and had taken firm
root in the socialist party and promising root in political
catholicism. A loosely united, inter-party, democratic reform
movement had thus emerged in German politics. In this
reform movement the socially conscious left wing of liberalism served as a linchpin. The war experience and the
indisputable, glaring bankruptcy of the old order during the
war had then suddenly made the idea of democracy palatable
to the large majority of Germans.

The translation of the idea into reality was, however, a
prodigious task in view of Germany's social and political

---

[1] Peter Gay, *Weimar Culture: The Outsider as Insider* (London, 1969), p. 1.

development and in view of the circumstances, both internal and external, surrounding the collapse of the imperial system in 1918. Even the propagators of the democratic idea could not agree on how to go about their task after they had assumed governmental responsibility. Hamstrung by ideologies which emphasized evolution, historical on the one hand and deterministic on the other, and by a past dominated by mutual distrust, liberalism and socialism adopted a defensive stance after the war and hesitated to undertake any radical reform. The form of politics was changed, the substance, however, was not. The democratic idea remained an idea, and for the populace at large it quickly soured. The popular mandate for extensive reform was retracted as early as the June elections of 1920.

The idea of the Weimar Republic continued to have its defenders; the reality of the Weimar state had no vibrant and devoted support. It turned out to be neither the state which Social Democrats envisaged nor the state which progressive liberals had hoped to create. By the right it was described as the bastard son of domestic and foreign treachery; by the left it came to be regarded as a child crippled by fanatical nationalism and the blind self-interest of the propertied few. For a decade the Weimar state was tolerated by much of the German middle classes. However, when the miseries of the depression followed upon the despair of the inflation, the malfunctioning democratic system was rejected with vigour by those social strata on which it depended for its life.

No group of Germans was more devoted to the idea of the Weimar Republic and at the same time more aware of the void between the idea and the reality than those journalists who formed the spiritual core of the German democratic press. Many of them regarded the idea as their trust and their burden. Before and during the war they had helped nurture and propagate the vision of a tolerant, cosmopolitan, rationally ordered society. Immediately after the war a number of them briefly took the initiative to try and realize this vision. Thereafter they struggled to preserve their own ideals.

They gave their readers an unending feast of reason and decency. Many of them were Jews, but the progress of mankind was their religion. They were liberals in a venerable rationalist tradition; they were journalists in the spirit of the French *philosophes*. They believed in truth, they believed in human understanding, and they believed that truth and human understanding led to mastery. They lived and worked in an age of hitherto unexampled social change. They encouraged and applauded change, for they believed in modernity. And yet they never fully appreciated all the consequences of the social changes which they witnessed, for they still assumed that even in an industrialized pluralistic society the only method of arriving at truth was by a free and noble competition of opinion in the open market. The open market did not exist. Therefore there was more than a trace of Egmont in all of them. 'Gradually I realized', Bernhard Guttmann reminisced later, 'that we had lived in the spirit of the eighteenth century with its belief in freedom, humanity, and an ultimate harmony in creation and among men; we had lived in a spirit which the sequence of wars and revolutions of the nineteenth century did not justify.'[2]

A number of democratic journalists participated eagerly in the founding of the German Democratic Party, a party which they visualized as a bridge between the working class and the bourgeoisie, with a programme and an ethos advocating a humane synthesis of socialism and liberalism, of intellectualism and political realism. They themselves believed that they embodied this synthesis, in their work and in their thought. The party was to serve as the political corner-stone and ideological fount of the new Republic. Together with the moderate socialists the DDP would implement the reforms necessary for a well-functioning democracy. The experience, however, turned out to be radically different from the hopes. The adoption of an essentially defensive political attitude by the executive ranks of the DDP after 1919 offended the reforming ideals of many of the prominent democratic publicists; and their criticism of developments in the DDP offended the political instincts of the party functionaries, who felt that the press which shared the general aims of the party owed it more responsible and stricter allegiance. A process of alienation from the party, partly imposed and

[2] *Schattenriss einer Generation 1888-1919* (Stuttgart, 1951), pp. 342f.

partly self-inflicted, took place among the journalists who
had enthusiastically supported the DDP at its inception.
Gradually they became outsiders in the only political
grouping in the state with whose fundamental aims they felt
they could identify. Their isolation from the DDP magnified
their isolation from a political and social system in which
they found few heartening features. The DDP was not the
party that they had intended it to be; by corollary the
Republic could not be the political order which they had
hoped to help conceive. Ultimately this dissatisfaction and
latent political deracination meant that although many
democratic journalists could continue to defend intellectually
the ideals of democracy against its opponents, they could
not summon the conviction, the sense of commitment, or the
arguments to defend the existing state à outrance against its
foes; to descend from the symposium to the battlefield. The
ideals had become disembodied; in the end they rang hollow
even for their defenders. 'When I looked back on my life,'
Guttmann remembered, 'I could not shake off the feeling of
futility.'[3]

The political frustrations and doubts, and finally the
ideological malaise which afflicted democratic journalists,
were accompanied and intensified by structural defects and
unstable conditions within the press as an institution. The
decentralization of the German press as a whole rendered it
highly vulnerable economically, and this economic insecurity,
whether latent or actual, made economic considerations take
priority, as a rule, over political considerations in the thinking of those publishers whose papers were not strictly party
organs. An intense competitiveness governed the newspaper
business, and economic survival was the overriding concern of
most publishers. The precariousness of their economic
position made newspapers readily susceptible to interference
by outside interests, to the financial lures of big business,
to pressures from advertisers and from governments, and to
the political fancies of the reading public. The tenuousness of
a publisher's existence, let alone of his independence, pervaded the newspaper trade in the Weimar period. The

[3] Ibid., p. 342.

economic instability of the Weimar state made the inadequacies of liberalism painfully relevant to publishers. In this situation owners were either unwilling or unable to provide safeguards for editorial independence.

In the prominent democratic publishing houses, in the Mosse, Ullstein, and Sonnemann firms, the predominance of economic considerations was not as blatant or as crudely emphasized as in smaller newspaper enterprises. Editorial and management policies did not conflict in principle as long as political and commercial interests overlapped, and editors had far greater freedom and security than in most other firms. However, in the mid-twenties sources of friction began to multiply. The owners of the firms were by and large more conservative in their liberal orientation than the leading editors of their newspapers; they were usually more sympathetic to the idea of liberal unity and, in most cases, less discriminating about the manner in which it was achieved; and they were more cautious about advocating close cooperation between the socialist and liberal movements. In some instances the differences were merely a question of subtleties in interpretation, but for the publishers the subtleties stemmed from practical business considerations. With time, even minor differences assumed major proportions. Thus the two dominant issues which crippled organized liberalism and undermined its popular appeal also occasioned rifts in the large democratic newspaper firms, as economic difficulties either accumulated or loomed on the horizon. This divergence of commercial interests and editorial inclinations was evident before the depression struck with its full force; and the resulting administrative confusion which was an added hindrance to the pursuit of a resolute editorial line was a feature of the democratic publishing houses which predated the rise of political extremism. The depression and the overt political crisis which engulfed Germany at the end of the decade merely exacerbated existing difficulties. A crisis of constitutionalism in German politics would have arisen even without the serious economic slump of 1929-30. By the same token, the institutional crisis which surfaced in the democratic publishing houses after 1928 was not brought on but only aggravated by the depression.

The developments in the Mosse, Ullstein, and Sonnemann firms in the last years of the Weimar Republic followed different paths but the end result was the same: the political independence of the concerns, their internal cohesion, and their ideological self-confidence vanished. Viewed in broad perspective, the state of war between owner and editors in the Mosse firm, the fratricidal feuds in the Ullstein house, and the transfer of part-ownership in the FSD to the largest industrial complex in Germany, the dye-trust I.G. Farben, had common underlying causes and common ramifications. Economic and political disorientation provoked these crises and in the end left these firms devoid of political initiative and uncertain of their political role.

The establishment of the National Socialist dictatorship met with no notable opposition from the German democratic press. Within months of Hitler's advent to the chancellorship the three leading democratic publishing houses had coordinated their operations with the wishes of the regime, with relatively little direct pressure from without. The question of open resistance never arose, and in view of the developments in the democratic press in recent years, it could not arise. Democratic forms were not eliminated in Germany at one stroke; the Weimar constitution was not destroyed overnight; Hitler did not seize power by a *coup d'état*. He was accorded power in a state which had used up its available alternatives to a Hitler-led government. Government above parties had been tried; government by the army's political arm had failed. By January 1933 the Weimar experiment no longer had any semblance of a *raison d'être*. The constitution lay in ruins, and a political vacuum existed. In 1932 the majority of Germans had virulently denounced the Weimar state by voting for the Communists and the National Socialists. The Nazi take-over of power was not a 'seizure of power'; it was an assertion of positive wishes, of principles, of 'truth' in a vacuum of values, convictions, and political alternatives. In 1933 accommodation with National Socialism, with a political movement which displayed energy, purpose, and power, was an imperative necessity for the democratic press as a collective whole. This is what Hermann Ullstein meant later when he wrote: 'There is an inner logic in the fact that the house of Ullstein did not survive the collapse of the democratic German republic. Like that republic, it was unable to act decisively.'[4]

In a speech to journalists on 4 October 1933 Joseph Goebbels rang down the curtain on the democratic press of the Weimar Republic and on 'the other Germany': 'No one can assert that this government is comprised of stupid persons. For had they been more stupid than their opponents, then their opponents, by virtue of their greater intelligence, would probably have found ways and means of keeping us out of power.'[5] In 1934 the former democratic publishing houses passed out of the hands of the families which had launched them, but these transactions were in effect merely an epilogue to the story of the German democratic press and the collapse of Weimar democracy.

[4] 'We Blundered Hitler into Power', *Saturday Evening Post*, Nr. 213 (13 July 1940), p. 35.

[5] Cited in Hans Schmidt-Leonhardt, *Das Schriftleitergesetz vom 4. Oktober* (Berlin, 1934), p. 15.

APPENDIX I

THE POLITICAL ORIENTATION OF THE GERMAN PRESS

A. PERCENTAGE OF TOTAL NUMBER OF NEWSPAPERS[1]

	1898	1913	1917	1926	1928	1930	1932
Right-wing (incl. NSDAP, DNVP, DVP, and Economic Party)	24·1	22·6	16·8	23·6	27·3	22·5	26·7
Centre Party and BVP	9·6	11·6	13·8	12·8	10·8	12·9	12·9
Left liberals	19·6	14·2	16·9	5·5	4·1	3·0	2·9
SPD and KPD	1·7	2·2	2·7	5·7	5·1	5·5	4·8
Non-partisan	45·0	49·2	49·8	52·4	52·7	55·3	52·3

[1] The table up to 1930 is taken from *Handbuch der Weltpresse: Eine Darstellung des Zeitungswesens aller Länder*, ed. Deutsches Institut für Zeitungskunde (Berlin, 1932), p. 146. The figures for 1932 have been calculated on the basis of the statistics supplied in *Handbuch der deutschen Tagespresse* (1932), p. 27.

B. CIRCULATION OF THE POLITICAL PRESS COMPARED TO VOTING FIGURES
(IN MILLIONS)[1]

c=circulation; v=votes

Year	Nationalist right (DNVP, DVP, etc.)		Left liberals		Centre		SPD		KPD		NSDAP	
	c	v	c	v	c	v	c	v	c	v	c	v
1924	3·1	9·0	2·6	1·8	1·75	5·0	0·8	6·0	0·3	3·8	-	-
1928	4·2	7·2	3·7	1·5	1·8	4·8	1·1	9·2	0·4	3·2	0·05	0·7
1930	3·8	4·2	3·6	1·4	2·2	5·2	1·3	8·8	0·5	4·7	0·1	6·5
1932	2·7	2·8	3·2	0·4	1·7	5·8	1·2	8·0	0·6	5·2	0·7	13·8

[1] Compiled from Max Bestler, 'Das Absinken der parteipolitischen Führungsfähigkeit der deutschen Tageszeitungen, 1919-1932: Ein Vergleich der Auflageziffern mit den Wahlziffern der Parteien', unpublished diss. (Berlin, 1941), pp. 100ff.

APPENDIX II

CIRCULATION OF ULLSTEIN PUBLICATIONS [1]

	Vossische Zeitung	Berliner Morgenpost	Berliner Montagspost	BZ am Mittag	Berliner Allgemeine Zeitung	Tempo	Grüne Post	Berliner Illustrirte Zeitung
October 1926	59 080	566 450	160 860	197 610	52 710			1 579 190
October 1928	71 370	607 330	167 020	208 310	51 550		698 350	1 793 860
January 1929	69 680	614 860	160 250	190 860	52 320		857 690	1 842 300
April 1929	70 500	618 270	147 820	174 170	53 370		971 380	1 873 930
July 1929	70 960	615 730	154 330	192 130	51 980	100 940	985 150	1 883 010
April 1930	72 380	623 010	145 070	170 440	51 880	139 110	1 011 420	1 851 690
October 1930	79 660	601 540	178 110	197 230	48 930	144 510	1 033 200	1 809 420
January 1931	81 000	591 940	189 110	175 170	52 380	145 450	1 062 760	1 753 580
April 1931	73 970	572 770	174 370	159 220	51 910	124 650	1 122 460	1 819 130
April 1932	57 480	513 780	173 770	149 140	45 350	103 320	954 050	1 617 160
July 1932	56 700	487 190	184 930	155 380	44 470	112 400	924 630	1 603 220
October 1932	55 730	462 190	182 560	161 770	43 550	110 350	842 130	1 532 310
January 1933	53 500	449 710	160 400	139 390	44 220	96 920	832 660	1 502 090
April 1933	57 000	454 730	174 070	146 160	45 310	104 060	862 920	1 469 810
July 1933	59 910	423 400						1 293 180
October 1933	49 770	349 967	118 070	106 849	44 467		715 921	1 142 010
1934		323 000		99 810				1 080 000

1 From *Ullstein-Berichte*, October 1926 to April 1933. The figures after April 1933 have been gathered from the following sources: *Ullstein Geschäftsbericht* 1933; Eduard Stadtler to the Reich chancellery, 16 August 1933, Neue Reichskanzlei files, R43II/471; *Zeitungswissenschaft*, VIII (15 September 1933), p. 304; Joseph Wulf, *Presse und Funk*, p. 39.

BIBLIOGRAPHY

A. ARCHIVAL SOURCES

Bundesarchiv Koblenz

Reichskanzlei (R43I).
Neue Reichskanzlei (R43II).
Reichsministerium für Volksaufklärung und Propaganda (R55, incl. R55Zg.DC).
Reichsfinanzministerium (R2).
Reichssicherheitshauptamt (R58).
Reichsverband der Deutschen Presse (R103).
Deutsche Volkspartei (R45II).
Deutsche Demokratische Partei/Deutsche Staatspartei (R45III).
Sammlung Brammer (ZSg101).
Sammlung Sänger (Zsg102).
Winkler Denazification file (All. Proz. 2, VI–Winkler).
Nachlässe: Wilhelm Abegg, Gertrud Bäumer, Hermann Dietrich, Eduard Dingeldey, Anton Erkelenz, Bernhard Falk, Otto Gessler, Georg Gothein, Maximilian Harden (see also under Geheimes Staatsarchiv, Berlin), Alfred Herrmann, Siegfried von Kardorff, Erich Koch-Weser, Wilhelm Külz, Walter Lambach, Hermann Luppe, Friedrich von Payer, Rudolf Pechel, Hartmann Freiherr von Richthofen, Walther Shücking, Gustav Stolper (see also under Theodor Heuss Archiv, Stuttgart), Gottfried Traub, August Weber.

Politisches Archiv des Auswärtigen Amtes, Bonn

Nachlass Gustav Stresemann.
Büro des Reichsministers.
Politische Abteilung II, III.
Presse Abteilung.

Geheimes Staatsarchiv, Berlin

Reichsministerium des Innern (Rep. 320).
Staatsministerium des Innern (Rep. 90).
Nachlässe: Maximilian Harden (the main body of this Nachlass is in the Bundesarchiv Koblenz), Friedrich Meinecke, Eugen Schiffer.
Flugblätter und Broschüren, XII Hauptabteilung (DDP).

Hauptstaatsarchiv, Hamburg

Staatliche Pressestelle.
Nachlass Carl Petersen.

Bayerisches Hauptstaatsarchiv, Munich

Ministerium des Innern.
Staatsministerium für Wirtschaft.

Hauptstaatsarchiv Württemberg, Stuttgart

Nachlass Conrad Haussmann.

Berlin Document Center

NSDAP Master File.
Kulturkammer (personnel records of the Reichspressekammer).
Party Membership Correspondence.

Institut für Zeitgeschichte, Munich

Dr. Carl Jödicke, Dokumente und Aufzeichnungen betr. Ullstein-Verlag
    1933-45 (F501).
Hans Schäffer, Tagebücher und Anlagen (ED93).
Winkler, Dr. h.c. Max (ZS517).
P. aus dem Winckel, Aufzeichnungen (Zg1892).

Theodor Heuss Archiv, Stuttgart

Nachlässe: Theodor Heuss, Walter Goetz (consists only of correspon-
    dence with Heuss), Gustav Stolper (consists only of correspon-
    dence with Heuss).

*Werner-von-Siemens-Institut für die Geschichte des Hauses Siemens,
Munich*

Nachlass Carl Friedrich von Siemens.

Zentralarchiv der Frankfurter Allgemeinen Zeitung, Frankfurt a.M.

Biographical files (press cuttings, curricula vitae).

Archiv, Ullstein G.m.b.H., Berlin

Biographical files (press cuttings).

Archiv des Verlags M. DuMont Schauberg, Cologne

Büchner Protokolle—Redaktionssitzungen der Kölnischen Zeitung 22.
    März 1929 bis 2. Dezember 1935.

Institut für Zeitungswissenschaft, Munich

Sammlung Karl d'Ester (press cuttings; Ullstein file contains material on the Ullstein legal suit).
Ullstein Geschäftsberichte.

Institut für Publizistik, Berlin

Georg Bernhard, "Stellungen im Zeitungswesen", Ms.

St. Antony's College, Oxford

NSDAP Hauptarchiv (microfilm).

Leo Baeck Institute, New York

Biographical files (press cuttings, correspondence): Hans Lachmann-Mosse, Ullstein family, Theodor Wolff.

In private hands

Ernst Feder, Diary.
Nachlass Erich Eyck (selected correspondence was kindly put at my disposal by Professor Frank Eyck).
Business report of the Frankfurter Societäts-Druckerei 1926.

B. NON-ARCHIVAL PRIMARY SOURCES

Newspapers and Periodicals

Berliner Morgenpost
Berliner Tageblatt
Berliner Volks-Zeitung
BZ am Mittag
Blätter der Staatspartei
Der Demokrat
Das demokratische Deutschland
Deutsche Einheit
Deutsche Presse
Frankfurter Zeitung
Die Hilfe
Münchner Neueste Nachrichten
Das Tage-Buch
Die Tat
Tempo
Ullstein-Berichte
Vossische Zeitung
Die Welt am Montag
Die Weltbühne

Zeitungs-Verlag
Zeitungswissenschaft

Handbooks

Handbuch der deutschen Tagespresse, ed. Institut für Zeitungswissenschaft, Berlin; 4th edn., Berlin, 1932; 5th edn., Berlin, 1934; 6th edn., Frankfurt a.M., 1937.

Handbuch deutscher Zeitungen 1917, ed. Oskar Michel, Berlin 1917.

Handbuch der Weltpresse: Eine Darstellung des Zeitungswesens aller Länder, ed. Deutsches Institut für Zeitungskunde, Berlin, 1931; 2nd edn., Berlin, 1934; 3rd edn., Leipzig and Frankfurt a.M., 1937.

Handbuch über die Stadt Berlin, Berlin, 1929.

Handbuch der Zeitungswissenschaft, ed. Walther Heide, Berlin, 1940-3.

Jahrbuch der Tagespresse, vols. I-III, Berlin, 1928-30.

Müller-Jabusch, Maximilian (ed.), *Handbuch des öffentlichen Lebens*, Leipzig, 1925, 1929, 1931.

Sperlings Zeitschriften- und Zeitungs-Adressbuch, 52nd edn., Leipzig, 1926; 57th edn., Leipzig, 1931; 59th edn., Berlin, 1933.

Memoirs, Diaries, Collections of Documents, Contemporary Interpretative Literature (Selected)

Auerbach, Walter, *Presse und Gruppenbewusstsein*, Berlin, 1929.

Bab, Julius, *Das Erwachen zur Politik*, Berlin, 1920.

Baümer, Gertrud, *Grundlagen demokratischer Politik*, Karlsruhe, 1928.

Baum, Vicki, *I Know What I'm Worth*, London, 1964.

Bericht über die Verhandlungen des 1. Parteitags der Deutschen Demokratischen Partei abgehalten in Berlin vom 19. bis 22. Juli 1919, Berlin, n.d.

Bericht über die Verhandlungen des 2. ausserordentlichen Parteitages der Deutschen Demokratischen Partei abgehalten in Leipzig vom 13. bis 15. Dezember 1919, Berlin, n.d.

Bericht über die Verhandlungen des 2. ordentlichen Parteitages der Deutschen Demokratischen Partei abgehalten in Nürnberg vom 11. bis 14. Dezember 1920, Berlin, n.d.

Bericht über die Verhandlungen des 3. (ordentlichen) Parteitages der Deutschen Demokratischen Partei abgehalten in Bremen vom 12. bis 14. November 1921, Berlin, n.d.

Bericht über die Verhandlungen des 4. Parteitages der Deutschen Demokratischen Partei abgehalten in Elberfeld vom 9. bis 10. Oktober 1922, Berlin, n.d.

Bericht über die Verhandlungen des 5. Parteitages der Deutschen Demokratischen Partei abgehalten in Weimar vom 5. bis 6. April 1924, Berlin, n.d.

(Other party conference protocols were not published but are available in the NSDAP Hauptarchiv.)

Bernhard, Georg, *Demokratische Politik*, Berlin, 1919.

Die Kriegspolitik der Vossischen Zeitung, Berlin, 1919.

Die deutsche Tragödie: Der Selbstmord einer Republik, Prague, 1933.

Meister und Dilettanten am Kapitalismus im Reiche der Hohenzollern, Amsterdam, 1936.

Bernhard, Ludwig, *Der 'Hugenberg-Konzern': Psychologie und Technik einer Grossorganisation der Presse*, Berlin, 1928.

Bertkau, Friedrich and Karl Bömer, *Der wirtschaftliche Aufbau des deutschen Zeitungsgewerbes*, Berlin, 1932.

Betz, Anton, 'Die Tragödie der "Münchner Neuesten Nachrichten" 1932/33', *Journalismus*, II (1961), pp. 22-46.

Blume, Gustav, *Herr Theodor Wolff und das Ressentiment: Offener Brief an den Chefredakteur des 'Berliner Tageblatt'*, Berlin, 1920.

Bonn, Moritz Julius, *Wandering Scholar*, London 1949,

Brüning, Heinrich, *Memoiren 1918-1934*, Stuttgart, 1970.

Bussmann, Hans, *Untersuchungen über die Presse als Machtform*, Berlin, 1933.

Calic, Edouard, *Ohne Maske: Hitler-Breiting Geheimgespräche 1931*, Frankfurt a.M., 1968.

Carlé, Wilhelm, *Weltanschauung und Presse: Eine soziologische Untersuchung*, Leipzig, 1931.

Cohnstaedt, Wilhelm, 'German Newspapers Before Hitler', *Journalism Quarterly*, XII (1935), pp. 157-63.

Dovifat, Emil, *Die Zeitungen*, Gotha, 1925.

Duderstadt, Henning, *Vom Reichsbanner zum Hakenkreuz, wie es kommen musste: Ein Bekenntnis*, Stuttgart, 1933.

Eberle, Joseph, *Grossmacht Presse: Enthüllungen für Zeitungsgläubige, Forderungen für Männer*, Vienna, 1920.

Eigenbrodt, August, *Berliner Tageblatt und Frankfurter Zeitung in ihrem Verhalten zu den nationalen Fragen 1877-1914*, Berlin, 1917.

Facsimile Querschnitt durch die Berliner Illustrirte, ed. Friedrich Luft, Munich, Berne, Vienna, 1965.

Facsimile Querschnitt durch die Frankfurter Zeitung, ed. Ingrid Gräfin Lynar, Stuttgart, 1964.

Facsimile Querschnitt durch das Reich, ed. Hans Dieter Müller, Munich, Berne, Vienna, 1964.

Fechter, Paul, *An der Wende der Zeit: Menschen und Begegnungen*, Gütersloh, 1949.

Feder, Ernst, *Heute sprach ich mit . . .: Tagebücher eines Berliner Publizisten 1926-1932*, ed. C. Lowenthal-Hensel and A. Paucker, Stuttgart, 1971.

Fischart, Johannes (Erich Dombrowski), *Politische Köpfe*, Berlin, 1919.

Fritsch, Theodor, *Der jüdische Zeitungs-Polyp*, Leipzig, 1921.

(ed.), *Handbuch der Judenfrage*, Leipzig, 1937.

Fromm, Bella, *Blood and Banquets: A Berlin Social Diary*, New York, 1942.

G., R., *Prelude to the Past: The Autobiography of a Woman*, New York, 1934.

Die Gegenwart, XI/special issue (31 October 1956), entitled 'Ein Jahrhundert "Frankfurter Zeitung" 1856-1956'.

Gerlach, Hellmut von, *Von rechts nach links*, Zürich, 1937.

Geschichte der Frankfurter Zeitung, ed. Verlag der Frankfurter Zeitung, Frankfurt a.M., 1911.

Goebbels, Joseph, *Vom Kaiserhof zur Reichskanzlei*, Munich, 1934.

Groth, Otto, *Die Zeitung: Ein System der Zeitungskunde*, 4 vols., Mannheim, Berlin, Leipzig, 1928-30.

Guttmann, Bernhard, *Schattenriss einer Generation 1888-1919*, Stuttgart, 1951.

Hadamovsky, Eugen, *Propaganda und nationale Macht*, Oldenburg, 1933.

Hamburger, Richard, *Zeitungsverlag und Annoncen-Expedition Rudolf Mosse Berlin*, Berlin, 1930.

Heenemann, Horst, *Die Auflagenhöhen der deutschen Zeitungen: Ihre Entwicklung und ihre Probleme*, Berlin, 1930.

Herrmann, Alfred, *Hamburg und das Hamburger Fremdenblatt*, Hamburg, 1928.

Herz, Emil, *Denk' ich an Deutschland in der Nacht: Die Geschichte des Hauses Steg*, Berlin, 1951.

Heuss, Theodor, *Erinnerungen 1905-1933*, Tübingen, 1963.

Die Machtergreifung und das Ermächtigungsgesetz: Zwei nach-gelassene Kapitel der 'Erinnerungen 1905-1933', ed. E. Pikart, Tübingen, 1967.

Hildenbrandt, Fred, *. . . ich soll dich grüssen von Berlin: 1922-1932 Berliner Erinnerungen ganz und gar unpolitisch*, Munich, 1966.

Hiller, Kurt, *Köpfe und Tröpfe: Profile aus einem Vierteljahrhundert*, Hamburg and Stuttgart, 1950.

Hitler, Adolf, *Mein Kampf*, Munich, 1943.

Jacob, B. and Ernst Schilasky, *Die Juden und das Berliner Tageblatt: Ein Briefwechsel*, Berlin, 1920.

Jänecke, Walther, 'Der Übergang der Presse von der Weimarer Republik zum Dritten Reich', *Zeitungs-Verlag und Zeitschriften-Verlag*, Nr. 13 (1 May 1963), pp. 592-8.

Jameson, Egon, *Wenn ich mich recht erinnere: Das Leben eines Optimisten in der besten aller Welten*, Berne and Stuttgart, 1963.

Die Juden in Deutschland, ed. Institut zum Studium der Judenfrage, 3rd edn., Munich, 1936.

Kahn, Ernst, 'The Frankfurter Zeitung', *Year Book II* (of the Leo Baeck Institute), London, 1957, pp. 228-35.

Kaulla, Rudolf, *Der Liberalismus und die deutschen Juden*, Munich and Leipzig, 1928.

Kaupert, Wilhelm, *Die deutsche Tagespresse als Politicum*, Freudenstadt, 1932.

Kircher, Rudolf, *Powers and Pillars: Intimate Portraits of British Personalities*, trans. C. Vesey, London, 1928.

How they do it in England, trans. Frances, Countess of Warwick, London, 1930.

Klippel, Joachim, *Geschichte des Berliner Tageblattes von 1872 bis 1880*, Dresden, 1935.

Kober, A.H., *Einst in Berlin*, ed. Richard Kirn, Hamburg, 1956.

Kessler, Harry Graf, *Tagebücher 1918-1937*, Frankfurt a.M., 1961.

Koestler, Arthur, *Arrow in the Blue: An Autobiography*, London, 1952.

The Invisible Writing: The Second Volume of an Autobiography, 1932-40, London, 1969.

et al., The God that Failed: Six Studies in Communism, London, 1950.

Krell, Max, *Das alles gab es einmal*, Frankfurt a.M., 1961.

Lauinger, Artur, *Das öffentliche Gewissen: Erfahrungen und Erlebnisse eines Redakteurs der Frankfurter Zeitung*, Frankfurt a.M., 1958.

Lewinsohn, Richard, *Das Geld in der Politik*, Berlin, 1930.

Linke, Lilo, *Restless Flags: A German Girl's Story*, London, 1935.

Lüddecke, Theodor, *Die Tageszeitung als Mittel der Staatsführung*, Hamburg, 1933.

Meister, Anton (Adolf Dresler), *Die Presse als Machtmittel Judas*, 2nd edn., Munich, 1931.

Müller, Oscar (ed.), *Krisis: Ein politisches Manifest*, Weimar, 1932.

Paucker, Arnold (ed.), 'Searchlight on the Decline of the Weimar Republic: The Diaries of Ernst Feder', *Year Book XIII* (of the Leo Baeck Institute), London, 1968, pp. 161-234.

Pem (Paul E. Marcus), *Heimweh nach dem Kurfürstendamm: Aus Berlins glanzvollsten Tagen und Nächten*, Berlin, 1952.

Presse in Fesseln: Eine Schilderung des NS-Pressetrusts, Berlin, 1947.

Rosenberg, Alfred, *Dreissig Novemberköpfe*, Munich, 1939.

Schacht, Hjalmar, *My First Seventy-Six Years*, London, 1959.

Schay, Rudolf, *Die Juden in der deutschen Politik*, Berlin, 1929.

Schmidt-Leonhardt, Hans, *Das Schriftleitergesetz vom 4. Oktober 1933*, Berlin, 1934.

Schubert, Walter, *Freie Meinungsäusserung, freie Presse: Entstehung und Untergans eines liberalen Prinzips*, Würzburg, 1939.

Das Schwarzbuch, Tatsachen und Dokumente: Die Lage der Juden in Deutschland 1933, ed. Comité des délégations juives, Paris, 1934.

Sieburg, Friedrich, *Germany: My Country*, trans. W. Ray, London, 1933.

Simon, Heinrich, *Leopold Sonnemann: Seine Jugendgeschichte bis zur Entstehung der 'Frankfurter Zeitung'*, Frankfurt a.M., 1931.

Sinsheimer, Hermann, *Gelebt im Paradies*, Munich, 1953.
Stapel, Wilhelm, *Die literarische Vorherrschaft der Juden in Deutschland 1918-1933*, Hamburg, 1937.
Stolper, Toni, *Ein Leben in Brennpunkten unserer Zeit: Gustav Stolper 1888-1947*, Tübingen, 1960.
Stresemann, Gustav, *Von der Revolution bis zum Frieden von Versailles: Reden und Aufsätze*, Berlin, 1919.
Trials of the War Criminals Before the Nuernberg Military Tribunals, vol. VII (The Farben Case, Military Tribunal VI, Case 6), Washington, 1953.
Ullstein, Heinz, *Spielplatz meines Lebens: Erinnerungen*, Munich, 1961.
Ullstein, Hermann, *The Rise and Fall of the House of Ullstein*, New York, 1943.
    'We Blundered Hitler into Power', *Saturday Evening Post*, Nr. 213 (13 July 1940), pp. 12ff.
(Ullstein Verlag), *50 Jahre Ullstein 1877-1927*, Berlin, 1927.
    Der Verlag Ullstein zum Welt-Reklame-Kongress, 1929, Berlin, 1929.
Wolff, Theodor, *Pariser Tagebuch*, Munich, 1908; 2nd edn., Berlin, 1927.
    Vollendete Tatsachen, Berlin, 1918.
    Das Vorspiel, Berlin, 1924.
    Through Two Decades, London, 1936.
Wulf, Joseph, *Presse und Funk im Dritten Reich: Eine Dokumentation*, Gütersloh, 1964.
Zechlin, Walter, *Pressechef bei Ebert, Hindenburg und Kopf*, Hanover, 1956.
Zehn Jahre deutsche Republik: Ein Handbuch für republikanische Politik, ed. Anton Erkelenz, Berlin, 1928.

Selected Secondary Sources

Abel, Karl-Dietrich, *Presselenkung im NS-Staat: Eine Studie zur Geschichte der Publizistik in der nationalsozialistischen Zeit*, Berlin, 1968.
Albertin, Lothar, 'German Liberalism and the Foundation of the Weimar Republic: A Missed Opportunity?' in *German Democracy and the Triumph of Hitler*, ed. Anthony Nicholls, and E. Matthias, London, 1971, pp. 29-46.
    Liberalismus und Demokratie am Anfang der Weimarer Republik: Eine vergleichende Analyse der Deutschen Demokratischen Partei und der Deutschen Volkspartei, Düsseldorf, 1972.
Becker, Werner, *Demokratie des sozialen Rechts: Die politische Haltung der Frankfurter Zeitung, der Vossischen Zeitung und des Berliner Tageblatts 1918-1924*, Zürich and Frankfurt a.M., 1971.

'Die Rolle der liberalen Presse' in *Deutsches Judentum in Krieg und Revolution 1916-1923*, ed. Werner E. Mosse, Tübingen, 1971, pp. 67-135.

Bestler, Max, 'Das Absinken der parteipolitischen Führungsfähigkeit der deutschen Tageszeitungen 1919-1932: Ein Vergleich der Auflageziffern mit den Wahlziffern der Parteien', unpublished diss., Berlin, 1941.

Boveri, Margret, *Wir lügen alle: Eine Hauptstadtzeitung unter Hitler*, Olten and Freiburg i.B., 1965.

Bracher, Karl Dietrich, *Die Auflösung der Weimarer Republik: Eine Studie zum Problem des Machtverfalls in der Demokratie*, Villingen, 1964.

The German Dictatorship: The Origins, Structure, and Effects of National Socialism, trans. J. Steinberg, New York, 1970.

Wolfgang Sauer, and Gerhard Schulz, *Die nationalsozialistische Machtergreifung: Studien zur Errichtung des totalitären Herrschaftssystems in Deutschland 1933/34*, Cologne and Opladen, 1962.

Bramsted, Ernest K., *Goebbels and National Socialist Propaganda 1925-1945*, Ann Arbor, Mich., 1965.

Deak, Istvan, *Weimar Germany's Left-Wing Intellectuals: A Political History of the Weltbühne and Its Circle*, Berkeley and Los Angeles, Calif., 1968.

Diel, Helmuth, 'Grenzen der Presselenkung und Pressefreiheit im Dritten Reich untersucht am Beispiel der "Frankfurter Zeitung" ', unpublished diss., Freiburg, 1960.

Dietrich, Valeska, *Alfred Hugenberg: Ein Manager in der Publizistik*, Berlin, 1960.

Eksteins, Modris, *Theodor Heuss und die Weimarer Republik: Ein Beitrag zur Geschichte des deutschen Liberalismus*, Stuttgart, 1969.

'The Frankfurter Zeitung: Mirror of Weimar Democracy', *Journal of Contemporary History*, VI/4 (1971), pp. 3-28.

Engelsing, Rolf, *Massenpublikum und Journalistentum im 19. Jahrhundert in Nordwestdeutschland*, Berlin, 1966.

Fliess, Peter J., *Freedom of the Press in the German Republic 1918-1933*, Baton Rouge, La., 1955.

Gay, Peter, *Weimar Culture: The Outsider as Insider*, London, 1969.

Gottschalk, Regina, 'Die Linksliberalen zwischen Kaiserreich und Weimarer Republik: Von der Julikrise 1917 bis zum Bruch der Weimarer Koalition im Juni 1919', unpublished diss., Tübingen, 1969.

Greuner, Ruth, *Gegenspieler: Profile linksbürgerlicher Publizisten aus Kaiserreich und Weimarer Republik*, Berlin [East], 1969.

Wandlungen eines Aufrechten: Lebensbild Hellmut von Gerlachs, Berlin [East], 1965.

Grosser, Alfred, *Hitler, la presse et la naissance d'une dictature*, Paris, 1959.

Habermas, Jürgen, *Strukturwandel der Öffentlichkeit: Untersuchungen zu einer Kategorie der bürgerlichen Gesellschaft*, Neuwied, 1965.

Hagemann, Walter, *Publizistik im Dritten Reich*, Hamburg, 1948.

Die Zeitung als Organismus, Heidelberg, 1950.

Gründzüge der Publizistik: Als eine Einführung in die Lehre von der sozialen Kommunikation, rev. edn., ed. H. Prakke, Münster, 1966.

Hale, Oron J., *The Captive Press in the Third Reich*, Princeton, N.J., 1964.

Hartenstein, Wolfgang, *Die Anfänge der Deutschen Volkspartei 1918-1920*, Düsseldorf, 1962.

Heiber, Helmut, *Die Republik von Weimar*, Munich, 1966.

Heidorn, Günther, 'Zur Geschichte der Zeitungstypen in der Weimarer Republik', *Wissenschaftliche Zeitschrift der Universität Rostock*, II (1952-3), pp. 221-40.

Hepp, Fred, 'Der geistige Widerstand im Kulturteil der "Frankfurter Zeitung" gegen die Diktatur des totalen Staates, 1933-34', unpublished diss., Munich, 1949.

Hughes, Thomas Parke, 'Technological Momentum in History: Hydrogenation in Germany 1918-1933', *Past & Present*, No. 44 (1969), pp. 106-32.

Jones, Larry E., ' "The Dying Middle": Weimar Germany and the Fragmentation of Bourgeois Politics', *Central European History*, V (1972), pp. 23-54.

Kaznelson, Siegmund (ed.), *Juden im deutschen Kulturbereich: Ein Sammelwerk*, 2nd edn., Berlin, 1959.

Koszyk, Kurt, *Zwischen Kaiserreich und Diktatur: Die sozialdemokratische Presse von 1914 bis 1933*, Heidelberg, 1958.

Das Ende des Rechtsstaates und die deutsche Presse, 1933-1934, Düsseldorf, 1960.

Deutsche Presse im 19. Jahrhundert, Berlin, 1966.

Deutsche Pressepolitik im Ersten Weltkrieg, Düsseldorf, 1968.

Deutsche Presse 1914-1945, Berlin, 1972.

Krejci, Michael, 'Die Frankfurter Zeitung und der Nationalsozialismus 1923-1933', unpublished diss., Würzburg, 1965.

Krieger, Leonard, *The German Idea of Freedom*, Boston, Mass., 1957.

Kurucz, Jenö, *Struktur und Funktion der Intelligenz während der Weimarer Republik*, Berlin, 1967.

Lebovics, Herman, *Social Conservatism and the Middle Classes in Germany, 1914-1933*, Princeton, N.J., 1969.

Lindemann, Margot, *Deutsche Presse bis 1815*, Berlin, 1969.

Matthias, Erich, and Rudolf Morsey (eds.), *Das Ende der Parteien 1933*, Düsseldorf, 1960.

Mendelssohn, Peter de, *Zeitungsstadt Berlin: Menschen und Mächte in der Geschichte der deutschen Presse*, Berlin, 1959.

Moll, Helga, 'Der Kampf um die Weimarer Republik 1932/33 in der Berliner demokratischen Presse: Für und wider das "System"—

"Berliner Tageblatt", "Vossische Zeitung", 'Germania", und "Vorwärts" ', unpublished diss., Vienna, 1962.

Mommsen, Wolfgang J., 'Die deutsche öffentliche Meinung und der Zusammenbruch des Regierungssystems Bethmann Hollweg im Juli 1917', *Geschichte in Wissenschaft und Unterricht*, XIX (1968), pp. 656-71.

Mosse, Werner E., 'Rudolf Mosse and the House of Mosse 1867-1920', *Year Book IV* (of the Leo Baeck Institute), London, 1959, pp. 237-59.

(ed.), *Deutsches Judentum in Krieg und Revolution 1916-1923*, Tübingen, 1971.

(ed.), *Entscheidungsjahr 1932: Zur Judenfrage in der Endphase der Weimarer Republik*, Tübingen, 1965.

Paucker, Arnold, *Der jüdische Abwehrkampf gegen Antisemitismus und Nationalsozialismus in den letzten Jahren der Weimarer Republik*, Hamburg, 1968.

Ritter, Gerhard A., 'Kontinuität und Umformung des deutschen Parteiensystems 1918-1920', in *Entstehung und Wandel der modernen Gesellschaft: Festschrift für Hans Rosenberg zum 65. Geburtstag*, ed. G.A. Ritter, Berlin, 1970, pp. 342-76.

Robson, S.T., 'Left-Wing Liberalism in Germany 1900-19', unpublished diss., Oxford, 1966.

Schwarz, Gotthart, *Theodor Wolff und das 'Berliner Tageblatt': Eine Liberale Stimme in der deutschen Politik 1906-1933*, Tübingen, 1968.

Starkulla, Heinz, 'Organisation und Technik der Pressepolitik des Staatsmannes Gustav Stresemann 1923 bis 1929', unpublished diss., Munich, 1951.

Turner, Henry Ashby, Jr., *Stresemann and the Politics of the Weimar Republic*, Princeton, N.J., 1963.

'Big Business and the Rise of Hitler', *American Historical Review*, LXXV (1969), pp. 56-70.

Walter, Heinrich, *Zeitung als Aufgabe: 60 Jahre Verein Deutscher Zeitungsverleger*, Wiesbaden, 1954.

Wegner, Konstanze, *Theodor Barth und die Freisinnige Vereinigung: Studien zur Geschichte des Linksliberalismus im wilhelminischen Deutschland (1893-1910)*, Tübingen, 1968.

Werber, Rudolf, 'Die "Frankfurter Zeitung" und ihr Verhältnis zum Nationalsozialismus, untersucht an Hand von Beispielen aus den Jahren 1932-1943: Ein Beitrag zur Methodik der publizistischen Camouflage im Dritten Reich', unpublished diss., Bonn, 1965.

INDEX

8-Uhr-Abendblatt, 19, 105-6, 108, 111, 199, 230-1, 248, 267

Advertising, 14-5, 72-3, 226, 281; declines, 83, 222-3; importance of, 131, 234; competition for, 160

Agrarian League, 9

All Quiet on the Western Front, novel, 112; film, 216

Allgemeine Anzeigen G.m.b.H., 78

Allgemeine Elektrizität Gesellschaft (AEG), 50

Alsberg, Max (1877-1933), 181, 191

Alterum Kredit A.G., 79, 164

Amann, Max (1891-1957), 282, 294, 300, 302, 304

Der Angriff, 85, 258

Anschütz, Gerhard, 146

Anti-Bolshevik League, 288

Anton, Heinrich (pseud.), 124

Arens news service, 165

Army, see Reichswehr

Article 48, see Weimar constitution

Aschaffenburger Zeitung, 180

Association of German Department Stores, 188

Aus Wissenschaft und Politik, 77

Bachmann, Hermann (1856-1920), 23

Bäumer, Gertrud (1873-1954), 64, 67, 98

Bahr, Richard (1867-1936), 77

Banking, and press, 223, 259-60

Bauhaus, 192

Baum, Vicki, 112, 205

Bausback, Ferdinand (b. 1884), and Ullstein, 233, 288, 290, 296, 299-300

Bavarian People's Party (BVP), 141

Bebel, August (1840-1913), 24-5

Becker, Otto, 146

Benfey, Eduard, 233

Bergbaulicher Verein, 78

Berlin Association for the Provincial Press, 119

Berlin Fair and Exhibition Office, 227

Berlin Institute for the Study of the Press, 249, 281

Berlin Press Association, 119

Berliner Abendpost, 20-1

Berliner Allgemeine Zeitung, 21, 112, 314

Berliner Börsen-Courier, 35, 129; favours liberal unity, 144-5; idea of merger with *FZ*, 161-3

Berliner Börsen-Zeitung, 259, 293

Berliner Druck- und Zeitungsbetriebe A.G., 303

Berliner Handelsgesellschaft, 295

Berliner Illustrierte Nachtausgabe, 81, 111

Berliner Illustrirte Zeitung, viii, 21, 112, 131, 206, 294, 298, 314

Berliner Lokal-Anzeiger, 18, 81

Berliner Montagspost, 112, 314

Berliner Morgenpost, viii, 17, 20-1, 23, 56, 111, 112, 121-2, 234; circulation, 74, 269, 294, 314; readership, 136, 269; political purpose, 20, 136-7; and elections, 141, 198; and National Socialism, 244-5, 269, 271-2, 276

Berliner Morgen-Zeitung, 19, 111, 230-1

Berliner Tageblatt, viii, 17-9, 23, 32, 34, 51-2, 54, 56, 105-7, 117, 119, 190; and DDP, 93-6, 99, 102, 150, 154; circulation, 109; readership, 109-10, 134, 136, 283-4; compared to *FZ*, 126; influence, 134-7; and liberal unity, 146, 154; and idea of new party, 154-6; and I.G. Farben, 167; and political crisis, 196, 215-22, 248, 251-8; and State Party, 201-2; and 1930 elections, 202; owner's plans for, 225-6, 228-31. 258-60; and National Socialism, 240-6, 251, 253-7, 267-80, 283-8, 301

Berliner-Volks Zeitung, 19, 35, 107, 187, 287; character of, 110-1; circulation, 110, 231; readership, 136; political purpose, 136-7, 230; reorganization of, 225-7, 230-1; banned, 248

Berliner Zeitung, 20-1

Bernhard, Georg (1875-1944), x, 53, 71, 82, 114, 127, 133, 135, 272, 280; as editor of *VZ*, 23-4, 117-9, 147-8, 207; during war, 54-6, 145, 220; and DDP, 56-7, 93-4, 100-2; on role of press, 71, 73; as source of conflict, 117, 145, 147-53; personal character, 117-20; and liberal unity, 145-53; and Ullstein affair, 181-91, 207; leaves *VZ*, 185, 188, 231; and Radical Democratic Party, 218

Bernstein, Arthur, 29

Bernstorff, Johann Heinrich von (1862-1939), 146

Bethmann Hollweg, Theobald von (1856-1921), 32

Bethusy-Huc, Count, 31

Bismarck, Otto von (1815-1898), 4-5, 10, 17, 20, 25-6, 278

Das Blatt der Hausfrau, 112

Bleichröder bank, 76

Blomberg, Werner von (1878-1946), 268-9, 288

Blum, Léon (1872-1950), 184

Bonn, Moritz Julius (1873-1965), 24, 59, 125, 136

Bornstein, Josef (b. 1899), and Ullstein affair, 186, 190

Bosch, Carl (1874-1940), and *FZ*, 165-76, 179, 303

Bosch, Robert (1861-1942), 165, 171

Boulevardblatt, 14-5, 19, 21

Boxheim documents, 242

Brammer, Karl (1891-1964), 92

Brandenburg, Erich, 146

Braun, Heinrich, 24

Breiting, Richard, 264-6, 279

Brentano, Lujo (1844-1931), 125-6

Bretholz, Wolfgang (1904-1969), 253, 287

Broschek, Kurt (1884-1946), 163, 209

Brüning, Heinrich (1885-1970), 192, 202, 221, 226, 228, 245, 260-1; as chancellor, 195-7, 205, 213-7, 219, 238, 248; views on, 197, 215-7; and Hindenburg, 214-5; and Ullstein, 233-6; dismissal, 247, 252-3; and National Socialism, 255

Bülow, Bernhard von (1849-1929), 112,

Bürgerblock government, 141

Büxenstein printing firm, 82

Bureau International de Presse, 180

BZ am Mittag, 21, 112, 121-2, 206, 231; circulation, 294, 314; character, 136-7; and 1928 elections, 141; and NSDAP, 202, 245; changes in, 235-7

Carbe, Martin (1872-1932), 32, 49, 99, 105, 162, 167, 224; and conflict in Mosse firm, 106, 107-8, 225-9, 258; and State Party, 201

Carnegie empire, 192

Caro, Kurt, 230, 287

Caro, Michael, 111

Cautio G.m.b.H., 292, 300, 303

Centre Party, 6, 8-9, 10-2, 37, 56, 67, 141, 153, 243, 245, 258, 288; and press, 84, 85-6, 267, 269; and NSDAP, 255, 261, 266-7, 276

Clark, R.T., 68

Cohn, Emil, 19, 226

Cohnstaedt, Ludwig (1847-1936), 124; director of FSD, 161-3, 171

Cohnstaedt, Wilhelm (b. 1880), 40, 53-4, 125, 128, 133, 252, 280; and DDP, 93, 95

Concordia Literarische Anstalt, 292

Coudenhove-Kalergi, Richard Nikolaus von (1894-1972), 166

Council of people's commissars, 43, 48

Cura auditing company, 292

Daily Mail, 14

Die Dame, 112

Darmstädter und Nationalbank, 259

Debach, Hugo, 296

Delbrück, Hans (1848-1929), 33
Delbrück, Schickler & Co., 76
Democratic Club, 225
Democratic Union, 7, 96
Demokratische Beiträge, 77
Demokratischer Zeitungsdienst, 92, 250
Depression, 158, 216, 306; and press, 83, 85, 92, 160, 191, 222-4, 231-3, 258, 281, 294; and politics, 160, 214
Dessauer Zeitung, 165
Deutsche Allgemeine Zeitung, 72, 82, 91-2, 118, 177, 283-4, 293
Deutsche Bank, 295
Deutsche Politik, 47
Deutsche Union, 20
Der deutsche Volkswirt, 129, 206
Deutscher Aufstieg, 226
Deutscher Verlag, 300
Deutscher Verlagsverein, 78
Deutsches Nachrichtenbüro (DNB), 294
Diels, Rudolf (1900-1957), 298
Dietrich, Hermann (1879-1954), 88, 94, 236, 249, 292; and Bernhard, 187-8; and the political crisis, 222; ties to the press, 223; and sale of Ullstein, 297-9
Dietrich, Otto (1897-1952), 282
Dix, Rudolf (b. 1884), 191
Dohna, Alexander zu, 143
Dombrowski, Erich (b. 1882), 106, 258
Dominicus, Alexander, 146
Dovifat, Emil (1890-1969), 249
Dresdner Bank, 132; and Mosse, 259, 303
Dresdner Neueste Nachrichten, 144, 208
Bankhaus Dreyfus, 162
Dreyfus trial, 18, 33
Drill, Robert (1870-1942), 125
Duderstadt, Henning, 111
Duisberg, Carl (1861-1935), 167
DuMont Schauberg firm, 208, 260

Economic Association for the Furtherance of the Spiritual Forces of Reconstruction, 80
Economic Party, 148, 153
The Economist, 129
Editorial independence, question of, 72, 75-6, 79, 83, 104-5, 226

Editors' law, 274, 276, 298-9
Franz Eher Nachf. G.m.b.H., 294, 300, 304
Elbau, Julius (1881-1965), 119, 133, 234-5, 290; and liberal unity, 145, 157; and State Party, 200; as acting editor of *VZ*, 207; and Hindenburg, 220
Enabling law, 273
Engel, Fritz (1867-1935), 229
Erkelenz, Anton (1878-1945), 60, 66-7, 97-8, 120, 177, 287-8; and press, 90-1; joins SPD, 200-1, 212
Eschenburg, Theodor (b. 1904), 199
Eyck, Erich (1878-1964), 147

Faber, Robert, 75
Faktor, Emil (1876-1941?), 35
Fallada, Hans (1893-1947), 112
Fatherland Party, 55
February Club, 148
Feder, Ernst (1881-1964), 99, 106, 108, 109, 117, 133, 173, 176, 225-7, 244, 252, 259; on grand coalition, 194; and State Party, 201-2; and 1930 elections, 202, 210-1; leaves Mosse, 228-9; and NSDAP, 242-3
Fehrenbach, Constantin (1852-1926), 75
Feiler, Arthur (1879-1942), 40, 46, 54, 125, 128; radicalism of, 127-8; leaves *FZ*, 170, 175-6, 261
Feuchtwanger, Lion (1884-1958), 112
Fischbeck, Otto (1865-1939), 46
Fischer, Hermann (1873-1940), 88, 91, 143
Foerster, Friedrich Wilhelm, 39
Foreign office, and press, 72, 283-4
Frank, Leonhard (1882-1961), 112
Frankfurt am Main news service, 165
Frankfurter, Richard (1873-1953), 59, 190-1
Frankfurter Generalanzeiger, 161, 258
Frankfurter Nachrichten, 293
Frankfurter Societäts-Druckerei, viii-ix, 28, 104, 160, 309-11; origins, 25-8; and Verlag Neuer Staat, 90-2, 164; and DDP, 93-6, 103; development, 122-33; Jews in, 133-4; financial difficulties, 129-33, 160-1, 163, 175-6, 178-9, 260; and I.G. Farben, 165-79, 201, 238, 260,

303; and political crisis, 197-8,
215-22; and depression, 231-2, 238,
260; and National Socialism, 267-
80, 283-7, 288, 290-1, 303-4
Frankfurter Zeitung, viii, 25-8, 34, 40,
46, 48-9, 51, 53-4, 56, 66, 71, 152,
209, 300; readership, 26-7, 128-30,
134, 136; and DDP, 93-6, 102, 150,
158, 198; radicalism of, 122;
owner-editor relations, 122-3, 128;
circulation, 129-30; editors of, 123,
125-8, 170, 173-5; influence of,
134-7, 250-1; and liberal unity,
144, 146, 156-7, 158; and I.G.
Farben, 165-79, 238, 260; financial
difficulties, 129-33, 160-1, 163,
175-6, 178-9, 260; and political
crisis, 194-7, 212, 215-22, 251-8;
and State Party, 200-1; and elections of 1930, 202; and National
Socialism, 240-6, 254-8, 267-80,
283-6, 290-1, 303-4
Freisinnige Party, 5
Freisinnige People's Party, 7-8
Freisinnige Union, 7
French Revolution, 4
Frick, Wilhelm (1877-1946), 228, 264,
273
Fried, Ferdinand (pseud.), 239
Friedensburg, Ferdinand (b. 1886),
102
Fritsch, Theodor (1852-1933), 134
Front 1929, 148
Fürstenberg, Carl (1850-1933), 124
Funk, Walther (1890-1960), 293,
300-1

General congress of workers and
soldiers' councils, 48
Generalanzeiger, 14-5, 20-1, 28, 225,
270
General-Anzeiger, Dortmund, 93, 144,
218, 258
Gerlach, Hellmut von (1866-1935), 35,
51, 53, 59, 93, 102, 135, 156, 189,
272, 280; leaves DDP, 96-8, 100;
and liberal unity, 153-4, 155; on
1930 elections, 202-3; and Radical
Democratic Party, 218
Gerland, Heinrich (1874-1944), 49,
59; leaves DDP, 143
German Communist Party (KPD), 243,
268, 272, 310; and its press, 84-5,

221, 249, 266, 281; elections gains,
158, 203, 212, 248-9; and Hitler,
264, 266
German Democratic Party (DDP), viii,
68-9, 130, 163-4, 165, 175, 217,
226, 249, 291-4; founding of, 31-
58; ties to industry, 49-51, 64-5,
67; in elections, 51, 59, 89-90, 141,
209; and Berlin-Frankfurt press, 53-
4, 56-8, 90-103, 107, 127, 135,
198, 220, 252, 307-8; and press in
general, 77-8, 84, 87-103, 164, 205-
7; reasons for decline, 58-67, 89-90,
93-4, 141-2, 205-7; and government, 60, 67; influence, 60; divisions within, 64-7, 142; and liberal
unity, 142-58; and Ullstein affair,
186-8; merges with Young German
Order, 187, 198-9; and Mannheim
conference, 206-7
German Nationalist People's Party
(DNVP), 56, 102, 141, 144, 152-4,
211, 241, 289; elects Hugenberg
chairman, 81; and press, 84-6, 89;
in elections, 90, 141, 213, 273;
and rebels in, 157
German People's Party, to 1910, 4-6,
25-6, 163, 169
German People's Party (DVP), 1918-
1933, 44, 56-7, 88, 98, 101, 141,
211, 241, 289; and press, 78, 84,
86-7; and liberal unity, 107, 142-
58; and collapse of grand coalition,
194; and State Party, 199-200; in
1930 elections, 209
German Progressive Party, 4-6
German State Party, 93, 188, 226;
founding of, 187, 199-202, 209; in
1930 elections, 209; in 1932; 252;
splits, 211-2, 218; and press, 249-
50, 252, 258
Germania, 267
Gessler, Otto (1875-1955), 59, 88, 94,
177
Girardet, Wilhelm (1838-1918), 14
Goebbels, Joseph (1897-1945), 74, 85,
118, 237, 242, 258, 271; on role of
press, 85, 273-4; on Nazi press,
250; as propaganda expert, 264-5,
267, 273-6; and take-over of power,
282-7, 290-1, 293, 296-300, 302,
311
Göhre, Paul, 24

Göring, Hermann (1893-1946), 264, 270-1
Goldschmidt, Jakob (1882-1955), 226
Goldschmidt, Rosie (b. 1898), 147; marries Franz Ullstein, 151-3; and Ullstein affair, 180-90, 193
Goldschmidt, Sally (1869-1939), 125, 128
Gothein, Georg (1857-1940), 38, 40, 60, 94, 97-8, 257
Gräfenberg, Ernst, 151
Gräfenberg, Rosie, see Goldschmidt, Rosie
Grand coalition government, in 1923, 101; 1928-30, 141, 158, 194-5
Gregory, Alexander (pseud.), 124
Groener, Wilhelm (1867-1939), 234-6
Das Gross-Deutsche Reich, 289
Grossmann, Kurt, 202-3
Die Grüne Post, 112, 314; banned, 298-300
Guttmann, Bernhard (1869-1959), 133, 134, 307-8; heads Berlin bureau of FZ, 126-7, 128; leaves FZ, 170, 173-5, 176; on state crisis, 212

Haeuber, Erich, 287
Haas, Ludwig (1875-1930), 164
Haber, Fritz, 165
Hahn, Victor (b. 1869), 199
Hamburger Fremdenblatt, 35, 39, 144, 148, 163, 209, 236
Hamm, Eduard (1879-1944), 94
Hannover Anzeiger, 209
Hansabund, 64, 91
Harder, Adolf, 249
Harzburg Front, 81
Haupt, Walter, 302
Hauptmann, Gerhart (1862-1946), 112
Haushofer, Karl, 296, 299
Haussmann, Conrad (1857-1922), 18, 32-3, 43, 46, 52-3, 59, 60
Hearst press, 14, 192
Heberle, Rudolf, 242
Hecht, Wendelin (b. 1893), 303
Heine, Wolfgang (1861-1944), 24, 97
Heinze, Rudolf, 44
Hellpach, Willy (1877-1955), 68, 143
Heppenheimer, Heinrich, 111
Hermann, Fritz, 162
H.S. Hermann firm, negotiates with FSD, 161-3

Hess, Rudolf (b. 1894), 299
Heuss, Theodor (1884-1963), 47, 66, 95, 98, 187
Heydebrand und der Lasa, Ernst von (b. 1851), 118
Hieronymus, Robert, 35
Die Hilfe, 90
Hilferding, Rudolf (1877-1941), 254
Hilfspolizei, 270
Himmler, Heinrich (1900-1945), 298
Hindenburg, Paul von (1847-1934), 195-6, 216, 280; and Brüning, 213-4, 216, 247; and Hitler, 214-5, 221, 239, 243, 264, 268; trust in, 219-21, 245; and political crisis, 253-6
Hirsch, Felix (b. 1902), 211
Hitler, Adolf (1889-1945), 71, 81, 86, 202, 205, 213-4, 225, 236, 249; views on press, 134, 265; response to, 203-4, 240-6, 255-7, 268-72, 277-8; and presidential elections, 216, 221, 239; idea of 'taming' him, 244-5, 252-6, 260-3; and takeover of power, 247, 264-80, 282-9, 293-301, 303-4, 310
Reimar Hobbing printing firm, 82
Höllering, Franz (1896-1968), and Ullstein, 235-7
Hoesch, Leopold von (1881-1936), 180
Holsteinischer Kurier, 35
Holy Roman Empire, 3
Huck, August (1849-1911), 14
Huck, Wolfgang (1889-1967), 161, 207-10
Hugenberg, Alfred (1865-1951), 90, 158, 167, 213, 228, 289; development of press empire, 78-81, 89, 164, 205, 208, 292-4; and DNVP, 81, 157; and party press, 86
Hugo, Otto, 44
Hummel, Hermann (1876-1952), 163, 197, 303; interests in press, 164-5; I.G. Farben, 165-73, 175-6

I.G. Farbenindustrie, 165; and synthetic gasoline, 166-7, 238; and FZ, 167-79, 196, 290, 303, 310; and Brüning government, 238
Imprimatur G.m.b.H., 164-5, 172, 303
Independent Social Democratic Party of Germany (USPD), 227

Industry, and National Liberals, 5; and DDP, 49-51; and press, 75, 78-82, 88-9, 164-79, 223

Inflation, 306; and press, 75-6, 83, 87-8, 131

International Federation of Journalists, 119, 184

Inter-party committee, 10-1

Jacob, Berthold (1898-1944), 111

Jacobsohn, Siegfried (1881-1926), 118

Jewish Central Association, 230

Jews, in DDP, 47, 66; and democratic press, 133-4, 175, 229-30, 274, 287-8, 290, 306; and Young German Order, 201; under Hitler, 267, 276, 287-8, 290

Jödicke, Carl, 234, 261-2, 295, 299

Jungdeutscher Orden, see Young German Order

Kaas, Ludwig (1881-1952), 255

Kafka, Franz (1883-1924), 305

Kahl, Wilhelm (1849-1932), 143

Kahn, Ernst, 162

Kamper, Walter, 66, 128

Kapp putsch, 67

Keinath, Otto (1879-1948), 59, 143

Kempf, Rosa, 177

Kerr, Alfred (1867-1948), 133, 230

Kircher, Rudolf (1885-1954), 71, 125; Berlin correspondent of *FZ*, 174-6; and State Party, 200; on political crisis, 217, 252-3; and National Socialism, 243-4, 255, 257, 268-9, 275-6; on role of press, 250-1

Kirchhofer, Fritz (1895-1947), 211

Kirdorf, Emil (1847-1938), 80

Klages, Victor (b. 1889), 107

Kleefeld, Kurt (1881-1934), 49

Kloetzel, Cheskel Zwi (1891-1951), 111

Koch-Weser, Erich (1875-1944), 49, 65, 77, 94, 99, 163, 258; and 1928 elections, 141, 198; and liberal unity, 148-9, 157; and State Party, 198-9, on constitutional crisis, 217-8

Kölnische Volkszeitung, 248

Kölnische Zeitung, 260, 283; and liberal unity, 144; and State Party, 199-200; and Stolper, 208

Königsberger Allgemeine Zeitung, 208-9

Königsberger Hartungsche Zeitung, 144, 208-9

Koestler, Arthur (b. 1905), 133, 211, 231; dismissed by Ullstein, 237-8

Konzentrations A.G., 84

Koralle, 112

Korff, Kurt, 290

Krüger, Alfred, 111

Krüger, Otto, 233

Krumbhaar, Heinrich (1867-1939), 223

Krupp concern, 78, 192

Kuczynski, Robert, 202-3

Külz, Wilhelm (1875-1948), 98

Kuratorium for the reconstruction of German economic life, 49-51, 64

Lachmann-Mosse, Felicia, 105

Lachmann-Mosse, Hans (1885-1944), and Mosse firm, 105-9, 111, 224-31, 238-9, 258-60; and DDP, 107; and sale of firm, 301-2

Lambach, Walther (1885-1943), 157

Lammers, Heinrich (b. 1879), 293

Landsberg, Otto (1869-1957), 191

Leipziger Neueste Nachrichten, 265, 287

Leipziger Volkszeitung, 135

Lensch, Paul (1873-1926), 55

Lessing family, 299

Leuna works, I.G. Farben, 167

Levi, Paul (1883-1930), 152; and Ullstein affair, 181, 191

Levysohn, Arthur, 18-9

Lewinsohn, Richard (1894-1968), 71, 133, 290

Liberal Association, 143-4, 146-7, 156, 188

Liberalism, in the 19th century, 3-12; during Weimar, vii-viii, 211-2, 278-9. 305-8; and National Socialism, vii-x, 203-5, 210-1, 240-6; divisions within, 43-5, 64-7; question of unity, 7-8, 36-7, 42-5, 65, 107, 142-58; and socialism, 42-5, 65-6; resignation, 212, 278-9

Liebermann, Max (1847-1935), 146

Lippmann, Julius (b. 1864), 186-7

Locarno, 120

Ludwig, Emil (1881-1948), 192

Luppe, Hermann (1874-1945), 49

Magdeburgische Zeitung, 88

Mahraun, Artur (1890-1950), and State Party, 199-202, 211

Mann, Heinrich (1871-1950), 220
Martens, Theodor (b. 1897), 299
Mathis, Franz Carl, 91-2
Matthes, Joseph Friedrich (b. 1886), and Ullstein affair, 180-1, 184-8
Mehring, Franz (1846-1919), 19
Mein Kampf, 265
Meinecke, Friedrich (1862-1954), 42, 146
Meissner, Otto (1886-1953), 236
Meyer, Hans B., 107
Millaud, Moise-Polydore (1836-1892), 15
Misch, Carl (1896-1965), 117, 133, 290
Der Mittag, 226
Moeller van den Bruck, Arthur (1876-1924), 289
Mosse, Rudolf (1843-1920), 16-9, 22, 26, 34, 35, 105-6, 108, 111, 225, 229
Mosse firm, viii-ix, 28, 36, 78, 103-11, 131, 160, 162, 239, 248, 309-11; origins, 16-9; development of, 105-11; and Verlag Neuer Staat, 90-2, 164; and DDP, 93-6; Jews in, 133-4; and 1930 elections, 197-8; and political crisis, 215-22; during depression, 224-31, 232, 258-60; and National Socialism, 267-80, 283-8, 301-3
Müller, Hermann (1876-1931), 141, 158, 216
Müller, Richard A., 114, 191, 232, 261, 288
Müller-Hepp, Alfred, 226
Münchner Neueste Nachrichten, 34-5, 39, 88
Münzenberg press, 221, 235
Mutuum Darlehens A.G., 79, 164

Naphtali, Fritz (1888-1961), 128
National assembly, 48, 51, 59, 67
National Liberal Party, 4-12, 19, 39, 41, 43, 88, 142
National Social Union, 7, 126
National Socialist German Workers' Party (NSDAP), ix-x, 158, 167, 216, 222, 237, 310; growth, 71, 202-3, 209, 212-214, 225, 248-9, 254, 273; and press, 71, 81, 84-5, 249-50, 274, 281-304; views on, 202-5, 214-5, 235-6, 240-6, 251, 253-7, 261-3; appeal of, 238-9, 240-1; legality of, 242-3, 275; signs of decline, 255-7; in power, 264-80
Nationalliberale Beiträge, 77
National-Zeitung, 19
Naumann, Friedrich (1860-1919), 7, 9, 46, 59-60, 90, 126, 288
Thomas Nelson & Sons, 21
Neue Berliner Tageblatt, 20
Neue Leipziger Zeitung, 209
Neue Montags-Zeitung, 235
Neuer Tag, 293
Neurath, Konstantin von (1873-1956), 284, 288
Newspapers (see also Press), nature of, vii-viii; early development of, 12-6; decentralization, 13-4, 74, 81-2, 281; commercialization, 14-5; politicization, 15-6, 29; and question of independence, 28, 75-8, 84; during the war, 28-30, 54; and economic problems, 74-5, 78-9, 82-3, 104, 281; 'depoliticization', 75, 77-8, 270; and heavy industry, 78-82; under Nazi rule, 281-304
Nicolai, Walter (b. 1873), 55
Nicolson, Harold (1886-1968), 113-4
Northcliffe, Viscount (1865-1922), 14-5
Nouvelles Littéraires, 120
Novalis, 124
Nürnberg-Fürther-Morgenpresse, 165
Nuremberg war trials, 172
Nuschke, Otto (1883-1957), 35-6, 46, 52, 89, 110, 187; leaves Mosse, 225-6

Oberländer Zeitung, 249
Oeser, Albert (1878-1959), 126, 128, 170
Ohst, Wilhelm, 287
Olden, Rudolf (1885-1940), 133, 135, 211, 272, 280; on Ullstein affair, 190; on State Party, 201; dismissed by Mosse, 229
Oppenheim bank, 132, 288
Osborn, Max (1870-1946), 133, 290
Ossietzky, Carl von (1889-1938), 63, 111, 227; and DDP, 153; and Wolff, 155; on 1930 election, 203; on Ullstein, 236-7
Ostdeutsche Bank, 123
Osthilfe programme, 197

Palestine Symphony Orchestra, 124
Papen, Franz von (1879-1969), as chancellor, 235, 247-8, 252-5, 262, 266; views on, 252-4, 259-61
Payer, Friedrich von (1847-1931), 53-4, 94-5, 122, 132-3; as director of FSD, 161-2, 168, 171, 175-6
Peace League of War Veterans, 227
Petersen, Carl (1868-1933), 220
Pferdemenges, Heinrich, 296
Pinner, Felix (1880-1942), 258
Plutus, 24
Poincaré, Raymond (1860-1934), 121
Pol, Heinz (b. 1904), on liberalism, 211-2; leaves Ullstein, 234-5
Political parties, and press, 15, 72, 84-103
Potempa murder, 257
Praktische Berlinerin, 112
Press (see also Newspapers), power of, 70-1, 82, 96, 134-7, 205-7, 223, 248-51, 265; and government, 72, 127, 248, 273-4; in Third Reich, 281-304
Press agencies, 75, 76-7, 80, 83, 92
Preuss, Hugo (1860-1925), 49, 60
Progressive People's Party, 7-12, 37-8, 40-3, 51, 96, 156
Pro-Palestine Committee, 134, 189
Propyläen-Verlag, 112
Pünder, Hermann (b. 1888), 234, 236
Pulitzer press, 14

Querschnitt, 112, 295
Quidde, Ludwig (1858-1944), 39; rejects State Party, 200-1
Quigley, Hugh, 68

Radical Democratic Party, 201, 218
Räuscher, Josef, 258
Rathenau, Walther (1867-1922), 49, 59, 63, 156, 171
Reich Association of the German Press, 119, 298; and Ullstein affair, 186, 188-9
Reich economic council, 101, 119, 127-8
Reich Press Chamber, 282
Reich press law (1874), 70
Reich Union of German Newspaper Publishers, 75, 125, 223, 224
Reich Union of German Writers, 124
Reichsbank, 112

Reichsbanner, 68, 221, 262
Reichstag fire, 266, 270, 272
Reichswehr, 211, 214-6, 236, 245, 268-9
Reifenberg, Benno (1892-1970), 123, 126, 174
Reiner, Max (1880-1944), 219-20
Reinhardt, Max (1873–1943), 18
Reinhold, Peter (1887-1955), 295; joins Ullstein, 233-4; on NSDAP, 245, 253
Remarque, Erich Maria (1898-1970), 112, 216
Reparations, Lausanne conference, 252
Republican Party of Germany, 111, 155, 227
Republican Press Union, 119
Reusch, Paul (1868-1956), 82
Reventlow, Ernst zu (1869-1943), 118
Rheinbaben, Rochus von, 143
Richter, Eugen (1838-1906), 6-7
Richthofen, Hartmann von (1878-1953), 88
Ross, Fritz (1889-1964), 295-6, 299; and Ullstein affair, 181, 183
Rothschild brothers, 114, 192
Ruhr occupation, 70, 101, 129-30, 292

SA, 216, 253, 257, 268, 270, 273, 287; danger of, 235-6, 241-3
Sabersky, Fritz, 163, 168
Sarwey, Helmut, 201, 220
Schacht, Hjalmar (1877-1970), 31, 59, 283, 295-7
Schäffer, Hans (1886-1967), 256; and Ullstein, 232-4, 261, 271-2, 288; and Papen, 254
Schaumburg-Lippe, Friedrich Christian zu, 285
Scherl firm, 18, 78, 81, 110
Schiffer, Eugen (1860-1954), 59, 62; leaves DDP, 143
Schlegel, Robert, 249-50
Schleicher, Kurt von (1882-1934), 235, 239; influence, 214-5; as chancellor, 247, 254-6, 262, 266
Schmitz, Hermann (b. 1881), 172, 238
Schmutz- und Schundgesetz, 98-9
Schnitzler, Georg von, 172
Scholz, Ernst (1874-1932), 157, 200
Schotthöfer, Fritz (1871-1951), 125
Schumpeter, Joseph, 129

Schwab, Joseph, 106
Schwabach, Paul von (1867-1938), 76
Schwander, Rudolf (1868-1950), as director of FSD, 160-1, 168, 175, 176-7
Schwarzschild, Leopold (1892-1950), 193
Seebote, 249
Segall, Sali, 31
Sieburg, Friedrich (1893-1964), 152, 174, 284-5
Siemens, Carl Friedrich von (1872-1941), 59, 143, 179
Siemens firm, 50
Simon, Felix, 123
Simon, Heinrich (1880-1941), 27, 53, 128, 175-6, 178, 238, 285, 303; character of, 123-4, 125; and I.G. Farben, 168-71; on 1930 crisis, 212
Simon, Kurt (1881-1957), 27, 92, 303; character of, 123, 125; searches for partner for FSD, 161-3; and I.G. Farben, 168-71
Simon-Sonnemann, Therese, 27, 122-3, 132, 303
Sinsheimer, Hermann (1884-1950), 107
Social Democratic Party of Germany (SPD), 6, 8-12, 23-4, 37, 39, 42-5, 65-7, 77, 93, 101, 135-6, 153-4, 200-1, 202, 218, 221, 227, 243-4, 248, 254, 258, 306; and press, 84-5, 266, 281; and 1928 elections, 141; dissension within, 158; during political crisis, 194-5, 202, 212, 216-7; tolerates Brüning, 213; and Hitler, 266-7, 269, 272
Social Democratic Workers' Party, 25
Sonnemann, Leopold (1831-1909), 25-8, 53, 122-3, 126, 161, 169, 171, 178-9
Spahn, Martin (1875-1945), 288, 296
SS, 216, 253, 268, 270, 273, 287
Stadtblatt der Frankfurter Zeitung, 131
Stadtler, Eduard (b. 1886), and Ullstein, 288-90, 295-6, 300
Stahl, Leo, and Ullstein scandal, 180-1, 183-4, 190
Stahlhelm, 118, 270
Stark, Oskar (1890-1970), 176, 196, 258, 287
State Party, see German State Party

Steed, Henry Wickham, 291
Stein, August (1851-1920), 34, 126
Stein, Fritz, and liberal unity, 148-9; joins Ullstein, 236-7
Stein, Günther (1900-1961), 196, 229
Steinborn, Paul, 229
Stennes, Walter, 235
Stephan, Werner (b. 1895), 87
Stinnes, Hugo (1870-1924), 42, 47-8, 81-2, 87, 118, 165, 288, 293
Stöcker, Adolf (1835-1909), 96
Stolper, Gustav (1888-1947), 129; as potential liberal leader, 206-10
Strasser, Gregor (1892-1934), 241, 256
Strauss, Ottmar (1878-1946), 82
Stresemann, Gustav (1878-1929), 56-7, 88, 101, 112, 120, 143, 145, 192; and liberal unity, 43-6, 143-4, 148-9, 157, 198-9; views on press, 72, 87; and foreign policy, 121, 146; proposed as leader of new party, 154-5
Striegauer Anzeiger, 89
Stubmann, Peter (1876-1962), 68
Stülpnagel, Heinrich von (1866-1944), 239
Stuttgarter Neues Tageblatt, 144
Syndicated news columns, 75-7, 83, 165
Synthetic gasoline, I.G. Farben project, 166-8

Tägliche Rundschau, 239, 258
Der Tag, 81
Das Tage-Buch, criticizes *FZ*, 177-8; and Ullstein affair, 185-6, 193; and Brüning, 215; attacks democratic press, 221
Die Tat, 239, 259
Telegraph Union, 76, 79, 81, 294
Tempo, 112, 122, 239, 246, 276, 295; financial difficulties, 150, 233; circulation of, 294, 314; banned, 267
Le Temps, 128
Thomas, Hans (pseud.), 239
Thyssen, August (1842-1926), 47-8
Thyssen, Fritz (1873-1951), 47-8, 82
Times, London, 128
Times, New York, 128
Tirpitz, Alfred von (1849-1930), 19, 39, 55
Toller, Ernst (1893-1939), 202-3
Topf, Erwin, 196

Trade unions, Christian, 8-9, 199; Hirsch-Duncker, 42, 66
Treviranus, Gottfried Reinhold (1891-1971), 157
Trimm, Thomas (pseud.), 298
Troeltsch, Ernst (1865-1923), 59
Tucholsky, Kurt (1890-1935), 153

Uhu, 112, 295
Ullstein, Franz (1868-1945), 21, 55, 91, 114-6, 134, 279; and Bernhard, 117, 147-53; on liberal unity, 147-53; and Ullstein affair, 180-91, 227, 232; on firm's political involvement, 206, 279; on Hitler, 256; and sale of firm, 297, 299
Ullstein, Hans (1859-1935), 21, 114-6, 134, 147; and Ullstein affair, 181, 185, 190-1
Ullstein, Heinz (b. 1893), 119-20, 297; and family scandal, 181, 183, 191
Ullstein, Hermann (1875-1943), 21, 23, 113, 114-6, 134, 147, 246, 260-1, 289, 310-1; and family scandal, 181, 185, 191, 232-3; and his press circle, 205-10
Ullstein, Leopold (1826-1899), 19-22, 26, 115
Ullstein, Lotte, née Lehmann, 151
Ullstein, Louis (1863-1933), 21, 114-16, 117, 134, 147, 295; and family scandal, 181, 183, 185, 190-1, 227
Ullstein, Rosie, see Goldschmidt, Rosie
Ullstein, Rudolf (1874-1964), 21, 114-6, 134, 147; and family scandal, 181, 185, 190-1
Ullstein firm, viii-ix, 17, 28, 103-4, 108, 110, 131, 162, 309-11; origins of, 19-24; and DDP, 54-8, 93-4, 99; and State Party, 200; and Verlag Neuer Staat, 90-2, 164-5; and development in Weimar, 111-22, conflict within, 115-7; Jews in, 133-4; and liberal unity, 145, 150; and family scandal, 180-93, 229; and 1930 elections, 197-8, 211; political involvement of, 206, 210; and the political crisis, 215-22; during depression, 231-8, 260-1, 294-5; and government pressure, 233-4; staff changes in, 234-8, 239; and Hitler, 267-80, 283-90, 294-302
Ullstein news service, 113, 232

Ullstein photo agency, 113
Ulmer Tageblatt, 88
Union of Independent Democrats, 201
Universum Film A.G. (UFA), 288; acquired by Hugenberg, 79; and I.G. Farben, 167; and Ullstein, 234-5

Vera Verlagsanstalt, 78-9
Verlag Neuer Staat, 90-2, 164-5
Versailles treaty, 59, 68, 97, 117, 158, 291
Vetter, Karl, 111; role in Mosse firm, 227-31; on Hitler, 277, 287
Vögler, Albert (1877-1945), 80
Völkischer Beobachter, 85, 288
Vogelstein, Theodor (b. 1880), and founding of DDP, 31-2, 34-5; and *FZ*, 162
Volksnationale Reichsvereinigung, 211
Vollmar, Georg von, 24
Vorwärts, 212, 248, 267
Vossische Zeitung, viii, 17, 71, 82, 91, 112, 118-20, 206-7, 211, 231, 234, 239, 299; acquired by Ullstein, 22-3; and DDP, 55-7, 93-6, 100-2; circulation of, 117, 121, 294-5, 314; readership, 121, 136; compared to *FZ*, 126; influence of, 134-7; and liberal unity, 145-53; financial difficulties, 150, 233, 260; and Ullstein affair, 180, 182, 187, 189-90; and political crisis, 196, 215-22, 251-8; on 1930 elections, 198, 202; owners' plans for, 236-7; and National Socialism, 240-6, 254-7, 261, 267-80, 283-6, 294-5

Wall Street crash, 158
Warburg, Max (1867-1946), 257
Warmbold, Hermann, 238, 260
Weber, Alfred (1868-1958), 34-7, 41-3, 45-6, 47-8, 136
Weber, August (1871-1957), 143, 188
Weber, Max (1864-1920), 48-9, 59-60, 125-6
Weimar Coalition, 67, 198
Weimar constitution, 60, 67-8, 192, 271; on freedom of expression, article 118, 70-1, 266, 274; article 48, 70, 195-7, 213, 216-7, 247-8, 251, 264, 266, 270, 280
Weimar Republic, 305-11; weaknesses,

59-60, optimism in, 68-9; the electoral system, 50, 71
Weismann, Robert (1869-1942), 152, 244
Weiss, Bernhard (1880-1951), 226-7
Welk, Ehm (1884-1966), 298
Die Welt am Abend, 235
Die Welt am Montag, 23, 35, 93, 96, 218
Die Weltbühne, 118, 153, 203, 234; and liberalism, 211-2; and Brüning, 215; attacks democratic press, 221
Welter, Erich (b. 1900), 126, 128, 175-6, 261
Wiemann news service, 165
Wiener, Alfred (1885-1964), 230
Wiessner, Max (1885-1945), 34, 209; joins Ullstein, 300-1
Wilhelm II (1859-1941), 26, 31, 40
Winkler, Max (1875-1961), 291-4; and Ullstein, 296-7, 299-300; and Mosse, 302-3
Winnig, August (1878-1956), 55
Winschuh, Josef (b. 1897), 199
Wirth, Joseph (1879-1956), 101, 154-5
Wirtschaftsstelle für die Provinzpresse (Wipro), 79
Die Woche, 81
Woga A.-G., 259
Kurt Wolff Verlag, 295
Wolff, Otto (1881-1940), 82
Wolff, Theodor (1868-1943), 17-9, 23, 66, 97, 105, 133; as an editor, 18, 106-7, 109, 119; view of journalism, 18-9; and founding of DDP, 32-8, 40, 42-7, 110; resigns from DDP executive, 52-3; leaves DDP, 59, 96, 98-100; criticism of DDP, 93, 142, 154; attacks against, 94, 135, 239; and conflict with Lachmann-Mosse, 106-8, 225, 228-31; suggests new party, 154-6, 157-8; on liberal unity, 154; on break-up of grand coalition, 194; on 1930 elections, 197-8, 211; on State Party, 201-2; on Hindenburg, 220; and National Socialism, 255, 268-9, 272, 280; rumours about, 258-60
Wolff's Telegraph Bureau (WTB), 76, 294
Wollf, Julius Ferdinand (b. 1871), 208
World War I, 10-2, 28-30, 32-3, 96
Wulffen, Günther von, 296

Wynands, Franz, 287

Young German Order, 209; merges with DDP, 187, 199; views on, 201-2, 218; breaks with DDP, 211
Young Liberals, 8, 199
Young Plan, 158-9; referendum against, 81, 158

Zechlin, Walter (1879-1962), 221
Zehrer, Hans (1899-1966), 239
Zeitungsbedarf G.m.b.H., 292
Zimmermann, Friedrich (1898-1967), 239, 259
Zuckmayer, Carl (b. 1896), 112